Visual Arts	Literature	Philosophy
Phidias, Myron, Parthenon, Pantheon and Colosseum	Homer, Dionysian festivals; Sophocles, Aristophanes, Euripides, Horace, Cicero, Vergil, Plutarch	Socrates, Plato, Aristotle, Epicurius, Zeno, Boethius
Great cathedrals built, Giotto, Ghiberti, Fra Filippo Lippi, Botticelli, Donatello	Dante, Petrarch, Boccaccio, Chaucer	Abelard, Thomas Aquinas, R. Bacon
da Vinci, Van Eyck, Durer, St. Peter's built in Rome, Michelangelo, Raphael, Brueghel, Titian, Giorgione, Tintoretto, Veronese	Ariosto, Rabelais, Spenser, Marlowe, Shakespeare	Machiavelli, More, Luther, Erasmus, Montaigne
Bernini, Rubens, El Greco, Rembrandt, Velasquez, Van Dyck, Poussin, Watteau, Hogarth, Fragonard, Gainsborough	Cervantes, Pepys, Milton, Pope, Swift, Defoe, Gray	F. Bacon, Descartes, Grotius, Hobbs, Spinoza, Lock, Voltaire
David, Ingres	Goldsmith, Fielding, Burns, Goethe, Schiller	Hume, Rousseau, Kant
Goya, Gericault, Corot, Turner, Delacroix, Millet, Daumier, Manet, Degas, Renoir, Monet, Rodin, Seurat, Cezanne, Van Gogh, Gauguin, Homer	Coleridge, Wordsworth, Scott, Byron, Austen, Shelley, Keats, Pushkin, Heine, Cooper, Balzac, Hugo, Stendhal, Sand, Lytton, Dickens, Poe, Dumas, Thackeray, Longfellow, Hawthorne, Melville, Stowe, Whitman, Tennyson, Eliot, Tolstoy, Dostoevski, Browning, Twain, Ibsen, Stevenson, Wilde, H. James	Hegel, Mill, Comte, Kierkegaard, Schopenhauer, Marx, Engels, Thoreau, Spencer, T. H. Huxley, Emerson, Haeckel, Nietzsche
Duchamp, F. L. Wright, Matisse, Kandinsky, Braque, Picasso, Klee, Rivera, Orozco, Rouault, Mondrian, Miró, Chagall, Lipchitz, Moore, Pop art; Op art; chance painting	Maeterlinck, Zola, Kipling, G. B. Shaw, Masefield, Mann, Lawrence, Frost, Maugham, Lewis, T. S. Eliot, Joyce, Dreiser, Fitzgerald, France, Malraux, Hemingway, O'Neill, A. Huxley, Benet, Faulkner, Sandburg, Stein, Steinbeck, Thomas, Williams, Miller, Orwell, Cummings, Auden	Bergson, Dewey, Pierce, W. James, Spengler, Russell, Santayana, Sartre, Camus

THE UNDERSTANDING OF MUSIC

FOURTH EDITION

CHARLES R. HOFFER
Indiana University

Wadsworth Publishing Company
Belmont, California
A Division of Wadsworth, Inc.

Music Editor: Sheryl Fullerton
Production Editor: Jeanne Heise
Designer: Detta Penna
Copy Editor: Hinda Farber
Page Layouts: Wendy Calmenson, Cheryl Carrington

Cover: *Snowing, 1939;* Marc Chagall, Russian, 1889– ; Gouache on cardboard, 26½ x 20½ inches; Courtesy of The Saint Louis Art Museum, Saint Louis, Missouri.

Printed in the United States of America
1 2 3 4 5 6 7 8 9 10—85 84 83 82 81

A Study Guide has been specially designed to help students master the concepts presented in this textbook. Order from your bookstore.

Library of Congress Cataloging in Publication Data

Hoffer, Charles R
The understanding of music.

Includes index.
1. Music—Analysis, appreciation. I. Title.
MT6.H565U5 1981 780'.1'5 80-24040
ISBN 0-534-00915-8

ACKNOWLEDGMENTS

Photographs, paintings, cartoons, music examples, and quotations are reproduced with permission from the following sources. References are to page numbers unless indicated pl. (plate).

Photographs, Paintings, and Cartoons

The Art Institute of Chicago (pl. 15). Art Reference Bureau: Archives Photographiques (7), Alinari (111, 124, 125, 142, 245), Marburg (123), Archive für Kunst und Geschichte, Berlin (154, 247), Giraudon (224), ARB (127, 233), Bibliotcca Ambrosiana-Milan (126), Vaerihg (407), Louvre (290, pls. 9, 10), Ole Woldbye, Copenhagen (285). ASCAP (465). Austrian National Travel Office (201). The Bettmann Archive, Inc. (131, 194, 355, 399, 404). Boosey and Hawkes, Inc. (467). California Institute of the Arts (440). Capitol Records (487). Columbia Records (441, 458). Finnish National Travel Office (364). Foster Hall Collection (455). French Government Tourist Office (90). Ewing Galloway (99, 102, 104). German National Tourist Office (264). Horizon Press, New York: photo from the new edition of *The Encyclopedia of Jazz* by Leonard Feather, copyright © 1960 (481). Alan Hovhaness (470). Indiana University School of Music (228, 316, 320). Italian Government Travel Office (125). Library of Congress (215, 481, 483). Magnum Photos, Inc., New York (xviii, 368). Motown (491). Museum of the City of New York (453). Museum of Fine Arts, Boston (267). The Museum of Modern Art, New York (427, 436, 442, pls. 12, 13). National Gallery of Art, Washington, D.C. (325, 416, pls. 2, 3, 4, 5, 7, 8, 11). The New York Public Library at Lincoln Center, Dance Collection (464). Novosti Press Agency (387). Organization of American States, Washington, D.C. (397). Louis Ouzer, Rochester, New York (414). Richard Pflum (269, 308, 309). Philadelphia Museum of Art (456). RCA (373). Bill Ray (84). Rogers Organ Company (69). Royal College of Music, London (234). Scala, New York (pls. 1, 6). G. Schirmer, Inc. (393). B. Schott's Söhne (417). David Schreiber (412). Smithsonian Institution, Division of Musical Instruments, Hugh Worch Collection (183). St. Louis Art Museum (COVER, pl. 14). Susanne Faulkner Stevens, Avery Fisher Hall, New York (80). United Artists Corporation, copyright © 1962. Beta Productions, Inc. All rights reserved (494). United Feature Syndicate, Inc.: cartoon copyright © 1958 United Feature Syndicate (5). Universal-Edition A. G., Vienna (428). The University of Michigan School of Music, Stearns Collection (217). Vladimir Ussachevsky (438). The Walters Art Gallery, Baltimore (116).

Music Examples and Quotations

Associated Music Publishers, Inc.: Symphony no. 2, by Jean Sibelius, used by permission of Breitkopf & Härtel by Associated Music Publishers, Inc. (365-366); "Serenity" by Charles Ives, copyright © 1942 by Arrow Music Press, Inc. Copyright assigned 1957 to Associated Music Publishers, Inc., renewed 1969, and used by permission (396); *Bachianas Brasileiras* no. 5, by Heitor Villa-Lobos, copyright © 1948 by Associated Music Publishers, Inc., and used by permission (396). Belmont Music Publishers: *Variations for Orchestra*, op. 31, by Arnold Schoenberg, used by permission of Belmont Music Publishers, Los Angeles, California 90049 (423-424). Belwin-Mills Publishing Corp.: *Kleine Kammermusik für fünf Bläser*, op. 24, no. 2 by Paul Hindemith, copyright 1922 by B. Schott's Söhne, Mainz, renewed 1949 by Schott & Co., London, and used by permission of Belwin-Mills Publishing Corp. (418-420); trumpet solo based on "Black and Tan Fantasy" used by permission of Belwin-Mills Publishing Corp. (479-480). Boosey and Hawkes, Inc.: Concerto no. 3 for Piano by Bela Bartók, copyright © 1947 by Boosey & Hawkes, Ltd., renewed 1974, and reprinted by permission of Boosey & Hawkes, Inc. (381-382, 384, 385); *A Young Person's Guide to the Orchestra* by Benjamin Britten, copyright 1946 by Hawkes & Son (London) Ltd., renewed 1973, and reprinted by permission of Boosey & Hawkes, Inc. (61-62); *A Ceremony of Carols* by Benjamin Britten, copyright 1943 by Boosey & Co., Ltd., renewed 1970, and reprinted by permission of Boosey & Hawkes, Inc. (394); *Appalachian Spring* by Aaron Copland, copyright © 1945 by Aaron Copland, renewed 1972, and reprinted by permission of Aaron Copland, copyright owner, and Boosey & Hawkes, Inc., sole publishers and licensees (462-463); *The Rite of Spring* by Igor Stravinsky, copyright 1921 by Edition Russe de Musique; renewed 1958, copyright and renewal assigned to Boosey & Hawkes, Inc., and reprinted with their permission (410, 412). The H. W. Gray Co., Inc.: Cantata no. 140 by Johann Sebastian Bach, used by permission of the H. W. Gray Co., Inc. (33-35, 38, 163-165). Holt, Rinehart

CONTENTS

PART FIVE TWENTIETH-CENTURY MUSIC 369

PART SIX AMERICAN MUSIC 449

LISTENING GUIDES

ENRICHMENT BOXES

to Marjorie

PREFACE

What does an author do to improve an already successful book? It's a logical question, one that any author considering revision spends many hours pondering. In a sense, it's a simple matter: Keep what's good and change what isn't. But that doesn't get down to the hard questions of deciding what is good in the previous edition and how to improve what isn't so good.

In the case of THE UNDERSTANDING OF MUSIC, there was a solid foundation of features on which to build. Instructors and readers have responded favorably to the selection of basic information, the wide coverage of types and styles of music, the logic of a chronological approach, the clear and down-to-earth writing style, the "post-hole" technique of concentrating on a limited number of works that can serve as examples of other music, the relating of music to the larger culture, and the supplementary *Record Album* and *Study Guide and Scores* booklet.

However, improvements were needed to meet the changing emphases and audiences in music appreciation. Although previous editions stressed improved listening skill through short exercises, a chapter on listening, and the simplified scores in the *Study Guide and Scores*, many students needed extra help in following and concentrating on the music when a work is more than a couple of minutes long. To meet that need, the Fourth Edition contains sixteen *Listening Guides* that lead students in what to listen for in a particular work. The Listening Guides point out the main features and provide a timetable of when those features appear in the music. They have been tried out with many students for several years, and they have worked well.

In addition, to help motivate students and increase their interest in music, the Fourth Edition contains thirty-two short separate *enrichment boxes* on topics related to the text. These sections include interesting and useful information presented in a refreshing manner. One such box discusses Leonardo da Vinci as the premier example of the "Renaissance man," another explains the opportunities and traditions related to concert attendance, a third box describes the development of recordings, and another tells about Niccolo Paganini and his influence on nineteenth century music.

The writing has been touched up to make it as readable and alive as possible without sacrificing the depth or quality of coverage of topics. With the increased amount and quality of artwork, as well as a more attractive design, the Fourth Edition will be more accessible and appealing to both instructors and students.

Another change in the Fourth Edition is the increased number of chapters. Dividing many of the existing chapters into smaller units delineates topics more clearly, gives the book greater flexibility as a teaching tool, and makes each chapter more appropriate to the amount of material covered in each class period.

There are also the usual refinements in any new edition. Some works have been changed or added, including the chorus "For Unto Us a Child Is Born" from Handel's *Messiah,* three pre-Bach works, a song by Ives, and a folksong arranged by Copland. The treatment of music since 1945 has been strengthened with a work by Crumb and an electronic work by Subotnik. In some instances the same information is now presented more concisely.

The same question about revision and improvement also existed with the *Record Album* and the *Study Guide and Scores.* The six-disc album, prepared by Columbia Records, is now thoroughly integrated with the textbook through the use of the Listening Guides. The quality of some of the recordings has been improved. The *Study Guide and Scores* now has simplified scores for eight works. While few nonmusicians can read music, with a little practice most of them can follow simple scores as they listen. These scores are another way to keep the students' attention on the music and more aware of what's happening in it.

The improved *Instructor's Manual* includes suggestions for teaching, class activities, test items, and a list of books and films.

I would like to thank all those who encouraged me in my efforts to be a teacher and writer. I am indebted to the many students in my music appreciation classes, from whom I learned much about how to aid them in their understanding of music.

And I would like to express my appreciation to the reviewers who provided prepublication comments: Alexander Silbiger, University of Wisconsin, Madison; Larry W. Long, New River Community College; Carlesta Henderson, Keene State College; Patrick V. Casali, Oakton Community College; Rudolph Kremer, University of North Carolina, Chapel Hill; Ernest R. Woodruff, Northwest Missouri State University; Annette LeSiege, Wake Forest University; Irving H. Cohen, West Chester State College; Margaret B. McArthur, Texas A & M University; Kenneth Jewell, West Valley College; Chuck Iwanusa, C. S.

Mott Community College; Robert W. Froelich, Ashland College; Stanley D. Green, Oklahoma State University; William K. Gaeddert, Baker University; and Eleanor Ray Hammer, Los Angeles Valley College.

Finally, thanks beyond the power of words to express are due my wife, Marjorie, who, as a teacher of music appreciation courses, offered many valuable suggestions. With gratitude I recognize her encouragement and editorial advice.

Charles R. Hoffer

PART ONE

THE NATURE OF MUSIC

1

MUSIC AND PEOPLE

Each year people all over the world spend countless hours performing and listening to music, and they spend a lot of money for instruments, records, and record-playing equipment. People dance, sing lullabies, and whistle as they work in just about every part of the globe. It is estimated that in America over thirty million people play musical instruments regularly. Americans spend more money on music than on spectator sports. Music is present at weddings, ship launchings, and ball games.

Just about everyone likes some kind of music. "Music haters" seem to be as rare as people who dislike ice cream or soft drinks. But not everyone likes the same type of music, nor does everyone use it in the same way. People have different reasons for listening to or making music.

REASONS FOR MUSIC

There are many reasons why music is so much a part of people's lives. First, it can be a background for activity. It provides an environment of sound in much the same way that wallpaper provides a visual environment. Some people want sound around them almost all the time. If their portable radios or record players were taken away, they would feel uncomfortable.

Another use of music is to provide a special atmosphere for a nonmusical situation. Music is used in this way in motion pictures. The musical score enhances the mood created by the dramatic action, and by doing this it increases the impact of the film. Sacred music promotes a feeling of worship in religious ceremonies by encouraging an attitude of devotion and commitment to religious beliefs.

Music is also used to promote a feeling of group identity. People often prefer a type of music (or clothing or hair style) because they think it associates them with certain persons or ideas. The person who wants to be considered an "intellectual" may express to friends a preference for Bartók's string quartets and sophisticated jazz, while someone who wants to be known as "one of the crowd" might listen to country-western music.

People vent their feelings through music. It seems to make the world a little brighter and to ease pain and disappointments. Folk music often provides such a release of feelings. For example, the American folk song, "The Praties* They Grow Small," which was sung in the 1840s by Irish immigrants, has these words:

O I wish that we were geese, night and morn, night and morn,
O I wish that we were geese, for they fly and take their ease,
And they live and die in peace eatin' corn, eatin' corn.
O we're trampled in the dust over here, over here.
O we're trampled in the dust, but the Lord in whom we trust
Will give us crumb for crust, over here, over here.

Love songs and lullabies are also expressions of deep and personal feelings.

Music is often used as recreation, like a song sung for the sheer fun of it. There is a difference between recreational music and the expression of feelings that were just described. Emotional release implies the easing of some deep psychological need, while recreation implies refreshing or relaxing activity—a mere diversion or frivolity. Here is an example with absolutely no religious implications!

O the Deacon went down to the cellar to pray.
He found a jug and stayed all day.
O the Deacon went down to the cellar to pray.
He found a jug and he stayed all day.
I won't grieve my Lord no more.
I ain't a-gonna grieve my Lord no more.

The use of music to accompany work is less common in the United States than in other cultures. In Africa songs accompany almost all activities, including paddling a canoe and hunting animals. Music often provides rhythmic support for a recurrent physical action.

Another use of music is to invoke divine action. The rain dance found among some American Indian tribes is one example of this use. The difference between this type of music and the music that contributes to an atmosphere of worship is the fact that the rain dance is believed to have magical significance and is expected to yield a specific result—rain.

Background music in a motion picture, the chant at a rain dance, the hymn and anthem in a religious service, a popular song, the song calling for

---

* Potatoes

social action, and the ever-present music in public places all have a purpose that is easy to understand. That purpose is to fulfill some need beyond the music itself—to bring rain, to promote social justice, to express feelings, and so on. The quality of the music is not as important as the desired outcome. If one long monotonous sound will inspire people to support a cause, then one long sound would be considered sufficiently musical.

MUSIC AS A FINE ART

There is a type of music that exists for no practical reasons. It is music that people listen to because they find it intellectually fascinating and psychologically satisfying. It is music that is contemplated—that is, thought about studiously and considered with undivided attention. This "music for listening" is generally referred to as *art music.* The term does not mean music that is associated with paintings or sculpture; "art" has a broader meaning. The term *fine arts* refers to objects that are created simply for the visual or aural satisfaction they offer.

Many people find it hard to understand the importance of something that has no practical value and exists only for what it is. How can something have value if it doesn't do anything for us? Most things are created because they have some use. They are functional and have a purpose. But music and the other fine arts are different. Painting, sculpture, ballet, poetry, literature, and music exist only for the interest and fascination they hold for people. They have psychological—not functional—relevance.

What are people doing when they stop and look at the graceful shapes of clouds glowing in the sunset? They are pausing to enjoy the view and to contemplate its meaning *for the pleasure, satisfaction, and enjoyment of doing so.* What is valuable is the *experience* of contemplating the *qualities* of the sunset. This careful noticing of beauty does not ensure survival, earn money, improve health, or solve problems. In terms of human existence, viewing a sunset is a pointless thing to do; it's silly, in a way. Yet, contemplating the shapes of the clouds, the varied hues, the silhouettes of objects against the darkening sky is an enriching and satisfying experience for the viewer.

The inability to appreciate the nonfunctionl value of music is well illustrated by this "Peanuts" cartoon.

This nonfunctional type of experience—which can be called *aesthetic* —seems to rise above ordinary, everyday events. It touches the imagination and lifts the spirit, if one is sensitive to it. This passage from the book of Isaiah is an example:

> For you shall go out in joy,
> and be led forth in peace;

the mountains and the hills before you
  shall break forth into singing,
and all the trees of the field
  shall clap their hands.

Certainly these lines are not meant literally. Rather, the poet is telling the people how they will feel when God delivers them from Babylon. The poet could have said "You will leave feeling very happy." The message is there, but how much more stirring and effective it is to invoke some poetic imagination! The biblical version has rhythm, beauty, and color that attract and please the reader.

The arts are a distinctly *human* activity; it is one aspect of living that makes people different from the animals. The valuing of objects for their intellectual and psychological satisfaction calls for a higher type of mental activity than animals possess. As far as can be determined, animals have no sonnets, sonatas, or sculpture.

The difference between human and animal life is the difference between the words "exist" and "live." Human beings want to do more than exist; they do not want merely to survive in a cave and grub roots for food. Humans notice sights and sounds and have feelings about them, and they find life a lot richer because of these feelings.

The arts are created by people for people, and not because some intellectuals say so. Rather, music and art exist because in some way that is difficult to understand they are expressions of the human race at its best. There is plenty of evidence to support this claim.

From a Scientist. In writing about the evolution of the human race in his book *Human Destiny,* Lecomte du Nöuy says that the most important date in all human history was when the Cro-Magnons began putting pictures on the walls of caves and decorating tools, which became "proof of the progress of the human spirit in the direction of evolution, that is, in the direction leading away from the animal."

From a Philosopher. In seeking to prove logically the existence of the human spirit, William Ernest Hocking cites as evidence human creativity in the arts, specifically as exemplified by the music of Bach.

From Educators. Music has been deemed an essential part of a good education at least since Plato, who urged music in the education of every citizen. The universities of the Middle Ages included music as one of the subjects, and present-day educators and organizations like the Educational Policies Commission have recommended music study.

From the Common People. Since the Cro-Magnon period over 15,000 years ago, people have been looking at beauty in the world about them. They are fascinated by the shifting color of a sunset, the shape of a flower, the rhythm of the rolling surf. What's more, they create beautiful and artistic objects. They build parks and museums. They value paintings, symphonies, and poetry, and they seek artistic qualities in their everyday surroundings—in their clothing, homes, furniture, automobiles. A cardboard carton could serve as a lamp table; it would even have the virtue of being far cheaper than a piece of furniture. But human beings simply do not want to exist with drab objects; they want to live.

Since it is evident that the arts, including music, have so much significance in human life, a logical question is: why? To answer this question, one must delve into the areas of aesthetics, philosophy, and psychology. Several explanations can be found. One group of philosophers holds that in music and other arts, people experience in a symbolic way the events of life. The theory proposes that in the recurrent rise and fall of intensity in music, listeners find a parallel with the feelings associated with life. Other philosophers claim that music is "transfigured Nature," transcending the world and revealing "the realm of the ultimate Will (God)," to cite phrases from Schopenhauer. Whatever the reason, people find life richer because of the arts. Differing explanations of why this is so do not erase this fact.

The arts are not the only attempt to live rather than exist. Recreation—

"The Black Bull," a cave painting from Lascaux, France. This picture was painted in the Cro-Magnon period about 15,000 years ago.

playing tennis or cards, for example — is also an attempt to enjoy life. The difference between recreation and the arts is that the fine arts involve analyzing and contemplating objects to a much greater degree.

Why is the word "fine" used with the term "arts"? To answer that question think back to your elementary school days when you decorated a paper plate or carved a figure on a potato for block printing. Would you consider these efforts to be fine works of art? Probably not. Why? Weren't they sincere human creations? Well, yes, but they weren't really *that* good. Most people can do much the same thing. The arts-crafts project didn't represent unusual skill, devotion, or talent. If nearly everyone can do something, it may be art, but it is not fine art. Epic poems, symphonies, and marble sculptures, when skillfully created, arc of value partly because very few persons have the talent and energy to create them.

MUSIC AND CULTURE

Culture—of which music is a part—is all the product and practices of a large group of people. The patterns of sound called "music" were not preordained in the past, with the musician's task being the discovery of those patterns. A search for the perfect melody or the lost chord is about as likely to succeed as a search for the pot of gold at the end of the rainbow. People do not find music; they create it.

Since music is a human creation, it is a part of culture. This means that understanding a culture requires at least some understanding of that culture's music, and vice versa. If people are ignorant of their culture, they are not in the mainstream of its life and are somewhat alien and out of place. Suppose that you moved to India. Like most Americans you would probably find Indian music hard to understand. But if you are going to live there, you should learn something about its music. If you don't you will be a bit of an outsider in that society. You will find life in India a little duller, shallower, and less satisfying.

It is to your advantage to learn as much as possible about the music and other fine arts of your culture. And in a day of jet airplanes and instant communication, it is good to learn a little bit about the music and arts of other cultures as well, as you will in Chapter 8.

"I KNOW WHAT I LIKE"

It's a fact: not all people like the same foods, clothes, cars, or music. Should preferences in music be strictly a personal matter? In one sense the answer is yes. No one need feel ashamed of his or her preferences in any area. Feelings are private and personal, and they cannot successfully be imposed or dictated, even in totalitarian societies. And there seems little danger that today's college students will accept without question the opinions of "authorities" about what music is "good" and what isn't.

The matter of personal preference is complicated, because people generally like what they know and dislike what they don't know. If there is truth in the phrase "I know what I like," there is also truth in the words "I like what I know." Not only is familiar music enjoyed more, it is heard more fully and accurately. People who don't know a type of music simply don't hear some of its subtleties. So while people have individual feelings about what they hear, these feelings are strongly influenced by their cultural conditioning.

To demonstrate the effect of a familiar style of music, listen to two versions of the same work included in the *Record Album.* One is "Mendelssohn's 4th" by Tom Parker and Apollo 100, and the other is the first movement* of Symphony No. 4 by Felix Mendelssohn, performed by Eugene Ormandy and the Philadelphia Orchestra. The Apollo 100 version is in the rock-popular style, while the Philadelphia Orchestra performs the "straight," "square," or original version. The speed of the two versions is about the same, but the Apollo 100 version is played by popular instruments and is shortened by about three

*A *movement* is a large, independent section of a musical composition.

fourths. Listen first to "Mendelssohn's 4th" a time or two until you can remember it fairly well, and then attempt the first movement of the symphony. Don't worry if you can't fully understand the symphony after a couple of hearings. It will come up again in the next chapter.

Sociologists have identified some factors that appear to influence the type of music people prefer. Several of them are included in the discussion on page 10.

The fact that knowledge and preference are mutually dependent has some important implications. First it means that you should know something about a type of music before you make up your mind about whether or not you like it. Second, there are no inherently inferior types of music, only types that are unfamiliar. (Individual pieces within a certain type vary in quality.) Third, some kinds of music are created chiefly for listening, while other types exist mainly to advance nonmusical outcomes. This information should affect how a particular type of music is considered. Fourth, when some musical works seem more worthy of careful attention than others, the difference usually lies in the purpose of the music. Few pieces of art music are suitable for hearing or singing around a campfire, and few campfire songs are fascinating pieces for careful listening.

Usually the musical works that offer the greatest listening rewards are those that require some effort to get to know. Pieces that are easily comprehended on one or two hearings are usually too superficial and trite to hold our attention, and we soon become bored with them.

Although it is perfectly natural to like some musical works better than others, personal preferences should not keep you from learning music that you might find interesting and satisfying if you knew it better. Personal preferences should not be so narrow that you miss out on something good. Because a book can discuss only a tiny amount of all the music that has been created, each writer selects what he or she considers the best examples and most important information in the field. What is presented in any book in any course is just a sample of the total subject—a skimming off of the top of the content.

LEARNING ABOUT MUSIC

As with clothes, cars, and foods, people's musical preferences are learned, not inherited. People learn to like rock music, just as they learn to like Japanese music, country-western songs, or Broadway musicals. An understanding and liking for art music is also learned. Because it is not so familiar and is more complex, art music usually requires more effort to learn.

The type of information that is learned about music should be different from what is learned in most other courses. For instance, in science courses students learn a body of facts covering such diverse topics as the periodic table and the number of light-years to a distant star. In understanding music, however, the value of facts is not so clear. The pitch A above middle C is usually 440 vibrations per second. That fact is of little value in helping someone understand a piece of music, however.

The learning of facts does have a place in a music course because they can help you understand what you hear. The fact that Beethoven was born in

---

WHAT INFLUENCES MUSICAL PREFERENCES?

It's a fact: age and education do seem to affect people's preferences in music. It's not true for everyone, but it is for a lot of people. An especially clear example of this fact appears in the results of the National Assessment of Education, which is the first nationwide study of levels of achievement and attitudes of 9-, 13-, and 17-year olds, and persons between the age of 26 and 35. One question asked of the thousands of people selected on a scientific basis was "What one kind of music do you *most* like to listen to?" The findings were grouped according to the types of music the respondents said they liked best.

With the 13- and 17-year olds, rock music was the overwhelming choice. It was named by 62 percent of the 17-year olds; no other type of music received higher than 8 percent. The answers from the 26–35 age group were very different. Rock fell from 62 to 14 percent, which is an enormous dropoff. Instrumental art music more than doubled from 5 to 12 percent, and country music increased almost six times its former standing by moving from 5 to 29 percent. A parallel question about the type of music liked the least produced answers that rock was the least liked by 25 percent of the 26–35 age group, making it their winner of the "boobie prize" among all the types of music. Its least-liked score with 17-year olds was 11 percent, less than half of its later negative response.

Although there is no large-scale study comparable to the quality and size of the National Assessment of Education comparing the level of education and music preference, a number of studies strongly suggest that the audience for art music is mainly composed of people with a college education. Whether or not it is a desirable situation (and it isn't), people who have not attended college are rarely seen in the audiences for art-music events and seldom buy recordings of such music. The opposite is true: the vast majority of the audience for country music is made up of non-college graduates.

Do a college education and maturation cause one to become more interested in art music, or does college tend to attract those persons who are more likely to be interested in art music? No one knows the answer to that question. Perhaps both situations are true. The increased interest in art music by college graduates may also be due to the fact that many of them took a music or art appreciation course in the process of earning their degree. It looks like learning more about music in a college-level course increases a person's understanding of music, which in turn increases an interest in it.

It's nice to read some good news once in a while.

1770, died in 1827, lived in Vienna, met Mozart, played the piano brilliantly, composed nine symphonies, went deaf in his later years, and was an individualist is interesting to know. But it is more important that his works do not strike you as a jumble of sound when you hear them, because if that happens you have failed to understand Beethoven's *music.*

A sense of musical organization and pattern is called *syntax.* Musical syntax is similar to syntax in language. The words "arms her the girl lifted delicate beautiful" are hard to read, not because they are difficult words but because they don't fall into a logical pattern. When the words are arranged into "The beautiful girl lifted her delicate arms," they are easy to comprehend. Almost everyone knows some music and, therefore, has some sense of musical syntax. However, that sense usually does not include many of the types of music presented in this book. When the music is unfamiliar, more careful listening is required to build up a sense of pattern for that particular type of music.

Closely related to a syntactical sense is skill in listening to music. Without this ability to hear what is happening in a piece, listening to music is like having little vision and visiting an art gallery. Listening skill is so important that an entire chapter is devoted just to it. Equally important are the Listening Guides and the simplified scores in the *Study Guide and Scores.*

There is another area of learning in music. It is a mode of thought, a *way of thinking.* To understand music one needs to consider sounds somewhat as a musician considers them. This statement does not mean that a person must perform music, although that helps. Rather, it means that sounds are to be contemplated and valued for their own sake. Musicianlike thinking does not regard music as something to have in the background while studying or talking with friends. Musicians are interested in the sounds and how they have been treated by a composer or performer.

MUSIC AS A LANGUAGE

Musicianlike thinking also involves an understanding of what music can communicate. Except for words sung in vocal works or a few phrases of music associated with characters or ideas in an opera, musical sounds cannot convey specific meanings; so music is not a language in the usual sense of the word. Music can project certain overall moods to which we can try to attach words, but it cannot, for example, tell you to read Chapter 2 before the next class meeting. Written or spoken words are much better suited to this type of communication. Musical sounds "communicate" only themselves—a pattern of sounds taking place in a period of time.

What music has done in sound for hundreds of years, painting has finally approximated. Until the twentieth century, painters were called on to play the role that the camera does today. That is, they were to paint a scene or person so that the subject could be recognized. The better painters did more than that; they designed and interpreted as they made reproductions faithful to the original subject. Then came the camera, and faithful pictorial representation became a less important function of painters. They changed their orientation from the rendition of specific objects—pictures that "looked like something"—to works that could be valued for their artistic qualities. A painting such as Piet Mondrian's *Broadway Boogie-Woogie* (plate 13) and Picasso's *Three Musicians* (plate 12) have value purely for their visual qualities, and not because they are an accurate reproduction of a scene.

What about music reading? It is useful and valuable, but not absolutely necessary. People who are not musicians can get by without it. However, if they can comprehend musical notation, they will be able to learn more about music. For instance, the musical examples in this book will be more meaningful, which in turn will help in learning to listen.

QUALITY IN MUSIC

Asking the question "Are some musical works better for listening than others?" is like asking "Are some houses more attractive than others?" Questions about *quantity*—which piece of music is longer or which house is larger—are easily answered. Questions about *quality*—which house or composition is more attractive or has more interesting construction—are impossible to answer exactly. Yet, there are differences. Most people find some houses more attractive and some pieces more interesting to listen to.

A few points can be made about quality, however, even if complete answers are not possible. To be compared at all, the objects must be in the same category; apartment buildings should not be compared with single-family dwellings. Comparisons across cultures are not possible either, because each type of house or music has its own logic and style. A Georgian two-floor house cannot be compared with a Spanish villa. Furthermore, the differences in quality are a matter of degree rather than a matter of being obviously good or bad. Some houses are more attractive than others, but that does not mean that the less attractive ones are ugly.

The ability to sense quality in houses or in music requires experience and knowledge. Worthwhile judgments about the qualities of an architectural style cannot be made when seeing the style for the first time. It is necessary to see many examples of the style to make a good assessment. Knowledge and experience make a person an expert in an area. The assessment of the architect who has looked at hundreds of houses is better than that of a novice. One does not have to like or agree with the architect's judgments, but they should be respected.

The knowledge and perceptiveness of individual listeners are crucial to their understanding of a musical work. The composer treads a delicate line between offering listeners something new and something old. To a significant degree, the music must sound familiar; the established patterns must be followed somewhat. But compositions must contain something of interest, something new. If a work has too much novelty and variety, it is a senseless array of sounds; if the piece has mostly the expected patterns, it is boring. In the days of the silent motion picture, a favorite comedy device was for one character to pick up a custard pie and throw it in the face of another actor. Pie-in-the-face humor is funny—the first time it is seen. But after a while the routine loses its impact; it seems too obvious to be funny. Just how much pie in the face can be appreciated and in what setting depends, of course, on the sensitivity and sophistication of the viewer. The same is true of listeners' reactions to what they hear in a piece of music.

Sometimes works of art music seem long and complex, and some of the time they are. Often there is a relationship between the level of sophistication and length, although this is by no means always true. When you were a youngster, maybe you liked to read comic books (nothing to be ashamed of). You enjoyed their stock characters and predictable, simple stories. In a few years you probably grew bored with Batman, Wonder Woman, and whoever. The relating of a simple story no longer satisfied you; you preferred something with a more interesting plot and character development. An author needs space in which to provide these complexities; the result is a novel or a play. To express profound feelings and demonstrate skill at organizing sounds, composers usually need works longer than a minute or two and more than an attractive rhythmic pattern or catchy tune.

This chapter has presented a view of music as something more significant than merely a pleasant diversion or a background for other activities. In a way that no one fully understands, skillfully organized sounds are valuable to human beings. Such music exists for its artistic qualities, and it is often profound and complex. These facts mean that learning to understand and listen to art music is a challenge. Fortunately, the effort is well worth making. Music as one of mankind's great accomplishments yields much meaning and enjoyment to every person who can hear and understand it.

2
LISTENING TO MUSIC

While in college I had the good fortune to take an art appreciation course. One day the instructor projected a Rembrandt painting on the screen, and proceeded to point out Rembrandt's genius in his treatment of light and shadow, the overall design, the brushwork for the hands of one of the figures, and similar features. After about 10 minutes I was struck by the fact that every feature of the painting had been present when I had first looked at it. They were all there before his explanation, but I had not been aware of them; *I had looked but not really seen.* I realized then that I needed to be taught to see all that a fine painting has to offer.

It's much the same in music. Most people need to be taught to hear what a fine piece of music has to offer. The purpose of this chapter is to provide such help.

ATTITUDE

Making attitude the first requirement for appreciating music may seem surprising, but it is essential. You are the only person who can make yourself pay attention instead of daydreaming to music. You are the only one who can focus your listening on one part of the music and who can make yourself remember a musical pattern. No book or instructor can listen for you.

What makes up the right attitude for better listening to music? Partly it is the willingness to make an effort. It requires effort to move beyond a simple awareness of music to an understanding of what it has to offer.

A second aspect of attitude is the realization that quality music is usually not simple. If music were too obvious, it would fail in artistic expression. Certainly, an art that reaches to the very roots of human psychological character is not going to be understood easily.

Another feature of proper attitude is tolerance toward all music. Much of the music discussed in this book may be new to you. Some of it may seem strange and difficult to understand. But if you are openminded, if you assume the integrity of the creative artist, and if you give yourself a chance to understand the work, your chances of growing to like the music are greatly increased.

When some people have difficulty understanding a musical work, they rationalize their position by thinking "Since I don't understand or like the piece, something must be wrong with it." Even though a work may seem unusual or extreme, it should be regarded as an honest effort of the composer, and not the work of a charlatan. You should assume in works generally recognized as of good quality that you have probably failed to hear what's there, and that with more careful study and listening you will come to understand and like it better.

Further, an attitude of tolerance encourages learning. If your energies are devoted to deciding whether you like a work or not, you don't learn very much. Do *not* ask yourself at first "Do I like it?" Rather, ask "Is the melody being played now?" "How does it fit in with what I heard earlier?" "What is the composer trying to achieve in the work?" and similar questions.

TYPES OF LISTENING

Aaron Copland has spelled out three types or "planes" of listening. The types are discussed here as though they are separate and distinct, but of course they are not. Certain aspects of listening are more important than others at particular moments, but they are interrelated. An awareness of these types aids in learning to listen to music more fully.

The Sensuous Plane

The first type is termed "sensuous." This delicious word means "of or appealing to the senses." In music it refers to the purely physical effect that music has on its listeners. When the orchestra works its way to a climactic point and a chill runs up the spine, the effect is primarily a sensuous one. The same is true when people react to a stirring march by tapping their feet, or when a performer dazzles them with a breathtaking performance. Most of the time, however, sensuous qualities in music are not appreciated in such an obvious way. A rich-sounding chord in the music may cause a certain feeling, but the listener does not break into tears or cheers. The feeling is not that strong; and besides, our culture teaches us to control our emotions.

Hearing is an action involving a sense organ. Sounds are physical in nature, so the sensuous pleasures of music are not particularly intellectual. They should not be downgraded, however. There is real pleasure to be gained by listening to the tone of a violin or French horn, just as there is pleasure in looking at a beautiful blue color in a picture. The majestic sounds of an orchestra or large choral group have a certain inherent excitement about them, just as does the view from the top of a mountain. Sensuous pleasure is one of the values of listening to music.

Sensuous effects are not the main value of music, however. An emphasis solely on sensuous qualities eliminates from consideration many musical works of much merit. What's worse, depending on sensuous effects leads down a musical blind alley. A search for music with greater sensuous impact leads finally to music that is simply orgiastic. Such music usually has little artistic quality; it is merely an aural roller-coaster ride or cold shower.

Sensuousness in music also involves time and rhythm. Music, because it is perceived in a context of time, is relived with each hearing. It unfolds as the listener follows. A composer can take the musical resources available and spread them out to achieve the maximum effect. A musical work can have a sudden thunderous chord or the delicate tone of a flute sound at just the right moment. The timing of such effects gives music much of its sensuous impact.

The Expressive Plane

There is little doubt that music has expressive power by stimulating feelings in the listener. A particular phrase may evoke a psychological reaction similar to some previous reaction. But music is limited in its ability to designate specific thoughts. For example, music may give an impression of sadness, but it cannot describe what is causing that feeling. Nor can it designate objects. For most people, one sound does not represent "clouds," another "bread," and another "wheel." Music can provide general moods, but not specific thoughts.

The indefiniteness of music's meaning is to its advantage. A musical work may be heard by a thousand people, but each will hear it in a slightly different way, depending on that person's individual inclinations. Even more important, music can break through the barrier of words. Words are often too brittle, too inflexible, too conventional to allow for full expression. Between the words "anger" and "rage," for example, there are many shades of meaning. Also, anger is usually coupled with frustration or sadness, or both. As a feeling becomes more complex, it is harder to describe. When a loved one dies, a person feels emptiness, grief, remorse, and powerlessness. But these feelings cannot be fully communicated to someone else, no matter how many words are used or how carefully the words are chosen. Music conveys moods, and each listener can fill in the meanings from his or her personal reactions.

The Sheerly Musical Plane

The third plane or type of music listening is the one that nonmusicians tend to ignore. Copland calls it the "sheerly musical" plane. The phrase refers to concentration on what happens in the music—what notes are being played, at what speed, in what combination with what other notes, on what instrument, in what range—the aspects of music discussed in Chapters 3 and 4. It is on this plane that listeners can realize musical values. It is here that they reach a sophisticated stage of musical experience, a stage in which they appreciate the sounds and their manipulation unhampered by physical response or a search for expressive meanings. The acquisition of this type of listening requires more effort and training, but it offers greater rewards. And so this book concentrates primarily on this plane of listening.

Much of the success in hearing the musical qualities in a musical work depends on a different kind of listening, which is the topic of the box on page 18. Partly it depends on the development of listening skills, and this important topic takes up the rest of this chapter.

IMPROVING LISTENING SKILL

The ability to hear music can be improved in several ways. The suggestions here are general, and they are not presented in order of importance.

1. *Concentrate very hard on the musical sounds.* Listening in a half-hearted way isn't good enough. And listening intently for two minutes isn't good enough when the piece is ten minutes long.

2. *Concentrate on the main themes of the piece.* When listening to a work that is unfamiliar, don't try to comprehend everything the first time. Learning to listen is like learning to drive a car. When first learning to drive, one's total attention is directed toward executing a few basic actions, like keeping the car on the road and not hitting other cars or pedestrians. With increased experience, however, the driver can safely do other things—notice the scenery or carry on a conversation with a passenger. Had all these activities been tried too early in learning to drive, a catastrophe might have occurred! The same principle applies to art music; instead of a collision, however, the end result is confusion and a dislike of music.

How can the important features of a piece be determined before hearing it? In this book the main themes and sections are indicated; "road maps" or "guided tours" of sixteen compositions are provided in the form of Listening Guides. If you are listening at a concert or to a recording of a work not covered in this book, you can read the notes on the concert program or record jacket. Such commentary can be helpful, if well written.

On page 23 you can see the first theme of the first movement of Felix Mendelssohn's Fourth Symphony. Try following as you listen to the recording in the *Record Album* (Record 1, Side 1).

The second theme, which also appears on page 23, enters about 1:33 into the music. (It is not included in the Apollo 100 version of the work.) The third theme, on page 24, enters about 3 minutes into the work.

3. *Remember the main themes of the work.* Memory is absolutely necessary for the comprehension of music. At any particular instant, only one sound can be heard. It may be a single tone or several sounds occurring simultaneously. In any case it can be perceived only for a moment, and other sounds are heard in succeeding moments. To make sense out of these brief sounds, a listener must rely on memory and anticipation. Even anticipation involves memory because it is a prediction of what will happen in the future based on what has happened in the past.

Visual experiences do not involve the element of time. An entire

---

LISTENING IN A DIFFERENT WAY

When trained musicians use the word "listen," they do not mean merely hearing or being aware of some sounds. They are referring to an activity involving intense concentration. If you were majoring in music, you would take a course called "ear training." In that course you would listen to melodies, rhythms, and chords, often played by the instructor on the piano, and then you would put what you heard into notation. While taking ear training, many music majors have discovered an important fact: Until they needed to listen in order to pass the course, they had seldom really listened carefully before. They had *heard,* but not genuinely *listened.* As the course progressed, they began to be aware of things in the music that they had never heard before.

Many everyday experiences in hearing encourage us *not* to listen carefully. The mind has a way of "tuning out" sound that it does not want or need to hear. The ticking of a clock, the noise of traffic, and the sound of a refrigerator turning on and off can be ignored. People become good at ignoring music, too. With supermarkets, banks, eating places, and even doctors' offices offering a continual stream of music, to say nothing of all the time radios and records are playing, much of the time all of us must learn to *not* notice music. So, we have learned very well how to "tune out" music, and have little experience in trying to listen intently to music. This is a satisfactory situation with most of the music we hear, but not with art music.

Not only does careless hearing become an established habit, but certain qualities of most popular music are not helpful in teaching you to listen to art music. These qualities are:

---

picture can be seen in a moment. (Closer analysis and full appreciation will require a longer period of viewing, of course.) Suppose that memory and anticipation are made an integral part of the viewing experience. It might be done like this. Assume you are to see an unfamiliar picture that is entirely covered except for a thin vertical slit. Then the slit is drawn slowly across the picture. Your knowledge of the picture will have to be the result of (1) your memory of what you have seen, (2) the slit-sized portion you are presently viewing, and (3) your guess as to what will be revealed in succeeding moments. Difficult? Yes. But that is the way music is perceived, and that is why memory is so necessary.

As a general rule, the more frequently you experience something, the better your recall will become. Think again of the picture analogy. The fifth time the slit is drawn across the picture, you will have a much clearer idea of what the picture is like than you had the first time. The same is true of music. The more often you hear a piece, the better you will remember it and the more fully you will understand it. Repeated hearing of a musical work is the surest way to gain greater understanding of it.

Occasionally listen to short sections of a work several times. This practice is especially useful in places that seem disorganized. Between

---

1. Most popular music is played at a loud dynamic level. By comparison, art music may seem weak and anemic.

2. Most popular music works are short, often about 2½ minutes long (except for music played at discos). In art music the listener must pay attention and remember what has been heard for periods as long as 15 or 20 minutes without a break. To someone not accustomed to art music, listening to it may be like watching a film of a basketball game in slow motion.

3. Few popular works of music present any development of themes, something that is a feature of art music. The main musical idea in a popular song is presented in the first 30 seconds; after that it consists of that idea repeated and a little contrasting material.

4. Popular music often presents more activity and threatrical features. Performers move around a great deal and make their actions and facial expressions quite obvious. Flashing lights are often a part of the setting. Art music has little theater, except for opera or ballet. Instead, the attention is centered on the sounds being produced.

For these reasons, learning to listen to art music usually requires some different listening habits. In effect what you will need to do is listen to most music in the usual lackadaisical way, but adopt a different way of listening to art music.

Yes, it can be and is done by many people.

Yes, it's well worth learning to listen carefully to art music.

---

playings, attempt to run through the music in your mind by shutting your eyes and trying to rehear it mentally. Repeat this process of actual and imagined hearings, several times if necessary, until your mental rendition of the portion is accurate.

Memory can be aided in several other ways. Actual participation helps one to learn music more thoroughly and remember it more accurately, so sing, play, and whistle themes when possible.

4. *Notice what happens to themes and musical ideas as the music goes along.* In his Fourth Symphony Mendelssohn does some masterful composing that can easily be overlooked unless attention is directed toward it. From both the first and third themes he extracts small melodic ideas, or *motives.* From the first theme he takes the opening three or five notes, sometimes changing the rhythm slightly. From the third

theme he takes five notes and the rhythmic pattern. These motives bob

in and out of the music and, in the process, act as unifying ideas for the movement. More than that, at two places well along in the movement Mendelssohn has the two motives vie with each other, almost as though there was a contest between them. Listen to the movement again, and notice the two places where first one motive and then the other is heard in alternation. The contesting of the motives adds much to this already vibrant piece of music.

5. *If you have trouble following and remembering the main themes and what happens to them, listen to the work again—and again, if necessary.* Only a few people can really hear an artistic work of music once and grasp its themes and form, so don't be surprised or discouraged if you can't do it. After all, how many times do you hear a popular song during the weeks it's at the top of the charts? Even though it may not be complicated or long, you can't remember it completely after several hearings.

6. *Apply knowledge to what you hear.* It has been said that knowledge leads to understanding. If a section of a work is in a certain form, knowing the characteristics of that form will help you follow its design and grasp more of its meaning. Information about music helps you know what to listen for and, equally important, what not to listen for.

The first movement of Mendelssohn's Fourth Symphony uses sonata form, which will be explained more fully in Chapter 15. The overall plan of the form is three large sections: one in which the themes are presented, one in which the themes are developed or "worked over," and then one in which the themes from the opening section are presented again. In this symphony the opening third of the movement is repeated before moving on to the middle or development portion of the form. However, the repeat sign is often ignored in performances, as it is on the version in the *Record Album.*

7. *Try to be more aware of the more subtle and smaller features of the music.* Although following the main themes of the music is helpful, don't stop there. Musical works written for artistic reasons have skillful manipulations of sounds and many subtleties. A slightly changed chord, a brief interruption of the rhythmic pattern, a new combination of instruments, the sounding of a fragment of the theme—such apparently insignificant techniques can spell the difference between an ordinary piece and an exceptional one.

8. *Encourage your reactions to music.* This suggestion should *not* be taken to mean that you should emote or talk to yourself when hearing a piece. Rather, you should be aware of your feelings about what you hear and let them be active. Consciously notice your responses while listening.

Feelings are private and are impossible to communicate fully. Because feelings are so difficult to describe and because no one can be sure what another's feelings are, music cannot be accurately expressed by highly subjective adjectives. "Sad" music to one may be "devout" music to another. It is not accurate to say "This music should make you feel sad." Although a person may correctly say "It makes *me* feel sad," such a statement can apply only for that individual. Some aspects of music are more objective and "public" and, therefore, are appropriate for discussion and examination. "The music is loud" is a far more verifiable statement than "The music is sad." What happens in the music can be discussed objectively; how an individual reacts to the music cannot.

As you listen to the first movement of Mendelssohn's Symphony No. 4, select a short section and try to notice the subtle reactions it encourages in you. For example, in the first three measures of the first theme the opening pattern of three notes is repeated immediately and exactly. The second appearance makes the melodic figure seem more emphatic. The figure is heard a third time, only this time its upper note is higher than before and a bit longer, which makes it seem even more emphatic. Also listen to the energetic accompanying music played by the orchestra just ahead of and during the first theme. It seems designed to grab the listeners' attention. Now, what has just been described is but 3 measures lasting not more than 2 seconds among the 563 measures in the movement. Virtually every measure of this music offers something to which you can and should respond—like the way the music quickly leads up to the first note in the second line of the first theme example, just to indicate another place.

9. *Don't conjure up visions or fantasize when listening to music,* unless it is a work specifically composed for that purpose. Sometimes students in elementary school are given listening lessons dealing almost exclusively with "program" music—music in which the composer consciously attempts to associate his work with a particular story or scene. This type of music is in many ways well suited to the requirements of guided listening experiences in the early grades. Unfortunately, however, students sometimes begin to assume that for every piece there must be a picture or story. They conclude that music is incomplete by itself.

As was pointed out earlier, the most rewarding listening is in terms of musical treatment of sound. Trying to imagine a tender love scene or a ship plowing through the waves only distracts from the sound of the music itself. Instead of listening the mind is engaged in creating fantasies. Pictorial association can easily become an invitation to daydream.

10. *Practice learning to listen to music more effectively.* There are several ways in which you can do this. One is to follow the suggestions in this chapter.

Another is to utilize the Listening Guides for various pieces of music located throughout this book. These guides outline the main features of a musical work such as changes of melody, prominent solos, form, and so on. On the left-hand side of each guide appears the time at which the feature appears in the recording in the supplementary *Record Album.* Other recordings will have similar but not identical timings. (Whether you follow a watch or clock as you listen is a matter of personal preference.) Listen to the recording while following the Listening Guide as many times as you need to be able to follow along without losing your place. When you can listen and keep your place in the guide, you can be reasonably sure that you are hearing the main features of the work, although the more subtle aspects may remain to be uncovered by later listening efforts. Don't try to listen to any work more than twice in one day; spread the listening practice out over a number of days by doing some each day rather than "cramming" immediately before examinations. In fact, start practicing listening today! A Listening Guide for the first movement of Mendelssohn's Symphony No. 4 is included on pages 23–24.

LISTENING GUIDE

MENDELSSOHN: SYMPHONY NO. 4, "ITALIAN"

First Movement (Record 1, Side 1)

Exposition

0:02 First theme (*A*) played by violins.

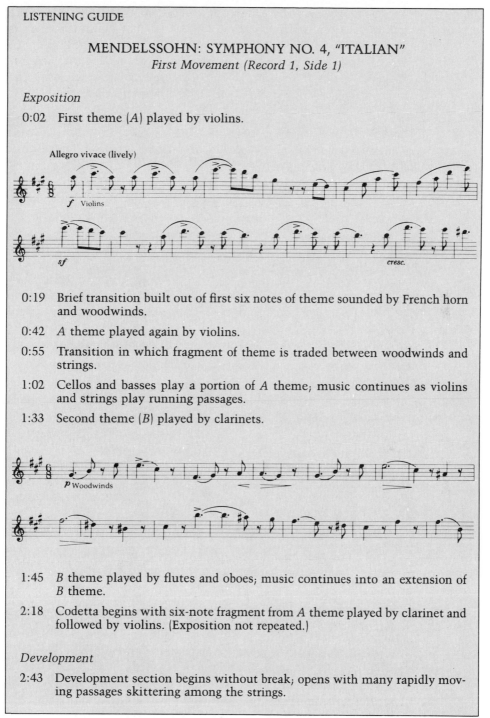

0:19 Brief transition built out of first six notes of theme sounded by French horn and woodwinds.

0:42 *A* theme played again by violins.

0:55 Transition in which fragment of theme is traded between woodwinds and strings.

1:02 Cellos and basses play a portion of *A* theme; music continues as violins and strings play running passages.

1:33 Second theme (*B*) played by clarinets.

1:45 *B* theme played by flutes and oboes; music continues into an extension of *B* theme.

2:18 Codetta begins with six-note fragment from *A* theme played by clarinet and followed by violins. (Exposition not repeated.)

Development

2:43 Development section begins without break; opens with many rapidly moving passages skittering among the strings.

(continued)

2:56 Third theme (*C*) begins in the second violins; is soon imitated by first violins, violas, and then cellos and basses.

Music grows more contrapuntal.

3:34 Fragment of *A* theme sounded by woodwinds; music increases in intensity as both *A* theme and *C* theme vie with each other.

3:59 *C* theme sounded by orchestra.

4:14 *C* theme repeated at loud level by orchestra. Fragments of *A* theme are heard again.

4:30 Music becomes quieter as *A* theme fragment is heard more clearly.

4:44 Oboe sounds long note that leads into *A* theme fragment and transition into final section of the movement.

Recapitulation

5:05 Theme *A* played by violins.

5:25 Transition of rapidly moving notes played predominantly by violins.

5:37 Theme *B* played by violas and cellos; clarinet and flute play rapidly moving contrasting figures.

5:50 Theme *B* played by violins and later extended.

6:25 Coda begins with appearance of *C* theme played softly by woodwinds.

6:49 Theme *C* and fragment of theme *A* are played at same time, *A* in the violins and *C* by the flutes and oboes; then the themes alternate.

7:14 New melodic material introduced in viola and cello parts, and first violins have rapidly moving notes; music begins to build again.

8:17 Movement closes with fragments of *C* theme and a series of brief chords.

A third way this book helps you improve listening skill is through the simplified line scores that appear in the supplementary *Study Guide and Scores.* These scores take the twenty or more lines of an orchestral score and reduce them to one or sometimes two lines that present the most noticeable and significant aspect of the music at that point. Also, they indicate the instruments heard most clearly and describe the form and other features. While you may not be able to read music, you will probably be able to follow a line score as you listen. (The material on page 25 offers a little help and encouragement in doing this.) As with the Listening Guides, it is suggested that you listen as many times as needed until you can follow the music without getting lost.

LOOKING AT MUSIC NOTATION

Your reaction when first looking at the music examples for Mendelssohn's Symphony No. 4 and other works that appear later in the book might have been best expressed in two words: "Good grief!" Are you supposed to be able to read music? Are you expected to understand every symbol and word that appears in the examples?

Well—yes and no. No, it is not necessary that you understand every symbol and word in the examples. No, you are not expected to be able to perform the examples from reading the music. But, yes, you can get an impression of how the music goes from looking at the notes, probably much more of an idea than you may realize.

To begin with, the five horizontal lines (called the *staff*) are like a graph that shows how high or low a note is. When the notes extend beyond the top or bottom of the five-line staff, short lines are added to extend the range of the "graph." Therefore, you can sense in what direction and how far the notes are moving. For example, in the first theme of the first movement of Mendelssohn's Symphony No. 4 (page 23), you can easily tell that the first three notes are immediately repeated exactly. You can also tell that the third group of notes is like the first two, but goes up higher.

Rhythm is indicated by adding a vertical line (called a *stem*) to the notehead, or by adding horizontal lines to the stem, or by filling in the head of the note to make it solid rather than a circle, or by adding a dot to the right of the notehead. A number of things about the music affect how fast the sounds actually happen, but *in general* the more the noteheads are filled in and beams added, the faster the music will sound. The note that is just a circle is the longest type; a circle with a stem is half the length of the circle; a note with a stem and solid head is half again as long; a solid head with a stem and horizontal line or a waving line called a *flag* is half again as long, and so on. Therefore, you can tell that the first note in the second theme (page 23) is noticeably longer than any of the two notes and a rest that follow it, and that the note in the sixth measure is significantly longer than any others on that line. The dot, by the way, adds half the value to the note.

Many of the signs and words tell the performer how the music is to be performed. Some of these are quite guessable. For instance, in the example for the second theme of Mendelssohn's Fourth Symphony there are two rather long horizontal lines below the notes that come together as the music progresses. These lines indicate that the music should grow softer. The chevron-shaped marks above the notes in both the first and second themes indicate that the note should be accented, or "punched out" somewhat louder. The dots over or under (*not* beside) notes, as can be seen in the third theme, tell the performer to make the notes clearly separated—like dots. Traditionally the verbal directions in the music are in Italian. Some of these are also guessable. "Espressivo" means "expressively" and "risoluto" means "resolutely." "Appass." is an abbreviation for "appassionato," a word that every college student should be able to guess. "Cantabile" means "singing-like," which may not be quite as easily guessed unless you have studied French or Spanish. In this book these words are followed by an English translation in parentheses.

If you want to know more about music notation, the topic is presented in Appendix B.

You can also work with another person to develop listening skill by pinpointing changes in short rhythmic or melodic figures. For example, play a four-note pattern on the piano. Then repeat the pattern, but change one note. Ask the other person to say whether the first, second, third, or fourth note was altered. Tap out two rhythmic patterns, making one change in the second pattern. The length of the melodic or rhythmic patterns can be increased as skill improves.

Tests of Good Listening

How can you tell if you are really hearing what a piece of music has to offer? There is no easy answer, but these practical questions can be raised:

Does the music seem sensible?

Does it move along without seeming to be dead and stagnant?

Do you hear specific details of form, rhythm, and melody?

Do you keep your attention focused on the music almost all the time?

Do you get some reactions or feelings from the music as you hear it?

Do you like to listen to the music? Do you enjoy it? Does it seem interesting?

If the answer to all these questions is "yes," there can be little doubt that you are hearing the music as it should be. Composers intend that their music be enjoyed, that it be found interesting and meaningful. They want their skill at handling music to be appreciated, and they want to produce music that will have lasting attraction. They realize that music will cause feelings in the listener. When people hear music more fully and with feeling, they are understanding and appreciating it.

3

WHAT IS MUSIC? MELODY AND HARMONY

Music is one form of sound. Sound results when a vibrating string, reed, or vocal cord sets air molecules in motion. The molecules bump into one another, something like billiard balls, each setting the next in motion. This chain reaction continues until it strikes the eardrum, where the nervous system picks up the impulses and transmits them to the brain. Some of these sounds are considered music and others are not. What makes the difference?

WHAT IS MUSIC?

To be music, sounds must seem organized and meaningful. The letters t-t-h-r-s-e-c are all letters in the alphabet, but unless arranged into s-t-r-e-t-c-h, they have no meaning. They are not organized. Music, therefore, is organized sound. Random sounds cannot be music except by sheer accident, although in some types of music the performer is given some choice of what to do and/or when to do it.

Most musical sounds possess pitch—recognizable levels of highness and lowness. But not all musical sounds have pitch. The snare drum and the cymbal have been recognized members of the orchestra for 200 years, yet these and a few other similar instruments do not play different pitches. In recent years sounds have been synthesized on tape recorders and electronic equipment, and pitch is not always present in such music. *Music,* then, *is a combination of sounds that are organized and meaningful, occurring in a prescribed span of time and usually having pitch.*

Because music is organized sounds, what composers do with and to sounds is crucial. Sounds are to music as cloth is to a piece of clothing. Just as tailors cut and shape fabric to create an article of clothing, composers can manipulate and form sounds to create a musical composition. Composers, and, in some kinds of music, performers, can treat sound in several ways:

They can make it high or low.

They can place it before, after, or among other sounds in a series.

They can combine sounds so that several are heard simultaneously.

They can regulate the duration of a sound.

They can make a sound stronger or weaker.

They can change the quality of a sound in countless ways.

Finally, they can use any combination of these six possibilities.

For somewhat different reasons, musicians and students learning about music need to think about how sounds are organized into music. Musicians consider what can be done with sounds because it is the substance with which they work. Students of music need to learn some basic terms that describe the various ways in which sounds are manipulated. Although these terms are needed in discussing music, they are even more important in helping you to think about music. Words are implements that permit us to classify objects and ideas and to organize our thinking. For example, if you understand the word "timbre" (which you will after studying Chapter 4), you can consider more effectively why one particular quality of sound was chosen instead of another for a certain portion of music. When you are conscious of the choices, you will be thinking the same way as a musician, and you can begin to understand and appreciate better the musical decisions represented in the musical work.

PITCH

The degree of highness or lowness of a sound is referred to as *pitch.* Pitch can be measured scientifically, since it is determined by frequency of molecular vibrations, with a more rapid vibration giving the sensation of higher pitch. Highness as the word is used in music has nothing to do with height in terms of space. In many non-Western cultures the word that refers to highness has the connotation of smallness, and in some cases, femininity. Among many Americans, there is a prevailing misconception that "high" means "loud" and "low" means "soft."

Musicians use the term *interval* to describe the distance between two pitches. The most fundamental interval is the *octave.* It gets its name from the fact that the duplicate of any note is eight notes away from the original, and for this reason it is given the same letter name. Two pitches an octave apart, if sounded together, blend so well that they sound almost like one pitch. The naming of intervals is discussed in Appendix B.

MELODY

Melody refers to pitches sounded one after another in a logical series to form a satisfying musical unit. For most people melody is experienced in simple, short pieces of music that exist primarily because their melodies are pleasing to hear, play, or sing. People recognize and respond to many melodies, ranging from "The Star-Spangled Banner" to folk tunes and popular songs. (The word *tune* is often used as a less formal synonym for melody.) There are also many more complex pieces that are valued mainly because of the quality of their

---

SOUND AND VIBRATIONS

The violin string demonstrates a principle of sound discovered by Pythagoras in ancient Greece. He found that when half the length of a string is sounded, it produces a pitch one *octave* above the original pitch of the string. The octave has twice the number of vibrations of the lower pitch and blends very closely with it. Pythagoras also discovered two more simple ratios of vibrations in addition to the 2:1 ratio of the octave, but could have had no way of establishing the many other parts of the fundamental sound that go along with it.

The number of times the string vibrates each second determines the pitch of the sound. However, not only is there the fundamental vibration of the full length of the string from the bridge to the saddle next to the pegs, there are also many less-powerful vibrations of the string into halves, quarters, eighths, thirds, sixths, and so on. The picture illustrates the complex patterns of the string as it vibrates. The number and strength of these *partials* of the fundamental determine the quality of the sound.

The width or size of the vibration of the string largely determines how *loud* the sound is. A soft sound vibrates over a narrow range, while a loud sound moves back and forth over a wider area.

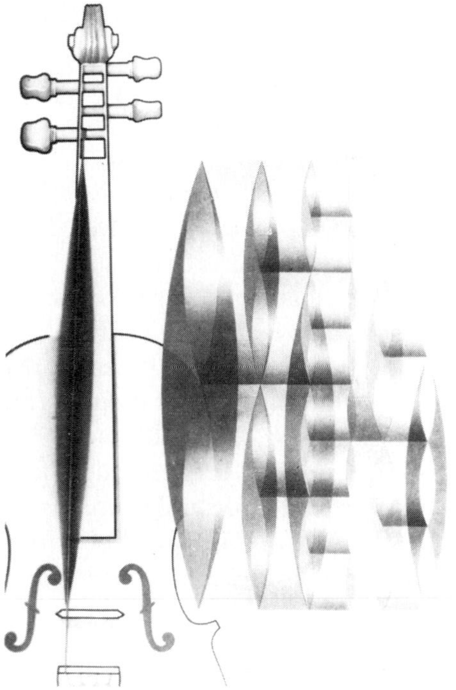

The function of the box under the string on the violin is to give the sound "body" and to amplify it. Other instruments have other means of making and amplifying sounds, but the same principles of pitch, partials, and loudness are still true.

---

melodies. These works tend to be short, usually not more than a few minutes in length. Although long works such as operas appear to refute the previous statement, most of them are actually made up of shorter pieces, each with a distinctive melody.

There is, however, another aspect of melody that is not so familiar. A melody can become the basis for a long work of music. Such a melody is called a *theme* to indicate its function as a central musical idea for the piece. The manipulation of melodies is one of the more important features of music composed for artistic purposes.

A theme may or may not be "tuneful." There are many examples of mediocre tunes that become the themes for great works of music. In other words, a theme is often important not so much because of *what it is* but because of *how it is developed and what it becomes.* One of the best-known examples is the short theme from the first movement of Beethoven's Symphony No. 5:

The three G's and an E flat that make up the theme are hardly much as a melody, but what Beethoven does with this melodic figure is nothing short of genius.

To illustrate how melodies form the basis of a rather large work, listen to *Nocturne* by the nineteenth-century Russian composer Alexander Borodin (pronounced *Bor*-o-deen) (Record 1, Side 1). The music was originally for string quartet, but today is usually performed by a string orchestra. Its melody is the basis of the song, "And This Is My Beloved" from the Broadway musical *Kismet* of some years ago. It is presented in the Listening Guide on page 32.

One musical symbol that is a bit less common but is prominent in the second theme of Borodin's *Nocturne* is *tr.* It is the abbreviation for *trill,* which is the rapid alternation between a pitch and the pitch immediately above it.

Melodies do not exist by themselves; for several reasons, they are heard as part of a total musical work. First, melodies are played on an instrument or sung with a voice. So the features of the voice or instrument—its tone quality, its adaptability to the requirements of the melody—contribute to the effect of the melody itself. A melody that is well suited for the violin may be a poor one for the flute, and vice versa. Second, since melodies must exist in a dimension of time, they all have rhythm. The duration of the notes and their placement in time are as vital as their pitch. One awkwardly placed rhythmic value can ruin an otherwise good melody; on the other hand, a distinctive rhythmic pattern can enhance a rather average tune. Third, almost all melodies

Alexander Borodin.

have other pitches sounded with them. The kind of accompaniment given a melody makes a lot of difference. Fourth, other music usually precedes and follows the melody. The right kind of musical buildup can make an everyday melody sound beautiful. Fifth, most melodies tend to center about one particular pitch. There is a sense in which the music moves away from and returns to a "home" pitch. More will be said about this important fact in the discussion of harmony.

Melodies come in a wide variety of shapes and sizes. Some are long, giving the impression of ever-flowing melody that never quite repeats itself. Others seem to be a collection of short fragments. Some are easily sung; others are impossible to perform except on a particular instrument. Strangely, some melodies are difficult to remember. These melodies are found in some twentieth-century music, in which the pattern of sounds is unfamiliar.

COUNTERPOINT

Some melodies can be combined. The combination of two or more melodic lines simultaneously is called *counterpoint.* The word comes from the Latin *punctus contra punctum,* meaning "point against point." (In medieval times, notes were called "points.") The adjective form of the word is *contrapuntal.*

LISTENING GUIDE

BORODIN: *NOCTURNE*

from String Quartet No. 2, (Record 1, Side 1)

0:00 *A* theme played by cellos over throbbing, syncopated accompaniment.

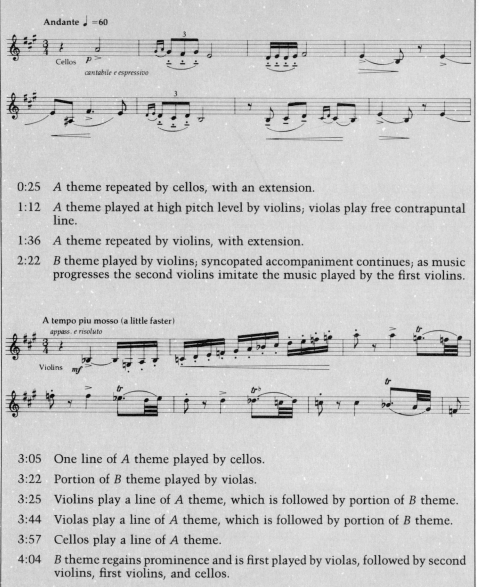

0:25 *A* theme repeated by cellos, with an extension.

1:12 *A* theme played at high pitch level by violins; violas play free contrapuntal line.

1:36 *A* theme repeated by violins, with extension.

2:22 *B* theme played by violins; syncopated accompaniment continues; as music progresses the second violins imitate the music played by the first violins.

3:05 One line of *A* theme played by cellos.

3:22 Portion of *B* theme played by violas.

3:25 Violins play a line of *A* theme, which is followed by portion of *B* theme.

3:44 Violas play a line of *A* theme, which is followed by portion of *B* theme.

3:57 Cellos play a line of *A* theme.

4:04 *B* theme regains prominence and is first played by violas, followed by second violins, first violins, and cellos.

4:34 *A* theme played by violas, with portion of *B* theme following.

4:55	*A* theme returns very much as it appears in opening of work, except that solo cello and solo violin play it in imitation.
5:20	*A* theme played in imitation by entire cello and violin sections.
6:06	First and second violins play *A* theme at high pitch level in imitation.
6:28	Violins repeat playing of *A* theme in imitation, and portion concludes with fragment of *B* theme.
7:12	Coda begins with violas playing portion of *A* theme, which is "answered" by a portion of the *B* theme.
7:27	Cellos play the *A* theme, which is followed by portion of *B* theme.
7:40	Violins play portion of *A* theme; fragment of theme is passed among the string instruments.
8:52	Concludes very quietly at a high pitch level.

Counterpoint is essentially linear music. That is, the composer intends for the listener to perceive these sounds as two or more concurrent melodies. Even though some harmony is produced as the lines of counterpoint are sounded, the sense of line is more important.

All that has been said about melody also applies to counterpoint. What is true of a single melody can also be true of melodies when sounded together. Rhythm, instrumental or vocal characteristics, and musical context are all involved.

A clear-cut example of counterpoint is a section from the Cantata No. 140, *Wachet auf, ruft uns die Stimme* ("Wake Up, Call the Voices"), by J. S. Bach. In the fourth section, which begins with the words "Zion hears the watchmen calling," one melody is played by the strings in the orchestra. Try singing the melody, or play it on an instrument. Performing the melody will help you remember it. If you can't perform it, follow the notated music closely as you listen to the piece. Notice that the melody gives the impression of easy, graceful motion. The lines bracketed together on page 34 occur simultaneously, so follow them together.

CANTATA NO. 140

Fourth Section

10
Tenors
Zi - on hört die Wäch - ter sin - gen,
Zi - on hears the watch - men call - ing,
Violins
das Herz thut ihr vor Freu - den sprin
her heart with - in her leaps for glad
20
gen, sie wa - chet und steht ei - lend
ness, she wakes and stands to has - ten
auf.
forth.

After the melody in the strings has been played once, Bach brings in the chorale melody on which three sections of the cantata are based. (A *chorale,* pronounced "coh-*rahl,*" is a Lutheran hymn tune. Bach did not compose the chorale melodies, but he wrote all the other parts of the cantatas.) This melody is sung by a section of male singers. A listening score for the entire section is included in the *Study Guide and Scores.*

Borodin's *Nocturne* also contains counterpoint. Toward the end of the work when the opening melody returns, the violins play it at a high pitch level while the cellos perform it at a low pitch level. The two sections play the melody in a follow-the-leader fashion, much as people do when performing a round. Then the two violin sections play it in this manner. The musical terms for this are *strict imitation* or *canon.*

HARMONY

Another way to manipulate sounds is to combine them, usually to enhance a melody. The practice of adding accompanying sounds is called *harmonizing.* Harmonizing takes place when a folk song is sung with guitar accompaniment. The folk song may consist of an attractive melody, but sung alone it is likely to seem a bit barren. The harmony part contributed by the guitar provides an appropriate setting and adds to the effect of the song.

The word "harmony" itself is sometimes confusing, due to its somewhat different use in everyday language. If the students in a dormitory get along well, they can be said to be living together harmoniously. In music, harmony refers *only* to the simultaneous sounding of pitches, regardless of whether the effect seems pleasing or not.

The difference between counterpoint and harmony is largely one of viewpoint. Counterpoint reflects a linear, horizontal view of music. *Harmony,* on the other hand, stresses the vertical aspect, the effect of sounds heard simultaneously. But counterpoint and harmony are not as distinct as the two viewpoints might indicate. The lines of counterpoint do form simultaneous combinations of sound, and every group of vertical sounds occurs in relation to other groups that have preceded and will follow it. In music there is almost always an element of the horizontal (the progression of music in point of time) and the vertical (the effect of sounds at any particular instant). The difference between harmony and counterpoint, therefore, lies in the amount of emphasis given to each dimension.

The term *texture,* as it is used in music, refers to whether the music is essentially linear or chordal. Texture might be expected to refer to the degree of smoothness or roughness of sound, but in music the word is not used in that way. Linear music is called *polyphony* (po-*liff*-o-nee); music made up of a melody and chords is known as *homophony* (ho-*moff*-o-nee). These textures will be examined more thoroughly in Chapters 9 and 11.

An understanding of harmony can be aided by defining a few basic terms. One is the word *chord.* A chord is the simultaneous sounding of three or more pitches. Chords are the basis of harmony. The most familiar chord consists of three notes selected on the basis of an alternating pattern somewhat like the black and red squares on a checkerboard. If every other white key is played on the piano, the result will be a chord of some type. In musical notation such a chord can be written so that the notes appear in a line-line-line or space-space-space arrangement. (Spaces as well as lines are used in the musical staff.)

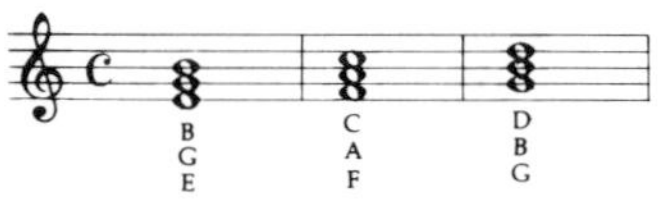

The "every other" pattern can further be observed in the alphabetical names of pitches in a chord—A C E or B D F, for example.

Sometimes the same three notes in a chord are rearranged. For example, a low C may appear as a high C instead. This rearrangement may hide the basic pattern from the eye of a person looking at the notation, but the ear can hear the similarity, and the chord is still essentially the same.

The "every other" pattern of chord construction is so basic that it is frequently found outlined in melodies as well as in chords. The first seven notes of "The Star-Spangled Banner" are an example of this.

If the sounds give the listener the impression of repose, equilibrium, or agreement, they are called *consonant.* If they give the impression of harshness, tension, or disequilibrium, they are called *dissonant.* But words can't really describe these two concepts. They are given meaning only through the hearing of actual chords, and even then there is no clear-cut distinction between consonance and dissonance. It is more accurate to speak of *degrees* of consonance and dissonance.

Chords are heard not only as units containing consonance and dissonance, but also as single sensations of sound. Composers, especially in the last one hundred years, have sometimes added pitches to chords to achieve a desired "color." The effect is enriched sound rather than tension.

Most music tends to relate to a pitch center, and this tendency is especially true in harmony. Chords contribute to a sense of relationship with the home tone, which is called the *key center* or *tonic.* Music usually reveals a continual ebb and flow away from and toward a key center, and this process establishes a sense of *key* or *tonality.* Interruption of the forward movement within a key gives the listener a feeling of dissatisfaction, and yet expected motion can become dull if it is never varied. Therefore, a composer or arranger cannot select chords in a haphazard manner. The progression of chords to and from the tonic must be planned so that the desired effects can be achieved.

Even while chords are being heard as units, they are implying horizontal motion as well. For this reason, a series of chords is called a *progression.* Here is a simple chord progression that gives a strong sense of forward motion. Play it or have someone play it for you.

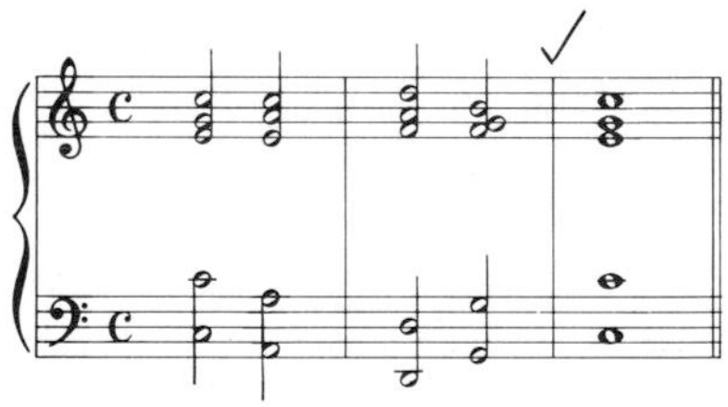

During one playing, stop at the checkmark without sounding the last chord. The incomplete feeling that is created will be easily sensed.

The purpose of harmony in music is to enrich the musical effect. If a folk singer strums the wrong chords on a guitar, he or she can ruin the impact of the singing. For example, if an important note in the melody, say a B, is sung, but an A C E chord is strummed, a severe dissonance will be created. Or the player could play an A C E chord when C E G is needed to return to the tonic. In a more sophisticated musical work with more complex harmony, the skillful handling of chords is just as critical. Harmony is comparable to the setting for a play. The effectiveness of the actors' lines in Shakespeare's *Macbeth,* for example, depends much on whether the scenery and costumes indicate the location as a street corner in twentieth-century America or a gloomy medieval castle. The harmony and the melody must jibe; they must complement each other.

To delve further into the topic of harmony at this point would require lengthy and technical discussion. To pursue further aspects of harmony, consult the material in Appendix B.

Let us again refer to the chorale melody Bach used for his Cantata No. 140. Usually the last section of a cantata is the singing of the chorale melody by the congregation and choir. (The cantata as a musical form will be studied in Chapter 12.) Bach takes the same melody to which he previously gave contrapuntal emphasis and now he harmonizes it. In other words he applies two concepts—counterpoint and harmony—to the same melody, but in different portions of the cantata.

In this harmonization the melody is in the top notes in the *soprano* part. The three remaining parts, reading downward, are called *alto, tenor,* and *bass* (pronounced "base"). The soprano and alto parts are usually sung by women and the tenor and bass by men.

Seventh Section

Soprano
Alto
Tenor
Bass
Glo - ri - a sei dir ge - sun - gen
Glo - ry now be sung to praise Thee
mit Men - schen und eng - li - schen Zun - gen,
with tongues of all man - kind and an - gels,
mit Har - fen und mit Cym - beln schon.
with harps and cym - bals sound - ing forth.

If you can sightread the alto or tenor lines, or hear them performed without the other parts, you will notice that they lack the melodic interest of the chorale melody. It is clear that these inner parts are subordinate to the main melody. The bass line has more musical interest. Although its wide interval leaps make it seem less smooth than the chorale melody, it does have melodic character. The outer voices (soprano and bass, representing the highest and lowest parts) are more easily heard by the listener, so it is logical that Bach made these parts more interesting.

Melody, counterpoint, and harmony have something in common: They are all made from pitches. The differences among them lie in whether or not the pitches are sounded together and the way in which the pitches are organized. As important as pitches are, they are not the only aspect of sound. These other aspects are the subject of the next chapter.

4

WHAT IS MUSIC? RHYTHM, LOUDNESS, TIMBRE, TEXTURE, AND FORM

Three dimensions of sound were discussed in the preceding chapter: pitch, the formation of a consecutive series (melody), and simultaneous combinations (counterpoint and harmony). A fourth way to manipulate sound is in terms of time. Time can be controlled in two ways: (1) by altering the length or duration of a sound and (2) by adjusting its placement in relation to sounds occurring before and after it. The organization and management of time in music is very important because music is an art that exists in time.

RHYTHM

The word that refers to the flow of music in terms of time is *rhythm.* It does not refer only to a recurrent pattern, orderly movement, or a repeated situation, as it sometimes does in everyday usage. The word "rhythm" is a broad term that has several aspects.

Beat

One such aspect is *beat,* which many people incorrectly think is a synonym for rhythm. The beat is the recurrent throb or pulse in music. It is felt more strongly in some pieces than in others, but it is present most of the time. In fact, if by some mechanical means a piece of music could be performed without a feeling of beat, the listener would tend to put one there anyway.

There are usually subdivisions and multiples of the beat that are sensed along with it. The beat and its divisions and combinations are something like a large wave on the ocean. Not only is there the main swelling of water; there are also numerous smaller formations apparent on the wave, and larger tides affecting all the waves. Because there is more to rhythm than just the beat, a piece with a throbbing, pounding beat may actually have little rhythmic interest, at least to the musician, while a quiet-sounding work may have an elaborate rhythmic structure.

The beat remains basically steady, like a heartbeat. A heartbeat that jumps from a couple of fast beats to a few slow ones and then to one or two fast beats again is a sign of physiological disorder. Music with an unstable beat is equally disturbing and unpleasant. (Try to sing a familiar song while purposely speeding up and slowing down the beat. The effect is irritating and unsettling.) Occasionally, of course, it may be desirable to change the beat suddenly, but only if the composer and performer think it is right for that piece of music.

The beat is the unit of measurement for the duration of musical sounds. In music a sound is not judged as lasting for "three seconds" or "one-half minute." It is described as lasting for several beats, one beat, or a fraction of a beat. The time allotment for a note is called the *value* of the note. Note values are listed in Appendix B.

Meter

In most music, beats are organized into patterns called *meter.* There is a natural human tendency to organize sounds into patterns. The sound of a clock becomes "tick-tock" in our minds, even when all the sounds are the same. Meters are created by emphasizing certain beats: "ONE-two, ONE-two" gives the listener a two-beat pattern; "ONE-two-three, ONE-two-three" gives a three-beat feeling, and so on. Poetry often contains metrical patterns (called iambic, trochaic, etc.). Here is an example from Stephen Vincent Benét's "The Ballad of William Sycamore":

My father, he was a mountaineer,
His fist was a knotty hammer;
He was quick on his feet as a running deer,
And he spoke with a Yankee stammer.

In music notation each group of beats is marked off into a separate unit called a *measure* by vertical bar lines on the staff. Each measure contains all the notes to be sounded over the span of time ticked off by two beats, three beats, or whatever the number of beats in the meter.

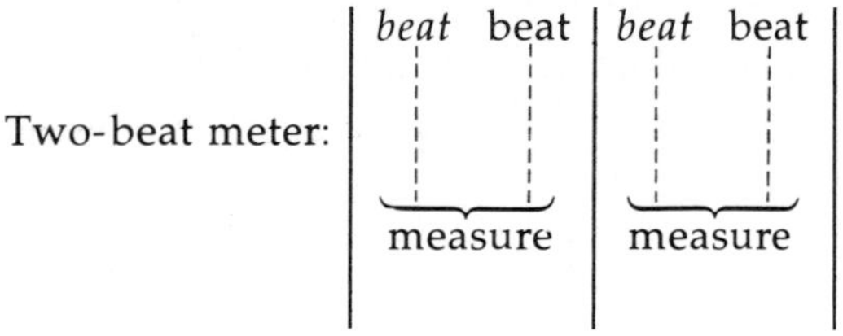

At the beginning of almost every piece, and sometimes within it, can be seen two numbers in the staff, one on top of the other. These numbers are known as the *meter signature* or *time signature,* and they tell the musician how the beats are going to be grouped and how they will be indicated in the notation. Generally, the top number tells how many beats are in each measure, and the bottom number tells which note value represents the duration of one beat. Exceptions to the rule of meter signatures exist, and these exceptions are explained in Appendix B.

TEMPO

The word *tempo* in music refers to the rate of speed at which the beats (*not* the notes) recur. In other words, it is the pace of the beat. Tempo can be indicated accurately by use of the metronome, commonly seen as a pyramid-shaped object whose inverted pendulum can be set to tick at varying speeds. (Electrical models are rapidly replacing their wind-up predecessors.) Some pieces of music display a marking like this at the beginning: ♩ = M.M. 120. The initials M.M. stand for Maelzel's Metronome; Maelzel patented the work of another man and had the device named for himself. The number refers to the number of ticks that are to be produced per minute. The quarter note means that each quarter note should last for one "tick," with other note values being in direct proportion.

Since the metronome was an invention of the early nineteenth century, composers before that time were not able to specify the desired tempo so exactly. They indicated the tempo in a general way by the use of a word such as "fast" or "slow." Even today, when a metronome marking may be written in the music, it is still customary to include verbal indications for the desired tempo. These words give the performer some flexibility in establishing the speed of the piece, and this freedom tends to make for more inspired and imaginative performances.

The words indicating tempo are generally written in Italian, although in the last 100 years some composers with strong feelings of nationalism have chosen to write directions in their native language. The terms for tempo are especially significant because they are usually listed in concert programs and on record labels to identify the movements of a longer work. Here are some of the common terms:

ITALIAN TERM	MEANING
Largo	Very slow, broad
Grave	Very slow, heavy
Adagio	Slow, leisurely
Andante	"Walking," moderate tempo, unhurried
Moderato	Moderate speed
Allegretto	"Little allegro," moving easily
Allegro	Moderately fast, moving briskly
Allegro molto	"Much allegro," very brisk
Vivace	Lively
Presto	Very fast
Prestissimo	As fast as possible

Composers often couple other directives with the tempo indications. These additions usually have more to do with style than with speed (such as *con fuoco,* "with fire or force"; *sostenuto,* "smooth, sustained"). Within the broad framework of a specific tempo there may be indications of slight tempo changes (such as *meno,* "less"; *più,* "more"; *poco,* "a little"; *rit.* or *ritard,* "gradually slower"; *accel.* or *accelerando,* "gradually faster").

Beats and Notes

The speed of the beats and the speed of the notes are not the same thing. They are related, of course. A fast tempo usually has more notes in a given span of time, but not always. Even though a piece may have a rapid tempo, the sounds may be in long note values, giving an impression of slowness. And the opposite can happen: A phrase of music with a slow tempo may have short note values and appear to be quite fast. Other things being equal, a note will last longer at a slow tempo than at a fast tempo.

In most music the sounding of the notes themselves provides the only clue as to where the beats occur. A drum doesn't need to tap out the beat so that the listener can feel the pulse of the music. Most of the time the note patterns fit the underlying metrical pattern. If this doesn't happen, the music has been incorrectly written. Putting the measure lines in the wrong place is like putting the periods and commas in the wrong place when writing a paragraph. Imagine reading: "The music of Bach is. Very interesting to, hear it makes much. Use of. . . ."

But if a piece of music always follows a predictable pattern, it doesn't have much rhythmic interest. In such music the composer must make sure there is enough that is interesting in the harmony and melody so that the listener will want to hear it.

Syncopation

Sometimes the composer or performer deliberately misplaces the rhythmic emphasis and puts emphasis—called *accent* in music—where it's not expected or removes it where it is expected. This alteration of the accents is termed *syncopation.* It appears in most types of music to some extent, but it's especially prominent in jazz and twentieth-century music. In the song "Dixie" there is syncopation on that word in the phrase "I wish I was in Dixie." If you sing the word *Dixie* in that phrase so that the second syllable occurs exactly on the second beat, it will be a duller piece of music.

Many popular songs contain a kind of syncopation. The normal pattern for accented and unaccented beats in two- and four-beat meter is 1 2 3 4, or 1 and 2 and. However, many popular songs have those beats performed 1 2 3

4, or 1 *and* 2 *and.* The first theme in the first movement of Beethoven's *Pathétique Sonata* (Chapter 19) contains syncopation when the second note in the third measure occurs off the beat.

"Mambo" and "Cha-Cha" from West Side Story

Almost no single musical work includes all the different aspects of rhythm. Leonard Bernstein's two dances from *West Side Story* are excellent examples with which to summarize a discussion of rhythm. Both "Mambo" and "Cha-Cha" are Latin American dance patterns, and both are incorporated in the original Broadway version of the musical in a dance sequence called "The Dance at the Gym" (Record 1, Side 1).

"Mambo" certainly demonstrates the excitement that rhythm can create. It achieves this partly through a rather fast tempo, although that is not the main reason for the tremendous energy of the music. The more important causes are the simultaneous appearance of more than one rhythmic pattern and the frequent and rapid use of syncopation. The color provided by the trumpets, voices, and percussion also contribute to the overall sense of excitement.

"Mambo" is filled with examples of interesting rhythmic writing, but perhaps the best one appears at about 1:11 into the recording in the *Record Album.* In this example the notes are placed so that the progression of sound at any point can be seen from the pattern of sixteenth notes at the top. These fly by at the rate of *four* in *less* than *half a second!*

The "Cha-Cha" is the opposite of "Mambo." It contains a little syncopation, but it is quite subtle. The four-beat meter is followed regularly. Actually, much of the rhythmic interest of "Cha-Cha" lies in the rests, in which finger snapping takes place on the recording in the *Record Album.* The melody, by the way, is a version of the song "Maria," which appears a little later in the musical.

LOUDNESS

A fifth means of manipulating sound is to alter its strength. In music the word *loudness* or *dynamics* refers to the amount or strength of sound. It is perhaps the most easily understood dimension of music. Good composers and performers make skillful use of loudness shading, so that the music reveals an almost constant interplay between loud and soft sounds.

A change of loudness is one of the most common and most effective means of musical expression. In interpreting a piece of music, performers speak of *phrasing,* which refers to the way musical segments, called *phrases,* are performed. Phrases in music are comparable to phrases found in language. The performer studies a musical phrase and decides which notes should be emphasized. These notes are performed more loudly; they are emphasized. The rhythm and tone color may also be altered slightly, according to the demands of the phrase. All of these refinements cause the phrase to take shape and be musically logical. Small but skillful gradations of loudness can make the difference between a sensitive performance and one that is matter-of-fact.

The relationship between meter and loudness was pointed out previously in this chapter. Without a change in loudness it would be difficult to sense a meter.

The method of indicating loudness in the music is rather simple. Two Italian words are basic: *p* or *piano,* "soft"; and *f* or *forte,* "loud." The words can be made more extreme: *ff* or *fortissimo,* "very loud"; *pp* or *pianissimo,* "very soft." Or they may be made more moderate by adding the prefix *mezzo* (pronounced *met*-zo), meaning "medium": *mf* or *mezzo forte,* "moderately loud"; *mp* or *mezzo piano,* "moderately soft."

Gradual changes of loudness are indicated by *crescendo* or its abbreviation *cresc.,* "get louder"; and *decrescendo* or *decresc.,* "get softer." The latter term can be indicated equally well by *diminuendo* or *dim.* Frequently the *crescendo* is represented by the sign < and the *decrescendo* by the sign >.

TIMBRE

Another way to change a sound is to alter its quality or "color." The technical word for tone quality is *timbre* (*tam*-ber). It is to music as color is to art. Many instruments can play middle C (violin, clarinet, flute, trumpet, trombone, cello, and others), and most people can sing that note. Yet, each instrument mentioned and each person will sound the same pitch with a somewhat different quality. The reasons for this are described on page 47.

Differences of quality can also be achieved on a single instrument. A phrase played at one pitch level may sound quite different if played at another level on the same instrument. For example, the low notes on the clarinet have a resonant but mellow quality, while the very high notes are shrill and piercing.

Good composers use the colors of voices and instruments to achieve the desired effect. If a stirring, strong sound in an instrumental work is wanted, a trombone may be called for; if a lyric, high sound is wanted, a flute or violin may be specified. Not only do composers use the colors of voices and instruments individually; they also combine different qualities to achieve new colors. French horns and cellos playing together produce a certain quality; add clarinets, and the quality is changed slightly; add bassoons, and it is changed again. The possibilities are almost limitless for composers who know instruments and voices and how to write for them.

In recent years composers have become even more intrigued with timbre. They are exploring sounds other than those made on traditional musical instruments, which already offer a myriad of possibilities. Different qualities of sound can form the basis of entire pieces of music that contain little except timbre produced in a planned order and span of time. Although such pieces may seem strange when first heard, they demonstrate the inventiveness of the human mind and the vast possibilities available through the use of tone color.

COMBINING THE ELEMENTS: MUSIC

Music is created when its elements—pitch and rhythmic patterns, loudness and tone colors—are organized and combined in such a way that the hearer finds the listening experience rewarding and meaningful. The resulting combination is greater than the sum of its parts because each element is reinforced and enhanced by another. So the work of manipulating the elements is crucial in music.

How the Composer Works

Where do composers begin? How do they start? In some respects they go about writing music in the same way you go about writing a paper for English class. Before composers can begin, they need sufficient technical skill in writing music, just as you need to have familiarity with spelling, punctuation, and grammar in order to write clearly. They have a general idea about what they want to put into sound, just as you have an idea about what you want to say in words.

Composers vary in their methods, just as students in English vary in how they work out their compositions. Some spend much time thinking before

---

TONE QUALITY

Fortunately for music, no instrument except for an electronic synthesizer can produce a perfectly pure sound. The tuning fork is pure but not very interesting to hear. It is dull because it lacks the rich spectrum of partial pitches found in the sounds of musical instruments and voices. As is shown in the picture of the violin string on page 29, every voice or instrument produces a number of other pitches in addition to the fundamental pitch. These other pitches always follow a specific pattern. Here is the pattern for the first five in the pattern for the note G.

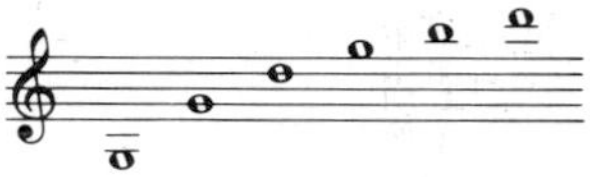

As you can see, the pitches are closer together in the higher notes, but they also become softer as they get higher.

The number and strength of these partial sounds (also called *harmonics* or *overtones*) determine the particular timbre or tone quality of a voice or instrument. The oscilloscopic pictures of the timbres of three woodwind instruments demonstrate their strikingly different timbres. The flute (a) has the clearest quality, the one closest to the tuning fork. The clarinet (b) has a rich and unique pattern in which the partial an octave above the fundamental is vurtually absent. The oboe (c) presents the jagged contour that contributes to its reedy and plaintive timbre.

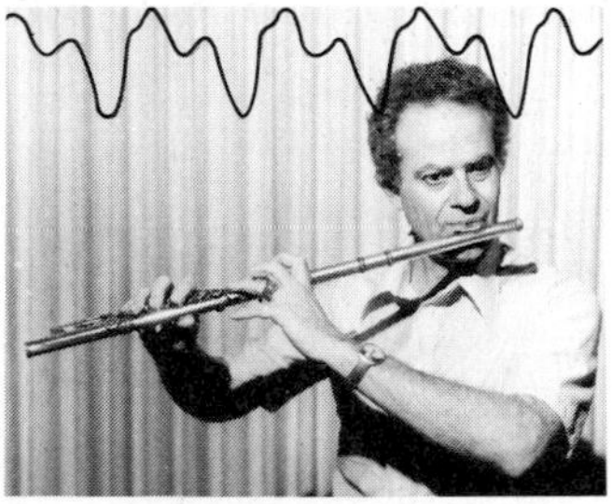

a

b

c

---

putting anything on paper; others make trial runs with ideas; still others work up an outline. Quite early in the process, most composers are thinking of the medium for which they are writing: a song, a symphony, a piano sonata. Aaron Copeland, the eminent American composer, says he begins with a musical idea—a melody, an accompanying figure, or a rhythmic pattern. He takes this idea and begins to develop it into a musical composition.

One thing composers do *not* do is languish about, waiting to be "inspired." Creative ideas do not just happen. Creative efforts involve false starts, revisions, and much hard work. One need only look at Beethoven's manuscripts, for example, to see in the anguished scrawls and messy erasures the struggles that he went through in order to create. It seems inaccurate, therefore, to credit composers with superhuman and mysterious powers. True, most composers are creative artists who possess much natural talent. To them, however, writing music is a logical and expected activity; it is their work. If there is a mystery in composing, it is in the marvelous ability of the human mind to create. The creative and planning mind, then, is the most important factor in the formation of music.

Form

The word *form* in music refers to the overall pattern that can be heard in relatively long segments of a composition. It can also describe the nature of complete works—symphony, oratorio, concerto—or the pattern of shorter sections and lines of music. Although the term "form" can be used in three different ways, each use of the term still refers to the organization of sounds as revealed through patterns in music.

The presence of form can be sensed, even though the particular form may not be identified by name. Such sensing indicates that to some degree you are recognizing the organization of musical elements. You need not be able to say, on hearing a Mozart symphony, "Why, that's in sonata form, and right now the second theme of the exposition is being played." If you can recognize the form to that extent, however, you are far more likely to understand the music than is a person who cannot. You probably have a much better idea of what you are hearing, and consequently you will enjoy it more.

Rhyme schemes for poetry are often indicated by letters of the alphabet. The procedure is much the same for analyzing lines or short sections of music. The familiar carol "Deck the Halls" illustrates a common form. The first line of music is:

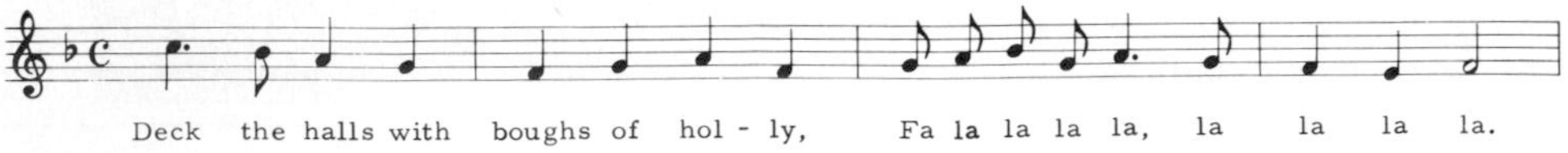
Deck the halls with boughs of hol - ly, Fa la la la la, la la la la.

The first line is usually called *a.* For more lengthy sections of a work, capital letters are used. In any case, these letters have nothing to do with names of pitches. They merely denote the order of appearance of phrases or sections.

The music for the second line of the song is exactly like the first, so this line may also be indicated by an *a:*

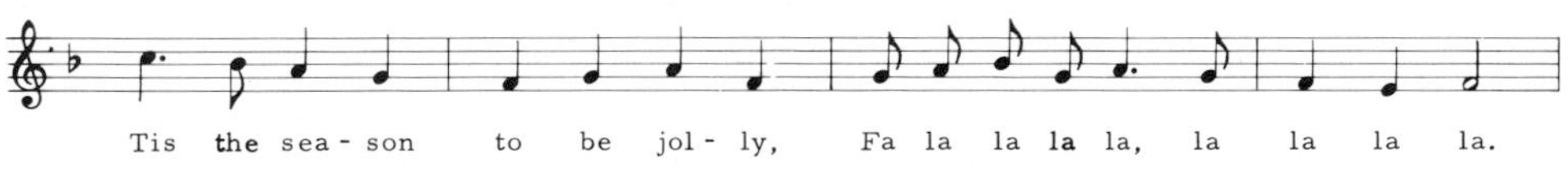
Tis the sea - son to be jol - ly, Fa la la la la, la la la la.

The third line is different, so it is indicated with the letter *b:*

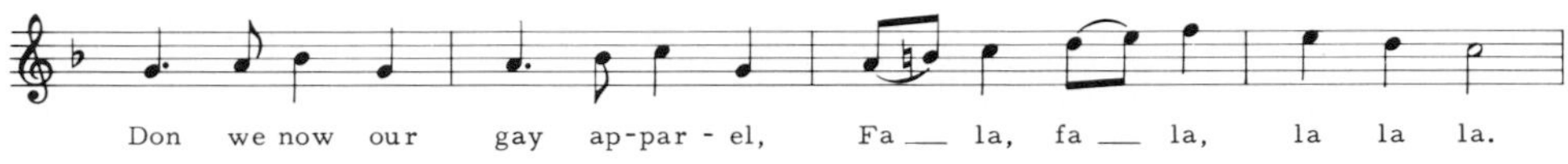
Don we now our gay ap-par - el, Fa — la, fa — la, la la la.

The music for the first half of the last line is identical to the first two lines, and the last half is similar:

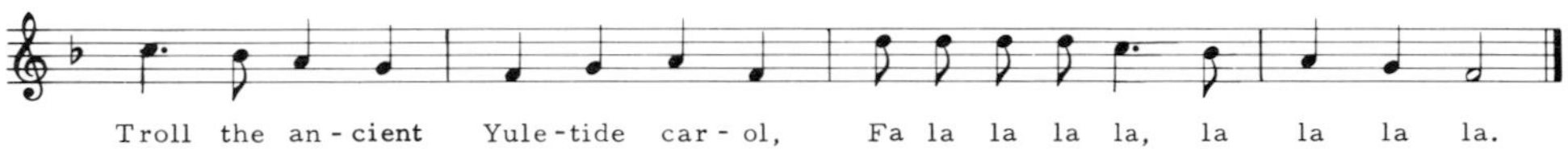
Troll the an - cient Yule-tide car - ol, Fa la la la la, la la la la.

This fourth line is like but not identical to the first, so it is indicated as *a′*. The prime mark (′) denotes some alterations but not enough to warrant a different letter.

The form of "Deck the Halls," therefore, is *a a b a′*, or basically *a b a* with *a* repeated. It contains the seeds of contrast and unity necessary for attractive musical compositions. The *a* line is heard twice, so that its second appearance provides an element of familiarity and unity; the *b* part provides contrast.

The coalescence of musical elements is crucial to composers, performers, and listeners. Here is the advice given to his colleagues by Frédéric Chopin, an outstanding pianist and composer of the nineteenth century: "An artist should never lose sight of the thing as a whole. He who goes too much into details will find that the thread which holds the whole thing together will break, and instead of a necklace, single pearls will remain in his stupid hands."

5

MUSICAL INSTRUMENTS: ORCHESTRAL AND BAND

There are hundreds of different kinds of instruments in the world, and they can be grouped in a variety of ways. This chapter presents instruments associated with the band and orchestra.

ORCHESTRAL INSTRUMENTS

The instruments of the symphony orchestra can be divided into "families" on the basis of similar design and principles of sound production. There are four families: strings, woodwinds, brasses, and percussion.

Strings. The strings are the backbone of the orchestra, and they constitute about half of its membership. The violin, viola (vee-*o*-la), cello (*chel*-o, officially the violoncello), and the double bass have essentially the same design. The main difference among them is one of size and, consequently, the general pitch level at which they sound. The player produces sounds by plucking the strings with the finger or, most often, by drawing a bow across the strings. When the hair of the bow is examined under a microscope, tiny depressions can be seen. The uneven surface catches on the string to set it vibrating. The player applies rosin to the bow to help it drag more firmly on the string.

The body of the instrument is largely hollow. The wooden bridge visible on the top of the instrument props up the strings and transmits their vibrations to the body, which amplifies the sound and provides the distinctive tone quality of the instrument.

Extending out from the body of the string instrument is the neck, on which is glued a black fingerboard. The player presses the string down firmly on the fingerboard to change the pitch. The shorter the string—that is, the smaller the distance between bridge and finger—the higher the pitch. The four strings are of different materials, thicknesses, and tension. Tension is regulated by the pegs at the scroll end of the instrument. When the player tunes, a

The violin. Isaac Stern, concert violinist.

tightening of the string produces a higher pitch, while loosening the tension causes a lowering of the pitch. The instruments are tuned so that there is an interval of five notes between the pitch of each string and the one adjacent to it; on the double bass the interval is four notes.

Although a performer usually plays a single pitch at a time, it is possible to play two or even three notes at one time, a technique called *double* (or *triple*) *stops.* The bow in this instance is drawn across adjacent strings in a single stroke, so that they vibrate simultaneously.

The string player controls pitch with the fingers of the left hand and manipulates volume and phrasing with the bow held in the right hand. The more pressure that is applied to the bow and the faster it is drawn over the strings, the louder the sound will be. The bow can be drawn smoothly, or the strokes can be separated to produce a variety of styles.

All good string players vibrate the left hand in a slight, rapid motion when playing. This motion creates *vibrato,* which adds warmth to the tone quality by causing fast but small changes of pitch. The tone can be made softer and more mellow by the use of a mute—a wood or plastic device that is fitted over the bridge.

The violin is the smallest and highest pitched of the four string instruments. Its range covers well over four octaves from its lowest note, which is G below middle C. There are two sections of violins in the orchestra: first and second. There is no difference in the instruments themselves; the distinction lies in the way the music is written for them. The first violin part is generally higher, more difficult, and more easily heard in the total orchestral sound.

The viola is somewhat larger, but like the violin it is held under the chin. Its general range is about five notes lower than the violin's.

The cello rests on the floor and is supported lightly between the player's knees. It is pitched an octave below the viola. In general its range is comparable to that of a baritone singer, and it is especially well suited for warm, melodious passages.

The double bass is known by several other names: contrabass, string bass, and bass viol. When playing, the performer either stands or partially rests his weight on a high stool. The double bass is seldom heard alone, although its tone is not unpleasant in the slightest.

The harp is also a member of the string family. Its sounds are made by plucking the strings with the hands. There are only about half as many strings on a harp as there are keys on a piano. But the harp compensates by means of a pedal mechanism, which can change the length of the strings almost instantaneously to provide different pitches.

Woodwinds. As their family name implies, these instruments use wind to produce their sounds and are (or were) made of wood. Their strong point is

The cello.

The double bass.

the varied timbres they produce. In a symphony orchestra one usually finds two flutes and a piccolo, two oboes and an English horn, two clarinets and a bass clarinet, and two bassoons and a contrabassoon. Saxophones seldom appear in a symphony orchestra.

All woodwind instruments consist of bodies that are hollow tubes. Holes along the length of the tube are opened and closed either by the fingers or by small pads attached to key mechanisms. As the holes are opened closer toward the source of air, the pitch gets higher because the air column inside the instrument is being shortened. At a certain point a key is opened to permit the instrument to move into a still higher range, and the holes and keys can be used for a new set of pitches. Woodwinds are articulated by the player's tongue, and each instrument can normally produce only one note at a time.

The flute changed its wooden body early in the twentieth century in favor of a metal one, which is usually of a silver-nickel alloy. The metal construction gives the instrument a more brilliant tone. The flute and its diminutive version, the piccolo, are unique in that they produce sound on the stopped-pipe principle. Many a youngster has made a sound by blowing across an empty pop bottle. The flute operates in a similar way. What happens is that the air going into the pipe collides with the air returning from the stopped end, and a sound results. The flute's range is from middle C up about three octaves, and the piccolo's range is one octave higher.

The oboe is made of wood that, like the wood in the clarinet and bassoon, has been carefully treated to prevent warping and cracking. The distinctive tone of the oboe is produced by a double reed. The reed is similar to bamboo cane.

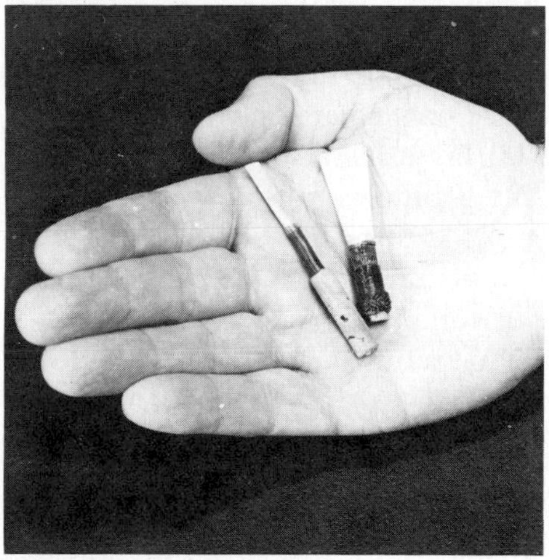

Oboe and bassoon reeds.

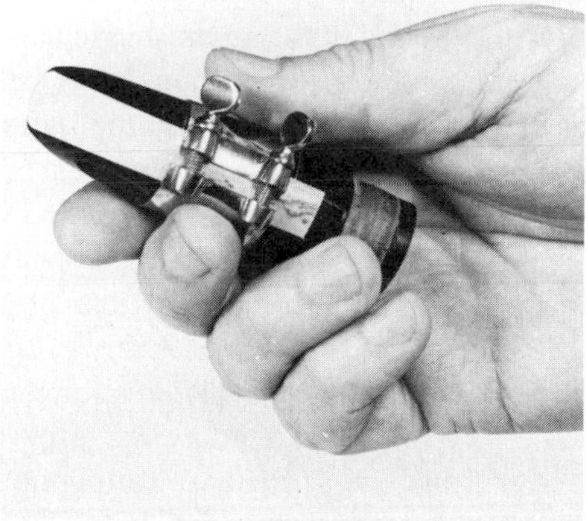

Clarinet reed and mouthpiece.

It is shaved, and the two small reeds are wired together so that the insides of each reed face each other. The instrument does not have a wide range; it extends only a little over two octaves. Its best notes lie around an octave above middle C, where they can easily be heard. The English horn is neither a horn nor English. It is basically a large oboe with a bulb-shaped bell, and it sounds five notes lower than the oboe.

The bassoon is also a double-reed instrument. It can play from more than two octaves below middle C to at least one octave above it. Its tone is highly distinctive, but not powerful. The range of the contrabassoon is an octave lower; its lowest pitch reaches almost to the lowest note on the piano.

The clarinet has the most varied timbre in its range of more than three octaves. Its low notes have a quality quite different from its high notes. It has only one reed, which is placed on a mouthpiece. Clarinets come in a variety of sizes, but only three are found regularly in the symphony orchestra: the B-flat soprano, A soprano, and the B-flat bass, which looks like a black wooden saxophone.

The saxophone is the newest instrument in the woodwind family. There are eight different sizes of saxophones. The instrument appears only occasionally in orchestral music but is a regular member of concert and jazz bands.

Brasses. Sounds on brass instruments are produced by "buzzing" or vibrating the lip membranes on a cup-shaped mouthpiece. This buzzing sound is then amplified through a metal tube with a flared bell at the end. Today all brass instruments have curves in them so that they can be held more easily. Also, all of the orchestral brasses have some means of changing the length of the tube by the use of valves or a slide mechanism.

A bugle is not an orchestral instrument, but it can illustrate an important principle of brass instruments. The bugle has no valves, so all its different pitches must be produced solely by changes of tension in the player's lips. This limitation means that the bugle can produce only a certain series of pitches, the familiar ones heard in bugle calls. All brass instruments achieve these different pitches by lip manipulation, but if pitches outside the series are desired, the length of the tube must be changed so that a new series is possible—one that contains the desired pitch. This is the function of the valves on most orchestral brasses: By pushing down various combinations of valves, the player opens or closes different portions of tubing so that the air column can be made the desired length for a new series. Like the woodwind instruments, the brasses are articulated by the player's tongue.

Generally an orchestra uses three trumpets, four French horns, two tenor trombones, one bass trombone, and one tuba. The trumpet is the highest pitched brass instrument. It has three piston valves, which when activated change the length of tubing used. Its range is not extremely wide, extending from a few notes below middle C up somewhat over two octaves. What the instrument lacks in range it makes up in power. The cornet is similar to the trumpet except for the conelike tapering of its tube or bore. (The trumpet bore is more like a cylinder.) The shape of the bore accounts for the mellower sound of the cornet. A mute for cornet or trumpet can be inserted into the bell. It softens the tone and makes it sound more pinched. The most common is a fiber mute, although there are other materials and several variations of the basic mute.

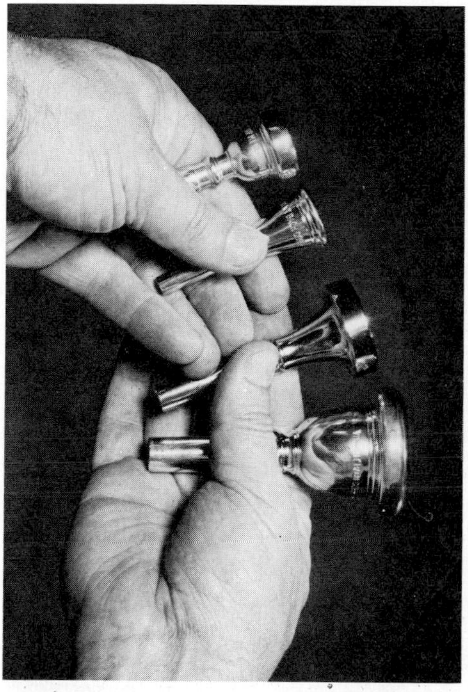

(Top to bottom) Trumpet, French horn, trombone, and tuba mouthpieces.

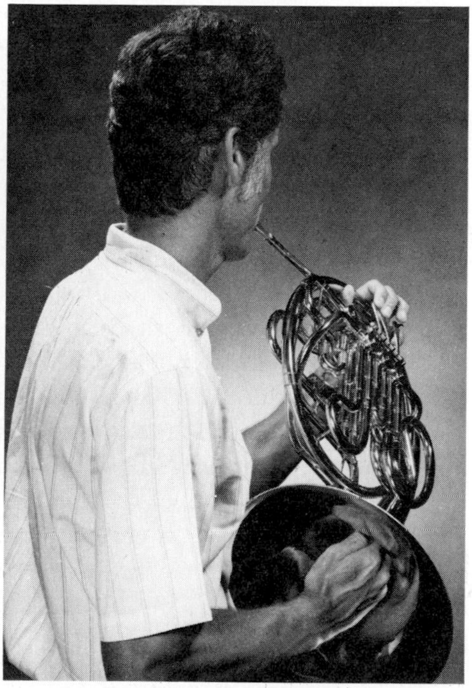

The French horn. The photograph shows the position of the player's right hand in the bell.

Extreme accuracy of lip tension is required in order to produce the desired pitch on the French horn. It can sound more than an octave lower than the trumpet, and its overall range is wider. Its valves, which are operated by the player's left hand, are of a rotary type. The valve mechanism turns to open up lengths of tubing. As is shown in the pictures on this page, the player inserts his right hand into the bell to modify the timbre. A mute is occasionally used.

The trombone is an octave lower than the trumpet. It is unique in that it has a slide to regulate the length of its tubing. The trombone has great power. The bass trombone is somewhat larger than the usual tenor trombone and plays a few notes lower.

The tuba is comparable to the double bass in its musical function. It seldom gets to play a solo, although when played well it has a pleasing timbre. Like most brasses, it can produce quite loud sounds, as well as a subdued dynamic level.

Percussion. All percussion instruments produce sound by being struck or rattled. They may be further grouped into those that play definite pitches and those that do not. Consider first those that can produce definite pitch.

A kettledrum is a large copper bowl over which is stretched a plastic head. Around the rim is a ring that regulates the tension of the head when the small protruding handles are adjusted: The tighter the drumhead, the higher the pitch. The problem with this procedure is that it takes a minute or two, which means the performer must stop playing for that period of time. Until about the middle of the last century, composers had to consider the inconvenience of retuning when they wrote for the instrument. Today there is a pedal mechanism that regulates pitch very quickly. The sticks have padded heads. To permit a variety of tone qualities, the player has available several pairs, all having a different firmness.

Kettledrums do not appear singly. A minimum of two is required, and more are often necessary, each of a different size and tuned to a different pitch. The name "timpani" is plural and is synonymous with kettledrums. The instruments are positioned around the timpanist in semicircular fashion for ease of playing.

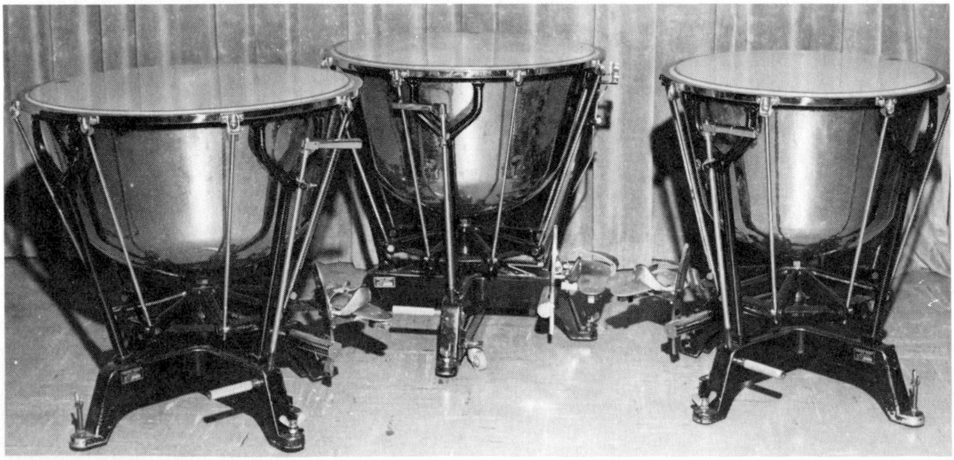

Timpani. The pedal for each drum is at the side of the instrument.

The glockenspiel, xylophone, marimba, and vibraphone are similar. All have tuned bars arranged in the pattern of a piano keyboard, and the player strikes them with mallets. The glockenspiel is highest in pitch and has metal bars that produce a light, tinkling sound. The xylophone has wooden bars and produces a dry, brittle tone. The marimba also has wooden bars, but below them hang hollow metal tubes that permit the sound to resonate for a few moments after a bar is struck. The vibraphone also has tubes, but has in addition an electrically powered device that produces a vibrato in the sound.

The piano and celesta are keyboard instruments that produce sounds by percussive means, as is described on page 67. Sounds on the piano are produced when a felt hammer, activated when the player depresses a key, strikes the strings. Because of this striking action, the piano is included among the percussion instruments despite the fact that its tones are produced by the vibration of strings. The celesta looks like a small spinet piano, but it is essentially a glockenspiel operated from a keyboard. Its steel plates are struck by hammers.

Chimes also produce definite pitches. The player hits the top of a hollow metal tube with a wooden hammer.

Percussion instruments of indefinite pitch are many in number. Most important is the snare drum. It is hollow, with calfskin or plastic heads stretched over both top and bottom. On the underside are several strands of wire that rattle against the lower head when they are tightened sufficiently to touch it. These are the snares, and they give the drum its characteristic crisp sound. The snares can be loosened to produce a heavier sound. The snare drum is played with a pair of wooden sticks.

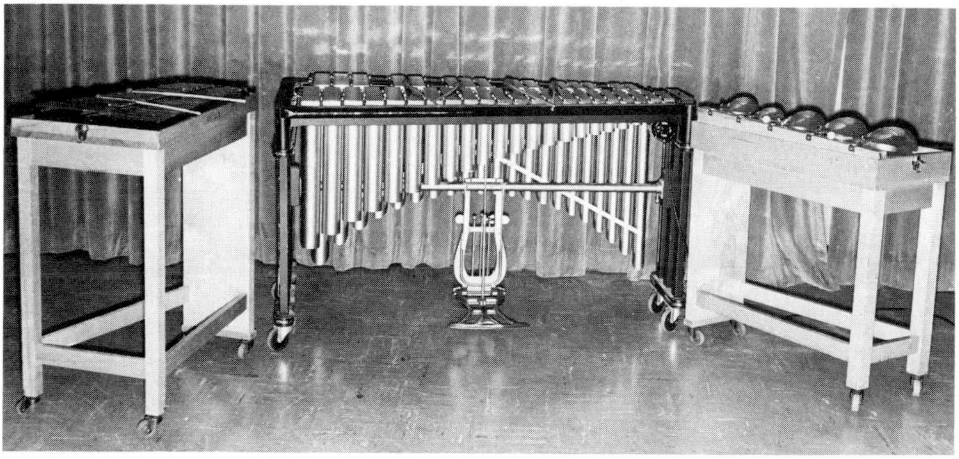

(Left to right) Xylophone, vibraphone, and Chinese temple blocks.

The bass drum is the largest percussion instrument, and it is placed on its side for playing. It is struck with a single stick or "beater" with a round padded head. When hit hard the bass drum has tremendous power.

The cymbals are large metal discs that are often struck together as a pair. A cymbal can also be suspended from its center and struck with a stick. A gong is a large metal disc of thicker metal than a cymbal. It is suspended from one edge and struck with a beater.

The triangle is a three-sided metal frame suspended from one corner. A small metal beater activates the sound. The player can produce single strokes on one of the sides or can produce a more sustained effect by placing the beater inside one of the angles and moving it rapidly back and forth between the two adjacent sides.

The tambourine has a calfskin head stretched over a wood or metal rim, around which are placed small metal discs that rattle. The player shakes the instrument or taps it against his fist. Castanets are hollow pieces of wood or plastic that are clicked against each other.

The percussion player is assigned many unusual instruments. He hits the wood block, cracks a whip (which consists of two large, flat wood pieces that are slapped together), shakes maracas (hollow, dry gourds in which metal pellets have been placed), and even gets to blow whistles.

Britten's Young Person's Guide to the Orchestra

To become acquainted with the sounds of the various musical instruments that make up the orchestra, there is no better work than *The Young Person's Guide to the Orchestra,* Op. 34 by Benjamin Britten, a twentieth-century English composer (Record 1, Side 2). A Listening Guide for the work is included in this chapter. In spite of its title, the work is *not* juvenile in any sense. For the theme, Britten chose a melody by the most esteemed English composer of the seventeenth century, Henry Purcell.

The first section of *The Young Person's Guide to the Orchestra* is a set of variations on Purcell's theme. Britten makes following the instruments especially easy because he first introduces the full orchestra, then the woodwinds, then the brasses, then the strings, and finally the percussion. He closes this section with the full orchestra again. Having presented the full orchestra and each family of instruments, he proceeds through each section from the highest pitched instrument to the lowest.

The last section of *The Young Person's Guide to the Orchestra* is a fugue (pronounced "fewg"). The fugue form will be discussed in greater detail in Chapter 13, but the idea can be introduced here by stating that it is essentially an intellectual round. In the fugue Britten presents each section and

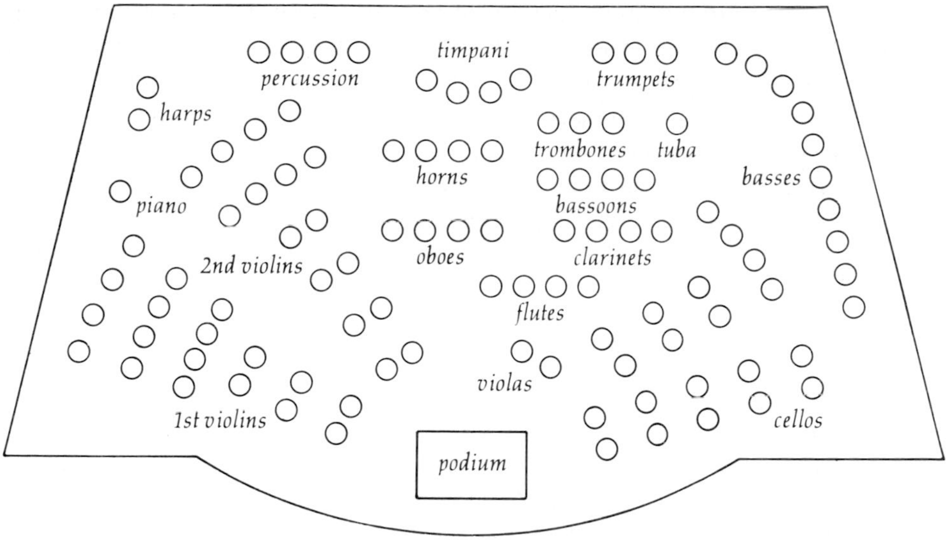

Seating Plan of Symphony Orchestra

Strings:	*Woodwinds:*	*Brass:*	*Percussion:*
18 first violins	*3 flutes, 1 piccolo*	*4 horns*	*2 kettledrum players*
16 second violins	*3 oboes, 1 English horn*	*3 trumpets*	*3 players alternating on*
12 violas	*3 clarinets, 1 bass clarinet*	*3 trombones*	*side of bass, and tenor drum,*
10 cellos	*3 bassoons, 1 contrabassoon*	*1 tuba*	*glockenspiel, celesta,*
10 basses			*triangle, cymbals*
harps			

instrument in the same order in which he featured them in the variations, which means that the fugue theme is introduced by the piccolo. The music closes with the full orchestra sounding Purcell's theme.

BAND INSTRUMENTS

Band instrumentation is far less standardized than orchestral instrumentation. Several instruments have been tried out in bands at various places and times and have been dropped from the organization—the flügelhorn, the saxhorn, the bass saxophone, and others. Bands vary in size from as small as 30 players to well over 100 players. Arrangers and composers cannot be sure of what kind or size group will play their band arrangements or compositions.

For many years the band was thought of in "town band" terms; that is, a small but noisy group that existed primarily to give concerts on hot summer nights in a park. Nobody took the group very seriously. Following World War I and on into the 1940s, the band took on a new dimension. It became a much larger organization and played a heavy diet of arrangements of orchestral music. When the band was good, the effect was something like the sound of a mighty organ. Since World War II another idea has appeared in bands and band music. Often called a "wind ensemble," this concept strongly favors original compositions and a much smaller group. Gone are the rich, heavy sounds of the early twentieth century. They have been replaced by music that is more intellectual.

OP., K., BWV, Etc.

Concert programs and record jackets usually list a work by the composer's name, the title of the work, and some letters and numbers. What do those letters and numbers mean?

Op., standing for *opus,* meaning "work" in Latin, is the most frequently seen set of letters. Since the early 1800s most composers (or sometimes their publishers) have put opus numbers on each work to indicate its place in their list of compositions. The number may refer to the order in which the work was composed or the order of publication. While not always an accurate indication of chronological order, at least the number distinguishes works by a composer with the same title such as "prelude" or "fugue."

For composers whose music does not carry meaningful opus numbers, scholars have numbered the music for them, and in doing so earned themselves an abbreviated version of immortality in concert programs. The best known of these scholars is Ludwig Köchel (*Keh-shul*), a Viennese botanist and amateur musician who assigned each of Mozart's compositions a number on a generally chronological basis. Today, every Mozart work is identified by a number preceded by the initial *K.* for Köchel. Some of Köchel's work has been corrected on the basis of later research.

Other musicologists (scholars in music, especially in music history) who have an initial associated with a composer's works are O. E. Deutsch, who is responsible for the *D.* in the identification of Schubert's music, and A. van Hoboken, who is responsible for the *H.* or *Hob.* associated with Haydn's works.

J. S. Bach's music is cataloged by themes in a book with the forbidding German title *Thematisch-systematisches Verzeichnis der musikalischen Werke von Johann Sebastian Bach.* It is easy to understand why this title is abbreviated to the letters *BWV*!

Although the correct identification of musical works may not always be easy, in some ways it is less prone to error than the identification of paintings. Painters seldom actually put the title of the painting on their work. For this reason, some paintings are known by more than one name. Occasionally both painters and composers make revisions or new versions of works, often those completed early in their careers. In music, works are sometimes arranged by the composer or an arranger for another medium; for example a piano work may be arranged for orchestra or part of an opera arranged for performance without voices.

So, what's in a name? Sometimes it is hard to tell, but the Op., K., and other cataloging symbols help.

LISTENING GUIDE

BRITTEN: *THE YOUNG PERSON'S GUIDE TO THE ORCHESTRA, OP. 34*

"Variations and Fugue on a Theme by Purcell" (Record 1, Side 2)

Theme and Variations

0:00 Theme presented at loud dynamic level by orchestra; a stately, solid melody:

0:28 Theme played by woodwinds.

0:54 Theme played by brasses.

1:17 Theme played by strings.

1:38 Theme played by percussion, especially timpani.

1:57 Theme repeated by entire orchestra.

2:20 Variation 1—flutes and piccolo; playful, with many notes.

2:53 Variation 2—oboes; plaintive, songlike melody.

3:50 Variation 3—clarinets; many arpeggios and runs.

4:30 Variation 4—bassoons; marchlike, with a little songlike melody.

5:24 Variation 5—violins; rhythmic accompaniment and dancelike melody.

5:59 Variation 6—violas; songlike melody with a wide range.

7:01 Variation 7—cellos; rich, flowing melody.

8:14 Variation 8—double basses; melody in which the three-note pattern ascends one note with each appearance; after the middle it basically descends one note each time.

9:13 Variation 9—harp; presents the theme upside down (inversion).

10:00 Variation 10—French horns; variation built around chords.

10:53 Variation 11—trumpets; marchlike figures.

11:23 Variation 12—trombones and tuba; heavy and majestic.

(continued)

12:40 Variation 13—percussion; timpani opens with portion of theme; followed by bass drum and cymbal, tambourine, triangle, snare drum, Chinese blocks, xylophone, castanets, gong, and finally the whip.

Fugue

14:32 Subject played by piccolo:

14:38 Subject played by flutes.

14:47 Subject played by oboes.

14:52 Subject played by clarinets.

15:03 Subject played by bassoons.

15:13 Subject played by first violins.

15:15 Subject played by second violins.

15:23 Subject played by violas.

15:29 Subject played by cellos.

15:33 Subject played by double basses.

15:45 Subject played by harp.

15:57 Subject played by French horns.

16:03 Subject played by trumpets.

16:11 Subject played by trombones and tuba.

16:17 Subject played by percussion.

16:27 Purcell's theme played loudly in long notes by brasses; upper strings and woodwinds continue contrasting material based on fugue.

16:57 Percussion enters loudly.

17:16 Closes with long, full-sounding chord.

Until well into the twentieth century there was a lack of quality music written for band. Very few of the great "name" composers wrote music for a group of wind and percussion instruments. And of the few works that were available, none was considered a major contribution of the composer. Some improvement is evident in the last fifty years, however. Several recognized modern composers have been commissioned to write works for wind band, and a few are making it their primary medium of musical expression.

The concert band is largely an American institution. Bands are seldom found in schools and colleges in the rest of the world. Most bands in Europe and Asia are adjuncts of military organizations, and the few permanent professional bands in any country are armed services bands. There is no "New York Philharmonic Band" or anything like it in any city of the United States or the world.

The main difference between the instrumentation of the band and orchestra is that the band includes no violins, violas, or cellos. Larger concert bands often include one or two double basses. Bands use a greater variety of some of the instrument types: there are often cornets in addition to the usual trumpets and tenor and baritone saxophones in addition to the alto saxophone. There are the regular clarinets, alto clarinets, bass clarinets, and sometimes even a contrabass clarinet. Bands are likely to include a baritone horn, which is almost never found in an orchestra. The baritone horn is in the same range as the trombone, but it has a slightly different bore and piston valves. Because tubas are extremely difficult to carry while marching, an instrument of a comparable range and sound was developed in the band of John Philip Sousa and appropriately named the sousaphone. The sousaphone is coiled over the player's shoulder and can be carried far more easily than the tuba. Sousaphones are often used by school bands in concert as well.

SUGGESTIONS FOR LISTENING TO ORCHESTRAL AND BAND INSTRUMENTS

Flute:

Bach—Sonatas for Flute and Harpsichord (any of seven)
Griffes—*Poem for Flute and Orchestra*
Mozart—Concertos for Flute, K. 313 or K. 314

Oboe:

Handel—Concertos for Oboe (any of three)
Mozart—Concerto in C Major for Oboe, K. 314
Poulenc—Sonata for Oboe and Piano

Clarinet:

Brahms—Sonatas for Clarinet and Piano (either of two)
Debussy—*Première Rapsodie for Clarinet*
Mozart—Concerto in A Major for Clarinet, K. 622

Bassoon:

Hindemith—Sonata for Bassoon and Piano
Mozart—Concerto in B-flat Major for Bassoon, K. 191
Vivaldi—Concertos for Bassoon and Orchestra (any of several)

Saxophone:

Debussy—*Rapsodie for Saxophone and Orchestra*
Glazounov—Concerto for Saxophone
Ibert—*Concertino da Camera, for Saxophone and Chamber Orchestra*

Trumpet:

Haydn—Concerto in E-flat Major for Trumpet and Orchestra
Hindemith—Sonata for Trumpet and Piano
Purcell—Sonata for Trumpet and Strings

French Horn:

Hindemith—Sonata for Four Horns
Mozart—Concertos for Horn, K. 412, K. 417, K. 447, or K. 495
Strauss—Concertos for Horn (either of two)

Trombone:

Hindemith—Sonata for Trombone and Piano
Poulenc—Trio for Trumpet, Trombone, Horn
Rimsky-Korsakov—Concerto for Trombone and Band

Tuba:

Vaughan Williams—Concerto for Bass Tuba and Orchestra

Percussion:

Chávez—Toccata for Percussion
Harrison—Canticle No. 3 for Percussion
Milhaud—Concerto for Percussion and Small Orchestra

Harp:

Handel—Concertos for Harp, Op. 4, Nos. 5 and 6
Mozart—Concerto in C for Flute and Harp, K. 299
Ravel—*Introduction and Allegro for Harp, Flute, Clarinet, and String Quartet*

Violin:

Beethoven—Concerto in D Major for Violin, Op. 61
Chausson—*Poème for Violin and Orchestra,* Op. 25
Prokofiev—Concerto No. 2 in G Minor for Violin, Op. 63

Viola:

Bartók—Concerto for Viola and Orchestra
Hindemith—*Trauermusik for Viola and Strings*
Vaughan Williams—*Flos Campi, Suite for Viola, Orchestra, and Chorus*

Cello:

Bloch—*Schelomo—Rhapsody for Cello and Orchestra*
Haydn—Concerto in D Major for Cello, Op. 101
Schumann—Concerto for Cello

Double Bass:

Dittersdorf—Concerto in E for Double Bass
Koussevitzky—Concerto for Double Bass

Guitar:

Rodrigo—*Concerto de Aranjuez for Guitar and Orchestra*
Villa-Lobos—*Chôros No. 1*
Vivaldi—Concerto in D for Guitar and Orchestra

Band:

Hindemith—Symphony in B-flat for Band
Holst—Suites No. 1 and 2 for Band
Hovhaness—Symphony No. 4
Milhaud—*Suite française*

Orchestra:

Bartók—Concerto for Orchestra
Ravel—*Bolero*
Rimsky-Korsakov—*Capriccio Espagnole*

6

MUSICAL INSTRUMENTS: KEYBOARD, FOLK, AND POPULAR

Band and orchestral instruments are used mainly in groups; very few pieces have been composed for unaccompanied solo trumpet, for example. Keyboard, folk, and some popular instruments are different. They are more likely to be played alone, especially keyboard instruments, and only occasionally are they played in large groups.

KEYBOARD INSTRUMENTS

Keyboard instruments that produce sounds by activating strings can be divided into two types. One produces sound by means of a quill that plucks the string when the key is depressed; the other produces sound when a key mechanism causes a felt-covered hammer to strike against the string.

Harpsichord. The harpsichord and virginal both operate on the principle of the plucked string, as shown in the diagram and explained on page 67. The main difference between these two instruments is that the virginal is a smaller, simpler instrument that sits on a table.

The harpsichord looks somewhat like a grand piano, although smaller. The case or body is much the same. The keyboard has fewer keys but they are in the usual black and white key arrangement, sometimes with the color scheme reversed. Later harpsichords, those built in the seventeenth century, had two keyboards plus stop knobs. These knobs can "couple" a key so that it sounds pitches an octave above or below the key being depressed.

Neither the harpsichord nor the virginal mechanism allows the player to alter the volume by the finger pressure applied to the keys. The only way to change the dynamic level is for the harpsichordist to play on the second keyboard or, on the more complicated harpsichords, to engage a knob that doubles the pitches an octave higher or lower. In either case, the change of loudness is abrupt because no gradual shadings are possible.

Clavichord. The mechanism of the clavichord is similar to that of the piano. It consists of a shallow box with strings running the width of the instrument. The strings are secured on the left by pins in a block of wood and

---

TWO KEYBOARD ACTIONS COMPARED

Although the larger harpsichords have two keyboards, many harpsichords look quite a bit like grand pianos. Despite their similar outward appearance, they are very different inside, and they certainly do not sound alike.

The harpsichord sounds the strings by a plucking action. In the detailed drawing of the mechanism for one key, there is one string (1) (some larger harpsichords have two) and a jack (2) that connects the key to string and damper. The jack holds the plectra (3) which are made of quills from feathers, hard leather, or, today, plastic. The sound is produced when the plectra pluck the string by moving up and down.

The piano has a considerably more complicated mechanism than the harpsichord. The principle is a hammer covered by a rather firm piece of felt bouncing against the string. To keep the string from ringing and blurring the sound, there is also a damper that prevents unwanted ringing. The drawing on this page shows that when the key (1) is depressed, the damper body (8) is activated, which raises the damper (9). *At the same time* the rest of the mechanism—(4) the hammer shank support, (5) repetition lever, (6) jack, and (7) set off button—bounces the hammer head (3) off the string. The hammer does not remain touching the string or else only a weak, dull sound would result. The damper remains off the string as long as the key is depressed, or all dampers can be lifted by means of a foot pedal.

Both the harpsichord and piano have pleasant and distinctive tone qualities. However, the piano supplanted the harpsichord in the late eighteenth century because the piano has a larger sound and because the player can control the amount of loudness of each note by how hard the key is depressed. The harpsichord has enjoyed somewhat of a revival of interest in the twentieth century.

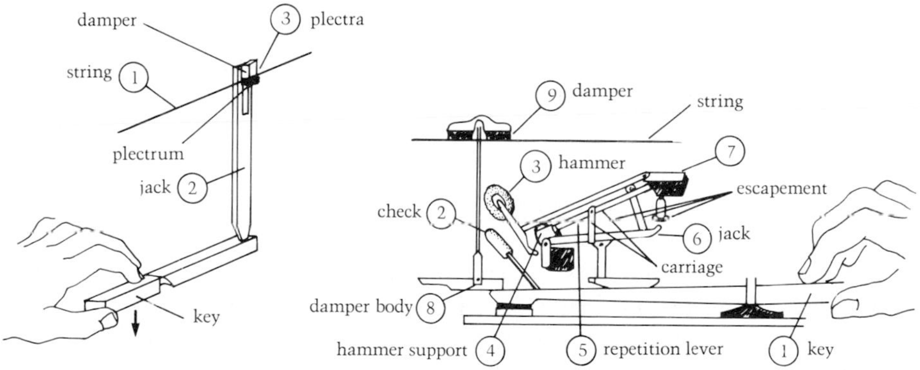

Action of a harpsichord *Action of a piano*

---

are sounded by brass tangents that strike the strings when a key is depressed. The clavichord has a weak tone, but the player has some control of the degree of loudness.

Piano. The piano came on the musical scene relatively late. It was first constructed about 1709, and the early models were unimpressive. The piano did not gain prominence until the last half of the eighteenth century.

The piano has a flat table of wood called the soundboard, the purpose of which is to amplify the sound from the strings. The strings themselves are strung over a cast-iron frame, which is absolutely rigid, enabling them to stay in tune for relatively long periods of time. They are tuned by means of pins that are sunk into a block of wood. The tuner merely twists the pin with a wrench to raise or lower the pitch. The keyboard mechanism itself is more complicated than it appears to be, having about twenty-seven pieces of metal and wood for each key, as illustrated on page 67.

Most pianos have three pedals. One pedal allows the sounds to ring after the fingers have left the keys. Another pedal allows only certain strings to vibrate—those whose keys are depressed at the moment the pedal is activated. A third pedal moves the entire keyboard mechanism slightly so that the hammer cannot strike all the strings for each note, resulting in a somewhat softer sound. On upright pianos this pedal moves the hammers closer to the strings, shortening and therefore weakening the hammers' strokes.

Pianos come in two types. The grand piano is long and flat. Because of its large size, its sound is superior to the upright. The upright piano has its strings mounted vertically, and the low strings are shortened in order to fit into a smaller space. Therefore, it has a less powerful sound and is a little more difficult to keep in tune. Concert music is always performed publicly on a grand piano. Throughout history keyboards have been constructed with differing numbers of notes. The modern piano is standardized at eighty-eight black and white keys.

Organ. The sound of the organ is made when air is blown into pipes. Even a minute change in the design of a pipe causes a change of tone quality. Each timbre must have its own set or rank of pipes, one pipe for each pitch in the rank. It is not unusual for a large organ to have as many as 100 ranks; medium-sized organs have 40 to 60. Each rank is brought into play by pulling a knob. Various knob combinations can be activated by pushing a button with the hand or foot. As can be seen in the picture, the knobs are on both sides of the keyboards, and the buttons are below the keys and on both sides of the center pedals. Even when the organist depresses only one key, many more pipes can be sounded, depending on which knobs have been activated.

Several keyboards are visible. An organ usually has at least two keyboards, called *manuals.* Each manual has sixty-one keys, fewer than the piano. The different manuals facilitate the use of different ranks of pipes. There is not time during the playing of a piece for the organist to adjust the knobs for each of the manuals. This work must be set up ahead of time.

Footwork on the pedals is nearly as important to an organist as finger technique on the keys. As can be seen in the picture, on the floor are black and blond wooden slats. The slats form another keyboard, the pedal board, which is played with the feet. Most pitches sounded by the pedals are low. Playing music with the feet is not easy, but good organists can perform remarkably difficult passages on the pedals.

Organists' feet also push the expression pedals. These pedals, which look like the accelerator pedal on an automobile, increase and decrease the level of loudness. Expression pedals are a more recent invention and were not available in Bach's time. In the Baroque period changes in loudness were made by adding or subtracting the number of pipes playing and by opening and closing a set of shutters around the pipe enclosure.

The twentieth century has brought forth many inventions, among them the electronic organ. Many pipe organists object to the electronic version. Their objection is based on the fact that its synthetic tones simply do not sound like an organ as it is traditionally conceived. The tone quality of most electronic models is very different from that of Bach's instrument. The organ

The console of a large pipe organ.

of Bach's time is considered the standard for organs built today. Good modern pipe organs have copied it in nearly every detail. They are custom-made and extremely expensive.

FOLK INSTRUMENTS

Folk instruments can be grouped into four large categories. One category is composed of those instruments that are played with the breath. The most common instruments of this type are flutes. Some flutes are played sideways; others are played straight out from the player's mouth. The nose flute, a type of flute played by the natives of Oceania and Hawaii, is literally blown with the nose. There are double-reed instruments similar to the oboe and single-reed instruments similar to the clarinet. The *pungi* played by the snake charmers in India is another example in the reed category.* A few simple brass instruments are also found in nonliterate cultures.

A second classification of instruments involves percussion instruments other than drums. Included in it are bells, chimes, xylophones, rattles, and the Jew's harp, which is a flexible metal strip attached to a small horseshoe-shaped frame. Its original name may have been "jaw's harp."

A third group includes all kinds of drums, which involve a stretched membrane of some kind. Drums are constructed from many materials, including wood, metal, coconut shells, and dried gourd, and they come in shapes ranging from the hourglass drums of the Cameroons to friction drums, on which sound is made when a piece of hide is rubbed across the drum skin.

The fourth classification includes all the string instruments. Most of these are plucked—zithers, lyres, and harps, for example—but some are struck with mallets and a few are bowed like a violin.

The instruments of a culture are usually constructed of materials readily available to that culture—animal horns or bones, skins, wood, gourds, and so on. The availability and complexity of instruments also depend on the knowledge of such crafts as smelting metals and shaping wood. Some folk instruments are unreliable in producing pitches and can be played only softly.

POPULAR INSTRUMENTS

Guitar. The guitar probably came from the Near East. The instrument was popular in France by the 1500s, and soon it became well known in Italy

*Actually, the music is wasted because cobras have no hearing. They respond to the swaying of the charmer's body.

Musical instruments of India. (Front to back) Sarod, tabla (smaller drum) and bayan (larger drum), and tambura.

and Spain. Early guitars had only four strings, but today six is standard. Except for acoustical improvements the modern guitar has not changed much in the last several hundred years. The guitar has two somewhat divergent relatives. One is the ukulele, which is basically a small guitar. The other is the banjo, which has a parchment skin stretched over a hoop and no back. The banjo has a much more brilliant sound than the guitar. It may have come to America with the slaves from Africa, but its ancestry is probably Arabic.

Electric Guitar. The electric guitar is very much used in current popular music, and its timbre contributes to the distinctive sound of rock. The electric guitar is only distantly related to the traditional acoustic guitar just described. Instead of having a hollow sound box that amplifies the sound, it has an artificial box that serves for decoration and as a site for mounting the control knobs. The sound is amplified by electronic means. By turning knobs the player can adjust the volume level, change the timbre of the sounds, and produce a vibrato. The electric guitar comes in basically two sizes. Like the acoustic guitar, the electric guitar has metal strips or *frets* that cross the fingerboard. They help the player place his or her finger to achieve a certain pitch.

Drums. The percussion in pop groups usually consists of a drum set played by one person. The set includes one or two suspended cymbals that are hit with a stick or a brush. There are three or four drums without snares or a bottom head. The absence of snares gives the drum a more "tubby" sound. The largest drum in the set is a small bass drum, which the player hits by pressing a pedal mechanism with his foot. Often this drum has a felt pad braced against one side to muffle the sound and cut down the reverberation. Much showmanship is involved in such drumming.

Accordion. The accordion has enjoyed several waves of popularity in the United States, and it is still quite popular in some European countries. The accordion is constructed so that air is forced through the instrument to activate metal reeds. The accordion has a short keyboard for playing the melody. The accompanying chords are produced by pushing buttons that sound entire chords; there is one button for each type of chord in each key. An accordionist with a quality instrument may achieve different timbres by pushing different buttons. The varied timbres of the organ can be duplicated in a limited way.

Human Voice. Whether or not the voice is a musical instrument in the precise sense of the word, it is certainly important in music. The material on pages 73–74 explains how it functions.

INSTRUMENTS TODAY

The most important new instrument is not an instrument at all in the usual sense of the word. It is the tone synthesizer—an electronic instrument that can produce almost any type of sound and timbre and is used in conjunction with a tape recorder. The player-composer usually does not actually interpret the work while the audience listens, as in traditional music. Instead, a piece is prepared on the synthesizer and the sounds recorded onto a tape. Then the

THE VOCAL INSTRUMENT

It may seem odd to talk about the voice as an instrument, but in many ways it is. It is a device composed of several parts that function together to make musical sounds. What may cause us to think of the voice as unlike other instruments is the fact that we're born with it and we learn to use it to some extent without formal training, something usually needed on the violin or trombone.

The drawing of the mechanical being below shows the parts of the body that go into making up the vocal instrument.

In the drawing, air is drawn into and forced out of the lungs (1) by the up–down motion of the diaphragm (2), which is a "floor" of muscle under the lungs. As the air is forced up, it passes through the vocal cords (3) causing them to vibrate. The speed of the vibration, and therefore the pitch, changes according to the length and the tension of the vocal cords. The tone quality is affected by the body and the chest, but even more by the resonating cavities in the head, including the sinuses (4). The tongue formation and cheeks (5)

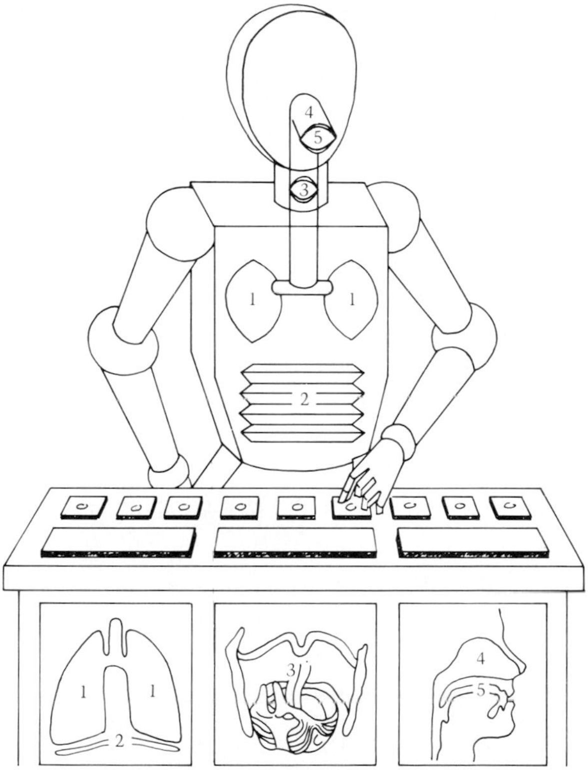

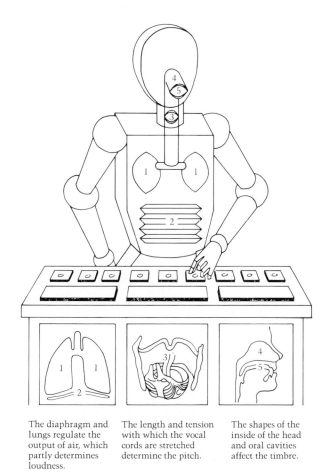

The diaphragm and lungs regulate the output of air, which partly determines loudness.

The length and tension with which the vocal cords are stretched determine the pitch.

The shapes of the inside of the head and oral cavities affect the timbre.

(continued)

also affect the timbre, including forming the particular vowel sound that is being sustained.

The difference between men's and women's voices is largely the length and thickness of the vocal cords. A man's vocal cords are normally about twice as long as a woman's, and they are also thicker, which contributes to a heavier timbre. The longer vocal cords of the male require a larger voice box or larynx, which results in the more prominent "Adam's apple" in the adult male.

The vocal instrument is similar to other instruments in one other way. To use it to its fullest capacity in making music, training is usually required (although not for everyone who succeeds as a singer of art music). To sing a difficult piece of music, one needs a great deal of muscle development and sensitive coordination of the various parts of the body, which calls for special training.

---

composer works with the tape to produce the composition. Some synthesizers are extremely complex, as the picture on page 74 indicates. One almost has to be an electrical engineer and acoustician to develop music for them. Simpler synthesizers are now being used in rock bands, and some high schools have them available for their students. Although many synthesizers are almost exclusively "solo" endeavors, the instrument is used in some popular and rock ensembles, as well as in art music.

Like the synthesizer, the tape recorder is not an instrument in the usual sense of the word. It can only reproduce sounds that are fed into it. The composer's job is, of course, to decide which sounds should be recorded. One of the chief sources of sound for the tape recorder in contemporary music—in addition to the tone synthesizer—is the world of commonplace, everyday sound: the cry of a baby, the chirp of a bird, the drip of a faucet. Sounds from conventional instruments are also used. The performer-composer then manip-

Synthesizer.

ulates the tape by increasing or slowing down the speed, by splicing the tape, by rerecording sounds on top of one another. Radically different effects are created by freely experimenting with the tape. This type of music has been called *musique concrète* (moo-*zeek* cone-*kret*). It alters natural sounds by means of the tape recorder itself.

Minor improvements in instruments will continue to be made, of course. Different materials will be tried and other refinements will be attempted. In a few cases electronic versions of presently existing instruments will be created, something that has already happened to the piano.

7

MUSICAL PERFORMANCE

Suppose a painting had to be recreated for each viewing. Instead of looking at a completed masterpiece, the viewer would need to watch a contemporary "performing painter" repaint the picture from directions left by the original artist. After every stroke, the painting would fade away—impermanent but indispensable to a vision of the painting. Furthermore, the impression of quality of the original masterpiece would depend largely on the quality of the "performing painter's" rendition. Music, except for electronic music, is presented in this manner. Performance is the necessary link between composer and listener, and the performer has a crucial role. Such an intermediary can enhance the composer's work through a good performance or distort it through a bad one.

When music is being performed, it is being recreated. There is a sense of immediacy and aliveness surrounding such an undertaking. It is an experience that covers a definite span of time during which things happen, and the listener feels involved in the unfolding of these "musical events." This type of experience is not shared in the relationship between painters and viewers, for example.

FACTORS AFFECTING PERFORMANCE

Several elements affect the recreation of musical works, including artistic problems such as a performer's ability and mundane matters such as money needed to hire musicians to perform.

The Performer's Skill. Foremost among the factors affecting musical performance is the skill of the performer rendering the music. Any amateur can read the lines of a play and follow stage directions. But such attempts cannot compare with the performance of a first-rate actor or actress, who knows how to make every inflection and every movement convey the intent of the playwright. The same differences in performance levels are true with music. Two performances of the same piece can vary to such an extent that what is exciting and moving when performed by one person or group can be dull and bland when performed by another.

The Live Performance. There is a difference between hearing a "live" performance of a work and listening to a recording of it. As a rule, live performance is superior because it gives a greater sense of involvement and enables the listeners to hear the direction of sounds coming from one portion or another of a large group.

There is also advantage in seeing a performer whose stage presence and physical motions can augment the effect of the music. Viewing is particularly important in opera, in which the singer-actor must move about and create a visual as well as aural impression. It is also a factor in instrumental playing. Whether the bow strokes of a violinist are vigorous and fast or slow moving and delicate, the listeners' awareness of how the music is being played is heightened by watching the performer at work.

More important, however, is the fact that a live performance is usually heard without distortion. It is heard as the composer and performer intend it to be. Recordings often do not reproduce the full sound as it really existed. The sounds produced by a group covering many square feet are compressed and amplified through a few inches of speakers. To compensate for this reduction, recording manufacturers sometimes exaggerate the reverberation, emphasize the bass tones, or tamper with the original sound in other ways. For these reasons, concert attendance is very helpful in learning about music. Some useful information concerning attending performances, including the unwritten traditions, are represented on pages 77–78.

The fact that a piece is being performed live by competent singers or players does not guarantee that the music is being heard properly. The acoustical environment in which the music is heard has a significant effect. Rooms or concert halls can be too large or small, have too much or not enough reverberation, or have "dead" spots where the sound is only weakly heard. The one

ATTENDING MUSICAL PERFORMANCES

It is possible, of course, to have music by playing a recording. However, as is pointed out in this chapter, recordings do not provide the sense of involvement that actually being present does. Listening to a recording is like watching a movie or television version of a play, it's more detached and less immediate.

When attending a musical performance, it is important to keep in mind the main reason for being there, which is to listen to the music. In doing so, it is hoped that you gain the psychological satisfaction and enjoyment described in Chapter 1. It is easy to be distracted by other things at a performance such as what to wear, when to applaud, how to act, and so on. These are really secondary matters, just as trying to be seen at a concert by the "right" people is secondary. If the secondary matters become primary concerns, being at the performance will probably not be enjoyable.

Assuming that you (or your instructor) have decided that you will attend a performance or two, what performance should you go to? There are many different kinds. Some are quite formal like symphony orchestra concerts and chamber music performances; others are less formal, such as jazz performances. Usually there is only one type of music performed at a performance. Rarely is a symphony orchestra followed by a rock band.

Performances also differ in length. Usually a recital (which implies that it is for a soloist or small group) is about an hour and a half long, with probably an intermission. An orchestra concert is somewhat longer, and a rock and jazz performance can be quite a bit longer. Longest of all, usually, are operas and oratorios, which can last for three hours or more.

Concerts of instrumental music usually don't have a great deal of visual interest. The players sit and play, and that's it. Opera has the visual elements of scenery, costumes, and actions. Popular music concerts are often "choreographed" with motions and dancelike routines.

There are some differences among performances in the use of the printed program and the behavior of the audience. Both of these matters will be discussed shortly.

It should be pointed out that the opportunity to attend performances of music will never be so convenient or inexpensive (that's right) again after you finish college. Colleges offer performances of students, faculty, and often bring in outstanding professional performers in a concert series. Most of the on-campus performances are free, especially those presented by students. Also, the students would love to have a larger audience. The professional performers (with the exception of popular music performers) who appear on campus can usually be heard by students at reduced ticket prices.

Now, what are some of the traditions associated with audience behavior? At performances of art music do *NOT* talk, whisper, rustle a program, or cough while the music is being performed. (Experienced concert-goers seem to have trained themselves to hold back all coughing and related activity until the end of a movement or work.) If the main point of attending a performance is to listen to music, then there should be nothing that intrudes on the concentration of anyone.

As for applause, *never* (well, almost never) applaud between the movements of an instrumental work. Save it until the entire work is completed. In an opera there is applause after duets, solos, and choruses. Sometimes the verbal cheering of "Bravo" (pronounced "*Brah*-vo") is in order. There is much applauding in jazz and rock concerts at the ends of songs and after individual solos. If you are in doubt about

(continued)

when to applaud, just hold back and imitate what others at the concert do.

The conductor is given special treatment at the performance. He or she is the last to enter and is applauded by the audience (but not the performers unless it is a guest conductor). The conductor also bows after the performances and acknowledges the members of the orchestra by shaking the hand of the first violinist, who is referred to as the *concertmaster.* Individual members of the group are acknowledged by standing and being applauded if the performers have had an especially important part that was performed well. Quite often the entire group is asked to stand.

Soloists rate even higher on the "recognition order" than the conductors. They enter last and leave first, and usually take some bows alone.

Most performances have a printed program listing the music to be performed. Usually it will be given to you when you enter the hall. Seldom are the works to be performed announced from the stage, except at popular music programs. Even the traditional extra number or *encore* played or sung at the end of the performance is often not announced.

On page 79 you will find a program containing a minimum amount of information. It lists the names of the group or the individuals if there are only a few of them. On one side of the page it lists the name of the composition; and on the other side lists the composer and/or arranger, sometimes giving the years that the person lived. For works with several movements, each movement is listed by its main tempo marking. Song recitals have programs listing each song by title and composer, and oratorios list each recitative, aria, and chorus. Opera programs look more like the program for a play, with a listing of acts and scenes and a short phrase about the time and place. Opera programs often contain a synopsis of the story. Some programs for professional performances contain notes interspersed among the advertisements. These remarks may be helpful, and then again they may not; it depends on how well the writer communicates with nonmusicians.

The dress of both the audience and performers is somewhat dictated by tradition. Instrumentalists wear a conservative suit or dress for afternoon performances and black for evening performances. They do this to keep their attire from drawing attention from the music. Choirs often wear robes for the same reason. In popular music there is an emphasis on the personality of the performer, so much variety of dress is almost expected.

The tradition that the audience wears tuxedos and long dresses to performances of music has long since passed in most places. Usually you will be wearing the right thing if you put on a coat and tie or dressy outfit for Sunday and evening concerts. Other performances are less formal and almost anything clean is appropriate.

Yes, traditions or no traditions, musical performances can be enjoyable.

INDIANA UNIVERSITY
SCHOOL OF MUSIC

Five Hundred Sixty-Eighth Program of the 1979-80 Season

Symphony Orchestra

Keith Brown, *Conductor*

Katsuhiko Watanabe, *Conductor*

Overture to *Meerestille und glückliche Fahrt* . . . . Felix Mendelssohn
(1809-1847)

Symphony No. 35 in D Major, K. 385 ("Haffner") . . . . . Wolfgang Amadeus Mozart
(1756-1791)

Allegro con spirito
[Andante]
Menuetto
Finale: Presto

Katsuhiko Watanabe, *Conductor*

INTERMISSION

Ein Heldenleben, Op. 48 . . . . Richard Strauss
(1864-1949)

Keith Brown, *Conductor*

Musical Arts Center
Wednesday Evening
March Fifth
Eight O'Clock

Avery Fisher Hall at Lincoln Center in New York.

characteristic that all good concert halls have is "presence," giving listeners a sense of being close and involved with what is going on.

The Inadequacy of Music Notation. A playwright can indicate the words the actor is to say and can give general directions about how the words should be spoken, but the author cannot tell the actor the exact voice inflection and timing *by means of writing.* The situation is much the same in music. Music notation tells the performer what pitch is to be produced and when, and it supplements this information with a few general directions regarding loudness and expression. The performer must then determine the musical inflections that seem most likely to recreate the composer's intent. The incompleteness of any system of music notation places much importance on the ability of the performer.

Even if notation could indicate fully how the music should be performed, it might not be desirable from the standpoint of both listeners and performers. All performances of a work would be identical, which would reduce the freshness caused by slightly different interpretations. Even more serious would be the absence of the many subtle shadings and nuances that make music a human rather than a mechanical means of expression. For instance, even the most capable concert performers do not play the rhythms and pitches exactly as written. (Keyboard players are an exception because pitches on keyboard instruments cannot be varied at will.) If these performances were subjected to scientific scrutiny, many slight deviations of pitch and rhythm would be found. However, the performance sounds better for these deviations, because a split-second's hesitation at one spot or a slight raising of pitch at another makes the music more effective.

Part of a musician's training consists of learning the traditions of performance that are not written down. The musician learns, for example, that a particular rhythmic figure is performed in a number of slightly different ways, depending on the period in history or the country from which the music originated. Singers and instrumentalists learn that slightly different tone qualities are more suitable in different kinds of music. There is nothing in music to demand that a performer slavishly follow the practices of the past, but a musician needs to know and consider them in order to be a good performer.

Preparation before the performance. Seldom are performances by good musicians presented without benefit of careful preparation. Difficult works cannot be given the best performance when the notation is read at first sight, even by very able musicians. The correct notes and rhythms need to be worked out, and the performer must decide upon the dynamic shadings, the proper tempos, and the many subtleties involved with performance.

Professional musicians speak more often about "rehearsing" music than "practicing." The distinction between the two words is not great. When a youngster begins lessons on an instrument, there is much talk (chiefly from parents) about practicing. Practice connotes learning the technical skills necessary for performance. It also suggests individual work. Rehearsal, on the other hand, implies group effort—the relating of various parts to one another and the perfecting of the whole. Each performer in a group needs to know what the others are doing and needs to be familiar with all that goes into the piece. A unified interpretation has to be established so that the group performs with consistency of phrasing and style.

The task of coordinating a group is especially difficult in the case of instrumental music. An orchestra has many different instruments requiring different parts, often more than twenty. A choral group usually has only four parts, almost never more than eight. Instrumentalists are usually called on to perform longer pieces and music requiring much faster execution of notes than are the singers in a choral organization. Another difference lies in the manner in which vocal and instrumental music is printed. In a choral group, all the singers look at complete copies of the music. Each performer can see how one part fits with the others and can anticipate the overall effect of the combined sounds. An instrumentalist, however, sees only one part, be it second clarinet, first violin, or tuba. Therefore, it is not possible to know what anyone else is doing, so each player must become familiar with the piece through rehearsal.

In music for more than two instruments, the only person who knows everyone's part is the conductor, who has a master copy of all parts, called a *score.* The size and complexity of the score explains why instrumentalists are given only their own parts to read. Scores are bulky and expensive to print. Following a score while the music is in progress requires technical knowledge and frequent page turning. On page 83 is the first page from the score to *Don Juan* by Richard Strauss; this work is present in more detail in Chapter 22.

Not only does Strauss' score present twenty-two lines to follow simultaneously; it also demonstrates the common phenomenon called *transposition.* That is, the player reacts to a printed pitch, but mechanical characteristics of the instrument cause the actual sound to be heard at a different pitch level. When the French horn sounds its C, the listener hears F, five notes lower; when the clarinetist plays C on the most common type of clarinet, the listener hears B-flat, one note lower. Many instruments do not transpose, however. The origins of transposition are rooted in a tradition that allowed players to change easily between instruments with identical fingering systems. Transposition also enables more of an instrument's notes to be written *within* a staff, rather than extended far above or below it. So much is now invested in methods books and printed music that it is not feasible to replace transposition just so that every instrument sounds the same pitch that is read.

THE CONDUCTOR

Large performing groups are always conducted. Many people, however, misunderstand the conductor's function. A good professional orchestra can start with a nod from one of the players and proceed to play a symphony acceptably. So why have a conductor? The conductor's position is comparable to that of a baseball or football coach. A good team can play quite well without a coach—for a while. But problems inevitably arise, and decisions have to be made. In a musical organization as well as a ball team, the situations requiring decisions do not usually lend themselves to resolution by group debate or vote. A knowledgeable and respected leader must be in charge to instruct, to be the guiding spirit for the team's efforts, and to galvanize the group into action.

A conductor's most important job, however, is to decide on and implement the interpretation of the music. Prior to directing a piece, therefore, the conductor studies the score to determine in advance the tempos, styles, and

Allegro molto con brio
2 Flutes
3rd Flutes & Piccolo
2 Oboes
English Horn
2 Clarinets
2 Bassoons
Contrabassoon
1-2 Horns in E
3-4 Horns in E
1-2 Trumpets in E
3rd Trumpet in E
1-2 Trombones
3rd Trombone
Timpani
Triangle
Cymbal
Becken mit Holzschlägel
Glockenspiel
Metr. ♩=84
Harp
glissando
Allegro molto con brio
Violin 1
Violin 2
Viola
Cello
Bass

nuances. This preparation is necessary for telling the performers, in rehearsal, the style in which they are to perform the piece.

The conductor keeps the performance together by starting the group concisely, maintaining the tempo, and giving cues—visual indications that an important passage is to begin at that moment. Gestures are used in conducting because they are silent and do not interfere with the sound of the music. The conductor's right hand sets the beat. The basic patterns are simple:

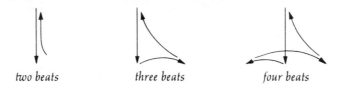

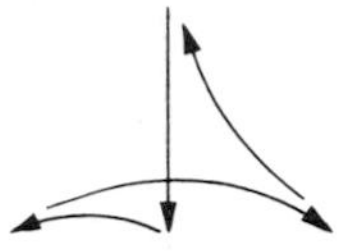

Most music falls into one of these three patterns, although some meters involve only one beat per measure and others involve more than four beats. The conductor's left hand indicates loudness and cues the various parts. Sometimes the conductor does not beat the patterns clearly. Why? Because a freer style enables the motions to be more expressive and less mechanical. Students of conducting are often told to "look like the music," meaning that their facial expressions and bodily motions should project the feeling of the music.

Unfortunately conductors do not operate in a vacuum. They are seldom free of matters pertaining to the public's reaction to the performance and to themselves. Too often the public's acceptance is not based on valid musical considerations. Some people recall that a conductor's hair flopped about or that the performance was conducted from memory or that the director did not use a *baton* (the small stick used to help clarify the beats of the right hand). These and similar observations are irrelevant to the sound of the music itself.

TIME AND MONEY

Time is a critical matter in putting together a performance. For instance, the professional orchestra today can seldom spend a week preparing for a single concert. Frequently there are other performances, such as educational concerts, recording sessions, and out-of-town appearances, that cut into rehearsal time. If a weekend concert features a concerto with a soloist, rehearsal time with the soloist is needed to coordinate and unify the interpretation. (In general, the soloist's views on interpretation prevail.) The other numbers on the program, perhaps a symphony and a long overture, can be given only cursory attention, sometimes as little as one run-through of the music.

The reason for limited rehearsal time is economic. The hours of em-

These pictures of Zubin Mehta show the forcefulness and expressiveness of his conducting. Photos by Bill Ray, New York.

ployment are carefully spelled out in a contract between the musicians' union and the symphony's board of directors. Extra rehearsal time can be had, but for an orchestra the cost is over a thousand dollars per hour, a figure that financially hard-pressed symphony orchestras can seldom afford.

The same situation exists in opera, except that the problem is worse. Stage productions involve the employment of many craft-union workers such as electricians, carpenters, and stagehands. These persons usually earn more than most of the performers, so the financial implications are far-reaching. These economic realities require the professional musician to perform well with little or no rehearsal, and they occasionally cause the public to hear a performance that has not been adequately prepared.

Financial Support of Musical Groups

The United States differs from European countries in the way it provides for the performance of music. In Europe most professional opera companies and orchestras operate under some direct subsidy from the government, both local and national. In America the arts have traditionally been supported entirely through private donations and ticket sales. Only in recent years has public money been made available to the arts, and the amounts have been small. Most governmental support has been for specific projects: performances in remote or less affluent communities, performances of new musical compositions, and concerts for school students.

When a person buys a ticket to the symphony or opera, it is usually assumed that the amount covers the actual cost of the program according to the number of seats in the concert hall. Unfortunately, this assumption is not true. Of every dollar received for the operation of a symphony orchestra, only about thirty cents comes from the sale of tickets. The total operation of the musical organization could be met through ticket sales only if the admission price were about triple its present level. There is a reluctance to increase the admission charge, because people of moderate or lower income would be "priced out" of musical events.

Traditionally the difference between income and expenditures has been made up by subscription drives and other forms of donation. Today it is impossible for a few wealthy patrons to provide sole support for an orchestra or opera company, although monied people are still necessary for the continuance of musical organizations. Since about 1960 a new form of arts support has emerged: the arts council and its fund drive. The arts fund drive operates in a manner similar to the united health and welfare drives. The various arts organizations pool their efforts into one united campaign. Such united drives have the advantage of receiving support from a broad section of the public. The arts council helps coordinate and promote artistic events as well as articulate the goals and needs of the arts to the community. When governmental assistance has been made available, it is often channeled through arts councils.

The shortage of funds for the arts in America has been an inhibiting factor in the cultural life of the nation. Many musical works, especially new ones, have never been performed publicly, and the number of performances of music in general has been limited.

The pattern of support for music in America has produced some curious inconsistencies. One is the position of the professional musician, who was one of the first to suffer from technological unemployment. Many theater musicians were put out of work when sound films were introduced at the end of the 1920s. The situation was further aggravated by the depression of the 1930s.

Then, after World War II came the vastly improved techniques of sound recording. People could hear excellent performances in their living rooms, so the need to attend a live concert was reduced. As a final blow to the performer's livelihood, television replaced the few remaining radio orchestras. By the 1950s only a small minority of the membership of the American Federation of Musicians was made up of people who earned the major share of their livelihood as performing musicians. Pay scales for most performing musicians were low, but have improved significantly in recent years with arts council support and other grants.

The present situation presents composers with the best and worst of times. It is possible for them *as composers* to earn a good living, something even Bach, Mozart, and Liszt could not do. Private foundations offer them grants and help them find avenues of performance for their works. An organization called the American Society of Composers, Authors, and Publishers (ASCAP) helps protect their legal rights to their work and gives them access to a complex system of profit sharing. In addition, there are more and better positions at universities as the demand increases for teachers of composition and related subjects. Never have composers had more freedom to write exactly what they feel like writing. Today's composers, however, sometimes find that their efforts are greeted coolly by the public and occasionally even by the performers themselves. Where there isn't antipathy, there seems to be apathy.

THE ROLE OF MUSIC EDUCATION

Music is now too complex a creation to be passed along informally from one generation to another, as is done in primitive societies. In a culture such as ours, dependent on a system of formal education to teach the younger generation, it is not surprising that the curriculum incorporates many aspects of our heritage, artistic as well as scientific.

The purpose of music in the school curriculum has not always been made clear to the public. Simply stated, schools offer music for the same reason that they offer languages and science: All are areas of knowledge, of human endeavor that students should know. Music classes exist primarily to instruct students in music, not to provide free entertainment for the community. Children learn songs because in so doing they gain an understanding of the organization and arrangement of musical sounds.

One aspect of American music education has perhaps been overemphasized. Because wind instruments are more easily learned and are louder and because much attention has been focused on bands and marching activities, many schools offer no instruction on string instruments. This trend has restricted the type of music that students can study.

Music education, because its benefits are intangible, has too often been justified on nonmusical grounds. It is said to improve character, teach teamwork, build healthy bodies, and establish good public relations for the school. Such reasons have not been substantiated and only obscure the true purpose of music education.

REVIEWS OF MUSICAL EVENTS

Most daily newspapers hire critics to write reviews of musical events. In New York City the would-be concert artist presents a recital, then anxiously waits for several hours to find out what judgment the critics have passed on the possibilities of a career as a performer. (The fact that the newspaper critics sometimes do not agree with one another has not discouraged this custom.) In other cities, the reviews are not taken so seriously, although they can affect the morale of a local amateur group.

Traditionally the main purpose of reviews was to guard artistic standards. For example, if an opera was produced poorly, then the public was so advised by the expert reviewer. The question may arise: Why review a performance that is presented only once? After all, there is no opportunity in such cases for the performers to improve their presentation or for attendance to be affected by the review. The answer probably lies in the fact that some readers like to read and talk about musical events, just as some enjoy discussing football games. What a critic said makes a topic for conversation, even if one disagrees with that opinion. In addition, for people who do not know what is happening in the musical world, reviews are an easy way to become "informed."

Not all reviews appearing in print are necessarily authoritative. Few people are expert in all phases of music, from opera to organ, from medieval to modern. Sometimes, in small cities, the music critic also reviews plays, books, and art shows and is responsible for evaluation in such learned fields as philosophy and education. Expertise in all these areas seems more than can be expected from anyone. Furthermore, critics usually have little time to write their reviews, and the reviews are often subject to cuts or last-minute alterations because of space limitations.

In spite of the pitfalls inherent in artistic criticism, newspaper and magazine reviews are usually a positive force. They do stress artistic quality, and they help the art of music by acknowledging the essential place of performance.

PART TWO

EARLY AND BAROQUE MUSIC

8

FOLK AND ETHNIC MUSIC

For much of human history there has been only folk-ethnic music; art music evolved only over the past 600 or 700 years, and did so largely in Western civilization. Folk music predates art music. Some types of folk music have probably changed little over the thousands of years, and yet some kinds are always changing, at least to some degree. So folk music is both old and new.

Music is found in every part of the world. It is a universal human activity. No one knows how much music there is, but the amount must be tremendous. The forms and styles of the music people produce are as varied as their languages and ways of life. Folk music is a fascinating and significant area of the world of music.

THE NATURE OF FOLK MUSIC

The words *folk* and *ethnic* are not synonymous. "Ethnic" refers to music identified with a particular group of people. "Folk" refers only to music actually created or adopted by the common people. A Hungarian peasant song about harvesting hay is a folk song, and because it is characteristic of that country, it is also ethnic music. The *raga* of India is not folk music; it is not the music of the common people but rather of a highly trained musical elite. It is characteristic of India, though, so it is ethnic music. Therefore, all folk music is ethnic, but not all ethnic music is folk music.

Generally speaking, folk-ethnic music is functional music. It is usually valued not for its musical qualities, but rather according to how well it fulfills its task of persuading spirits, accompanying the telling of a story, or providing a sense of group solidarity. The music may have considerable beauty in itself, but artistic expression is not the chief goal for most folk-ethnic music.

CHARACTERISTICS OF ETHNIC MUSIC

Creation. Contrary to popular belief, there is little "community composition"—music created by a group of people sitting around a campfire or marching into battle. Individuals create ethnic music, just as individuals compose art music. But there the similarity ends. The creators of ethnic music are almost always unknown. In fact, the individual might not admit to the accomplishment even if he or she could be located. In many areas of the world songs are supposed to be gifts from the gods revealed in dreams or visions or created on "orders" from a supernatural being. Besides, in most cultures people neither care nor remember who was first responsible for a song.

Oral Tradition. Once created, the music is perpetuated through *oral tradition,* whereby individuals hear the music, remember it, and perform it for others. If no one except the originator likes the song, it passes into oblivion. This tradition ensures the survival of only those songs that are liked by the particular culture. Oral tradition also means that the music is subject to many changes. Suppose that three people hear a song and that one of them is very musical. That person remembers it clearly, but decides to make a few small "improvements" in it. The second person also remembers the song clearly. But he or she belongs to another culture and adapts the song for use in that culture by setting new words to it and altering its rhythm and melody. The third person is not so musical, forgets half of the song, and inaccurately sings the remembered portion. The result is that what started out as one song is now three songs. And each of these versions will in turn be subjected to a similar process of revision and alteration.

Nonliterate societies have no system of musical notation. Even in the advanced societies of ancient India and China, only a system of visual cues was developed. Without a system of notation or recordings, music cannot be preserved accurately. For this reason, folk music is ever changing, which may be one of its strengths. It is both old and contemporary; it represents the heritage of the people and also their current tastes.

Relationship with Culture. The thorough study of ethnic and folk music is a complicated undertaking. The music is only the beginning. The total culture must be included—language, customs, thought forms, and so on. Ethnic music cannot be separated from the culture in which it exists. For example, among the Yoruba tribe in Africa, each type of drum represents one or several deities, and each deity has its own distinctive rhythm. The rituals can be understood only by a person who knows the particular drums, rhythms, and the appropriate god. Some Indian scholars object to attempts to illustrate *ragas* in musical notation and to discuss their musical aspects. To do so, they maintain, is to leave out the vital spiritual aspects of the music.

Complexity. Most of the folk-ethnic music of the world is less complex than art music. Why? First, most of it is confined to short works, usually songs. True, some African rituals last for hours, but the same music tends to be repeated over and over, with only slight variations. The Indian *raga* is also long, but it is an exceptional kind of music. Without a system of notation, musical works are usually rather short-winded. The short length allows for little formal or thematic development, something that is important to art music.

When ethnic music does display complexity, such as the rhythm of African music, it tends to do so with only one aspect of the music, leaving the other aspects relatively undeveloped. By contrast, art music consists of complicated combinations of pitch, harmony, rhythm, timbre, dynamics, and form.

CHARACTERISTICS OF NON-WESTERN MUSIC

What makes much of the ethnic music found throughout the world different from most of the music familiar to us? Let's start with the rhythm.

Rhythm. As was pointed out in Chapter 4, most of the rhythms in the music of Western civilization have regular patterns of accented and unaccented beats. Measure after measure is linked like beads on a string. Much of the rest of the world's music exhibits unequal rhythmic patterns. Sometimes the rhythm is free, especially in epic songs, funeral lamentations, and religious ritual. The rhythm usually conforms to natural speech patterns, so that the words are not adapted to a given metrical pattern as they are in most Western music. When no regular pattern is necessary, it is easy to make the music match the syllables of the words.

Here is a simple children's play song from the Ewe tribe in Ghana in West Africa.

EWE CHILDREN'S SONG

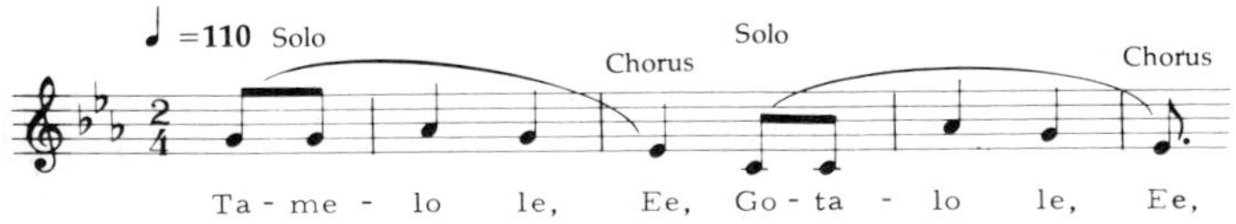

From A. M. Jones, *Studies in African Music*, vol. II (London: Oxford University Press, 1959), p. 1. Used by permission. Translation: The Water-crocodile, oh! The Land-crocodile, oh! School children ran away! Swiftly, swiftly.

Solo
Chorus
Su ku vi wo mi- fa du, gba - sa - srã, gba - sa - srã!

The accenting of the word *gbasasra* breaks the regularity of the pattern. This change does not bother the Africans because they do not think *1—2, 1—2* as Western-trained musicians do. In the example single bar lines have been added to show where the stress occurs.

Melodic Structure. Two important differences exist between most Western and non-Western melodies. One concerns the tuning of pitches. The interval of an octave has a solid basis in the physical laws of sound, and it is found throughout the world. The higher of the two pitches is produced by twice as many vibrations as the pitch one octave lower. All other intervals are altered in the present system of tuning, so the splitting of the octave into twelve equal parts was an arbitrary decision by Western musicians. Non-Western music generally does not divide the octave into twelve equal semitones. *Microtones,* which are pitches less than a semitone apart, are found in the Near East and Far East and, to some extent, in Africa. The octave is divided into twenty-two parts in India; in the Moslem world it has been variously divided into twenty-five, seventeen, and fifteen parts. To a listener who is not accustomed to them, microtones can sound hauntingly expressive or just plain out of tune.

The other difference is the type of scale on which the music is based. A *scale* is a series of ascending and descending tones that follow a specific pattern of intervals. Usually the top and bottom notes are one octave apart. A scale with all its pitches sounded in order for an octave or more seldom appears in the melody of a song. Instead, it is the underlying "formula" for the pitches appearing in a particular section of music. The *major* and *minor* scale patterns are predominant in Western music today, although other seven-note scales called *modes* are favored in folk and popular songs. A common scale in folk music is the *pentatonic* scale, a five-note pattern that duplicates the pitches of the black keys on the piano keyboard. ("Penta" means "five.") This is the basic scale of much Oriental music. It is also heard in the music of the American Indians, the Bantus in central Africa, and, occasionally, in some eastern European music. Many other scales are found throughout the world.

In addition to the variable tuning of notes and the wide diversity of scales, certain notes can be altered or ornamented by the performer in some musical systems. These aspects of pitch are part of the reason why non-Western music often sounds different to us.

Harmony. Most of the world's music contains very little harmony, something that is an important aspect of art music. Some melodies are never intended to have other sounds occurring with them. If harmony is found, it is in one of two forms. One form is a *drone,* a single continuous sound lasting throughout a piece. The Scottish bagpipe produces one of the few examples of a drone in Western music. The other type of harmony is produced by adding a duplicate melodic line that moves strictly parallel to the original melody. This harmony part is often a fourth or fifth below the melody. Sometimes it is a third away, which is the usual interval in Western harmony.

Form. Most ethnic songs are too brief to allow for much form. However, short sections are often arranged in various patterns. One type is the leader-response found in African music. The result is a game of "musical tennis" in which sections of music are alternated between a soloist and group. In many parts of the world the music is subjected to a simple variation treatment in which the basic melody is varied slightly and repeated many times.

Improvisation. Almost all art music is written in notation. The performer's main task is to recreate the notes on the page and adhere to the composer's intent. Not so with most of the world's music. No accurate system for notating music exists outside the West, and most composers of ethnic music are unknown, so the performer is encouraged to create new music while playing or singing. Performing music spontaneously, without the aid of notes, is called *improvisation.* The performer does not often improvise "out of thin air"—that is, without any guidelines at all. Usually there are melodic or rhythmic patterns and performance traditions that provide guidelines. In contrast to art music, in which the ideas of the composer prevail, much ethnic music is geared to the performer. Improvised performances are never quite the same twice, and often reflect the inspiration of the moment.

Instruments. Folk instruments are described in Chapter 6.

SOME SIGNIFICANT TYPES OF ETHNIC MUSIC

The topic of ethnic music is so vast that it could occupy many books. To keep this chapter within reasonable limits, it is necessary to leave out many types of music.

Europe. As might be expected, the folk music of Europe resembles Western art music more closely than do other ethnic musics. Wide differences can be found within the European continent, however, especially in isolated rural areas. One characteristic of European folk music is the singing of different lines of words to the same melody. Such songs are called *strophic.* A few pentatonic scales are encountered, especially in Hungary and eastern Europe, but major and minor scales and modes predominate. The rhythm is metrical, with somewhat more freedom of meter in eastern European music.

An old man in Java (Indonesia) playing a rebab, a two-stringed instrument that is often used in native instrumental groups called gamelan.

European folk songs include a greater percentage of epic tales and love sentiments than do the songs of other cultures. There are some folk hymns and songs revolving around turning points in a person's life such as birth or marriage. The French have songs to urge children to eat and teach them to count. Songs about agriculture are common, especially in eastern Europe. Dance music is prevalent, too.

India. Probably the most sophisticated music outside Western civilization is found in India. It is not folk music, but an ethnic music that requires much training for both performer and listener. Indian music is very much intertwined with religious belief and practice. It began at least a thousand years B.C., and it continues today. Despite several invasions by the Muslims over the centuries and the British occupation in the nineteenth and twentieth centuries, it is believed that the music has not changed much since its inception.

At the heart of Indian music is the *raga,* which is a melodic formula resembling a scale. It also embraces important Indian religious concepts. Indian musicians believe that the vibrations of the *raga* must be in tune with the universe, and that other arts such as poetry and painting must fit with music into the great cosmic scheme. For example, there are *ragas* that should be performed only in the morning, others only in the evening, others only in the rainy season, and so on. Theoretically, thousands of *ragas* exist, but only about fifty are used frequently. *Ragas* vary in length; the average is about twenty to twenty-five notes. Two tones tend to stand out in each *raga,* one being four or five notes higher than the other. Here is a *raga* from North India, notated as accurately as possible. The rhythmic values of the notes indicate importance, not length. The very small noteheads indicate slides or zigzag figures, and the brackets over the line mark off the phrases.

RAGA MIYAN-KI-MALLAR

From Walter Kaufmann, *The Ragas of North India* (Bloomington, Ind.: Indiana University Press, 1968), p. 3. Used by permission.

The next significant element in Indian music is its rhythm, which is built around the *tala.* Each *tala* is a rhythmic cycle of from 3 to 128 beats, although most are from 5 to 8 beats long. Each *tala* is divided into smaller groups. A *tala* is not a unit like a measure described in Chapter 4; it is a pattern. For example, a 7-beat *tala* might be made up of 3 beats + 2 beats + 2 beats. If an Indian musician taps his foot as he plays, it is not a regular tapping but an indication of the unequal divisions of the *tala.* Furthermore, the first beat in a *tala* is not stressed more than the other beats. Like each *raga,* each *tala* is named.

Using the *raga* and *tala* as guides, the performer improvises while singing a religious poem from one of the holy books. Because the musical system is so complicated, there is a dazzling array of melodic and rhythmic possibilities—enough to last a lifetime. The pleasure for the listener lies in hearing the performer create music within the guidelines of the system.

The *raga-tala* improvisations are organized in a loose form in which the *raga* is introduced and then followed by sections that feature the *raga* in different ranges of the voice and instruments. A simple bass pattern of three notes is sounded throughout to provide the listener with a constant reminder of the tonal centers of the *raga.* The *tala* pattern is played on small drums. If several players participate, a flute or oboe or *sitar* can be included. The *sitar* is a complicated string instrument with five melodic strings, two drones, and thirteen more strings that sound in sympathy with the melodic strings. It looks like a large guitar with pegs along the neck of the instrument. It is played while sitting on the floor, as are all Indian instruments.

Today in India a prospective musician studies either Western or Indian music; few musicians know both types. Indian music is often learned from a religious teacher or *guru* who knows music and who traditionally receives no pay for his lessons. His purpose is to guide the disciple spiritually through the study and performance of the music.

Indian music is one of the few types that has remained unchanged despite the influence of Western music. In fact, elements of Indian music have sometimes appeared in Western popular music in recent years. Still, the style seems very different to persons accustomed to Western music. Whatever one's reaction, it certainly cannot be considered a primitive type of music.

China. China's musical heritage is as old as India's. Because China had a system of writing words (not music), accurate accounts about its music throughout its history are available. Like Indian music, Chinese music was closely related to philosophy and religion. In fact, one early emperor ordered musicians and astrologers to work together in calculating the length of the pipe that was to be the standard pitch for all music; he wanted his reign to be in harmony with the universe.

The Chinese developed a theoretical system that provides for twelve pitches within the octave. Their basic melodic pattern, however, was the pentatonic scale, the five-tone pattern described earlier in this chapter.

In addition to an intricate theoretical system, the Chinese developed several exotic instruments. One was a model of a crouching tiger with a serrated ridge or set of wooden slats along its backbone. It was sounded by dragging a bamboo stick across the bumps or slats. Another instrument was a mouth organ with seventeen bamboo pipes.

In some periods of China's history music thrived, but in other eras it hardly survived. Much of the music was created for the official court, often for banquets. But like Indian music, Chinese music is not folk music. A few large orchestras existed in China—a situation rare outside of the West. Many theatrical, operalike productions were presented also.

Over the years, Chinese opera has developed to include preludes of crashing cymbals, acrobats, female impersonators, and solo songs. Hero roles are sung with a rasping sound, and heroines sing in a high, thin voice. Mastery of Chinese opera style requires years of rigorous training and practice. The lines of music consist of rather short phrases separated by instrumental interludes. A drum maintains a steady rhythm, and sections of the music are concluded with a cymbal crash.

In 1911 the last Chinese dynasty fell and the country was declared a republic. The ensuing years have been hard ones for music, largely because of political strife and repression. Since 1949 the Communist party has controlled the mainland and sophisticated music has been discouraged. More in favor is the unison singing of politically oriented songs such as "Up the Mountain Come the Manure Carriers" and "Hearts of the Frontier Guards Turn to the Party"—actual titles of songs heard in China in 1973. Quite recently there has been much more contact between China and the Western nations in all areas, including music. Some of the Chinese musical tradition is being preserved on Formosa, but the influence of Western music is strongly felt there.

Arabian Music. The Arabian world extends 4,000 miles from the north coast of Africa (just across the Strait of Gibraltar from Spain) to the borders of Pakistan. Although most Arabs share the same religious faith—Islam—their culture and music have never been well unified. Four main groupings of Arabian music can be identified. One is Persian, which centers in Iran. A second is Arab, centering in Egypt. A third is Andalusian; it exists mostly in North Africa. The fourth is Turkish. To further complicate matters, Arabian music has complicated and confusing music theories that vary from country to country. And when performed, the music often differs from the stated musical theories.

Much music from the Arabian world is vocal and is characterized by a tense, nasal quality. Some call and response between chorus and soloist is found. Accompaniment often consists of hand claps or tambourines. Mohammed, the prophet of Islam, did not approve of music in the mosque, so it is restricted in orthodox Islamic worship. A few restrained prayers and chants are "sung" in the mosque, but because they are not officially considered to be music, they are acceptable.

In Iran the music is constructed on a *gushe,* which is similar to the Indian *raga.* Usually playing a flute, the performer improvises a highly decorated line based on the *gushe.* The rhythm is free and allows the performer time in which to follow his musical inclinations.

Important Arabian instruments include the *tombak*—a drum in the shape of an hourglass and played with the hand and fingers, the *ud*—a string instrument with a pear-shaped body, and the *rebab*—a direct ancestor of the violin.

Although there are some professional musicians in the Arabian countries, there are few concerts in the Western sense of the word. Cafes are the usual setting for music performances, and one may sip a drink while listening. As an added attraction, the more thoughtful numbers may be interspersed with the gyrating female dancers for which the Arabian world is noted. Artistic musical qualities are difficult to maintain against such competition.

Jewish Music in Israel. Because the Jews were for so long scattered throughout the world, their nonreligious music has acquired many non-Jewish characteristics. Even the pre-Christian music of the Jews was influenced by both the East and the West because Jerusalem was a crossroads for caravans traveling between the two worlds. It is not unusual for German Jews to sing German or Yiddish songs or for Armenian-Russian Jews to sing songs of their former homeland. The Arabian world, which nearly surrounds Israel, has also had its influence. Many Jews, however, sing Arabian songs in a different style from the one they use for Jewish music.

Jewish religious music has remained rather well unified. Judaism was not so evangelistic as Christianity. It tended to keep its faith within the group, and it seldom incorporated local music into its worship. Its religious music is intended for prayers and invocations, not anthems such as are found in many Protestant churches. The music varies somewhat according to the degree of orthodoxy. The more orthodox congregations permit only unaccompanied chanting by cantors, while more liberal congregations often employ non-Jewish instrumentalists and singers and allow them to perform adaptations of music written for Christian worship. The orthodox chanting style has a free rhythm and decorative notes. Some Jewish religious music is similar to Arabian music. A few Jewish melodies have been adapted as hymns in Protestant churches, and Judaic music was influential in early Christian music.

Since modern Israel was established in 1948, attempts have been made to create new folk traditions to help unify a multi-ethnic nation whose bonds are largely religious and political. New popular songs have been composed about economic and political topics. Arabian tambourines and hourglass drums accompany them, as well as guitars and accordions. Arabianlike scales are often harmonized with Western chords. Like its people, Israel's music is highly cosmopolitan.

Spanish-American. The term "Spanish-American" includes a wide variety of music, partly because the music of Spain itself is immensely varied. It includes the music of the Spanish gypsies and of the Basque people of northern Spain, Arabian influence resulting from 600 years of occupation by the Moors, and French influence from Provençal. With the Spanish conquests in the New World, elements of its music were transported to the Americas. Spanish music became mixed with native Indian music and the music of the blacks, especially in Cuba, Brazil, and the West Indies.

In the centuries since the Spanish entered Latin America, their music has been adapted so extensively that it has become impossible in many cases

A Peruvian Indian of the Hauncarjo Valley playing an instrument made from animal horns.

to tell from where a particular song came. Some Spanish dances have been adapted, also. For example, the *bolero* was originally Spanish, but in Cuba its rhythm has become more complex. Among other features that carry over from Spanish music into Latin American music are the frequent use of meters having three notes to the beat, the presence of a line moving parallel to the melody but three notes above or below, and melodies with a rather narrow range.

Mexican music is largely Spanish in character, more so than most other Latin American music. Some Mexican Indians have retained their own music, but the Indian influence is not significant in Mexico's music. The Mexicans have a narrative type of song called a *corrido.* Like the English broadside ballad, it relates a happening or tells a story. Instruments play an important role in Mexican music and are sometimes featured in instrumental interludes. The often-heard *mariachi* band consists of from three to twelve players playing violins, guitars, trumpets, and other instruments. The name *mariachi* comes from the French word *mariage,* because these musicians once played mainly for weddings.

Spanish-American music is well liked in the United States. Much of it, however, is "commercial" music. It is not authentic, and to a musician it is less interesting than the real music of the Spanish-American peoples. Fortunately, some Spanish-American folk songs have been incorporated into the musical heritage of the United States, and Spanish-American people have preserved many of their distinctive songs.

Africa South of the Sahara. The areas north of the vast Sahara desert are largely Arabian in character. To the south are the provinces of the black people, and it is their music that will be discussed here. For the sake of brevity the term will be shortened to "Africa" for the remainder of this book.

Africans make music a more integral part of their lives that do most of the peoples of the world. Music is called on to cure illness, appease gods, and celebrate the births of babies. Music is used for singing the praises of cattle, telling about an elephant hunt, or paddling a canoe either against the current or with it—there is a song for each direction. Some music is sheerly for entertainment and is performed by men whose livelihood comes from their music-making. In some tribes there is a small musical elite, usually drummers, who practice their trade from youth. They spend most of their childhood learning how to drum, and they do not perform "publicly" until they are young adults.

The Western idea of a performer and a passive group of listeners is not a part of African tradition. A musical performance is truly a participatory event in which everyone sings, claps, or dances. Furthermore, African musicians want the music to have an impact on the listeners. They do not particularly care whether or not the listeners consider their music "beautiful," but they do want the audience to share their feelings.

Music is even used for signaling. Sometimes the drum rhythms resemble a simplified Morse code, but the signals are also related to the pitch structure of the language. Many African languages are tonal. A sound, *ba,* for example, takes on a different meaning depending on the pitch level at which it is spoken. A drummer then approximates the pitch of the word being signaled by beating on different-sized drums or hitting a log drum at different places.

The form found in African music was mentioned earlier in this chapter. It is a short unit of music that is repeated, varied slightly, or alternated with group response. The "call-and-response" technique between leader and group is central to African music. It assures the participation of which Africans are so fond. The music continues for as long as the ritual requires or with other music for as long as the performer and audience wish.

Improvising variations of short musical units is common in African styles. Not only does the leader improvise; in some tribes the group members improvise simultaneously among themselves.

The melodies in African music are not too different from Western music.

An African drummer in Mumbasa, Tanzania.

The underlying scale contains seven different notes, but microtones and the pentatonic scale are also used. Glides and other ornaments are incorporated into the singing, and this ornamentation sometimes hides the true pitch of a note.

The main feature of African music is its rhythm. The Ewe children's song provided a simple example of the rhythmic freedom of African music. A feature of West African music is the musician's ability to maintain a steady tempo for minutes or even hours. Western musicians keep a generally steady tempo, but they make slight fluctuations in it. The exactness of the tempo in African music makes it easier to emphasize certain beats and rhythmic patterns.

A more spectacular feature of African rhythm is the sounding of two or more rhythms at the same time, called *polyrhythm*. If one person taps the rhythm of a waltz while another taps the rhythm of a march, they are producing polyrhythm. In African music the sounding of different rhythms at the same time occurs most often in drumming, but it appears in other types of music, too. Sometimes as many as six different rhythmic parts are sounding simultaneously. The effect is truly exciting.

African music contains simple harmony and counterpoint. Parallel movement is created by a melodic line and its duplicate. There are also two-part rounds. These rounds may have developed from instances in which either the leader or chorus was overly anxious and began before the other had finished. Instruments such as the xylophone or harp sometimes accompany a melody by persistently repeating a short melodic phrase that contrasts with the melody.

African music is interesting not only in itself, but also because of the influence it has had on American music. American art music is presented in Chapter 32, and American folk music is discussed in the next section of this chapter. Jazz is presented in Chapter 34.

AMERICAN FOLK MUSIC

The English Heritage. Since English is the language of the United States, it is not surprising that the main source of American folk music is the British Isles. Many songs were imported intact from Britain, and many other songs have been patterned after British types.

The most significant type of British folk song is the *ballad.* It is a narrative song of five to twenty or more stanzas. Traditionally the ballad had a common iambic meter and stanzas of four lines, in which a 4-foot line alternates with a 3-foot line. Here is an American example:

> When John Henry was a little baby
> sitting on his pappy's knee,
> He grabbed a hammer and a little
> piece of steel,
> Said, "This hammer'll be the death
> of me."

Ballads are often tragic. John Henry dies driving spikes for the railroad. Some ballads have happy endings, and some are humorous. In "The Farmer's Crust Wife," the wife is taken to hell by the devil, but she is so ornery that the devil returns her to her husband. In a ballad the narrator-singer is a third person relating a tale and is not involved. The music reflects this by conveying a calm and detached attitude.

In older ballads the music often uses a seven-note modal scale, not the major-minor system of today. The rhythm largely depends on the text, which means that a regular pattern is followed. Much of the ballad singing in the United States is unaccompanied, although in Kentucky an accompaniment is taken for granted and is provided by a banjo, guitar, or dulcimer. The dulcimer looks like a long, flat violin with three strings. It is laid on the player's lap and plucked with a quill. Two of its strings produce a drone.

An interesting type of ballad is called a *broadside.* The name comes from the old English practice of printing ballads on large sheets of paper called "broadsides," which were then sold in the streets. Broadsides were often about current events and famous personalities. About 200 broadsides were circulated in the United States. The poetry was not always the best, and some of the situations were clichés, but broadsides did reflect the interests of the people.

The ballad style is evident in many American folk songs associated with occupations—sailors, cowboys, lumberjacks, miners, farmers, and so on. The ballad's influence can also be seen in American religious hymns. It has been estimated that most songs in the English heritage descended from about fifty-five tunes or "tune families."

Non-British music also came to the United States with various immigrant groups. In a few cases it was incorporated into the culture and stands along with the British style music: *"Du, du liegst mir im Herzen"* is a German song that has been adopted into the culture; *"Alouette"* is a French-Canadian example; and *"Chiapanecas"* (sometimes called "The Mexican Clapping Song") is a Spanish-American contribution that is clapped and stomped at many major league ballparks. Some of these songs have had new words put to the music. The Pennsylvania song *"Marjets wann ich uffschteh"* became "Go Tell Aunt Rhody the Old Grey Goose is Dead." Unfortunately, much non-British music has been lost.

Types of American Folk Songs. Folk songs were and are found in a variety of situations in the United States. Work songs were not a feature of American folk music, except for sea chanteys (pronounced *shantey*). "Haul Away Joe" is an example of a sea chantey. Clearly, the words are of little importance.

Louis was the King of France before the
  Revolution,
    'Way, haul away, we'll haul away Joe.
King Louis got his head cut off which
  spoiled his constitution,
    'Way, haul away, we'll haul away Joe.

A second type of folk song was intended to accompany dancing. In America this frequently meant square dancing. Again, the words were of little importance; some, in fact, were added just to fill out a phrase. A well-known example of this is "Turkey in the Straw," in which one verse is:

As I went out to milk, and I didn't know how;
I milked a goat instead of a cow.
A monkey sittin' on a pile of straw,
A-winkin' his eye at his mother-in-law.
Turkey in the hay, turkey in the straw,
The ole gray mare won't gee nor haw;
Roll'em up and twist 'em up a high tuck-a-haw,
And hit'em up a tune called Turkey in the Straw.

Some "fun" songs were not for dancing. "The Deacon Went Down" cited in Chapter 1 is one example.

Many American folk songs tell a story. "Careless Love" has a story of woe that concludes:

Love, oh love, oh careless love,
See what careless love has done to me.
When my apron strings were long,
You passed my window with a song.
Now my apron strings won't tie,
You pass my cabin door right by.

Many songs, both folk and art, exist primarily to express feelings. The white spiritual is one example. The words to "The Wayfaring Stranger" are:

I'm just a poor, wayfaring stranger,
A-trav'ling through this world of woe,
Yet there's no sickness, no toil, no danger,
In that fair land to which I go.
I'm goin' there to see my mother,
I'm goin' there no more to roam,
I'm goin' over Jordan,
I'm just a-goin' over home.

Sometimes composers find songs that they consider worth arranging for concert or recital hall performance. They leave the original melody largely intact and devise an accompaniment for piano or orchestra. Aaron Copland did this with the Shaker song "Simple Gifts" (Record 1, Side 2). The song originates from the period between 1837 and 1847, and the text expresses the Shaker ideal of the simple, orderly life.

'Tis the gift to be simple, 'tis the gift to be free,
'Tis the gift to come down where you ought to be,
And when we find ourselves in the place just right,

'Twill be in the valley of love and delight.
When true simplicity is gained,
To bow and to bend we shan't be ashamed,
To turn, turn will be our delight
'Till by turning, turning we come round right.

The setting of the melody for "Simple Gifts" is in keeping with the text and melody by being very open and uncluttered. There are only very brief introductory measures based on the melody for each half of the song. Sometimes the chords are sounded off the beat in a subtle way, but generally everything is understated and plain.

American Indian Music. The functional nature of American Indian music is apparent in the names given to the ritual procedures. As the titles imply, a sun dance or rabbit dance is created for a specific purpose.

Traditionally, Indian instruments consisted of a variety of drums, usually played with sticks. Many types of rattles were developed. Several types of flutes were played, especially by the males, who performed love music on them to impress their chosen young women.

The Indian population was never large (not more than one or two million in all of North America), and it is spread over a vast land area. As a result, musical styles differ widely among the various tribes, a fact that is also true in other parts of the world. The Indians of the Pacific Northwest and the Eskimos have developed music characterized by nonstrophic forms, complex rhythms, and small melodic intervals. The Indians of California and the extreme Southwest sing with a harsh vocal sound. The songs consist of two or more separate sections that are repeated, alternated, and interwoven. A third general area includes Utah, Nevada, and the interior of Northern California. In this region the singing is more relaxed in style, and songs are made up of paired phrases with each phrase repeated. The fourth type of Indian culture is distinguished more by language than geography. It consists of the Navajo, Apache, and some western Canadian tribes. Their melodies have a wide range, and male singers freely perform in the high "false" voice. The Pueblo and Plains Indians display more tension in singing and favor a two-part song form. The Indians in the eastern and southern parts of the United States feature singing responsively, with shouts tossed back and forth between leader and group.

Indian music has not had a significant effect on other American music for two reasons. (1) Most Indians do not live close to non-Indians. They have lived apart on reservations, and their music has tended to remain there. (2) Indian music is quite different from Western music. In some respects it is more oriental than Western. When one culture incorporates music from another, the two styles are likely to be similar. Some change, but not too much, is accepted in music. In the few instances in which Indian music has been incorporated into American compositions, it has been changed quite a bit.

Occupational Songs. An important contribution to America's folk music heritage can be heard in songs about various occupations. In many cowboy songs the text and music are tinged with loneliness and melancholy, reflecting the fact that life on the frontier was neither easy nor a lot of fun. Some of the cowboy tunes originally had other words before being adapted by the cowboy.

The development of the railroad provided another source for occupational songs. Some of these songs are about the men who worked the railroads ("Drill, Ye Tarriers, Drill"), some describe famous personalities ("John Henry" and "Casey Jones"), and others tell about trains themselves ("The Wabash Cannonball"). Sailors have provided their share of occupational songs as well. But today's business offices and assembly lines do not encourage the development of song literature. One does not sing to a computer, and the assembly line noise drowns out most other sounds. So the occupational song may become a thing of the past.

Afro-American Music. In a complex and pluralistic society the sources of a cultural mixture are hard to assess, and so it is difficult to determine which aspects of Afro-American music were transplanted from Africa and which were developed in America. In any case, some of the African's rhythmic ideas, the call-and-response patterns, love of instruments, and improvisation are now a part of American music. Africans brought something perhaps more important than any technical features: a strong interest in music and a desire to involve the listener in the music.

Haiti in the Caribbean, the Guianas on the north coast of South America, and northern Brazil have large black populations. Because of the isolation of these people from the mainstream of society, their music has remained strongly African. The mutual influence between African and Western music has occurred to the greatest extent in the United States. Cuba, Jamaica, and Trinidad are next in the amount of musical interaction between African and native styles.

The African influence has been felt most in the area of performance. The spiritual is a good example of this fact. There are both black and white spirituals. Their texts and melodic ideas are identical. The main difference between the two kinds of spirituals is in the way they are sung. The black spiritual is more rhythmic and stresses call-and-response, with some improvisation; the white version is more lyric and polished. The performance differences are also apparent in other types of black folk music. Some were originated by blacks and some were simply taken from the white culture.

Another performance area in which the influence of African music is evident is in singing style. African singers produce more varied sounds when singing. Some tones are purposely harsh and raucous in order to imitate animals; some are tense and some are throaty, but generally the style is relaxed and warm.

The song designed to accompany work is definitely a contribution of the black culture. The song text is not always related directly to the job at hand; often the words supply only a pleasant accompaniment to labor.

As in Africa, instruments are prominent in Afro-American folk music. Some of the instruments are conventional, while others are intended to provide sound effects. Included in the latter category are washboards, pans, cowbells, bottles, various clappers, and the gutbucket (an inverted washtub with a rope pulled through it and connected to a stick; the pitch is varied according to the tension of the rope).

The greatest musical contribution of the American blacks is jazz. A chapter of this book is devoted to it.

Folk and ethnic music is important partly because there is so much of it and so many people find it appealing. It has influenced the development and content of art music. In some cases folk melodies have been incorporated into operas or symphonies, but more often a composer has been influenced by a rhythmic pattern or style of melody heard in folk music. Folk music can also stand on its own merits. It has a basic expressiveness that is fascinating.

9

EARLY WESTERN MUSIC

No one knows how or where music began, but it seems to be a part of life in every age and place. Pictures on the walls of pyramids and on Mesopotamian vases show people making music. In ancient Israel, David soothed King Saul with harp music. In early Greek civilization poets like Homer sang their tales as they accompanied themselves on simple string instruments.

Plate 1
Goddess of Music.
(Scala/EPA.)

This page from a fourteenth-century manuscript shows the goddess Music sitting and holding a portable organ. Other instruments common during the time are also pictured. Starting at the top center and moving clockwise they are: ''pig snout'' psaltery, a mandola, clappers, long trumpets, kettle drums tied around the waist, bagpipe held by the man and a double-reed instrument called a shawm held by the woman, a jingle drum, and a vielle.

Plate 2
Giotto di Bondone: *Madonna and Child.*
(Samuel H. Kress Collection, National Gallery of Art, Washington, D.C.)

The painting is part of a series or polyptych. Notice that it is more two-dimensional or flat than later paintings. The outlines of the Madonna, seen in three-quarter position, create an elegant Gothic shape broken only by the almost geometric figure of the Child. The gold background shows the influence of Byzantine or eastern European art.

Plate 3
Sandro Botticelli: *The Adoration of the Magi.*
(Andrew Mellon Collection, National Gallery of Art, Washington, D.C.)

This painting shows the Renaissance fondness for order and balance. A group of figures at the left of the painting is balanced by a group on the right, with the infant Jesus in the center. The converging lines of the Greek and Roman ruins add perspective to the painting and show the renewed interest in these ancient civilizations. Notice also the brightly colored clothing on the figures.

Plate 4
Albrecht Dürer: *Portrait of a Clergyman*.
(Samuel H. Kress Collection, National Gallery of Art, Washington, D.C.)

The Renaissance is often associated with Italy. The artistic accomplishments of northern Europeans during that time are sometimes overlooked. Dürer shows the influence of Bellini and other Italian painters in this portrait. It is the solid quality of northern European work that the nineteenth-century writer Goethe described as "engraving figures of wood." The painting dates from about 1516.

Plato considered music an important part of a citizen's education, although his use of the word "music" included some rhythmic activities and poetry. He even ascribed to music certain moral qualities and effects. The Greeks developed several instruments, including the lyre, which is seen on many music emblems today. Most impressive, however, were the acoustical discoveries of Pythagoras, the same man for whom the geometrical theorem is named. About 550 B.C. Pythagoras discovered that every interval—the distance from one pitch to another—can be represented by a mathematical ratio and that there is a relationship between this ratio and the degree of consonance or dissonance.

Our understanding of Greek music suffers from the same limitation that affects our knowledge of most music until about the twelfth century: It is impossible to know how the music sounded. No accurate system was devised for writing music; or if one existed, it has been lost. Only a few scraps of music notation have been found, and attempts to interpret these fragments are mostly guesswork. The Greeks talked about music a great deal, believed (falsely) that

Several musical instruments can be seen in this painting from an ancient Etruscan tomb.

it influenced a person's moral character, theorized about music and acoustics, but were not able to transmit a lasting indication of its sound.

The Romans had music, too. Probably most of it, along with much of Roman culture, was taken over from Greek civilization. The Romans emphasized military music more than did the Greeks.

With the fall of the Roman Empire in 476 A.D., the Christian church attempted to root out of society everything that had been associated with pagan Rome. One object of this reform was Roman music, which had so often been associated with festivals (and orgies). Almost all remnants of Roman music have been lost or destroyed.

Because Christianity began in the context of Judaism, early church music assumed much of the heritage of the Jewish temple. Daily prayer hours were adopted, along with the responsive singing of psalms between a soloist and congregation. As Christianity spread through Asia Minor into Europe and Africa, it accumulated other musical elements. The fact that the early Church incorporated singing into its worship activities is recorded in Matthew (26:30) and Mark (14:26) and in nonbiblical writings. It is probable that during the first three centuries after Christ there were no uniform musical customs.

GREGORIAN CHANT

From the fourth to the sixth centuries A.D., church music became more uniform and evolved into more Western-sounding music. Trained singers were given increasingly more responsibility for the music. Late in the sixth century, as a part of the organizing of all aspects of the Church, Pope Gregory I directed a recodification and compilation of the chants. He assigned particular chants to certain services throughout the year. Gregory's work was so highly esteemed that even today this entire body of music is called *Gregorian chant.* (It is also known as *plainsong* or *plainchant.*) When the compilation was completed, the Church had a *liturgy,* a body of rites prescribed for public worship. The most frequent worship service is the Mass, which is described on page 113.

The music that evolved from the centuries of modification and adaptation by the early Church and under Gregory's direction is one of the great monuments of Western civilization. It is a valuable part of our cultural heritage, and it is important to the understanding of the music that follows it.

Gregorian chant is different from most music heard in America today. In chant, only one line of music is heard, without the enriching sounds of harmony. Even the melodic line is different. In place of beats and regular rhythmic patterns, there is a flexible rhythm, and the familiar major-minor scale system is generally lacking. Compared to most of the music we hear today, Gregorian chant makes no attempt to appeal to the senses or to the listener's emotions. Only men's voices are used, and they sing in a more subdued way than is generally used for other styles of music. The words are in Latin.

THE MASS AND ITS MUSIC

The Mass is central to the practice of the Roman Catholic faith. It is a ceremony that reaffirms in a symbolic way the connection between the believers and the risen Christ through a reenactment of the Last Supper (Holy Communion) with its sharing of the bread and wine and the miracle of that moment. Many Protestant churches also have Communion services, but the parts of the service are not the same as the version in the Catholic Church and the beliefs associated with the service also differ. The term "Mass" comes from the phrase that ends the service, "Ite missa est," with which the worshipers are dismissed.

The Mass may be spoken or sung, and is generally spoken except in large churches. Only a limited number of priests are trained to sing the Mass.

The Mass is made up of a number of parts. Some portions of it vary according to the particular day in the Church year. These portions are called the *Proper,* because they are proper for a certain date in the Church calendar. Some portions, however, are repeated for nearly every Mass, and these sections are called the *Ordinary,* because they are ordinarily included. The parts of the Ordinary are:

Kyrie—A short prayer in Greek instead of the usual Latin. The words translated mean, "Lord, have mercy on us; Christ, have mercy on us."

Gloria—Offers praise to God in Latin with the words "Glory to God on high."

Credo—A rather long statement of belief ("I believe in one God," etc.) that is recited or sung in a reciting style.

Sanctus—This section is the climactic moment in the Mass, when at its conclusion the priest raises the bread and wine for everyone to see. The words of the Sanctus are, "Holy, holy, holy."

Agnus Dei—The words mean "Lamb of God" and refer to the symbolism of the sacrifice by God of his Son to take away the sins of the world.

Because the Ordinary of the Mass appears in almost all Masses, it has been selected by composers to set to music. Literally hundreds of composers over the past 600 years have composed Masses, including such "big name" composers from the past as Beethoven, Mozart, Haydn, Palestrina (who composed over 100 Masses), and Stravinsky in this century.

A *Requiem Mass* is a Mass for the dead. It omits the Credo and Gloria and adds a section called *Dies irae* ("Day of Wrath"). Many composers have incorporated a fragment from a *Dies irae* found in Gregorian chant into their music to indicate death and terror.

Until Vatican Council II (1964–67), the Roman Catholic Church specified the content and words for every service, but now that has been changed. More freedom is permitted in the amount and type of music that can be included in the service, and even more important, vernacular languages (non-Latin) have been accepted. Unfortunately, most chants and music for Masses lose effectiveness when translated, so much of the traditional (and beautiful) music is not heard so often today.

Gregorian chant is not concert music. The chant was created for one purpose only: to contribute to the spirit of worship. When sung by the religious in a seminary or monastery, however, it is strangely moving. The impression is created partially by the setting and the obvious religious devotion of the participants and by the knowledge that the music helps to put the listener in the procession of the faithful stretching back nearly 2,000 years. But part of the effect is due to qualities of the music itself.

The music example shows an *Ave Maria* (Record 1, Side 1). The same words have been set to music by many composers; the versions by Schubert and Bach-Gounod are well known. The text is translated: "Hail Mary, full of grace, the Lord is with thee; blessed art thou among women, and blessed is the fruit of thy womb." The music is shown here in two versions. One is the traditional four-line staff and square notes of the Roman Catholic Church; the second is a rendition in modern notation.

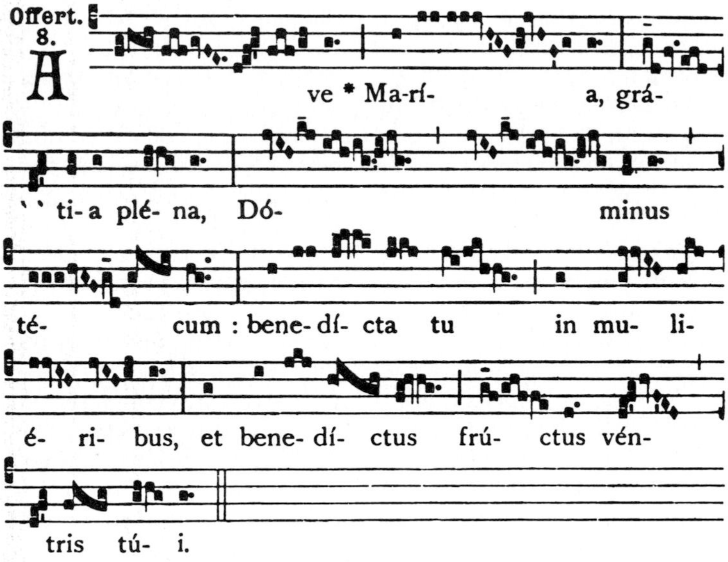

Even in modern notation, the music looks different. It has no meter signature. Almost all notes have the same rhythmic value, but the last note of each phrase is consistently longer. The grouping of notes is irregular; sometimes there are two in a group, sometimes three, sometimes more. The melody seldom moves very far from one note to another; its contour is smooth. It covers a range of about one octave, and it centers around the note G.* The piece is short, taking only about two and a half minutes to perform.

*The pitch is only approximate. The notes of Gregorian chant are not absolute pitches, such as are found today.

The unfamiliar sound of Gregorian chant can be partly attributed to its scale patterns. Today we hear many pieces of music that are in one of two patterns: major or minor. These patterns are called *keys* or *modes.* Originally, however, the term "mode" included several other patterns as well as major and minor. The notes of any mode, when lined up in order, result in a scale with its own characteristic pattern. In medieval times, musicians seemed to prefer the *non*major/minor modes, and these are the sounds heard in Gregorian chant. The same modal characteristics are sometimes found in folk music, and they are common in popular songs of today. It is easy to duplicate the sounds of these modes at the piano by playing scales *on the white keys only* from D to D, E to E, F to F, and G to G.

Gregorian chant seeks to convey a spirit, an attitude. Like the devout and pious persons who sing it, the music strives for a reverence worthy of acceptance by God. Although such an ideal may seem remote from the busy pace of contemporary American life, it is the ultimate goal of Gregorian chant.

Unlike other early music, Gregorian chant was carefully preserved in the monasteries by oral tradition and written manuscripts. This music has been painstakingly researched by musicologists.

A page of manuscript written in 1290 showing the old system of notation and beautiful decorations (illuminations). The picture in the decoration shows an early organ.

SECULAR MUSIC

Although Gregorian chant dominated the religious music of the times, music of a *secular* (worldly or nonsacred) nature also existed. Most of the secular music was not written down, so less is known about it. Most of the secular music was in the language of a particular country—French, German, English, Italian, Spanish—rather than in Latin. At first such music was largely performed by wandering musicians who traveled from place to place singing songs, reciting poems, and even exhibiting trained animals. Later, about the twelfth and thirteenth centuries, troubadours and trouvères dominated secular music in France. They were noblemen who were poets and composers but usually not performers, since they often hired minstrels to sing their songs. The music was for solo voice and was often sung with instrumental accompaniment. Most of the poems and songs were about an idealized type of love, with a passion more of the spirit than of the flesh. About 4,600 such poems and 1,660 such melodies have been preserved. Unlike Gregorian chant they have regular rhythmic patterns and they resemble folk melodies.

One of the manuscripts of secular music of the Gothic period that has been preserved is a *pastourelle* ("pastorale") with the title *Le Jeu de Robin et Marion* ("The Play of Robin and Marion") by Adam de la Halle (about 1230–1288). The text of a pastorale is always about a knight who tries to seduce a shepherdess. After some resistance, she gives in, and then screams for help, at which time her brother or lover rushes in to drive the knight away after some combat. At first pastorales were only spoken, but later actors, songs, and dances were added. Some of the songs were based on folk melodies, in whole or in part. The songs in the pastorale are short and simple. Each adheres to a rhythmic pattern or *mode.* These rhythmic modes, of which there are six, are similar to those used in classifying poetry today. The first song in *Robin and Marion* has the pattern of short–long (◡ —). In modern notation a portion of the song is:

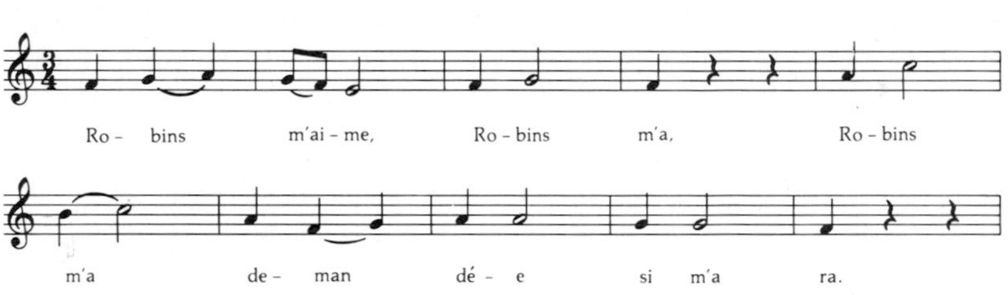

The music was probably accompanied by one or more of the instruments pictured in plate 1. The music for *Robin and Marion* does not sound overpowering or sophisticated, but rather simple and charming. Perhaps it is this quality of charm that encouraged such twentieth-century composers as Darius Milhaud (page 403) to write accompanying music to the melodies of Adam de la Halle of the thirteenth century.

POLYPHONY

Until about 1000 A.D. music consisted largely of a melodic line with an occasional improvised accompaniment. Although examples of the simultaneous sounding of pitches are found in early Western music, as well as occasionally in the music of other civilizations, these examples account for only a small amount of the total body of music. In the eleventh century Western music began to depart from the single line by indicating in notation the simultaneous sounding of different musical pitches.

Medieval musicians, many of whom were anonymous monks, accomplished the simultaneous sounding of pitches in a simple way. They merely took the lines of Gregorian chant they already had and added another layer of sound to the original. At first the added line ran exactly parallel to the original line at an interval of four or five notes below it. Since this did not allow for much musical freedom, over many years the added line was permitted to break out of its strictly parallel pattern and to assume a more independent character. When independent lines of melody were written for simultaneous performance, polyphony was accomplished.

Polyphony is an important concept in music. It is the combining of lines of nearly equal melodic interest; no line is more important than another. Listening to polyphony might be compared to watching a three-ring circus. Each act is equally interesting. Although it is not easy to look at all the acts at once, there are few dull moments during which little is happening.

In early polyphony notes of the same pitch, those an octave apart, and those four and five tones apart were considered to be consonant. (These intervals are the same ones Pythagoras had regarded as the most consonant.) The interval of a third, the interval upon which our system of chords is based, was regarded as a dissonance. It was, however, found in the folk music of that time, especially in England. It would be nearly 500 years before chords containing thirds would be considered consonant enough to appear as the important final chord of a piece.

MUSICAL STYLES AND PERIODS

The concept of style is very helpful in understanding music. A term such as "Renaissance," when applied to music, describes a style of music rather than a period of time. Even after a style has passed the peak of its use, composers occasionally return to it, sometimes centuries later. Entire works in old styles such as Renaissance and Baroque are still being written occasionally today, and certain elements of these styles appear in other pieces. Although a style of music is not confined to a particular time and place, it is named for the historical period in which it was predominantly associated. The designation of style periods can be made only after the actual years have passed, because such categorizing requires historical perspective. The dates of their beginning and ending can never be exact. Historic and artistic trends must always have approximate dates.

Literature, art, and music are generally given the same style period names, and the fine arts of a particular period do contain similarities of outlook and artistic goals. A word of caution: Much that appears in Gothic or modern art cannot be related directly to Gothic or modern music. Each art is influenced by technical matters peculiar to it, and each is affected by conditions that are not present in other fine arts. Until about 150 years ago, art and literature tended to be "ahead" of music in terms of reaching its eventual state of development. Several factors may have contributed to the developmental lag of music: the inadequacy of its notation, problems of instrument construction, the uncertainty of various tuning systems, and the lack of recording devices with which to preserve musical performance. Direct parallels, therefore, can seldom be drawn among the arts in the various style periods. Nor are the approximate dates for a period the same in the various arts. Throughout much of history cultural developments could not spread uniformly, largely because of limited communication and travel between countries. A highly popular movement in Italy could be virtually unknown in Germany, for example.

In spite of its drawbacks the concept of style in music can help in understanding music. With it you organize your thinking about music and recognize the way musical material is treated. Not only are concepts of styles useful, they are valid. The way in which musical sounds are handled in the various styles is the heart of art music. Also, an understanding of style helps you listen for the right things in music. Knowing that the Renaissance ideal was reverence and restraint of sound, you will not be surprised or disappointed by the lack of volume and flashing brilliance in Renaissance music. Brief descriptions of the various style periods are available for comparison and review inside the front and back covers of this book, as well as discussed at appropriate places in the text.

THE GOTHIC PERIOD AND MOTET

The period from about 1100 to 1450 has come to be known as the Gothic period. These centuries were marked by progress away from the otherworldly attitude that was characteristic of the preceding 1,000 years. The intellectual high point of the time was Scholasticism, a systemic philosophy culminating in the *Summary of Theology* by Thomas Aquinas. In his writings St. Thomas expressed and rationally developed with sophisticated logic the belief that the universe is an orderly unit governed for the purpose of making possible the fulfillment of the great Christian plan for peace and justice on earth and the salvation of mankind in a world yet to come. Scholasticism represents a balanced view of the importance of life here and now and an interest in matters of the spirit.

The Gothic age also held that government is the product of the social nature of the human race, and that when justice is the guiding principle of the ruler, government is good. It rejected the absolute power of kings, a belief that encouraged the Magna Charta in 1215. Another feature of the Gothic period was chivalry, which glorified women and idealized kindness and refined manners. Chivalry perhaps existed more as an ideal in literary works than it did in fact. There was an emphasis on the community—the guild, Church, or feudal manor; individualism was not encouraged. Many works of art and music were created by artists who did not attach their names to their works and whose identities are not known.

The Gothic period saw the founding of universities and the building of the great cathedrals. It also produced some significant literary accomplishments: the poems of the troubadours, the romantic legends of a Celtic chieftain named Arthur, and *The Divine Comedy* by Dante Alighieri (from which Delacroix centuries later drew his subject matter for *The Bark of Dante,* plate 10).

An excellent example of Gothic painting is the *Madonna and Child* by the great Italian painter of the time, Giotto (plate 2). The work is richly adorned, highly symbolic with its halos, and spiritual in its impact.

Gothic music is characterized, at least in France, by a sophisticated type of polyphony. At first the chant melody was sung or played at a slow tempo, while the added part sounded several shorter notes within the same duration. Later the chant melody and extra part were treated rhythmically according to the patterns of the rhythmic modes. Sometimes as many as four independent lines were combined in one work. When words were added to the lines, the piece became known as a *motet,* from the French *mot,* meaning "word."

The motet was a curious musical animal. First, it often combined various languages as well as sacred and secular texts. For example, one motet has two different sets of words for the top part, one in Latin, praising the Virgin Mary, and another in French, which reads: "When I see the summer season returning and all the little birds make the woods resound, then I weep and sigh for the great desire I have for fair Marion, who holds my heart imprisoned." The lower line typically utilizes a phrase of Gregorian chant. The length of the motet was determined by the length of the text. Usually it was not long. Second, the composers tended to concentrate on working out each line, relatively unconcerned about how it might sound when combined with the other lines. Some harsh dissonances were the result. Third, composers became fascinated, especially in the fourteenth century, by concealed meanings and relationships in the music. They took great delight in concealing a chant phrase in the upper lines. Or they set up a complicated scheme of rhythmic and melodic patterns, so that a rhythmic pattern might appear three times for every two times the melodic pattern was repeated. Such intellectual complexities interested the medieval musician, but they were generally lost on the listener. They can be comprehended only by looking at the music, not by hearing it. Such music was a form of intellectual puzzle. The fascination with intricate patterns and tricks (such as going through a melody backwards) is revived periodically, including in the twentieth century.

In summary, the Gothic motet featured rhythmic patterns adapted from secular music, but it was based on and developed from Gregorian chant. Some highly complex techniques of composition were employed. Various lines were added one upon another in layers.

While the Gothic motet was reaching its acme with the compositions of Guilliame de Machaut (Mah-*sho*), the pendulum was already beginning to swing away from this complex and intellectually oriented type of music. Actually, it had been largely a French development; composers in other countries evidently didn't care for the style or were not advanced enough to attempt composing in it. A blind Italian musician named Francesco Landini (Lahn-*dee*-nee) and an English composer named John Dunstable were writing music that was simpler and more listenable. Both men and their followers often used the same text for all parts. Their music enabled the words to be sung more or less simultaneously so that the text could be understood by the listener, something that was impossible with the Gothic motet. They also avoided harsh dissonances. A special contribution of Dunstable and other English composers was the use of simultaneous pitches three and six notes apart, the pattern that is still the most common in Western music. These intervals give the music a richer sound than the fourths and fifths of previous music. In fact, the works of Landini and Dunstable are a pleasure to hear today, six centuries later.

As the 1450s approached, the Gothic motet was rapidly disappearing, although Gregorian chant was continuing to influence other musical forms. Drawing to a close, however, was that long stretch of history called the Middle Ages. This period had not been "dark," as it is sometimes described. The years leading up to 1450 had laid the foundation for a new period, the Renaissance, as well as providing some great architecture and interesting music.

10

RENAISSANCE MUSIC

The word "renaissance" literally means "rebirth." Historically it referred to a revival of interest in the philosophy and arts of ancient Greece and Rome, although there was much more to it than just an admiration of a previous civilization. Music, however, had no ancient Greek roots to go back to. So the concept of rebirth in regard to music has little direct significance. In music it refers only to the style that predominated from about 1450 until 1600.

The intense interest of Renaissance artists and scholars in ancient Greek civilization led to a curious mixture of Greek and Christian belief. Michelangelo expressed this union of the pagan and Christian by decorating the ceiling of the Sistine Chapel with alternating figures of prophets and sibyls. Erasmus, the great philosopher, regarded Socrates as a pre-Christian saint, and once wrote, "St. Socrates, pray for us."

The Renaissance developed a number of intellectual outlooks that have become standard for our culture today. Among them are optimism, worldliness, hedonism (the importance of pleasure, especially physical pleasure, for its own sake), naturalism, and individualism. But most important is humanism: the glorification of the human and natural as opposed to the otherworldly or divine. Pride, considered to be a sin in the Middle Ages, was elevated to a virtue.

The results of humanism are well illustrated by the two treatments of the human body shown in this chapter. One is a piece of Gothic sculpture found on the cathedral at Chartres. Notice that this figure has a spiritual, otherworldly quality about it. The attitude of the head and eyes is serene, and the position of the body is formal. The proportions of the figure are distorted through exaggerated length, giving the body an emaciated look. The feet seem to dangle from the robes as though they are merely attached. Michelangelo's *David,* (pages 124–25), on the other hand, looks like a magnificent Greek god. (The figure of David stand over thirteen and a half feet in height.) The work suggests confidence and an admiration of the human body. David looks natural, almost casual and free. The body emerges from the withered state given it by medieval beliefs to the idealized status accorded it by Renaissance attitudes.

Sculptured figure of Christ on the Cathedral of Notre Dame at Chartres.

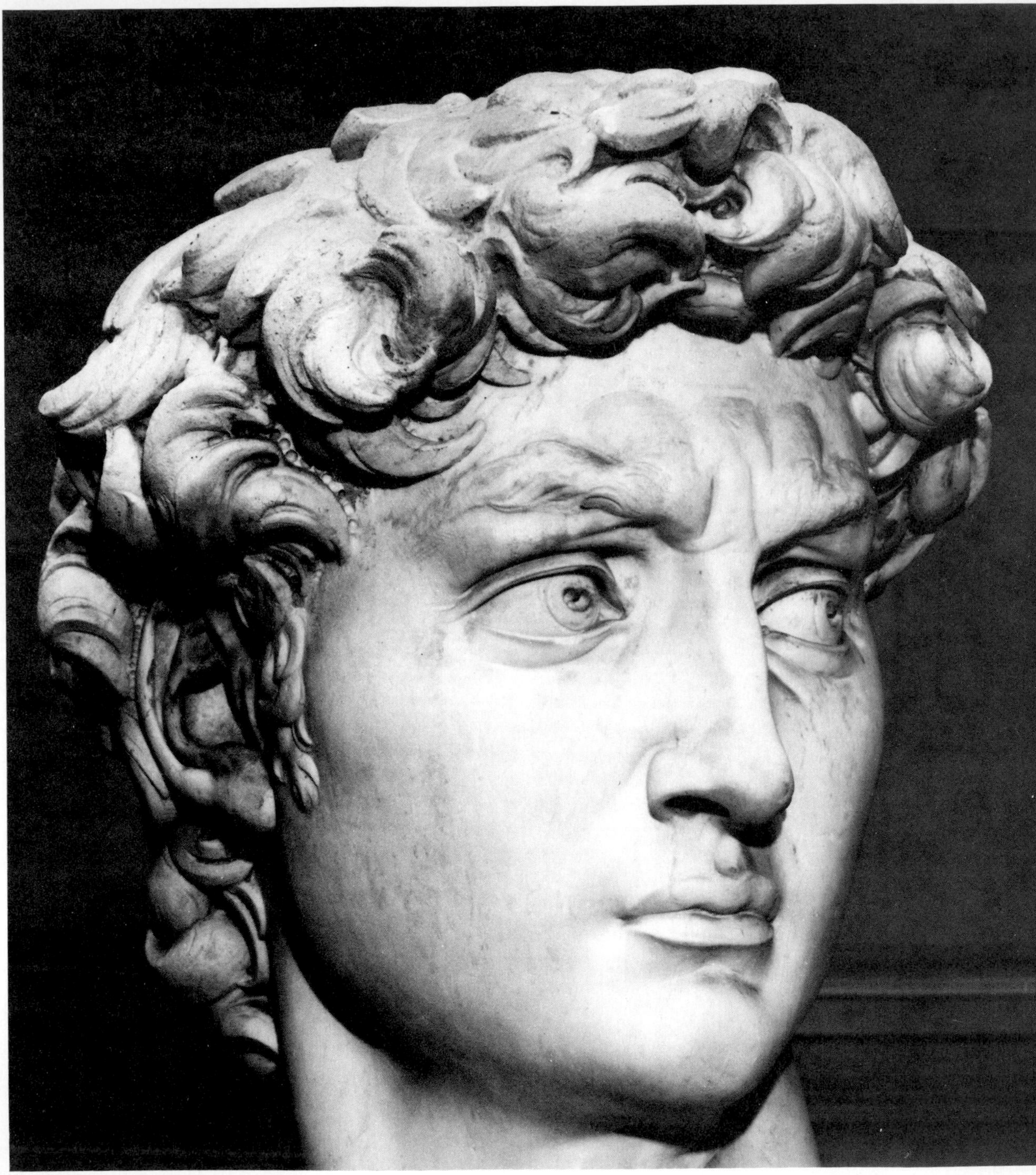

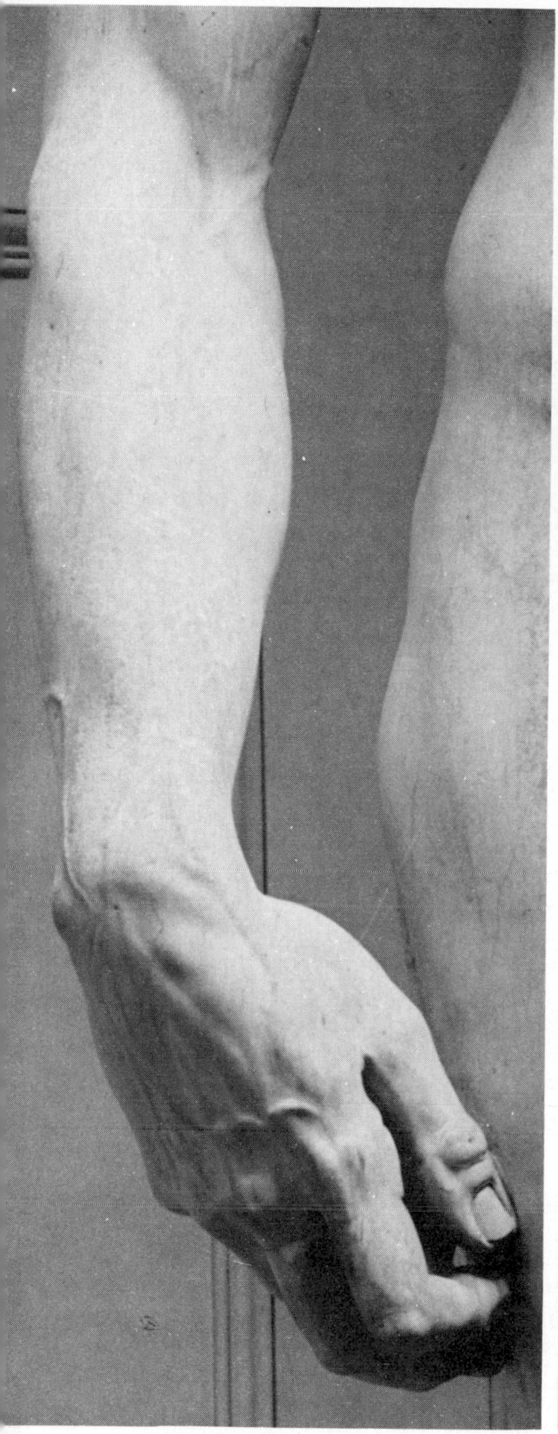
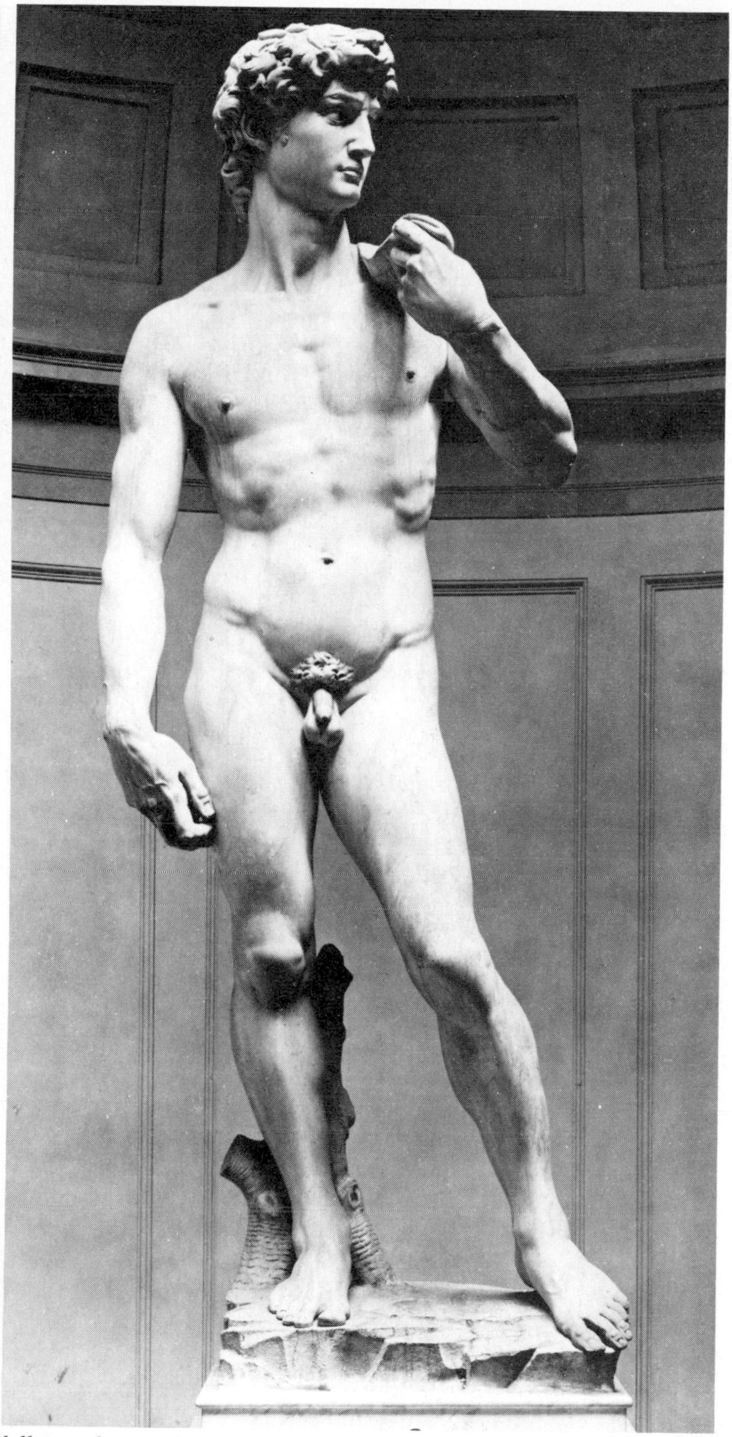

David by Michelangelo at the Galleria dell'Accademia, Florence, Italy.

LEONARDO DA VINCI

The epitome of the "Renaissance man" is Leonardo da Vinci (1452–1519). Born in the town of Vinci in northern Italy, he was the illegitimate child of a woman about whom virtually nothing is known and a man who was an accountant-notary. Bastards bore little stigma in Italy in those days, so his father, who later had four wives (not at the same time!), treated him very much as he did his other children, including having him baptized. Even as a boy, Leonardo was engrossed in botany, geology, and other physical phenomena. He was given an education (typical of the son in a good family, but not of the children of the masses) and acquired the curious habit of writing so that his words read from right to left and with the letters reversed; it is best read with a mirror.

Leonardo's father recognized his son's talents and at the age of fifteen took him from Vinci to Florence to apprentice in the studio of Andrea del Verrocchio, one of the best artists of the time. In addition to art, Leonardo's first biographer writes that he "could sing and improvise divinely" on the lute and was gifted in conversation.

When he was thirty he left Florence for Milan and the court of the Sforza family. They hired him, not for his artistic or musical ability, but rather as a designer of weapons. As it turned out, Lodovico Sforza never had any of Leonardo's weapons built, although he could certainly have afforded it. The Sforzas, Medicis, Borgias, and similar Italian families ruthlessly built small empires of wealth and power. The contradiction between their harsh politics and business practices and their support of the arts led someone to describe the Renaissance as "the pursuit of beauty—by thieves."

The Sforzas finally commissioned some paintings by Leonardo and employed him as a musician and reciter of stories and "prophesies." After eighteen years in Milan, Leonardo left when the Sforzas lost control of the city. He returned to Florence, where his reputation as an artist preceded him, so he had no trouble securing commissions, including his famous *Mona Lisa* . Six years later he returned to Milan, which was then under French control. By then his career as a painter was drawing to a close. Strange as it may seem, as one of the greatest painters of all time he produced only a little more than a dozen paintings. There are a number of reasons for this small output, but one stands out: He was busy doing so many other things that he didn't complete a number of works. For example, Pope Leo X once gave him a small commission, which ended in unpleasantness. Leonardo became interested in compounding a special varnish for the unpainted picture. The Pope grew disgusted, saying, "This man will never accomplish anything! He thinks of the end before the beginning."

As he grew older Leonardo became sullen and gloomy. At about the age of sixty-two he made the red-chalk drawing of himself seen on page 127 (the only likeness of him available today), and added at the bottom of the picture, "Leonardo da Vinci, portrait of himself as an old man." The final years of his life were spent in Amboise, France, in an honorary position to King Francis I.

In addition to painting and music Leonardo filled his notebooks with ideas and sketches. And what notebooks they are! They number 7,000 pages of mechanical ideas, anatomical and botanical studies, optics, mathematics, maps, plans for cities and irrigation canals, and painting and drawing techniques. In them he foretold flying machines and mass-production machines and a host of other inventions, made drawings of plant life so accurate that they could still be used in textbooks today, and was far in advance of his time for his anatomical studies. He was fascinated with sophisticated puzzles, especially ones like the polyhedron (see below) that might contain deep meaning. He thought proportions had fundamental importance not only for measurement and numbers, but also in weights, sounds, and almost everything else.

To him, painting was "the queen of all sciences," and art and science were inseparable. When he began his *Treatise on Painting,* he may have thought of writing down instructions for the correct representation of objects, but that led to considerations of perspective, proportion, geometry, and optics, and then further to anatomy and the mechanics of living and nonliving things, and ultimately to a search for principles underlying the operation of the universe itself. Sometimes such intellectual pursuits led him away from finishing a project, but they also earned him the reputation as one of the great geniuses of all time, the true "Renaissance man."

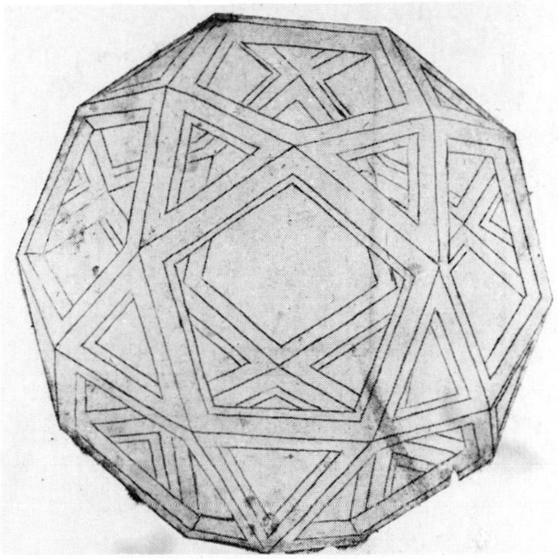

Leonardo was fascinated with the idea of flight. He was never able to solve its challenge. Today it is known that man's body weight is too great for Leonardo's ideas to have worked.

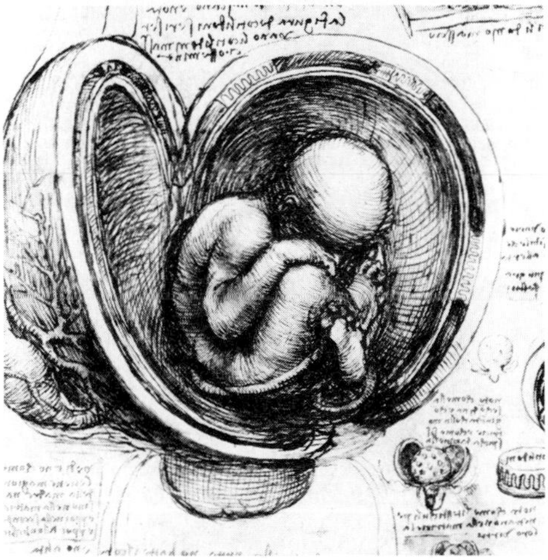

Leonardo's most famous anatomical drawing is this one of an embryo in the womb. It is faulty in a few places, but so accurate in others it can still be used in a medical text today.

With the increasing interest in the value of worldly life, there was a corresponding interest in the fine arts. A beautiful painting or piece of music began to have value for its own sake; it was no longer regarded only as a means to religious devotion. As a result of this change of outlook, the list of great Renaissance sculptors and painters is long—Botticelli, da Vinci, Michelangelo, Dürer, Raphael, Titian, Bruegel, Tintoretto. Botticelli's *The Adoration of the Magi* can be seen in plate 3.

Not only were works of art being enjoyed in a new climate of acceptance. The increasing affluence, especially in the cities of northern Italy and the Netherlands, meant that money was available with which to hire artists and musicians. The Church sought rich adornment for its buildings, one of several practices that led to the reform movement started by Martin Luther in 1517. An example of the art of this era is Dürer's *Portrait of a Clergyman,* plate 4. The effect of the Reformation on the world of music did not show its full impact until after 1600, but the seeds of change had been planted.

An event that reached into every area of human endeavor—education, religion, commerce—was Gutenberg's invention of printing from movable type. Printing made possible the wide dissemination of music, beginning with the appearance of the first printed music books in 1501.

The spirit of the times was one of optimism and discovery. The voyages of Columbus, Cabot, Balboa, and Magellan took place during the Renaissance. Copernicus was announcing his new discoveries about the universe. Rabelais, Machiavelli, Boccaccio, Montaigne, Thomas More, Francis Bacon, and Erasmus were exploring new ideas in literature and philosophy. However, no person embodied the ideal of the "Renaissance man" more abundantly than did Leonardo da Vinci, whose life and works are described on pages 126–127.

FEATURES AND TYPES OF RENAISSANCE MUSIC

The musical Renaissance started in the Netherlands, which then included Holland, northern Belgium, and part of northern France. The composers of the area had reached a level that was the envy of Europe. Composers from the Netherlands were lured away from their homeland to better-paying jobs in Spain, Bohemia, Austria, Germany, and especially the cities of northern Italy. The style and technique of the Netherlanders became internationally known and imitated. So cosmopolitan did composers become that they thought of themselves as musicians first and as citizens of a particular country second. For example, Orlando di Lasso (the name he used in Italy), alias Roland de Lassus (the name he used in Germany), wrote music in the German, French, and Italian idioms, as well as in the Netherlands style. A musician in that time had to be versatile, because his duties included not only composing but also performing, training a choir, and teaching.

The most esteemed composer of the early Renaissance was Josquin des Prez (Zhoss-can day *Pray*), who lived from about 1440 to 1521. Born in Flanders, Josquin was a choir singer in Milan, a musician in the service of the Sforza family, a member of the Papal Chapel, a choirmaster, and a musician in the service of Louis XII of France. In his compositions Josquin continued some of the techniques developed in the Gothic period. Like composers before him, he used the device of imitation, in which one line of melody appears in another part a measure or two later, somewhat like a round. But where his predecessors had obscured the imitation by having all parts singing continuously, Josquin emphasized the beginning of each imitative passage by having voices enter one after the other. By drawing attention to each successive voice in this way, he made the initial words sung by each entering part easier to hear. The music became clearer and assumed a phrase-by-phrase form.

More than any previous composer, Josquin was aware of a consistent organization of harmonies. Closely related to more sophisticated harmony was the development of a bass line. When composers started adding melodies to chant, they placed the chant around middle C (on a piano, this pitch is near the middle of the keyboard) and placed the additional melodies above it. This level of pitch and harmonic structure did not provide a convincing sense of chord movement. So about 1450 composers began to add another line *below* the chant to give the music a more solid foundation. This arrangement of voices remains to this day the standard for a choral group with men's and women's voices. At the time the sections were called "superius," "altus," "tenor," and "bassus"; today they are called soprano, alto, tenor, and bass.

It was the practice in the Gothic and Renaissance periods to select a phrase from Gregorian chant and sometimes from secular songs to form the *cantus firmus* or "foundation" melodic pattern for a vocal work. The musical setting of the Mass was then named for the Mass or song from which the phrase was taken. For example, Josquin composed a number of Kyries, but only one based on the phrase "Faysans regres" from a French secular song by an English composer named Walter Frye. In the Kyrie from the Mass *Faysans regres* Josquin combines the four-note phrase from the song with a Kyrie from a Mass. The original phrases of both are shown above Josquin's music. The two patterns are varied in rhythm and moved to different pitch levels.

The writing of the Kyrie is line against line, with each of the four parts having equal melodic interest. It is polyphonic, a term that was introduced in Chapter 3. Notice how the tenor imitates the bass phrase from the song, and how the soprano imitates the alto phrase from the Mass. The beauty of the

Kyrie from the Mass *Faysans regres,* Josquin des Prez

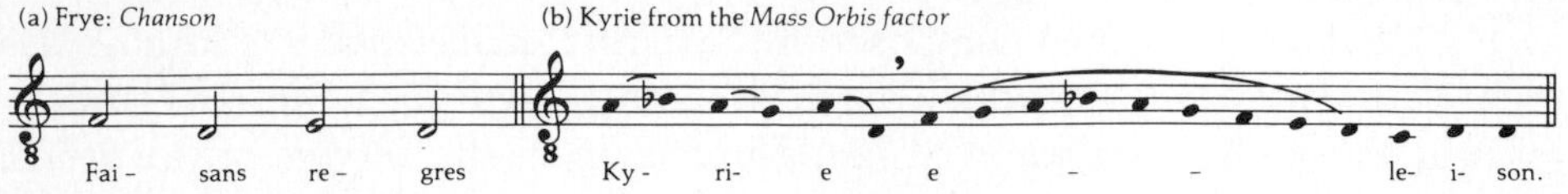

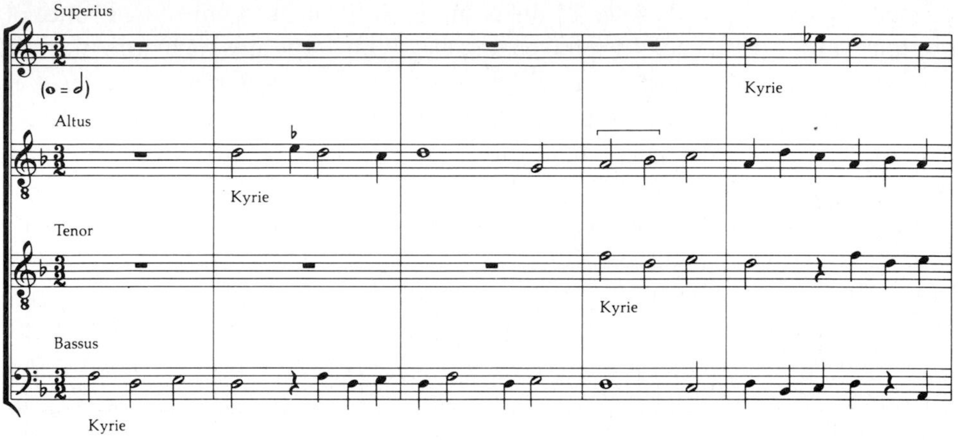

music lies in the skill with which Josquin was able to fit one line in contrast to the others, and not just in his cleverness in using fragments of melodies.

The most esteemed composer of the sixteenth century was Giovanni Pierluigi da Palestrina (c. 1525–1594). (Palestrina was the name of the small town in which he was born.) Many of the practices of Josquin des Prez reached their highest development in Palestrina's music. Unlike Josquin, who changed jobs frequently, Palestrina largely confined his career to Rome, where he held several positions, the most notable being that of choirmaster at St. Peter's. Undoubtedly Palestrina was familiar with the music of Josquin and other Netherlands composers. He utilized many of their devices such as imitation.

Historical circumstances encouraged Palestrina to be a conservative reformer instead of an innovator. One such event was the Council of Trent, held intermittently between 1545 and 1563. The Church felt threatened by the Reformation, so the Council met to respond to this situation and to acknowledge the need for some reform within the Church. One phase of the Church's life that came under attack was its music, which over the centuries had departed far from the Gregorian ideal. Complaints were registered about the use of secular tunes in music for the Mass, the complicated polyphony that made the words impossible to understand, the use of noisy instruments, and the carelessness and irreverent attitude of the singers. The Council directed that the chants be purged of "barbarism, obscurities, contrarieties, and superfluities" so that "the House of God might rightly be called a house of prayer."

In this old woodcut, Palestrina is handing Pope Marcellus his new Mass. Notice the style of notation on the pages of music.

Palestrina, therefore, composed for a Church that wanted to return to the purity of its earlier music. To his credit he achieved this goal *without* discarding the highly developed style of his predecessors.

The Renaissance Motet

The Gothic motet is a composition built on a line of Gregorian chant to which were added other melodies containing other words, often in more than one language. The motet of the Renaissance is quite different. It is a unified piece with all voices singing the same text. The Gothic motet is always based on Gregorian chant, but it contains secular words, too. The Renaissance motet, on the other hand, sometimes borrows from chant, but it conveys a spirit of reverence. The Renaissance motet is serious, restrained, and designed for the worship service.

Palestrina's *Sicut cervus* (page 134) is a good example of the Renaissance motet, and the work reveals many characteristics of his writing style (Record 1, Side 2). What are its significant features?

1. The text is in ecclesiastical Latin. It is a portion of Psalm 42, which in the *Revised Standard Version* reads:

> As a hart* longs for flowing streams,
> So longs my soul for Thee, O God.
> My soul thirsts for God, for the Living God.
> When shall I come and behold the face of God?
> My tears have been my food day and night,
> While men say to me continually, "Where is your God?"

2. The music is polyphonic. All of the lines are given equal attention and each has distinct melodic character.

3. Each voice usually enters in imitation of another. Look closely at the notes for the words *"Sicut cervus desiderat ad fontes."* First the tenor starts, followed by the alto two measures later, the soprano halfway through measure 4, and finally the bass in measure 6. All voices sing the pattern of the first four notes. The fifth note in the alto line is changed slightly to make it fit with other notes in the music, but in general the alto maintains the same melody. As the music progresses, the voices tend to move on to melodies of their own. At each addition of a new phrase of the text (*"ita desiderat," "anima mea,"* and so on), the process of imitation is repeated. Such imitative entrances enable the text to be understood. Palestrina and other composers of the time realized that if the listener knows the words, not every phrase of text needs to be heard to its conclusion.

---

*"Hart" means the male of the red deer, a stag.

4. The music does not have a strong feeling of harmonic movement. The chords lack the harmonic direction found in later styles. This lack is due partly to the polyphonic nature of the music, with its emphasis on the horizontal line.

5. The music does not have a strong feeling of meter or beat. *Sicut cervus* certainly does not encourage foot tapping. Even though present-day notation for *Sicut cervus* has measure or bar lines, the original probably did not. The bar lines have been added by editors for the convenience of the singers so that they can keep their place more easily. Most of the chord changes in Palestrina's music occur at moments of subtle stress, giving the music a gentle rhythmic flow.

6. Today the motet is usually sung without accompaniment, but during the Renaissance the voice parts were doubled by a few instruments. The performance ideal was to sing without accompaniment—a style called *a cappella* (meaning literally "for the chapel").

7. A small choir is most appropriate for the motet. Probably not more than two singers were originally assigned to each part. Boys, or men singing in falsetto voice, sang the high voice parts, since women were not allowed to participate in the Mass.

8. The melodies are very singable. The range of notes in any one part generally does not exceed an octave. Furthermore, the singers do not have to move far from one pitch to the next.

9. The form of this motet is derived from the structure of the psalm. Each verse is treated to its own polyphonic setting, and then the motet moves on to the next verse and different music.

10. The music has a restrained, unemotional quality. Bombast and emotionalism were considered insincere and not in keeping with the attitude of respect and awe that should prevail in the worship of God. Even though the text speaks of "longing for flowing streams," the music does not suggest sentimental display or pleading. When Palestrina does emphasize particular words, he does it so subtly that contemporary listeners may not notice it.

11. The melodic lines are fitted together with great craftsmanship. That is why Palestrina stands out among the composers of his era.

Part of the problem in listening to polyphony is the nature of the music. In homophonic music a listener can concentrate on the melody and merely sense the effect of the accompaniment. In polyphonic music, however, attention can be centered on any line with equal reward. For this reason repeated hearings of *Sicut cervus* are suggested, each time concentrating on a different voice part.

SICUT CERVUS

The Madrigal

The Renaissance period also had a distinctly worldly side. Many kinds of secular music were composed, several of them national in character. The main type of secular music was the *madrigal.** It has sometimes been described as a secular version of the motet, but there are significant differences between the two forms. The madrigal is in a vernacular language rather than ecclesiastical Latin. Its text often deals with sentimental and sometimes erotic love. Some madrigal texts have little literary merit, but many, especially the poems of Petrarch, are of exceptional quality.

Instead of being sung in church, madrigals were sung at courtly social gatherings and at meetings of learned and artistic societies. Madrigals were very popular, and an enormous number were composed. In England madrigal singing—with its requirement of music reading—was expected of an educated person. Since madrigals were written for situations not restrained by religious traditions, they contain greater freedom of expression than the motet, and they offered the composer more opportunity for experimentation. For instance, if the word "cuckoo" appears in a madrigal, it is not uncommon for a composer to write an imitation of the actual sound of the cuckoo.

Instruments often accompanied the singing of secular music. The madrigal, therefore, was frequently heard in conjunction with a lute or harpsichord. The instrumentalist simplified the written parts, reducing the complicated polyphony to chords. The lute, by the way, was the most popular instrument of the Renaissance. It has a pear-shaped body, frets, and a varying number of strings. Its pegbox is slanted back sharply away from the rest of the instrument. The lute is played by plucking, and rather intricate music can be executed on it.

The madrigal was largely an Italian development associated with composers such as Cipriano de Rore and Luca Marenzio. By the mid-1500s, madrigals had spread to other countries. Interest in the madrigal reached England late in the sixteenth century. When the first madrigals with English translations were printed in 1588, the response was a brief but brilliant period of original English secular vocal music. The English madrigal is especially enjoyable for three reasons: (1) Its text is in English and so no translation is necessary for American audiences. (2) Its composers had a knack for making the lines of music tuneful and singable. (3) The English had the delightful trait of not taking themselves seriously. No matter how sad the song may be, the listener senses a tongue-in-cheek quality.

---

*There were also a few religious madrigals called *madrigali spirituali,* which were nonliturgical pieces on religious topics, often songs to the Virgin Mary.

One well-known English madrigal is "April Is in My Mistress' Face" by Thomas Morley (1557–1602) (Record 1, Side 2). About half of the music appears here. The text is a wistful comment on life. In this work, "Mistress" does not mean "paramour," as it does today; "fiancée" is closer to the original intent. The complete text is:

> April is in my Mistress' face,
>   And July in her eyes hath place,
> Within her bosom is September,
>   But in her heart, a cold December.

The madrigal is similar to the motet in several respects. There are imitative entrances at the beginning of word phrases, and the texture is basically polyphonic. The vocal lines are smooth and singable. The harmony is not firmly established in one particular key. The use of instruments was optional during the Renaissance, but today both madrigal and motet are sung without accompaniment. The form is a phrase-by-phrase setting of the text.

There are significant differences between the two forms, however. For example, "April Is in My Mistress' Face" has a more metrical rhythm, which causes the moments of rhythmic stress to fall in a more regular pattern. The tempo is usually faster. There is a tendency to set the women's parts in contrast to the men's, which may or may not be an attempt to relate to the text. The language is English, not Latin. And in overall spirit Morley's madrigal is vastly different from Palestrina's motet.

APRIL IS IN MY MISTRESS' FACE

5
mf
in my Mis - tress' face, my Mis tress' face, A - pril is
mf
A - pril is in my Mis - tress' face, A - pril is
mf
in my Mis tress' face, A - pril is in my Mis-tress'
mf
in my Mis-tress' face, A - pril is in my Mis-tress'
10
in my Mis-tress' face, And Ju-ly in her eyes hath place,
in my Mis-tress' face, And Ju-ly in her eyes hath place,
cresc.
face, my Mis-tress' face, And
cresc.
face, my Mis-tress' face, And Ju-ly in her
15
cresc.
f
And Ju-ly in her eyes, in her eyes hath place.
cresc.
f
And Ju - ly in her eyes, her eyes hath place.
f
Ju-ly in her eyes hath place, in her eyes hath place.
f
eyes hath place, in her eyes hath place.

Morley's charming madrigal is only one of his many compositions. And Morley is only one of the many good English composers of his time, who in turn represent only a small proportion of the composers at work during the Renaissance. Partly to do justice to other composers, but more important, to provide additional names for music well worth hearing, the following annotated list is included.

COMPOSERS OF THE RENAISSANCE

English Composers		
William Byrd	(1543–1623)	probably the best English composer of the Renaissance; madrigals, church music, and keyboard music
William Cornyshe	(c. 1465–1523)	songs
John Dowland	(1562–1626)	lute songs and music, part songs
Robert Fayrfax	(1464–1521)	church music
Thomas Tallis	(c. 1505–1585)	church music
John Taverner	(c. 1495–1545)	church music
Thomas Weelkes	(c. 1575–1623)	madrigals
John Wilbye	(1574–1638)	madrigals
Netherlands Composers		
Jacob Arcadelt	(c. 1505–c. 1567)	*chansons* (rhythmic, simple, four-part songs), madrigals; influential teacher in Rome
Jacobus Clemens	(c. 1510–c. 1556)	church music
Heinrich Isaac	(c. 1450–1517)	church and secular music; international sources for texts
Orlando di Lasso	(1532–1594)	*lieder;* also wrote in French and Italian styles

Jacob Obrecht	(c. 1452–1505)	church music; used many devices of composition—canon, etc.; *chansons* also
Johannes Ockeghem	(c. 1430–1495)	church music; used many devices of composition—canon, etc.; *chansons* also
Jan Sweelinck	(1562–1621)	*chansons* in old style; known for keyboard music
Adrian Willaert	(c. 1480–1562)	influential composer and teacher at St. Mark's in Venice

French Composers

Clément Jannequin	(c. 1475–c. 1560)	chansons; fond of imitative sounds in music
Claude Le Jeune	(1528–1600)	motets, *chansons*
Claudin de Sermisy	(c. 1490–1562)	*chansons*

German Composer

Hans Leo Hassler	(1564–1612)	*lieder* (plural form of *lied,* a German version of the madrigal), church music

Italian Composers

Costanzo Festa	(c. 1490–1545)	early madrigals
Carlo Gesualdo	(c. 1560–1613)	madrigals with experimental harmonies
Luca Marenzio	(1553–1599)	madrigals
Philippe de Monte	(1521–1603)	madrigals
Claudio Monteverdi	(1567–1643)	madrigals written when a young man; important Baroque composer later

Giovanni Mario Nanino	(c. 1545–1607)	Palestrina's successor at Papal Chapel
Cipriano de Rore	(1516–1565)	madrigals

Spanish Composers

Antonio de Cabezón	(1510–1566)	keyboard music
Francisco Guerrero	(1527–1599)	church music
Cristóbal de Morales	(c. 1500–1553)	church music
Tomás Luis de Victoria	(c. 1549–1611)	church music in style of Palestrina

Renaissance Music in Perspective

The preceding list of composers is proof of the large amount of quality music written before 1600. If the music was plentiful and of a high caliber, why is it still largely unknown to the general public?

Renaissance music is not intended for the concert stage; its charm and subtle nuances are lost in an auditorium—the customary site for musical performances today. It is not big or colorful like much of the music to which we are accustomed. Furthermore, specialized skills are required to perform it well. A chorus may sing cantatas and other choral music beautifully and yet be unable to execute in proper style the polyphonic music of the Renaissance. Also, many types of music familiar today were unheard of before 1600; no concertos, symphonies, operas, or oratorios were composed before that time. Except for lute and a few keyboard works, little instrumental music was written down and preserved. Intervening centuries, then, have seen the development of new forms and media. As our musical heritage has expanded, our ability to pay attention to any one style has diminished.

These explanations for the lack of widespread popularity do not by any means indicate that Renaissance music is inferior. On the contrary, in the madrigal, motet, and other vocal ensemble music, Renaissance composers achieved a quality that has never been surpassed. In this regard Renaissance motets and madrigals are like Greek sculpture: Different pieces in different styles have been created, but the newer efforts have not diminished their predecessors.

11

BAROQUE VOCAL MUSIC: RECITATIVE AND ARIA

Even before 1600, the approximate beginning of the Baroque period, a new style and spirit had been emerging. It could be seen to some extent in Michelangelo's twisted statue *The Bound Slave* (page 142), in contrast to the objective quality of his *David* (pages 124–25). It could also be heard in Giovanni Gabrieli's massive works for brass instruments and two choruses. The Renaissance ideals of restraint and balance began to lose their appeal. The initial reaction to the new style is indicated by the term *baroque,* which was probably derived from a Portuguese word that meant "irregularly shaped pearl." The Renaissance was being replaced, not necessarily by better artistic works, but by creations in a different style. The result was a vast enrichment of the art of music.

Sometimes in everyday usage "baroque" means "extravagant," "grotesque," and "in bad taste," perhaps a carryover from its original meaning. In discussions of music, however, "baroque" refers only to the style of artistic expression prevalent from approximately 1600 to 1750, and that style was by no means grotesque or in bad taste.

The years from 1600 to 1750 saw such turbulence and change that it is impossible to characterize the period fully in a few lines. The following comments, however, provide at least some indication of the features of the Baroque.

CHARACTERISTICS OF THE BAROQUE STYLE

One of the most striking characteristics of the Baroque was its fondness for the large, the grandiose. In music this fact is exemplified by the prominent role of the pipe organ. In architecture this grandeur is illustrated in Lorenzo Bernini's monumental colonnades enclosing the vast piazza in front of St. Peter's Basilica in Rome. The huge columns reach out before St. Peter's like giant pincers seeking to draw everyone into the building. There are four rows of columns running parallel to one another. When standing in the center of the piazza,

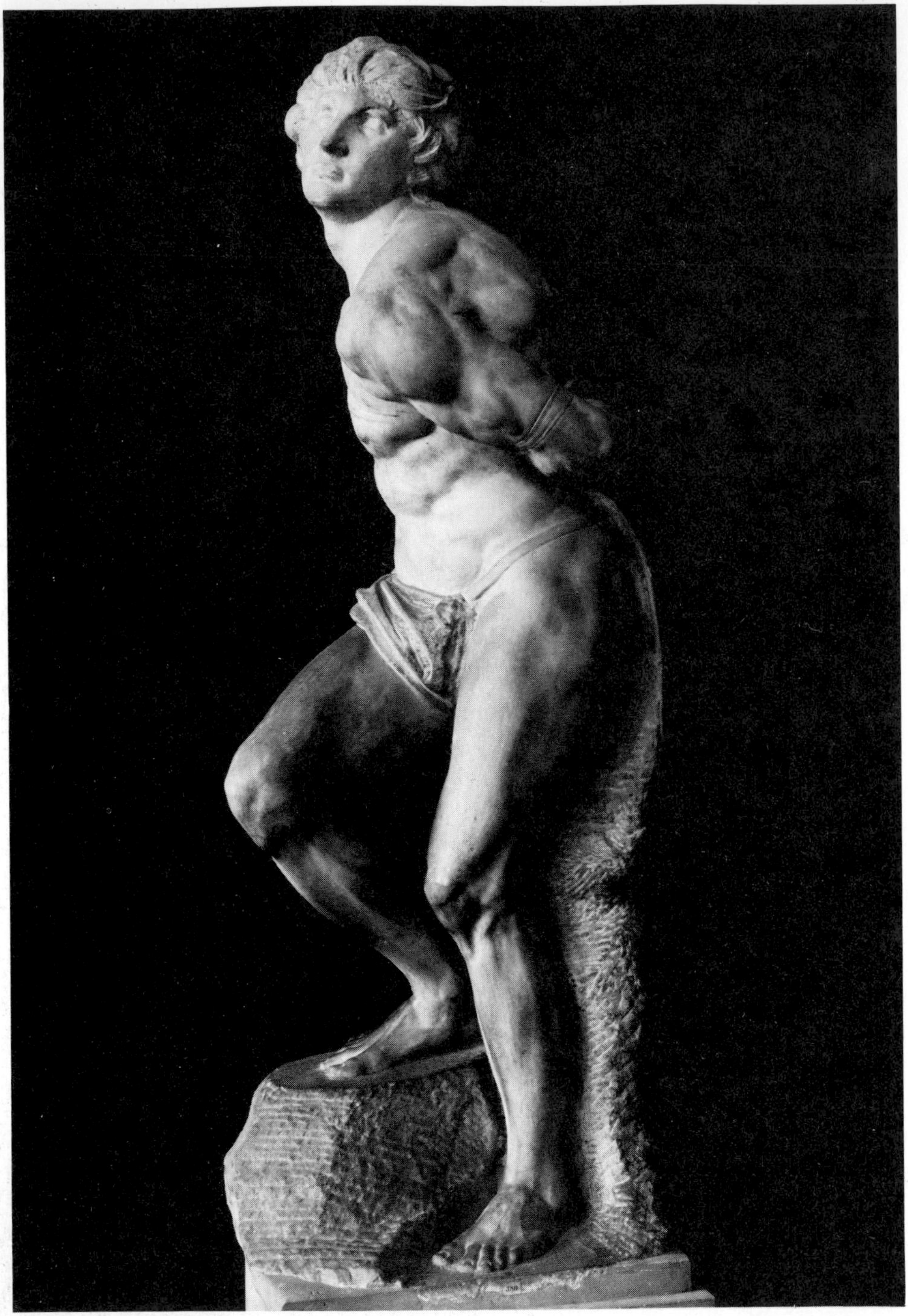

The Bound Slave *by Michelangelo.*

however, the viewer can see only a single row of columns since the other three rows are perfectly blocked from view. Measured across, the piazza itself exceeds the length of two football fields, and the colonnades are made up of 284 different columns. Statues of 140 saints sit on top of the columns. Baroque painters, architects, and composers seemed at times to want to overwhelm the viewer or listener.

A second notable feature of the Baroque period was its interest in the dramatic. Three major dramatic forms were developed in music: opera, oratorio, and cantata. Drama can also be seen in the twisted lines and struggling subjects in art works. Such treatment can be seen in Rembrandt's *The Descent from the Cross* (plate 5). Both size and twisting motion are evident in the ceiling of St. Ignatius in Rome (plate 6).

A third significant trait of the Baroque was its intensity of religious feeling, which tended to take two forms: Protestant and Catholic. The Protestant churches established themselves generally in northern Europe and on the British Isles. Protestant worship was devout, plain, and very serious. John

View of the piazza in front of St. Peter's in Rome from the roof of the Basilica. In the picture the huge colonnades designed by Lorenzo Bernini can be seen. The statues of Christ and the Apostles in the foreground are 19 feet high.

Milton's *Paradise Lost* and John Bunyan's Pilgrim's Progress were two monumental writings that expressed the Protestant attitude.

The Catholic faith was generally found in southern Europe. The Catholic Counter-Reformation developed in response to the Protestant Reformation, and a series of tragic religious wars between Protestants and Catholics followed. A happier result, however, was the encouragement of some outstanding religious art. An example is El Greco's *The Holy Family* (plate 7), which was painted in 1610.

Although it was marked by religious fervor, the Baroque era was also a time of significant advances in science. Among the famous scientists of the period were Sir Isaac Newton, who developed the theory of gravity; Kepler and Galileo, who developed Copernicus' theories about the movement of planets; William Gilbert, who introduced the word "electricity" into the language; Robert Boyle, who helped make chemistry a pure science; Robert Hooke, who first described the cellular structure of plants; Sir William Harvey, who described the circulation of the blood; Gottfried Wilhelm von Leibniz, who with Newton developed infinitesimal calculus; and René Descartes, who founded analytical geometry.

The Baroque saw the rise of a sizable merchant class, which was breaking away from the traditional society based on inherited land, title, and wealth. One result of this change was the inclusion of everyday scenes in paintings, novels, and comic operas.

Governmentally the Baroque was a mixture of petty principalities and absolute monarchies that were continually quarreling with one another. The Church still patronized the arts, but its role was less important than it had been in the Renaissance. The merchants and financiers ran the cities of northern Europe, while the Hapsburg and Bourbon families ruled in Austria and France.

In short, the Baroque era was a time of contrasts. Religious fervor existed side by side with scientific advances, drama, and grandeur. This quality of dualism, at times bordering on cultural schizophrenia, is also evident in Baroque music.

BAROQUE MUSIC

A period such as the Baroque, which saw burgeoning activity in many fields, could hardly pass without significant changes occurring in music, too. And music did change—greatly. It would be an oversimplification to say that Baroque music was unified in style. Some scholars have divided the Baroque into three periods: early, middle, and mature. Music in the early years tended to be experimental, while the middle and mature periods represent the style usually associated with the term "Baroque." The mature Baroque culminated in the music of Bach and Handel. It is largely through their compositions that Baroque music will be presented here.

Recitative. The practice of singing lines of music in a singsong, reciting style definitely did not begin in the Baroque era. Over 2,000 years earlier in ancient Greece Homer told his epic poems in this style, as had countless bards before and after him. The reciting style of vocal music, which is called *recitative (reh*-si-ta-*teev),* was refined and used in art music during the Baroque. The term "recitative" also refers to sections of oratorios and operas that are sung in recitative style.

The following musical example contains the entire recitative "The voice of him that crieth in the wilderness" from Handel's *Messiah.* It contains many of the characteristics of a recitative.

Expression of Text. As you may remember, one of the features of the Baroque period was an interest in drama. One of the results of this interest was a desire to make the vocal music expressive, to have it project the feeling of the text. Renaissance composers wrote so that several lines would fit well with one another. Since the words did not often occur at the same time among the various lines of music, they could not be easily understood and so their dramatic impact was limited.

A group of amateur musicians living in Florence around 1600 wanted to revive the ancient Greek practice of having musical declamations in dramas. They reasoned that a single line of melody would be freer to express the thought of the words. In early attempts at recitative the singers went so far as to grimace, act, and imitate the inflections of crying and gasping. Whatever the merits of such attempts at expression, they did open up for composers a new dimension in vocal music. The single melody could have a wider range, more chromatic movement (melodic movement by half steps), and freer rhythm than a line in a motet. For example, when Handel sets the word "crieth," he makes it the high point of the first phrase after building up to it with three pitch leaps. This makes it easier for the singer to emphasize "crieth." Notice that words such as "desert" and "highway" are treated in a more matter-of-fact way.

Homophony. Music that has a single melodic line with accompanying chords is called *homophony.* The concept of homophony can clearly be seen in Handel's recitative. All of the interest is in the melody sung by the tenor. The orchestra merely sounds some short chords.

Homophony existed long before the Baroque, but composers had given it little attention in serious musical works, so it had not been developed very much. By 1600 the polyphonic style of Palestrina had reached its optimum development. Composers began to feel that something new was needed. The process of change is evident in the books of madrigals by the outstanding, innovative composer Claudio Monteverdi (1567–1643). Between 1587 and 1603 Monteverdi published four books of madrigals in Renaissance style. In 1605, however, he published a book of homophonic pieces, some of which have accompaniments. By the eighth book (1638), Monteverdi's music calls for small vocal and string ensembles.

Melodic Quality. If recitative singing was to be closely related to dramatic speaking, the quality of its melodic line did not need to be tuneful in the usual sense of the word. The emphasis was to be on the dramatic rendition of the words rather than the quality of the melody. The reciting style presents a text as economically as possible. Often each note is coupled with just one syllable of a word. For this reason, recitatives are often short: "The voice of him that crieth in the wilderness" is only thirty seconds long.

Flexible Rhythm. The effort to achieve expression had another consequence: The idea of regular rhythm was discarded. Early Baroque composers seemed to reason that feelings should not be regulated by time. Their idea was to follow the inflections of the speaking voice. The singer was given the liberty of speeding up and slowing down, holding certain notes, and generally singing the words as he or she felt them, regardless of regular rhythm indicated by the music. The few chords that the accompanying orchestra or instrument did play were sounded at whatever moment was called for by the singer's performance. The Renaissance idea of an even flow of music was replaced in recitative by the new freedom of rhythmic interpretation allowed the performer.

Tonal Center. Handel's recitative also demonstrates the Baroque concept of harmony. Key and tonality were mentioned briefly in Chapter 3. A tonal center was one of the Baroque's significant contributions to music. Prior to that period, music was characterized by modal patterns that were neither major nor minor, and they were not harmonized in a systematic way. Any harmony was felt to be adequate as long as the sonority at any given moment was satisfying. There was little sense of *harmonic progression*—a logical succession of what chords would be used. Tonality in Baroque music, on the other hand, includes a system of chord relationships based on the attraction or "magnetic pull" of a tonal center. The chord progressions in "The voice of him that crieth in the wilderness" convincingly end with two chords. These chords, called a *cadence,* give a feeling of finality or conclusion, which is what Handel wanted. Knowing the tendencies of chords, composers can almost "punctuate" their music by inserting harmonic commas and periods to suggest varying degrees of conclusion.

Modulation. Handel's recitative demonstrates another musical fact: The tonal center can be changed. This process of changing from one key or tonal center to another is called *modulation.* It imparts variety and freshness to the music. Today listeners are so accustomed to hearing pieces modulate that they do not realize how monotonous music would sound without it. Music that does not modulate is like a room with beige carpeting, beige draperies, beige walls and ceiling, and beige furniture; there is no contrast, only uniformity and dullness. Even a simple, short song like "Deck the Halls" (page 48) suggests a new key briefly in the last two measures of the third line. It could be rewritten so that it would stay in the same key, but it would be less interesting. In the beginning of "The voice of him that crieth in the wilderness" the music centers around E, but it ends in A major.

Types of Recitative. Variety within the recitative style can be achieved in several ways. Later in *Messiah* the soprano, accompanied by simple chords, sings the recitative "There were shepherds abiding in the field, keeping watch over their flocks by night." This recitative is followed by another recitative, "And lo! the angel of the Lord came upon them, and the glory of the Lord shone round about them, and they were sore afraid." These lines are sung to a bright-sounding orchestral accompaniment. The pattern played by the violins is still chordal, but the notes are sounded in succession rather than simultaneously. The next recitative, which begins "And the angel said unto them, Fear not," again is accompanied by a minimum of chords, and gives an impression of steadfastness and calm. The fourth recitative in the series, which begins "And suddenly," projects the idea of excitement. The strings are playing a lively melodic pattern that is made up of notes found in the chords. Such expressive renditions of texts were not a part of the Renaissance outlook on music and would have been difficult to achieve in the polyphonic style.

Aria. A second type of homophonic vocal music developed in the Baroque period was the *aria* (*ar*-eeah). "Every valley shall be exalted" from *Messiah* is typical of this type of music. A Listening Guide for this aria appears on page 151. Arias differ radically from the recitatives just presented. They even look different in notation:

ex-alt
ed, shall be ex - alt ed,
shall be ex-alt

First, the aria is much longer than the recitative. (Less than half of it is included here.) In fact, "Every valley" requires about four minutes to perform, while the recitative that precedes it takes only about thirty seconds.

Second, the part for the orchestra or accompanying instrument is no longer confined to occasional chords. In an aria the accompaniment is likely to play portions of the music without the voice, and these phrases are musically interesting in themselves. The accompaniment may reiterate a figure that the soloist has sung or play its own melody.

A third difference is that in the aria the soloist often has to sing rapidly moving notes, or perform long phrases on a single word or syllable. The long runs of sixteenth notes (), such as appear on the word "exalted," illustrate one of the practices of Baroque music: *virtuoso singing.*

The word "virtuoso" refers to someone who has outstanding skill in performing. Early in the Baroque period much attention was given solo singers. Vocalists began to compete with one another for the favor of the audience by adding flashy runs to the music. The custom snowballed until the composer's music became merely a skeletal frame that each singer dressed up as he or she wished. Astonishing accomplishments in singing resulted, often to the neglect of musical quality. The situation had been corrected somewhat by Handel's time, but elements of the virtuoso style still existed. Audiences expected to hear some vocal display.

In "Every valley" tne runs do more than show off the singer's skill. Handel cleverly integrates them into the overall musical fabric so that they enhance the effect of the music. For example, it is easy to imagine that the singer's runs are an instrumental part adding a countermelody or variations on the melody. Handel also uses the virtuoso runs to bring out the idea of the words. In this aria the word "exalted" is treated to the long runs. "Exalted," meaning "raised or lifted up" in a spiritual sense, is the word that most appropriately expresses the main thought of the text. The low places will be raised up spiritually, says the poet in Isaiah 40:4. Not only does "exalted" have a crucial meaning within the text; it has an especially good vowel on which to sustain the singing: the "awe" or dark, broad "a."

The virtuoso passages in Baroque singing are sometimes baffling and disturbing to nonmusicians today, because it is hard to understand why a part of a word is stretched out over forty or more notes. "Exalted" can be sung with just three notes, of course, and these can even occur on a single pitch level, but the music wouldn't be as interesting. It is impressive to hear a skilled singer execute long runs, and it is also rewarding to hear the line fit into the music and to sense the emphasis that is given certain words. In everyday practical terms it is silly to use forty notes to sing one syllable, but musically it can be quite effective.

A fourth difference between an aria and a recitative is the relationship between length of text and length of music. The recitative "The voice of him" and the aria "Every valley" have texts of almost the same length. The aria takes about eight times as long to perform, however, because its text is spread

LISTENING GUIDE

HANDEL: *MESSIAH*

Tenor Aria: "Every Valley Shall Be Exalted" (Record 2, Side 2)

Form: A B A B

0:00 Orchestral ritornello (refrain) playing main melodic ideas from both main portions of aria.

0:23 Solo tenor sings "Every valley shall be exalted" *(A)*; short responses by orchestra:

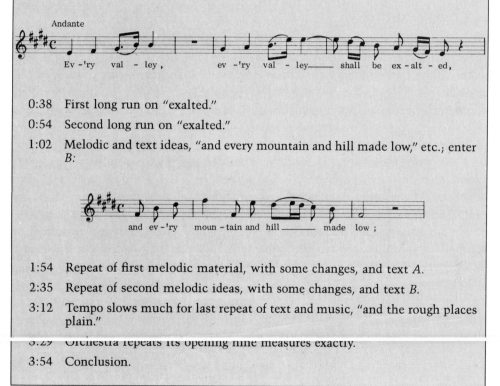

0:38 First long run on "exalted."

0:54 Second long run on "exalted."

1:02 Melodic and text ideas, "and every mountain and hill made low," etc.; enter *B:*

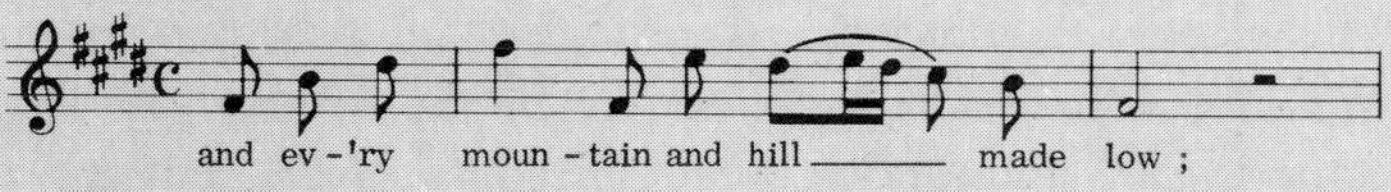

1:54 Repeat of first melodic material, with some changes, and text *A.*

2:35 Repeat of second melodic ideas, with some changes, and text *B.*

3:12 Tempo slows much for last repeat of text and music, "and the rough places plain."

3:29 Orchestra repeats its opening nine measures exactly.

3:54 Conclusion.

out by repeated words, by frequent runs, and by passages for the accompaniment alone.

A fifth difference between aria and recitative lies in the text. The recitative tends to keep the story going by describing an event. An aria often dwells on a single idea; sometimes it is a sung soliloquy.

A sixth difference between recitative and aria is the presence of form in the aria. Sections of an aria are usually repeated. The most frequent aria form is *A B A*. This design is often referred to as *da capo,* meaning that the second hearing of the *A* section is really a return to the beginning or the head of the piece. (The term *da capo* in Italian literally means "to the head.") "Every valley" has a form of *A B A B; A* is the melody for the words "every valley," and *B* is "the crooked straight." Although the printed musical example is incomplete, the form is apparent when the complete aria is heard.

Seventh, the aria and recitative have a different type of rhythm. The recitative allows for much rhythmic freedom, but the aria and other types of Baroque music follow strict metrical patterns and a steady beat. Except for unmetered recitatives and a few other free passages, Baroque music has strict rhythm, a characteristic that remained intact until the twentieth century. Changes of tempo were permitted only at the ends of sections in a long work, although holds were sometimes inserted, such as are present near the end of "Every valley." Baroque music has such a structured rhythm that it can be and usually was performed in the seventeenth and eighteenth centuries without a conductor. The custom was for the keyboard player to give the starting signal and set the tempo. Curiously, though recitatives were performed without a steady beat, composers wrote them with meter signatures, just as if they were to be performed strictly.

Eighth, the aria is intended to stand on its musical merit to a greater extent than is the recitative, which so often serves as a bridge between other numbers. Therefore, the composer usually gives an aria more memorable melodic qualities.

Both recitatives and arias are usually portions of oratorios, cantatas, or operas. The cantata and oratorio are presented in the next chapter and opera in Chapter 17.

12

BAROQUE VOCAL MUSIC: ORATORIO AND CANTATA

It's only logical that an age fond of drama would develop one or more dramatic forms of music. And so it was with the Baroque era. This chapter presents two of those forms, the oratorio and the cantata. Because of its role in the cantata and use in other music of the time, the chorale is also described. Since it is more interesting and effective to learn about aspects of music through the study of specific musical works, the oratorio is presented through Handel's *Messiah.* J. S. Bach's Cantata No. 140 serves as the medium for the study of that form.

GEORGE FRIDERIC HANDEL

George Frideric Handel (1685–1759) was a German by birth, the son of a well-to-do barber-surgeon in the city of Halle in Saxony. His father did not think music a suitable career and only grudgingly allowed his son to take music lessons. The boy showed proficiency in composition and theory, organ and harpsichord, and he also studied the oboe and violin. His father's early death permitted George to pursue his interest in music. After one year of college he went to Hamburg, where he took a position playing second violin in the orchestra, and where he became absorbed in the operatic style. By the age of twenty he had written his first opera.

Since Italy was the musical center during the Baroque period, it was the logical place for Handel to go. For three years he studied with the leading Italian composers and cultivated his friendship with patrons of music. He was well on the road to fame as a composer by the time he left Italy at the age of twenty-five.

In 1710 he returned to Germany to be musical director of the Electoral Court at Hanover. In his two years at Hanover he managed to take two leaves

George Frideric Handel, in a portrait by Philip Mercier.

of absence to go to London, where his musical style and his operas (despite their Italian language) were very successful. Although his second visit was made on the condition that he return to Hanover "within a reasonable time," he was still in London two years later when his master, the Elector of Hanover, was proclaimed King George I of England. Just how Handel took care of the embarrassing situation is not known. One story has it that he composed a group of pieces to be played while the king sailed in his barge on the Thames. These circumstances provided the title for his instrumental work *Water Music*.

For eight years Handel occupied a key position in the musical life of England as a director of the Royal Academy of Music. The enterprise, founded for the purpose of presenting Italian opera, had a stormy life. Cliques of musicians and temperamental singers squabbled, a situation that was not helped by Handel's overbearing and stubborn personality. Despite the turmoil of the Academy, Handel composed some of his best operas during this time.

In 1728 John Gay's *The Beggar's Opera* became popular. It was more nearly a play with inserted songs than a true opera and was an entertaining satire on political subjects. While Italian opera continued to be popular after the initial success of *The Beggar's Opera*, the support given Handel's Italian works was decreasing. Obstinate and unrelenting, Handel would not accept this fact. For another nine years he furiously wrote more operas, investing and losing money in them. At the age of fifty-two he could maintain the pace no longer. Victim of a paralytic stroke and heavily in debt, he acknowledged defeat and went abroad to recover his health.

And recover he did. After five more expensive operatic failures, he finally decided to turn away from opera. By doing so he ensured his immortality. Some years before, he had written one or two works in Italian operatic style, but with this difference: They were in English and were performed without actions, costumes, or scenery. This type of unstaged "opera," usually on a religious topic, is called *oratorio.* Within a few years he was again at the top of the English musical world. During the 1740s and early '50s there flowed from his pen a remarkable series of oratorios—*Messiah, Samson, Semele, Joseph and His Brethren, Hercules, Belshazzar, Judas Maccabaeus, Joshua, Susanna, Solomon, Jephtha*—over twenty-six in all.

By 1750, his sixty-fifth year, he was acknowledged to be the grand old man of English music. During the last nine years of his life he maintained a vigorous schedule of conducting and performing, although he became blind. In 1759 Handel collapsed following a performance that he had conducted. A few days later he died and was buried with state honors in Westminster Abbey. The German, who became an English citizen for the last forty years of his life, had earned a rightful place among England's national heroes.

THE ORATORIO

The oratorio was not an outgrowth of Renaissance forms, but rather a new type of music. In style it closely resembled opera, which was also a creation of the Baroque (see Chapter 17). In fact, the first works called "oratorios" were religious operas, complete with costumes and staging. By Handel's time the scenery, costumes, and actions had been abandoned, but the idea of drama was retained. Each soloist represented a specific character. Like opera, an oratorio was a work of considerable scope, requiring two or more hours to perform. It featured an accompanying orchestra and a chorus in addition to the soloists. Most of Handel's oratorios were drawn from religious sources, especially from the Old Testament.

Handel's Messiah

The oratorio *Messiah* is musically rather typical. It differs from other oratorios chiefly in that its text is entirely scriptural and it has no part for a narrator, who through singing describes the events of a story. *Messiah* is primarily a contemplation on Christian belief, starting with a section on prophecy and

Christ's birth, followed by His suffering and death, and concluding with the Resurrection and Redemption. Some of the conditions of its composition are described in the material on page 159.

Several traditions have developed regarding *Messiah.* At the first performance in London on March 23, 1743, King George II was so awed by the "Hallelujah Chorus" that he rose and stood at his seat. In those days, when the King stood, everyone stood. So the King's spontaneous action became a tradition that is still followed today.

Like other oratorios *Messiah* contains many individual musical sections—fifty-three in all. Generally the sections are one of three types: recitative, aria, or chorus. The aria and recitative were explained in Chapter 11.

The Chorus. The word "chorus" has two meanings in music. It refers to a group that sings choral music and also to the choral sections of an oratorio or opera. So a chorus sings a chorus.

In many ways the chorus portion of an oratorio is similar to the aria. It is a rather lengthy section, which presents about the same amount of text and features frequent repetition of words. Metrical rhythmic patterns are followed strictly, and the music requires some skill in singing. The accompaniment has a significant place in most chorus sections.

There is one fundamental difference between chorus and aria, however. If you study the music for the chorus "For unto us a child is born," you will see in the four measures in the middle of page 151 that while the tenors sing "For unto us" the sopranos are singing a run. Two lines of approximately equal interest performed together—this is what was found in Renaissance music! Sure enough, polyphony is present in the chorus. Again the Baroque is true to its nature in the presentation of extremes. While developing homophony—the expressive melodic line and its accompaniment—Baroque composers still retained the polyphonic style of the Renaissance and consciously wrote in both styles. Because of its different character, the term *counterpoint* is used for Baroque polyphony.

The counterpoint of the Baroque does not sound much like the polyphony of the Renaissance, however. Baroque music is built around tonality, around the major/minor key system. The simultaneous melodies of Baroque counterpoint are influenced by the same magnetic pull toward a tonal center that affects chords. Baroque counterpoint can modulate, too. Then there is the unflagging pattern of beats in its rhythm. So the same substance (polyphony) has been poured into two quite different molds.

The chorus "For unto us" (Record 2, Side 2) offers the listener three different moods, each of which fits the text (from Isaiah 9:6). The first feeling is tender, to suit the thought about an infant. It suggests the happiness felt at the birth of a child.

A
Soprano
For un-to us a Child is born,___ un-to us a Son is giv-en, un-to
us a Son is giv-en, For un-to
Alto
Tenor
For un-to us a Child is born,___
Bass
us a Child is born:
un-to us a Son is giv-en: un-to
B
For un-to us a Child is born,___
us a Son is giv-en:
For un-to

The second section has a more rugged, martial character. The words describe what lies in store for this infant: "And the government shall be upon His shoulder."

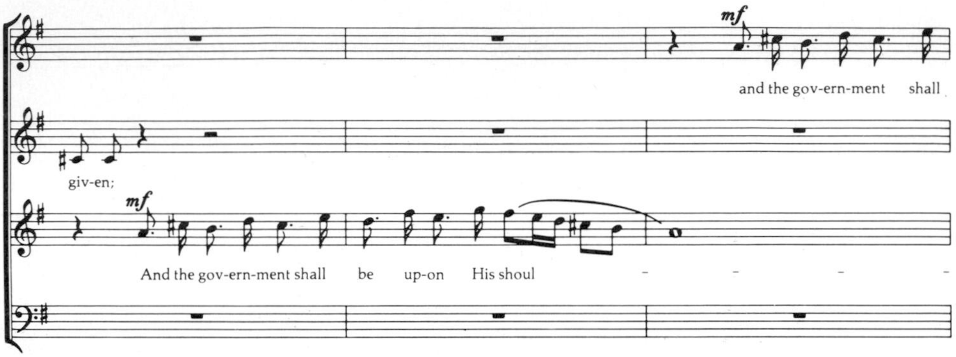

As these words are finished, the orchestra breaks into an excited, joyful melodic pattern. What are the words that call for such a reaction? "And His name shall be called Wonderful, Counselor, the mighty God, the everlasting Father, the Prince of Peace."

Handel then takes the three melodies and goes through them four times. The repetitions are never exact. The first time, for instance, the sopranos start the melody of "For unto us"; the second time the altos start it, and the third time it returns to the sopranos. The fourth time the basses start, and the sound is made even heavier and stronger when another section of the chorus is added to the line. In this way the piece has a sense of building toward a climactic finish.

Handel's good sense of fitting text and music is particularly evident in this chorus, especially on the phrase that begins "Wonderful, Counselor." First he establishes an excited figure in the accompaniment. Next he emphasizes the words, not by making them louder but by allowing them to stand alone with rests on either side. In this way he builds on the listener's expectations. Normally, the phrase would proceed, "And His name shall be called Wonderful, Counselor." But Handel wrote it this way: "And His name shall be called *(rest)* Wonderful, *(rest, rest)* Counselor." The beat or two of silence on both sides of

---

THE COMPOSING OF MESSIAH

The year of 1741 was not a good one for George Frideric Handel. He had poured most of his money into the revival of two of his Italian operas, *Imeneo* and *Deidamia,* and met with failure. His constant work and lack of sleep began to affect his health again. He had withdrawn from public life and lived in his quarters in Lower Brook Street at Hanover Square in London. Rather than brood his time away, he turned to writing the oratorio *Messiah,* and he worked on it with an intensity that he had never employed before. He must have labored constantly, and it is known that he paid little attention to the food the servant left at his door. After the completion of the "Hallelujah Chorus" a servant found him with tears in his eyes exclaiming, "I did think I saw all Heaven before me, and the great God Himself!"

Strangely, it is not certain who arranged the Bible verses for the oratorio. It is known who sent the text to Handel, a Charles Jennens, who is described as a "pompous, conceited, wealthy fop who imagined himself to be a literary genius." Dr. Samuel Johnson (1709–1784), famous for his use of the English language and a cutting tongue, said that Jennens was "a vain fool crazed by his wealth, who, were he in Heaven, would criticize the Lord Almighty." Johnson must have been right, because Jennens had the nerve to remark that Handel's music was "a fine entertainment" but "not near so good as he might and ought to have done."

Handel accepted an invitation to give a series of benefit concerts in Dublin, Ireland. He thought the change from London to Dublin might do him some good, as well as help his finances. Also, he was a generous man who was moved by worthy causes. The Dublin benefit was for the Society for Relieving Prisoners, the Charitable Infirmary, and Mercer's Hospital.

By the end of 1741 Handel had traveled to Dublin and led a series of concerts. He kept *Messiah* "up his sleeve" until March of 1742. An open rehearsal of the work a month before its premier helped to build public interest, so that hundreds of people had to be turned away from the first performance on April 13. Only 700 people could be squeezed into the hall, even though the advertisements asked the ladies not to wear hoops that made their dresses billow out and the men to leave their swords at home. The performance was a tremendous success.

Subsequent performances in London were not quite so enthusiastically received, perhaps because they were held in theaters. By 1750 the Foundling Hospital sponsored a performance of *Messiah.* A performance of *Messiah* became an annual attraction for the Hospital, a tradition that still continues today. Handel conducted his final performance of *Messiah* on April 6, 1759; eight days later he was dead. By that time both Handel and his oratorio had won a permanent place in the hearts of the English people.

---

the words make the difference between something average and something outstanding in the world of music.

The same passage also demonstrates the importance of rhythmic patterns and word accents. The word "wonderful" is sung with three-fourths of a beat on "won" and only one-fourth on "der." The final syllable receives the second beat of the measure. This rhythmic pattern approximates the spoken accents of the word, so Handel utilizes this pattern to make the word more natural and effective. He causes the important words and syllables to fall on the beat so that they can be emphasized when sung as when they are spoken. One such phrase is "the EV-er-LAST-ing FA-ther *(rest)*, the PRINCE of PEACE." To appreciate the importance of the placement of words in music, say the phrase to yourself in this way: "THE ev-ER-last-ING fa-THER."

Often Handel's choruses project a feeling of grandeur. The reverence of Renaissance choral music was exchanged for the drama and power of Baroque choral music. And, in fact, more singers were required for Baroque works. Handel gave the chorus an important place in the oratorio. But more than that, he established a standard for the oratorio in England and America, a standard that would last well into the twentieth century.

THE CHORALE

Just as Gregorian chant was an outgrowth of the belief and practice of the Roman Catholic Church, the chorale was a product of Protestant belief and practice. In the sixteenth century, when Martin Luther's break with the Roman Church had become final, Luther and some of his colleagues set about to provide music suitable for worship in the newly developed services. They wanted the members of the congregation to be participants in the service, not just observers as they were in the Mass. One way to involve them was to have them sing. But what should they sing? Chant was associated too strongly with the rejected Roman Church. Also, its flexible rhythmic style and subtle nuances are difficult for untrained singers to perform well. The answer was to create a new body of religious music. So from German religious songs, adaptations of chant and secular tunes, and from the pen of Luther and others came the *chorale.*

Luther believed not only that worshipers should sing but that their music should encourage the proper religious attitude. One purpose of the chorale, therefore, was to proclaim beliefs and to contribute to the spirit of worship. The Protestant religious attitudes of that time are clearly expressed in "A Mighty Fortress Is Our God," which Luther himself wrote. A translation of one verse is:

Though devils all the world should fill,
All eager to devour us;
We tremble not, we fear no ill,
They shall not overpower us.

For his analogy with God Luther chose the German word *Burg*, a medieval stone fortress, a symbol of austere strength. The chorale reflects, then, the deadly serious religious attitudes of the early Protestants. Each note in its melody stands like a block of stone in a medieval fortress.

On first hearing, a chorale, like Gregorian chant, may seem like dull music. It's true; both lack novelty and flashiness. However, religious music should express what the believer feels to be the ultimate and eternal. Music that is trivial and flashy does not express the idea of a God greater and more lasting than the universe. The music and the theology must be congruent. In both chant and chorale, reverence and a profound sense of respect are expressed effectively and beautifully.

Both chant and chorale today are important in traditional religious worship. An association between them and a religious attitude has been established. Whether or not this association is desirable, it does affect listeners and participants by giving a sense of being in the procession of the faithful who have gone before and by suggesting the timeless nature of their beliefs.

THE CANTATA

Because of their simple, strong qualities, chorale melodies are well suited for use as themes for other musical works. Several types of pieces for organ, which are discussed elsewhere in this book, have chorale melodies as their basis. Chorale melodies are often found in a *cantata.* Originally the word "cantata" meant any sizable work, sacred or secular, that was sung. By the time of Bach the cantata had become a short oratorio, with an instrumental accompaniment, arias, recitatives, and choruses. The cantata is much shorter and is written to be performed in a worship service, not a concert. Furthermore, it generally incorporates a chorale melody into some of its sections.

There was plenty of time in the service for a twenty-minute cantata in Bach's church in Leipzig. The principal Sunday service began at seven in the morning and lasted until about noon! In addition, there were three other short services on Sunday, as well as daily services and special religious celebrations. Altogether, Leipzig churches required fifty eight cantatas each year and other types of music for special occasions. During most of his career in Leipzig Bach composed about one cantata per month. About 200 of the 300 cantatas Bach composed during his career have been preserved.

Bach's Cantata No. 140

One of Bach's better-known cantatas has been mentioned on two earlier occasions in this book: Cantata No. 140, *Wachet auf, ruft uns die Stimme* ("Wake Up, Call the Voices"). The text, based on Matthew 25:1–13, tells the parable of the five wise and the five foolish maidens. The chorale melody appears at the beginning, middle, and end of the cantata. The opening chorus consists of variations on the chorale melody. Its text is:

Wachet auf, ruft uns die Stimme	Wake up, call to us the voices
Der Wächter sehr hoch auf der Zinne,	Of watchmen high up on the tower,
Wach' auf, du Stadt Jerusalem!	Wake up, thou town Jerusalem!
Mitternacht heisst diese Stunde;	It is now the hour of midnight;
Sie rufen uns mit hellem Munde:	They call to us with shining faces:
Wo seid ihr klugen Jungfrauen?	Where are you now, clever maidens?
Wohl auf, der Bräutgam kommt,	Cheer up, the Bridegroom comes,*
Steht auf, die Lampen nehmt! Alleluja!	Get up, and take your lamps! Alleluia!
Macht euch bereit zu de Hochzeit,	Prepare yourselves, the wedding nears,
Ihr müsset ihm ensprungen gehn.	You must go forth to welcome Him.

This chorus is the longest and most complex portion of the cantata. There is a driving, uneven rhythmic figure contrasted with a countermelody played by the violins. The chorale melody itself appears in long notes in the soprano. As these notes are sung, the alto, tenor, and bass sing contrasting musical lines in contrapuntal style. The orchestra plays a significant part.

This chorus illustrates the belief of Baroque composers in projecting the ideas of the text in the music. Called the *doctrine of affects* or *doctrine of affections,* this belief is evident in many Baroque works. Because the type of music associated with particular moods or ideas is not known by listeners today, the doctrine is mainly of historical interest. Examples in Bach's cantata of the application of the doctrine of affections include words such as *wach' auf* (wake up), *wohl auf* (cheer up), and *steht auf* (arise or get up). As they are

*In many cantatas, Jesus is referred to symbolically as the bridegroom, and the Church as his bride.

sung, the music usually leaps upward. The doctrine is also reflected in the consistent mood that is maintained throughout an entire section of a work.

CANTATA No. 140

Strings
der Wäch - ter sehr
of watch - men high
30
der Wäch-ter sehr hoch. . .
of watch-men up high . . .
der Wäch-ter sehr hoch. . .
of watch-men up high . . .
der Wäch-ter sehr
of watch-men up
hoch auf der Zin - - - -
up on the tow - - - -
hoch. . .
high. . .
- - - ne,
- - - er
40
1st Violins
Oboe
1st Violins
Wach' auf, du Stadt
Wake up, thou town
Wach' auf. . . Wach' auf, du Stadt Je - ru - sa -
Wake up . . . Wake up, thou town Je - ru - sa -
Je - ru - sa - lem!
Je - ru - sa - lem!
50

The second part of the cantata is a recitative for tenor. It sets forth the image of Christ as the Heavenly Bridegroom and tells about His coming. The third section is a duet for soprano and bass. It is in dialogue form with an important part for violin solo. The fourth section was cited on pages 33–35. A gentle melody is played by the strings while the tenors sing the chorale melody. After a recitative by the bass, another duet is heard. Again it is a dialogue between bass and soprano. The form is the typical *A B A* found so often in Baroque arias. In this duet the oboe has several important solos.

The final section of the cantata is a harmonization of the chorale melody. The music appears on page 38. It was customary for the congregation to join in the singing of this section. The chorales were familiar to the congregation and sung in the native tongue of the participants, which made the chorale and cantata more meaningful.

The concept of chorale singing was also influenced by the educational level of the worshipers. Many people in the Baroque era could not read or write, so pictures, statues, and music in churches were intended to be educational as well as beautiful. The text of a choral work was chosen for purposes of instruction as well as worship.

The cantata and oratorio are only two of the many types of vocal music written for Protestant worship services in the Baroque period. Another type is the *Passion,* which is like an oratorio except that its topic is the suffering of Christ on the cross. Bach's *St. Matthew Passion* was rediscovered and performed seventy-nine years after his death, and the event renewed interest in other Bach works. Like the cantatas, the *St. Matthew Passion* gives a prominent place to a chorale: "O Sacred Head Now Wounded."

There is a Baroque motet, too. It resembles the Renaissance motet in that it is unaccompanied, religious, and contrapuntal. In the Baroque style, however, it has a strict rhythmic meter and major/minor tonality. Its text is in a vernacular language.

The following chart summarizes the main differences between Renaissance and Baroque vocal music. Although the list of differences is sizable, it does not contain those that are associated with instrumental music. The next two chapters cover that area.

MUSICAL ASPECTS	RENAISSANCE	BAROQUE
Large vocal forms	Mass	Oratorio, cantata, opera, passion
Small vocal forms	Motet, madrigal	Chorale, recitative, aria, chorus, Baroque motet
Formal patterns	Phrase by phrase	*da capo* (A B A)
Texture	Polyphony	Homophony and polyphony
Tonality	Modes	Major/minor keys
Harmony	Not systematic but contains some feeling of a tonal center	Systematic with strong tonal center
Modulation	Rare	Frequent
Meter	Sacred music is not metrical; Secular music is often metrical	Strongly metrical
Beat	Steady but not strong pulse	Steady and strong beat, except for recitative
Expressiveness in singing	Restrained; some text could not be heard clearly	Very expressive; music adds to the feelings expressed in the text
Virtuoso singing	Almost none	Frequent in arias and choruses

OTHER BAROQUE COMPOSERS

Claudio Monteverdi

Claudio Monteverdi lived from 1567 to 1643. His life parallels the change from the Renaissance to Baroque styles in music. He was schooled in the Renaissance tradition and wrote well in the Palestrina idiom. His books of motets and madrigals, however, paved the way for the Baroque style and homophonic music.

Monteverdi held two important positions during his lifetime. One was in the court of the Duke of Mantua. Then in 1613 he was appointed choirmaster of St. Mark's in Venice, a post he held until his death thirty years later. Not only did he compose many religious works and madrigals, but he was also the most successful opera composer of his time. More than anyone else he promoted the ideals of opera and transformed it into a successful public medium. His contributions to opera include a reduction in the amount of recitative, which had predominated in early opera, and the addition of more beautiful melodic lines. He also infused his operas with more musical expression and encouraged instrumentalists to try effects such as tremolo (an agitated, back-and-forth movement of the bow on the string) to create more drama.

Heinrich Schütz

The life of Heinrich Schütz (1585–1672) also spanned the transition from the Renaissance to the Baroque. His music combines the cultures of Germany and Italy. His early life was spent in the service of a prince at Hesse-Cassel. Later he went to study in Venice with Giovanni Gabrieli, from whom he adopted the idea of composing for two choirs so that they contrast with each other. Schütz was interested in drama and became the first German composer to write an opera. His best works are in the area of church music. He composed settings of scriptural texts and Passions, several of which are still performed today.

Henry Purcell

Henry Purcell lived from 1659 to 1695 and holds a special place in the hearts of the English. He was the foremost composer of his time, and much of his music is still heard today. His brief career as a composer began in the court of Charles II and extended through the rather turbulent reign of James II into the period of William and Mary. Purcell was a successful composer in all forms, including opera, anthems, and instrumental music.

13

BAROQUE INSTRUMENTAL MUSIC: THE FUGUE

There are noticeable differences between the instrumental and vocal music of the Baroque period, a fact that distinguishes the Baroque from previous periods. Until the Baroque era a composition was not written particularly as a vocal or instrumental work. Except for a few keyboard and lute compositions the same piece of music could be performed entirely by voices, by instruments, or by a combination of the two. Baroque composers, however, wrote specifically for chorus or for a designated instrument. The nature of the instrument or voice was considered by the composer when creating the piece. So the composition can usually be recognized as being in an instrumental style or a vocal style.

The eventual distinction between the two styles was probably inevitable. Instruments and voices do not make music in the same way, and so each sounds best in different types of music. For instance, a violin or flute can easily produce sounds that are higher than the upper limits of the human voice; other instruments are capable of sounding below the range of the voice. Performers on most instruments can also play notes with a speed and clarity impossible for a singer to achieve. An instrument is more agile than the voice; it can move from high to low with ease.

In spite of the characteristic styles that emerged, the Baroque period saw quite a bit of interchange between them. After an aria was written, for example, it was not uncommon for the composer to make a transcription of that aria for harpsichord or violin. Making a musical *transcription* means adapting a piece written for an instrument or voice to another instrument or voice, or to a group of either. The musical success of a transcription depends on the composer, who must choose an appropriate piece for adaptation and then exercise skill in making the necessary changes to fit the new medium.

In general, Baroque instrumental music tended to be more contrapuntal than homophonic, while the opposite seemed to be true for vocal music. There is a logical explanation for this tendency. In vocal music composers tried to project a message. Recitative and aria were developed as a means of giving expression to the ideas contained in the text. Instrumental music, of course, was not affected by the specific words of a text.

TRANSITION TO BAROQUE STYLE

The change from the Renaissance to Baroque styles was gradual in the case of both vocal and instrumental music. The transition from one style to another also resulted in some interesting music by a number of highly gifted composers. Claudio Monteverdi's great contributions are mentioned in Chapter 11. Another group of important composers worked in Venice, which was throughout the sixteenth century an important and wealthy city.

Much of that city's musical activity centered around the Cathedral of St. Mark. The position of organist-choirmaster there was the most sought after in all Italy. Over the years the distinguished musicians who were employed there composed more and more for two choruses placed with the two organs on each side of the church. And not only were there singers and pipe organs, there were also such instruments as trombones, cornetts, and viols. The result was a powerful and exciting stereophonic sound with one group of performers answering the other. Giovanni Gabrieli (1557–1612) brought this technique to fruition in the early years of the seventeenth century. He was also the first composer to specify particular instruments for a part and the first to indicate the level of loudness in the music.

In 1608 a book of thirty-six *Canzoni per Sonare* was published, with G. Gabrieli having six entries in it. He actually wrote the canzoni at least twenty years earlier, and did not yet specify the instruments that were to play them. Because of his association with the brasses, this music has been somewhat preempted by brass players. Canzoni are instrumental versions of the vocal French *chanson.* They are short, contain much imitation among the parts, and have a lively character. The version in the *Record Album* (Record 1, Side 2) is played on modern brass instruments, which are much more powerful than the ones used in Gabrieli's day. Trombones at that time came in five sizes, and the cornett—not related to the metal cornet of today—was a wooden instrument with a cup-shaped mouthpiece. Although these transitional Renaissance-Baroque works originally had supporting keyboard parts, they add little to the music and are usually left out in performances.

The "Canzona per Sonare No. 4" opens with a short melodic figure that is typical of this type of music. The other three parts imitate it one after the other. The opening theme returns to conclude the canzona.

Other than that, the music consists of short sections that are treated in a contrapuntal way and not repeated. As was true of Morley's madrigal, the harmony that has been used so often over the past 300 years was not yet fully developed.

BAROQUE INSTRUMENTS

Two keyboard instruments were important in the Baroque period: the organ and the harpsichord. Both were described in Chapter 6. The organ had existed in rudimentary form for 1,500 years, but it reached its highest development during the Baroque. In fact, many organs built in the twentieth century represent attempts to replicate the organs of the eighteenth century. During the late nineteenth and early twentieth centuries, several ranks of pipes were added to organs to imitate the sound of trombones and other instruments. These synthetic efforts were seldom successful.

The harpsichord was frequently played in the Renaissance, but it became more important in the Baroque period. At about the time the Baroque period ended, the harpsichord faded in prominence and did not become popular again until the twentieth century. In the last several decades there has been a revival of interest in the harpsichord and new instruments are being manufactured.

Several orchestral instruments are featured in Baroque music. One is the whistle flute or recorder, which is played straight out from the player's mouth, rather than to the side as it is today. The flute was made of wood and had a lighter, less penetrating tone quality. The trumpet was given important solo roles during the Baroque period. It had no valves, and therefore the pitches had to be controlled entirely by the player's lips. Many of the Baroque trumpets were long and thin, which made it easier for the player to reach the very high notes heard in some Baroque compositions. The violin achieved a major role in Baroque music. It did not look quite the same as it does today. The fingerboard was shorter because players were not required to play very high notes. The bow stick curved slightly away from the hair, with a shape resembling an archer's bow, for which it was named. The hair tension was rather loose and the strings of the instrument were set on a flatter plane, making it easier for the violinist to play on more than one string at a time.

The quality of performance on orchestral instruments was probably not impressive by today's standards. Most players held other jobs, usually not associated with music, and the technical development of instruments was not advanced. The exceptions to this general situation were the trumpeters. It is likely that they performed very capably. The level of playing on the organ and probably the harpsichord was also very good.

Tuning

It was during the Baroque era that a significant breakthrough was made in tuning. Pythagoras' discovery of certain basic intervals did not solve the problem of exactly where the intervening notes were to be placed. The situation was complicated by a caprice of nature. Theoretically, if one plays a series of fifths, ascending or descending from a given note, the thirteenth note should duplicate the original pitch. But if the Pythagorean ratio for a perfect fifth is used and if the fifths are computed upward, the thirteenth note is noticeably higher than the original! This gap did not bother singers because they could easily make slight pitch adjustments, but the problem plagued keyboard-instrument makers. To get perfect tuning in some keys, they had to sacrifice the pitch accuracy in other keys. Keys with several sharps or flats were usually avoided, because keys with the fewest number of sharp or flats were favored. Opportunities for modulation and transposition were limited by this tuning system.

The problem was resolved when the size of the perfect fifth was reduced slightly, so that the distance between all half steps was equal, even if slightly imperfect. The Baroque period saw increasing use of this idea of *equal temperament,* the system of tuning still used today. To promote better systems of tuning, and to encourage a player's facility in all keys, a few composers, including Bach, wrote a series of pieces in all twenty-four major and minor keys. Bach's *Well-Tempered Clavier* was music of such high quality that it is frequently performed today.*

Terraced Dynamics

The gradual increase or decrease of loudness, which is so familiar today, was not common in music of the Baroque period. Renaissance composers had written no loudness markings at all in the music, and Baroque composers wrote very few. Often composers rehearsed and performed their own music, so extensive markings were not necessary. The few markings that are present, however,

*The word *clavier* referred to any keyboard instrument.

call for abrupt changes of level. A *forte* or loud level is likely to change suddenly to a *piano* or soft level. These changes are called *terraced dynamics.* One can only speculate on the reasons for the abrupt changes. Baroque artists and musicians were interested in dramatic contrasts, both visual and aural. Also, the keyboard instruments of the time could not make gradual changes, so a change in loudness level had to be achieved abruptly or not at all.

Basso Continuo

The harmonies in Baroque music became so well standardized that musicians devised a system of shorthand called *figured bass* to notate chords. The composer provided the bass line with cues in the form of numbers and an occasional sharp, flat, or natural to indicate the inner parts. The keyboard player was expected to read this "code" while performing the music.

The outer parts became the two important lines in Baroque music, with the melody being the most important. The bass part provided a foundation to the music. Because it sounded nearly all the time, it came to be known as *basso continuo* ("continuous bass"), which for convenience is usually shortened to *continuo.* The nearly continuous bass line is not too different from the bass lines found in jazz and rock today. Such a part contributes energy to the music.

Performance of Baroque Music

There were no professional orchestras during the Baroque period. The orchestras that did exist were associated with the courts and involved only part-time musicians. The orchestra was small—about twenty players. There was no conductor who stood before the group. The leader was usually the harpsichord player or first violinist, who began the music by giving the other musicians a nod. There were few public concerts. Performances of music were held in churches or in the courts of the nobility.

The choirs were also small by today's standards. For instance, Bach's choir at Leipzig sometimes numbered fewer than thirty singers. At one time he was down to three altos, and he wrote a letter to the town fathers asking for funds to employ a fourth alto. (The request was refused.)

Improvisation was an important aspect of Baroque musical performance. The fact that the figured bass had to be filled in by the keyboard player has been mentioned. A church organist was expected to improvise intricate and complex music. The improvisational ability of some Baroque composers, including Bach and Handel, made them legends in their time. A singer or instrumentalist would frequently add ornaments and embellishments to his line of music in an improvising manner. What is seen in the notation of Baroque music is in some cases only a skeleton of what was actually performed.

JOHANN SEBASTIAN BACH

The name of Johann Sebastian Bach seems to crop up in nearly every discussion of Baroque music. And well it should! He ranks as one of the musical giants of all time.

Bach lived an uneventful life, one not very different from that of many successful musicians of his time. The most notable feature about him was his lineage—he was one of a gifted musical family. Over a period of about six generations, from 1580 to 1845, more than sixty Bachs were musicians of some sort, and at least thirty-eight of these attained eminence as musicians. Included among the latter were Johann Christoph (1642–1703), who was a cousin of J. S. Bach's father, and several of J. S. Bach's own sons: Wilhelm Friedemann (1710–1784), Carl Philipp Emanuel (1714–1788), Johann Christoph Friedrich (1732–1795), and Johann Christian (1735–1782).

Johann Sebastian Bach was born in Eisenach in 1685, the son of a town musician. When the boy was ten, his father died. Johann's musical training was taken over by his elder brother, Johann Christoph, who was an organist. During his early career, Bach was known more as an organ virtuoso than as a composer. After two brief positions as organist, Bach was appointed to his first important post at the age of twenty-three, that of court organist and chamber musician to the Duke of Weimar (*Vy*-mar). He stayed nine years. It was during his Weimar years that he concentrated on organ, both as a performer and composer.

When the Duke failed to advance him, Bach accepted another position at Cöthen (*Keh*-ten). The prince at Cöthen was interested in chamber music, so the versatile Bach turned from writing church and organ music to composing primarily for instruments other than the organ. It was during this time that he wrote the famous Brandenburg Concertos. After the sudden death of his wife, Maria Barbara, he married and immortalized his second wife, Anna Magdalena, by writing a book of keyboard music for her.

The third and last portion of Bach's life began with his appointment in 1723 as organist-teacher of St. Thomas Church in Leipzig. Bach was not the first choice for the position. A member of the town council is reported to have said, "Since the best man could not be obtained, lesser ones will have to be accepted." The Leipzig position required the writing and direction of church music, so Bach again complied by changing the emphasis of his musical work. Not only were the Leipzig city fathers unaware of Bach's genius; they were stingy. His contract wouldn't find many "takers" today among competent composers or educators (see p. 176).

In spite of the annoyances of the position at Leipzig and tragedy in his personal life (six of his first eight children born in Leipzig died), Bach continued his endless stream of great music. Late in life he suffered a stroke and became blind. In 1750 he died, with his true stature still unrecognized. Interest in his music was renewed in 1829, when young Felix Mendelssohn rediscovered the *St. Matthew Passion.*

Except for a few brief journeys in Germany, Bach knew little of the world outside his immediate environment. He was not particularly well educated, and was very devout in his religious beliefs.* He created no new musical forms and instituted no new compositional techniques. His music was seldom heard

---

*He was fascinated with numerology, ascribing occult significance to coincidences of numbers such as the four letters in his last name, and he saw unusual significance in the number 14, which is derived when these letters are totaled according to their position in the alphabet.

Johann Sebastian Bach. Mezzotint by E. G. Haussmann.

Plate 5
Rembrandt van Ryn: *The Descent from the Cross.*
(Widener Collection, National Gallery of Art, Washington, D.C.)

Rembrandt painted *The Descent from the Cross* in about 1650. The work is dramatic in its treatment of light on the faces of the people. The light seems to be coming from the candle shielded by a man's hand, giving the scene an eerie pall. The cross is not in the center of the painting, as it would have been in Renaissance works. Jesus' body is twisted, another popular Baroque technique in painting and sculpture. The emotions of tenderness and grief are evident in the faces.

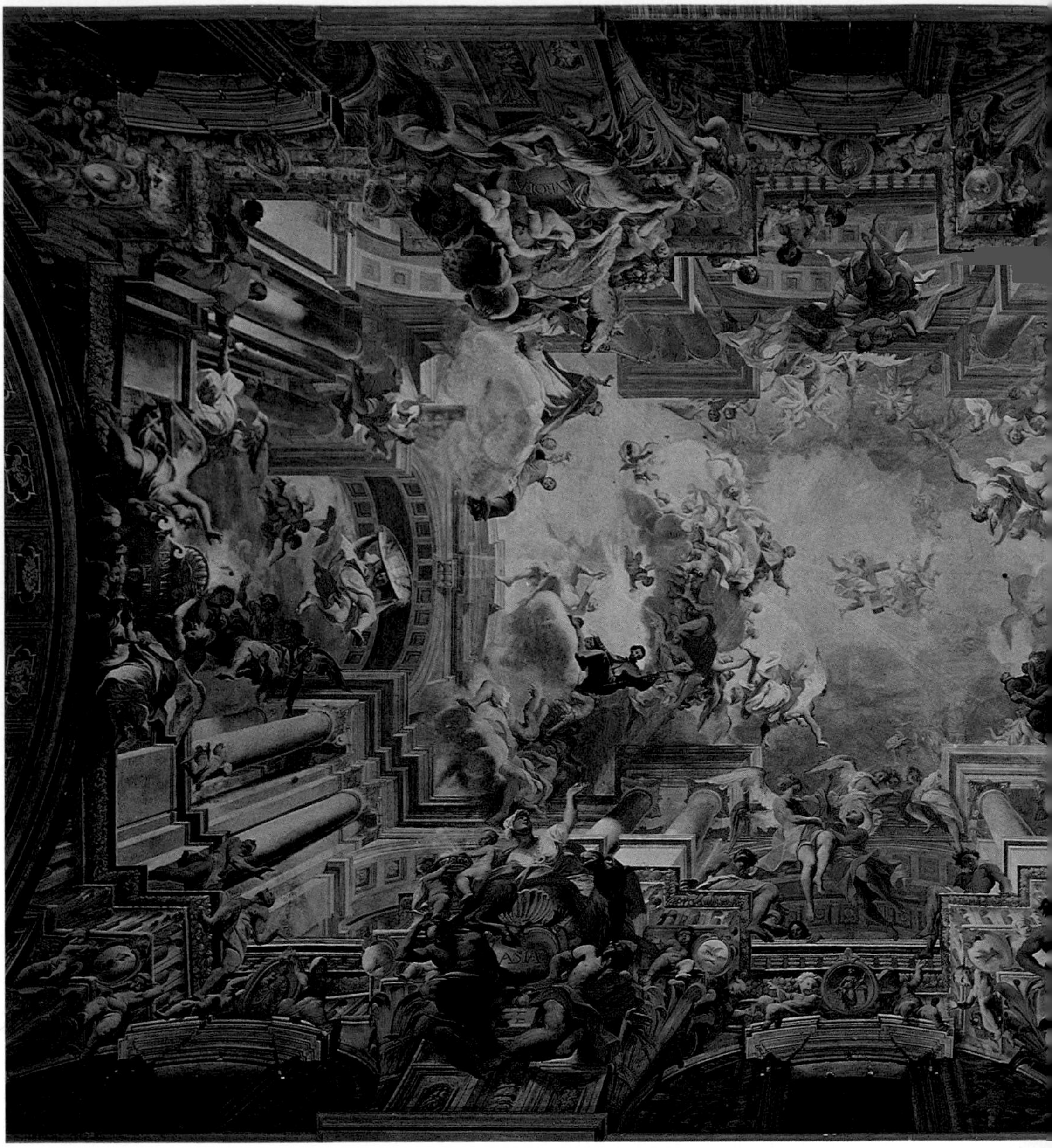

Plate 6
Andrea Pozzo: *Apothesis of Saint Ignatius.*
(Scala New York/Florence.)

Nowhere is the Baroque love of overpowering splendor more evident than in the elaborately painted ceilings of churches and palaces. Andrea Pozzo's mural covering the vaulting in San Ignazio (St. Ignatius) Church in Rome employs an ingenious ordering of perspectives. In the picture the sky seems to open up, with the Saint carried upward by a heavenly host, twisting and turning into infinity. Pozzo achieves an illusion of endlessness.

Plate 7
El Greco (Domenikos Theotokopoulos): *The Holy Family.*
(Samuel H. Kress Collection, National Gallery of Art, Washington, D.C.)

In some ways El Greco's *The Holy Family* is almost Gothic. The bodies have been elongated, giving a more spiritual appearance. But the flickering light marks its true Baroque character. Although it depicts a peaceful scene, the painting is more charged with emotion than Renaissance works such as Botticelli's *The Adoration of the Magi* (Plate 3). The difference is especially noticeable in the two skies.

outside of Leipzig during his lifetime, and even there it was probably not performed well.

Why is Bach so dominating a figure in music? The answer is that he wrote with such skill and effectiveness. Especially remarkable was his ability to write counterpoint. Words are inadequate to describe Bach's genius. Perhaps the late Dag Hammarskjold, Secretary General of the United Nations, expressed it best. In speaking of Bach and Vivaldi, another Baroque composer, he said, "Both have a beautiful way of creating order in the brain."

THE FUGUE

Because the organ can play in a wide variety of tone colors with tremendous power and range, Baroque composers began to write music specifically for the organ, and in the process they developed several forms of organ composition, of which the most prominent is the *fugue* (fewg).

The fugue, like most musical forms, did not appear full-blown. It evolved from less complex types of keyboard music. The fugue and its predecessors have one thing in common: They are conceived contrapuntally, with the lines of music imitating one another frequently. Imitation has been found in musical examples cited already in this book, including Palestrina's imitative entrances in the *Sicut cervus*.

Sometimes Bach and other composers included fugues as a portion of a longer work, which is what he did in the case of the fugue in Toccata, Adagio, and Fugue in C Major, BWV 564. The fugue opens with a melody that is divided into four distinct parts, each part being set off with rests around it. This melody serves as the basis for the remainder of the composition; in a fugue the main melody is called the *subject*. The music for this fugue subject appears in the Listening Guide on page 179.

At measure 10, the subject enters in another line. In a fugue these lines are called *voices*, even though they are to be played, not sung. The first voice begins with the notes C E, while the second voice begins with the notes G B. This change indicates that the music has modulated, in this case to the key whose center is five notes above the original. This is known as the *dominant key* because it is built around the fifth note in the key, which is nearly as important as the tonic or key center note.

While the second voice sounds the subject, the first continues with a line of counterpoint. This line is not as easily remembered as the subject, but it does have melodic character. It is called the *countersubject*, and the music for it also appears in the Listening Guide. Notice that it fills in the places where rests appear in the subject and that it has a quite different character.

The third voice then enters in the original key, while the second voice has the countermelody. The first voice begins free contrapuntal material.

At measure 28 the fourth voice enters in the pedal part. Its notes indicate a modulation to the dominant key again. The first and second voices continue in free counterpoint, while the third voice has the countersubject.

The fourth voice completes the subject at the beginning section that includes the initial presentation of the subject in all voices of the fugue. This portion is known as the *exposition.* From this point until its end, the fugue presents the subject in different keys and voices, and it contains epi-

---

BACH AT LEIPZIG

Although you may not think so when you read the contents of this section, the position of Cantor at St. Thomas Church and School was one of the most desirable ones in all of Germany. The job was a combination minister-of-music and teacher, which was typical of such a position during that time. It was the third appointment that Bach held for a significant amount of time, and the one he retained the longest, for the twenty-seven years from 1723 until his death in 1750. The school was a combination elementary and music school. Since only boys sang in church choirs in those days, there were no girls in the school.

The contract reads: Whereas the Honorable and Most Wise Council of this town of Leipzig have engaged me as Cantor of Thomas School and have desired an undertaking from me in respect to the following points, to wit:

1) That I shall set the boys a shining example of an honest, retiring manner of life, serve the School industriously, and instruct the boys conscientiously;

2) Bring the music in both the principal Churches of this town into good estate, to the best of my ability;

3) Show to the Honorable and Most Wise Council all proper respect and obedience, and protect and further everywhere as best I can its honor and reputation; likewise if a gentleman of the Council desires the boys for a musical occasion unhesitatingly provide him with the same, but otherwise never permit them to go out of town to funerals or weddings without the previous knowledge and consent of the Burgomaster and Honorable Directors of the School currently in office;

4) Give due obedience to the Honorable Inspectors and Directors of the School in each and every instruction which the same shall issue in the name of the Honorable and Most Wise Council;

5) Not take any boys into the School who have not already laid a foundation in music, or are not at least suited to being instructed therein, nor do the same without the previous knowledge and consent of the Honorable Inspectors and Directors;

6) So that the Churches may not have to be put to unnecessary expense, faithfully instruct the boys not only in vocal but also instrumental music;

7) In order to preserve the good order in the Churches, so arrange the music that it shall not last too long, and shall be of such a nature as not to make an operatic impression, but rather incite the listeners to devotion;

---

sodes with free counterpoint. In this particular fugue Bach brings in the subject with unusual frequency, and often the countersubject appears with it. The fugue closes with a final playing of the subject and a short concluding section.

The basic design of the Fugue in C Major can be diagrammed as shown on page 178.

This fugue has four voices. It could have had two, three, or five; more than five is not common. The order in which the voices enter is a matter of choice for the composer. Composers often vary the structure slightly to suit their desires for the piece.

---

8) Provide the New Church with good scholars;

9) Treat the boys in a friendly manner and with caution, but, in case they do not wish to obey, chastise them with moderation or report them to the proper place;

10) Faithfully attend to the instruction in the School and whatever else it befits me to do;

11) And if I cannot undertake this myself, arrange that it be done by some other capable person without expense to the Honorable and Most Wise Council or to the School;

12) Not go out of town without the permission of the Honorable Burgomaster currently in office;

13) Always so far as possible walk with the boys at funerals, as is customary;

14) And shall not accept any office in the University without the consent of the Honorable and Learned Council;

15) Now therefore I do hereby undertake and bind myself faithfully to observe all of the said requirements, and on the pain of losing my post not to act contrary to them, in witness whereof I have set my hand and seal to this agreement.

Done in Leipzig, May 5, 1723
Johann Sebastian Bach

All this for about $7,000 a year!

Lithograph of St. Thomas Churchyard in Leipzig.

EXPOSITION					DEVELOPMENT
Voice I	S	CS	FM		Return and development of subject and countersubject
Voice II		S	CS	FM	
Voice III			S	CS	
Voice IV				S	

S = subject   CS = countersubject   FM = free contrapuntal material

The subject is the unifying element of the fugue, and the exposition presents it clearly. The interlacing of counterpoint around a central subject (with its contrasting countersubject added for interest) reminds one of a complicated mathematical formula working itself out to a beautifully correct conclusion. It was to this quality of creating order in the brain that Hammarskjold was referring in the quotation cited earlier.

A procedure typical of Baroque music is illustrated in the measures from the Fugue in C Major shown in the next example.

Notice that each measure is essentially the same music, except that each measure is at a higher pitch level than the one before. The top line in the first measure begins on E, in the second measure on F, in the third on G, and in the fourth on A. In the lower bass-clef part the first note in the first measure is C, in the second it's D, in the third E, and in the fourth F. The technique of repeating a melodic figure at a different pitch level is called *sequence,* and it is a "bread and butter" technique of Baroque composers. It is encountered again and again in Baroque works.

LISTENING GUIDE

BACH: TOCCATA, ADAGIO, AND FUGUE IN C MAJOR, BWV 564

Fugue (Record 2, Side 1)

Exposition

0:00 Subject, in four distinct phrases, is presented in first voice alone, at moderately high pitch level:

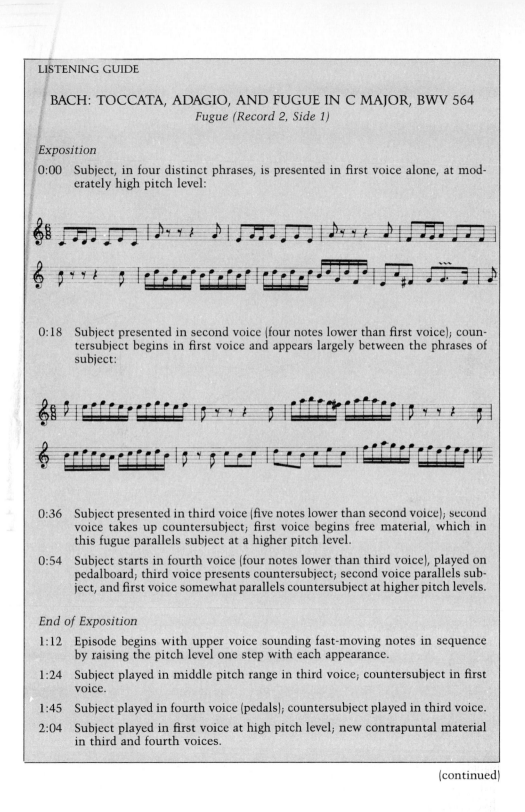

0:18 Subject presented in second voice (four notes lower than first voice); countersubject begins in first voice and appears largely between the phrases of subject:

0:36 Subject presented in third voice (five notes lower than second voice); second voice takes up countersubject; first voice begins free material, which in this fugue parallels subject at a higher pitch level.

0:54 Subject starts in fourth voice (four notes lower than third voice), played on pedalboard; third voice presents countersubject; second voice parallels subject, and first voice somewhat parallels countersubject at higher pitch levels.

End of Exposition

1:12 Episode begins with upper voice sounding fast-moving notes in sequence by raising the pitch level one step with each appearance.

1:24 Subject played in middle pitch range in third voice; countersubject in first voice.

1:45 Subject played in fourth voice (pedals); countersubject played in third voice.

2:04 Subject played in first voice at high pitch level; new contrapuntal material in third and fourth voices.

(continued)

2:25	Episode similar to first episode, with third voice sounding rapidly moving notes sequentially.
2:38	Subject played in second voice; first voice has running notes derived from countersubject.
2:56	Subject played in third voice (in minor key); second voice partially imitates subject one measure later; first voice continues running notes in sequence.
3:15	Episode uses figures in sequence, outlining chords similar to free material appearing earlier with subject, except that patterns basically ascend instead of descend.
3:22	Subject returns in fourth voice (pedals) rather loudly; countersubject in third voice.
3:40	Episode begins in first voice, with fast notes in sequence; very similar to initial episode; followed by sequence that descends.
4:09	Subject makes final appearance in fourth voice, loud, doubled with low pitch level; other three voices sound free material.
4:27	Free material containing a figure repeated in sequence; long, low pedal tone sustained until nearly the conclusion.
4:56	Closes with a rather low-pitched chord.

The conclusion of the Fugue in C Major offers another example of sequence and another technique associated with the organ.

Sequence appears in the treble-clef part and then in the upper notes of the upper bass-clef part in the second line. This time the pitch moves down one step with each beat and finally even more often. The technique associated with the organ is the long low note in the lower bass-clef part, the part played on the pedals. This steady, long pitch is called *pedal point.* The effect of such a note is interesting. It starts as a note fitting in with the chord, but then it doesn't change as the chords above it change. Still it persists, and eventually it "wins out" as the music works back to a chord in which it is a member. The pedal point technique is easy to play on the organ because of the pedalboard and the strong low notes available on the instrument. It is so associated with the organ that the technique is called pedal point even when written in orchestral compositions.

OTHER ORGAN FORMS

The fugue is not the only form that is particularly well suited to the organ, although it is perhaps the most important. Two others are based on the chorale: one is called *chorale variations;* the other, the *chorale prelude.* Variation technique will be discussed later in this book. For the present it can be described as the treatment of a theme that is repeated several times in succession but with modifications each time. The chorale prelude is a contrapuntal piece built around a chorale melody.

A third type of music well suited to organ is the *passacaglia* (pah-sa-*cahl*-yah). It begins with a statement of the theme, usually in the bass and without accompaniment. This melody, in triple meter, is repeated over and over in its original form, but new variations are added in other voices each time. The melody is likely to stay in the bass throughout. (The pedals are ideal for maintaining the rather slow-moving melody, leaving the hands free to play the faster, higher-pitched lines of music.) The continuous repetition, combined with continuous variation, can lead to a fascinating composition. One of Bach's finest organ works is his Passacaglia in C Minor.

Some types of pieces that were common for the harpsichord were also written for organ. One such type was the *toccata,* a flashy work with many rapid scale passages. The *prelude* was another; in the Baroque the word simply meant a short piece of instrumental music.

14

BAROQUE INSTRUMENTAL MUSIC: THE SUITE AND CONCERTO GROSSO

The organ is strongly associated with church music. There was, however, another kind of instrumental music during the Baroque: secular music written not for the organ but for orchestral instruments and for the harpsichord. This nonorgan music took three forms—suite, sonata, and concerto.

THE SUITE

The word *suite* (sweet) simply means a series or set of items that belong together—a suite of rooms or a suite of furniture. In the Baroque period, a suite referred to a collection of dances that were intended for performance as a group.

These dances were *stylized;* that is, they were "dressed up" to make them interesting pieces for listening. Composers wrote their own music for them, but meter, tempo, and other characteristics were like dance types. A contemporary composer might do the same thing by taking a popular dance of a generation or more ago, say the fox trot or Charleston, and writing similar music with more interesting melodies and harmonies while retaining the essential rhythm and style of the original dance music. This is what Bach and other Baroque composers did. They took several contrasting dances that were no longer in vogue and stylized them for listening, not dancing.

Many different dances were incorporated into suites. The four most common dances were the allemande, courante, sarabande, and gigue. The *allemande* (*ahla*-mahnd) (which means "German" in French) probably came from Germany. It has a moderate tempo and a rather continuous pattern of eighth or sixteenth notes. The *courante* (koo-*rahnt*) was French in origin. It moves a little more rapidly than the allemande. The *sarabande* (*sah*-ra-bahnd) is a slow dance. It was probably imported by the Spaniards from Mexico. The *gigue* (zheeg) originated in Britain, where it was called "jig." It is lively and is appropriately placed as the final dance in a suite. It also tends to be more contrapuntal in character than most dance types. With elements drawn from many countries, the Baroque suite is an international music form.

Other dances less frequently found in the suite are the bourrée, minuet, gavotte, loure, polonaise, and passepied. Often a composer wrote a *double*—a variation of the dance preceding it. Many times a suite is preceded by a prelude or overture. It is customary for all the dances in a suite to be written in the same key, with the double in the parallel major or minor key. The composer achieves variety by arranging the movements so that the faster dances contrast with slower ones. Most dances are in two-part form, with each part repeated.

Suites originally were composed for keyboard instruments, but later they were written also for orchestra.

Harpsichord by Johannes Daniel Dulcken, Antwerp, 1745.

Bach's Suite No. 3

One of the best-known suites for orchestra is Suite No. 3 by Bach.* The orchestra consists of strings (violin I, violin II, viola, and cello, with double bass doubling the cello part), keyboard, two oboes, three trumpets, and timpani. The addition of trumpets and timpani gave rise to the term "festival" orchestra. The keyboard player was the leader of the orchestra and normally the other musicians sat on either side of him.

In Bach's time the overture was more than a short introductory section; it could and often did stand as an independent composition. The overture for Bach's Suite No. 3 is typical of the form. It is the longest movement of the work. It begins in a slow tempo and has a massive, throbbing quality. The middle portion is contrapuntal and in a quick-moving tempo. The overture closes with a portion of the music that was used at the beginning of the piece.

The middle portion of the overture illustrates a concept of string playing that was prevalent in the Baroque era. The traditional style of playing in the early development of the violin was a rapid back-and-forth rubbing motion of the bow on the strings. Smooth, sustained playing was a later development. Partly because of tradition and partly because of the bow's construction, Bach and other composers wrote string parts with many repeated notes and measure after measure of continuous eighth and sixteenth notes. This style of playing adds a certain charm to Baroque music.

The second movement of the suite is an *air*. Like an aria an air is melodious. This one contains some of Bach's most beautiful writing. The movement is widely known as Air for the G String, so named after an arrangement for violin solo. The arrangement was done not by Bach but by a nineteenth-century violinist. Sometimes it is performed in a manner that conveys a sentimentality not intended by Bach.

In the original version of the Air the first violins play a gentle melody:

*Designations were not consistent during the Baroque period. Bach often called suites "overtures," and this work was originally so titled. In the present discussion, the term "overture" refers only to the opening movement of the composition, and the word "suite" refers to the entire work.

The third measure in the example begins with a long A. Its motion swings down and back up again. The interest of the melody is increased through the repeating of a two-note descending figure occurring at successively higher pitch levels. To emphasize the pattern further, rhythmic stress is felt on the circled notes. The same pattern is repeated in the next measure, but one note lower.

The musical success of the Air lies as much in the other parts as it does in the melody itself. The violin II and viola lines weave together effectively with the melody. The motion of one tends to answer the motion of another. When the melody sustains a long tone, another part usually has a moving figure. Cellos and basses outline the chords in simple eighth notes. The line sounds almost as though it were walking gently, first moving down the scale and then easing its way back to where it started. Rather then repeat each pitch at the same level, Bach writes the second note to sound either an octave higher or lower, a simple technique that adds just the right amount of interest.

In fact, the whole work is simple, so superbly simple. Bach creates a mood of serenity and yet adds enough motion to hold the listener's interest. This music illustrates the manner in which a great composer uses the usual patterns of chords and notes and adds to them the proper proportion of change and imagination.

The Air is followed by two *gavottes,* each with the typical two beats per measure that characterize this dance type. The gavottes are followed by a *bourrée* (boo-*ray*). The bourrée also has two beats to a measure, but it moves more quickly than the gavotte. The suite concludes with a gigue, which was favored as the last movement in suites because of its light mood and fast tempo.

In some respects Bach's Suite No. 3 is not typical of the form. Only one of its dances, the gigue, was a standard component in the average suite. Furthermore, the work was written for orchestra instead of for a keyboard instrument. Composers in Baroque times did not always specify which keyboard instrument they wanted. In Bach's famous *Well-Tempered Clavier* the word "clavier" does not refer to a special kind of piano; rather it means simply "keyboard." The pieces in that collection might have been played originally on the clavichord, harpsichord, or organ.

Bach's English Suite No.2

The lighter sound of the harpsichord and the mechanism of its action are especially conducive to the playing of rapid decorative notes. Since the harpsichord figured so prominently in the Baroque period, decorative notes became an integral part of Baroque keyboard music. These ornaments were sometimes indicated by an elaborate set of stenographic symbols; at other times they were notated in full by the composer. Both methods can be seen in the following two excerpts. Sometimes composers wrote a second, ornamented version of a stylized dance. Bach did this with the sarabande from Suite No. 2 of the English Suites. Here is an excerpt from the less decorated sarabande:

Here is the ornamented version of the same passage.

The arrows in the foregoing excerpts point to the ornament symbols, and the circled notes in the second excerpt show two passages with the ornamentation notated.

The piano and harpsichord both have the same characteristic: As soon as a sound is produced, it begins to fade away. It is impossible, therefore, to increase the volume of a tone after it is first sounded. Even the use of a sustaining pedal cannot maintain the tone at a constant level of loudness. A composer often writes many notes in pieces for the harpsichord and piano, partly because of the instruments' inability to sustain sound, and partly because many notes can be played at about the same time. In the Bach sarabande cited earlier, seldom does a beat pass without the appearance of a second note sounded shortly after the first.

An even clearer example of this practice is Bourée I (Record 2, Side 1) from the same suite:

Here Bach uses the notes that are found in a particular chord, but instead of having them sound together (and then fade together), he strings them out one after another, to produce what are called "broken" chords. One such chord has been circled and is also shown in its normal form.

In the Suite No. 3 by Bach and in most Baroque music the levels of loudness are indicated only occasionally. During this time the performer was given considerable freedom in deciding how the music should sound. In fact, the performer was often also the composer, so there was no need to write out how the music should be performed.

There is another reason for the lack of detail in the composer's directions. It is hard for us today to appreciate the demand for new music during the eighteenth century. There were no established "classics" from which performers could draw. The result was a prodigious output from many composers. Since they were under pressure to turn out large amounts of music, which, like magazine articles, would soon outlive their usefulness, composers did not fuss over each detail.

The harpsichord slowly passed from the musical scene after Bach's death. It was replaced by the piano, with its more flexible loudness levels and its more solid and forceful tone. The twentieth century has seen a revival of interest in the harpsichord.

THE BAROQUE SONATA

In the Baroque period the word *sonata* referred to an instrumental piece. This definition is admittedly broad, but it is about the only one that can be stated without qualification. Early Baroque sonatas involved several instruments and tended to evolve into two types: one developed along the lines of the suite, and the other, which came to be known as the sonata, included several subtypes. One, called *trio sonata,* had three parts played by four performers and will be explained later in the book. Another subtype involved one instrument plus accompaniment. A third type figured prominently in the music of Bach: a sonata for one unaccompanied instrument.

The sonata was generally made up of movements that alternated between slow and fast tempos. A three-movement sonata had a fast-slow-fast arrangement, while a four-movement sonata was likely to be arranged into slow-fast-slow-fast segments.

THE CONCERTO GROSSO

A favorite musical effect during Baroque times was the contrast between groups of instruments or what is called *concerted style,* and it took two forms. One of these stressed the contrast between types of instruments, such as woodwinds versus strings. The other, and more common, technique was the contrast of a large group against a small group or an individual player. This form later developed into the *concerto:* a large group contrasted with a single player or small group.

The more common type of concerto during the Baroque period was the *concerto grosso* ("grand concerto"), in which a small group was pitted against a large group. There is little difference in instrumentation or in the music that each group performs. No attempt is made to have the small group "show off," as is true in later concertos. The small group remains seated and often plays along in unison with the large group. Usually concerti grossi are composed for strings, with a harpsichord helping out on the harmonies. A few wind instruments are sometimes included in the small group. For example, four of the six frequently heard Brandenburg Concertos by Bach contain solo parts for winds.

The fact that the same or similar instruments play the same music sometimes makes it difficult to distinguish which group is playing. The orchestra of Bach's day was small, so the larger group was not large by today's standards. Also, three or four good string players can produce a healthy, vigorous sound. Recordings tend to make the groups less distinguishable by taking away most of the physical distance that is present in live performances.

Corelli's Christmas Concerto

Arcangelo Corelli's Concerto Grosso, Op. 6, No. 8 (*Christmas Concerto*) is one of many concerti grossi written in the seventeenth and early eighteenth centuries. The "Christmas" part of the title comes from the inscription on the music: "Composed for the night of the Nativity, 1712." The other connection with Christmas is the last movement, the pastorale. It is intended to give the feeling of the bagpipe music of the shepherds who visited the infant Jesus. The solo group consists of two violins and cello accompanied by a string orchestra and keyboard, a typical instrumentation for a concerto grosso. The music is typical also in the contrasting tempos that distinguish its various sections.

The first movement (Record 3, Side 2) opens with a fast, short introduction that is followed by a slow, deliberate section featuring the full orchestra throughout.

The pattern of the first two pitches of the theme is imitated as the parts enter. The music is quite contrapuntal.

The first movement continues with a fast tempo featuring the two solo violins. The melody is built around a short fragment that is only two measures long and contains only four different pitches.

As indicated by the brackets, the fourth and fifth measures are similar to the first two, except that most of the pitches are higher than they were the first time—an example of sequence. In this particular movement the two violin parts weave around each other in contrapuntal fashion. Many times there is a dissonance that resolves to a consonance on the second half of the beat. Hearing the interplay of consonance and dissonance is one of the pleasures of listening to this type of music.

The second movement consists of three sections in a slow-fast-slow pattern of tempos. Again the violins are featured, and again sequence can be heard. In the notation of the theme, a bracket has been put over the figure that appears sequentially at different pitch levels. The theme is not heard immediately; the movement opens and closes with an accompanying figure.

The third movement is fast, and has a meter with three rapidly moving beats per measure.

In the fourth movement the second violins imitate a portion of the first violin part. As the music moves along, a soft, flowing figure alternates with full sounding chords.

The fifth movement is a pastorale, a gentle rocking melody in 12/8 meter. Pastorales were popular in Baroque music; Handel's *Messiah* includes one.

OTHER BAROQUE COMPOSERS

Jean-Baptiste Lully

Jean-Baptiste Lully lived from 1632 until 1687. Though he was Italian by birth, he made his way into the court of the French kings by wit and luck. There he changed his name from Italian to the French version by which he has been known throughout history. Lully was a supreme entertainer in what at the time was the most sumptuous court in Europe. He staged dance spectaculars that were the favorites of the king of France. His major musical contribution was the development of the *French overture.* It is an instrumental form with a slow introduction in a heavy style with dotted rhythms, a middle section with imitation of a short melody, and occasionally a third section in a slow tempo. The story of Lully's death is apparently true. To keep the performers together he would beat time by pounding a stick on the floor. One day he happened to hit his toe with the stick, his foot became infected, and he died.

Arcangelo Corelli

Arcangelo Corelli, the leading exponent of Italian violin playing, lived from 1653 until 1713. Educated in Bologna, he spent most of his life in Rome, where he was admired as a violinist and composer. His music promoted the technical and tonal capabilities of the instrument. He is known only for his sonatas and concerti grossi. His body lies in the Pantheon in Rome, not far from that of the painter Raphael.

Antonio Vivaldi

Vivaldi (c. 1675–1741) is much admired by musicians, but is not so well known by the general public. He was a prolific composer who turned out an enormous amount of music of practically every type. He was born in Venice and was the son of a violinist. As a young man he was ordained a priest, but a few years later he decided on a musical career. The job he held for most of his life was as a teacher in a girls' music school. He wrote many works for the girls to play or sing, including concertos for violin, flute, bassoon, guitar, mandolin, and piccolo. One of his most famous works is *The Four Seasons,* which is a group of four concerti grossi with a solo violin part; each depicts a different season of the year. One can almost hear the people's teeth chattering in winter and feel the warm breezes of spring.

Georg Phillipp Telemann

Telemann was born in 1685 and lived until 1767. He was one of the most famous composers of the first half of the eighteenth century. Most of his life was spent around Hamburg. He left behind an enormous amount of music—40 operas, 44 Passions, 12 Lutheran services, and more than 3,000 works of other types. He was adept at composing instrumental music, including a number of well-known flute works.

PART THREE
CLASSICAL MUSIC

15

CLASSICISM, CLASSICAL MUSIC, AND SONATA FORM

By the time of Bach's death in 1750, the Baroque style had faded in popularity. In fact, Bach's own sons thought of their father as something of an out-of-date old man, a not unknown attitude of sons toward their fathers. But the world *was* changing. Passing was the intensity of religious feeling. Gone was the love of the dramatic and grandiose. A new age had arrived, one that would see significant changes in the style of art and music.

THE ROCOCO SUBPERIOD

As with all stylistic periods in music, the Classical period did not have a clearly marked beginning. An early instance of the gradual departure from the heavy, complex Baroque style was the *Rococo* or *galant style,* which began early in the eighteenth century in the courts of Europe, especially France. It was the art of the aristocracy, of the people at the lavish courts of Versailles and similar places. Like the aristocracy, Rococo music and art were light, elegant, and frivolous. In painting the Rococo was represented by Fragonard, Watteau, and Boucher. Their subject matter was often fanciful love, and their pictures were laced with figures of cupids and thinly clad nymphs. Boucher's *Venus Consoling Love* (plate 8) is typical. Rococo furniture and clothing were highly decorated. The lace cuff and the powdered wig were in vogue, and elegant manners were cultivated.

François Couperin (1668–1733) is probably most representative of Rococo composers. He wrote a large amount of music, mostly suites, for the clavecin, the French version of the harpsichord. These compositions served as models for Bach when he wrote his French and English Suites. Couperin's music was highly embellished, with many ornaments added to the happy, short melodies.

Although music and art in the Rococo style were not profound, they served as a pleasant diversion for the aristocracy during much of the eighteenth century. More important, the Rococo represented a break away from the complex counterpoint of the Baroque, and it ushered in a new type of music.

THE CLASSICAL ATTITUDE

During the Classical period, which scholars consider to be roughly from 1750 to 1825, several conditions in society influenced the artist and composer. The first of these was a new intellectual outlook of such scope that the period came to be called the Age of Enlightenment or the Age of Reason. The trend was strongly influenced by Descartes, Diderot, Moses Mendelssohn (grandfather of Felix Mendelssohn, an important composer of the Romantic period), Spinoza, and others who revived and added to the idealistic, idea-centered philosophy of ancient Greece. In fact, the word "classical" traditionally refers to the reason and restraint found in the life of the ancient Athenians.

Briefly, the philosophy of the eighteenth-century thinkers was this: First, truth can be realized only by the process of reason, so an emphasis must be placed on learning and intellectual pursuits. Second, the universe is a machine governed by inflexible laws that human beings cannot override. Therefore, what is true is true throughout the world; it is universal. Third, emotions as a guide to truth are false, so rational intellect should control human behavior. The intellectuals of the Classical period were not impressed by the unknown, since they believed that in time they would come to know it through thought and knowledge. They rejected the past, especially the Middle Ages, because they felt mysticism had stifled natural human capacities. Reason, not faith, was to be mankind's beacon.

The American Declaration of Independence written in 1776 is a thoroughly Classical document. It is difficult for us, who tend to think of revolutionaries as bomb-throwing zealots, to consider Jefferson, Washington, Adams, and the others as revolutionaries. But revolutionaries they were, even though their demands and statements of purpose were shaped in the language of reason and Classical thought. These individuals were cultured, intelligent, reasonable men, and their Declaration shows it. Although at its conclusion they pledge "our Lives, our Fortunes, and our Sacred Honor," the Declaration is essentially a legal brief, a list of the colonists' grievances against the King of England. Instead of screaming "Death to the tyrant!" Jefferson begins "When in the course of human events, it becomes necessary for one people to dissolve the political bands which have connected them with another. . . ." At a moment that would seem to require a display of emotion—the declaring of national independence and the pledging of one's life to a cause—the intellectual and political leaders were dispassionate, restrained, sensible, logical.

Another example of the Classical spirit comes from the world of painting: Jacques Louis David's *The Oath of the Horatii* (plate 9).

Patronage

Although it was beginning to wane, patronage was very much a part of the Classical era. The patronage system was one in which a composer accepted exclusive employment under the auspices of a patron. Patrons were either the wealthy (and sometimes decadent) aristocracy or the Church. The more frivolous taste of the aristocracy gave impetus to the movement away from the heaviness of Baroque counterpoint and toward the lighter style of the Classical period. When a composer found a good patron, a secure position and an audi-

---

JEFFERSON AND THE ENLIGHTENMENT

As Leonardo da Vinci is the example of the "Renaissance man" (see page 126), Thomas Jefferson (1743–1826) is the best personification of the Enlightenment and the Classical age. Like Leonardo, Jefferson could do many things extremely well. While he was not a painter, he was a good architect. He designed his home, Monticello, on the principles of the Italian Renaissance architect Andrea Palladio, and that basic design can be seen today in the Jefferson Monument and the Library of Congress. He was a cultured man, a fine violinist, and a good singer and dancer. He was well educated and had a real love of knowledge. He founded the University of Virginia, and it was Jefferson's personal library that was the nucleus for the Library of Congress. Fluent in six languages, he was a first-rate scholar in the classics. He translated several books from their original language, including the Bible. He had a talent for mathematics and mechanical things. Among his inventions are a swivel chair, a major improvement in the blade of the plow, a dumbwaiter, a four-way music stand for string quartet playing, and many other conveniences that can be seen at Monticello, just outside Charlottesville, Virginia. Also, he applied science to farming and was knowledgeable about meteorology.

Today, Jefferson is best remembered for his great influence on the development of the United States and his contributions as a statesman. In addition to being the author of the Declaration of Independence, he served as ambassador to France, Secretary of State, Vice President, and third President. The Louisiana Purchase was the result of his insight and efforts. Although he believed in God, he opposed strongly any connection between church and state. Five years before such ideas were included in the United States Constitution he secured the passage of the Virginia Statute for Religious Liberty, which guaranteed religious freedom and made it il-

---

ence for his compositions was assured. The writing of new works was expected. At its best, patronage was a good incubator for creative talent.

There were liabilities, however. Most serious among these was the fact that composers had to please their patrons, or else they found themselves helping in the stables or looking for a new patron. The result was much trivial music written according to standard formulas. Too, the patronage system regarded composers not as unique creative artists, but as the source of a product for the privileged classes to use and enjoy. Since the relationship between composers and their work was taken lightly, it was common practice for composers to borrow themes and ideas from one another. In fact, plagiarism was understood to be a form of flattery and commendation. Legal niceties such as copyrights and royalties were unheard of. Not until the advent of the Romantic philosophy of the nineteenth century did composers feel compelled to create in a way that was uniquely individual.

---

legal for any Virginian to be compelled to "support any religious worship, place or ministry whatsoever." Though unable to abolish slavery, he was able in 1778 to get the Virginia legislature to pass a law prohibiting the importing of slaves.

So rich and diverse were Jefferson's talents and accomplishments that President John F. Kennedy was prompted to say to a White House reception for 125 distinguished scholars, including 42 Nobel Prize winners, "This is probably the greatest concentration of talent in this house except for perhaps those times Thomas Jefferson ate alone."

Monticello, Thomas Jefferson's home at Charlottesville, Virginia. Designed by Jefferson himself, the building shows the symmetry and balance typical of the Classical period.

WOLFGANG AMADEUS MOZART

Of all the names in the Classical period, Wolfgang Amadeus Mozart stands out. His music has about it a clearness, delicacy, and simplicity that seem to defy analysis. His music is so—musical!

Mozart was born in 1756 in Salzburg, Austria. His father, Leopold, was a recognized violinist and composer in the court of the archbishop. The elder Mozart was quick to realize and capitalize on his son's extraordinary talents. Under his father's teaching, young Mozart showed remarkable mastery of the piano and to a lesser extent the violin. By the time he was five he had composed his first pieces, and at six he performed at the court of the Empress Maria Theresa. When he was seven Mozart and his sister, who was four years his elder, went on a tour of Europe that included Paris, London, and Munich. By the age of thirteen he had written concertos, symphonies, and a comic opera; at fourteen he was knighted by the Pope.

The most phenomenal aspect of Mozart's musical talent was his memory for music and his ability to work out whole pieces in his mind. He once wrote, "Though it be long, the work is complete and finished in my mind. I take out of the bag of my memory what has previously been collected into it. For this reason the committing to paper is done quickly enough. For everything is already finished, and it rarely differs on paper from what it was in my imagination."

Mozart never enjoyed the stability of a good appointment as a composer to a patron. For a while he worked for the Prince-Archbishop of Salzburg. The Archbishop was a difficult man, and the high-spirited Mozart resented the restrictions of the patronage system. (He wrote his father, "The two valets sit at the head of the table. I at least have the honor of sitting above the cooks.") He quarreled with the Archbishop and was dismissed. At the age of twenty-five he left Salzburg to pursue his career in Vienna.

Since Mozart did not fare well under the patronage system, he spent the last ten years of his life, as he put it, "Hovering between hope and anxiety." Due in part to his impractical and overgenerous nature in financial affairs, he had to eke out an existence by teaching, giving concerts, composing, and borrowing from friends.

In 1791, at the age of thirty-five, Mozart died of uremic poisoning. Because he was so deeply in debt, he was given the cheapest funeral and buried in a pauper's grave.

Despite his short life and its disappointments, Mozart composed over 600 works: 22 operas, 25 piano concertos, 12 violin concertos, 14 concertos for other instruments, 24 string quartets, 60 solo works for piano, 27 choral works, and 52 symphonies. Mozart never used opus numbers, although some were added later by publishers. His works were catalogued by a Viennese botanist and amateur musician named Köchel (see page 60).

SONATA FORM

The composers of the Classical period developed several forms for the individual movements of compositions. The most important of these was the *first movement, sonata-allegro,* or, more commonly, *sonata form.* This form proved so satisfactory that it served for practically all the first movements of Classical symphonies, concertos, sonatas, and string quartets, for some fourth movements, and even a few second movements. With modifications it has served composers until the twentieth century, and it is still used occasionally today. Its widespread acceptance came about without deliberate promotion; no convention of composers was called at which time it was decided that the musical plan called "sonata form" was to be the prescribed form for first movements. Rather, composers write in patterns that seem musically satisfying to them, and the result is a frequent use of the pattern known as sonata form.

Sonata form should not be confused with the term "sonata" meaning an entire piece. Sonata form involves only *one* movement. A sonata has several movements. Although Classical and Romantic sonatas usually have at least one movement in sonata form, the form is not limited to compositions called sonatas.

Mozart's Symphony No. 40 in G Minor, K.550, is an excellent work

Wolfgang Amadeus Mozart. An unfinished painting by Joseph Lange, his brother-in-law.

through which to examine the symphony and sonata form. The symphony was written in the summer of 1788 along with two other symphonies, Symphony No. 39 and Symphony No. 41, the *Jupiter.* The year was probably the most disappointing one of Mozart's personal life. Little is known about the circumstances that precipitated the writing of these symphonies, but it is probable that Mozart never heard them performed. The instruments called for in Symphony No. 40 are violins, violas, cellos and double basses (different parts were not yet written for the latter two instruments), a flute, two oboes, two bassoons, and two French horns. Mozart himself later added parts for two clarinets. The orchestra is noticeably smaller than the modern symphony orchestra. There are fewer kinds of instruments and the string sections are smaller. When playing Mozart symphonies today, most professional orchestras do not use all of their regular string players.

First Movement—Sonata Form. The first movement of Symphony No. 40 is in sonata form (Record 3, Side 1). With no introduction, it opens in a moderately fast tempo with this first theme:

Several interesting points can be made about these nine measures:

1. The theme is broken into two equal parts, the second being nearly identical to the first, but one note lower. Each half is further divided in half, the first portion sounding like a melodic statement and the second like a musical answer. So the melody contains symmetry.

2. With its many rapidly moving notes, the theme would not be well suited to singing, but it is well suited to the violins that play it.

3. The theme is disarmingly simple. This same rhythmic pattern appears in each of the four phrases. Similar rhythmic patterns can easily be found in other musical works. The quarter notes suggest basic chords: D D D B-flat (G minor), G E-flat C C (C minor), and so on. To this simple structure Mozart adds some musical "pepper"—a little dissonance. The eighth notes marked with an X in the example are not in the harmony of the chord. Since they are short and do not occur on the beat, the effect is not one of harshness. It is rather like a quick nudge.

4. The repeating of the three-note figure in the melody creates a sense of forward movement, a quality that is necessary for interesting music.

5. The melody is in a minor key, which adds its own particular mood to the piece. Many composers of the Romantic period used the sound of minor to achieve gloomy, bleak music, but not Mozart. He uses it to add only a tinge of color; never does it become sticky and sentimental.

6. The melody is, in a sense, a collection of several melodic fragments. It is not a sweeping, overarching array of tones. It is neat and precise. Not only does this type of melody fit well with the Classical attitude; it is also very suitable for development.

After a few closing chords, the theme begins to be repeated. But this time, halfway through, the music shifts to some solid chords and rapid, running scales—a *transition* of fifteen measures. The transition acts as a bridge to the second theme and a new key. It might seem that a transition does not need to have much musical interest in itself, if its function is merely to join one theme to another. However, a fine composer like Mozart can make a transition musically quite interesting. The end of the transition is easily identified by its two closing chords followed by a measure of rest. These clear-cut demarcations of form are typical of the Classical style.

There are two reasons for transitions. One is that in sonata form the second theme is almost always presented in a different key, so a modulation is needed. The first theme is in the *tonic* key, the key that predominates in a movement. If the tonic key is a major, the second theme will almost always be in the key that is centered five notes higher (the dominant key). If the original key is minor, as in the case of this Symphony No. 40, the second theme is usually in the relative major, the major key that uses the same key signature but has a tonal center one and a half steps higher.

There is another reason for the existence of a transition. Composers found that presenting a new theme on the heels of the first one was not musically satisfying.

The second theme is played between the violins and the woodwinds:

It differs from the first. It has longer note values and does not contain the repeated rhythmic pattern. There are few skips up or down to other notes. The theme is more difficult to remember than the first. In fact, it comes dangerously near being innocuous. The two themes in sonata form are seldom similar in mood or style; one contrasts with the other.

When the second theme of this movement has been completed, a transitionlike passage appears. Interspersed in it are fragments of the first theme, which are sounded alternately between the clarinet and bassoon. At this place in sonata form, composers have some options. Sometimes they introduce a third theme, at other times they engage in an extended transition, and occasionally they borrow a fragment of one of the preceding themes, which is what Mozart does here.

The transitional section following the second theme concludes with a *codetta.* It is simply a short concluding section. Often a brief melody is associated with it.

Exposition. So far only the first third of the movement has been presented. In it Mozart presents or exposes the musical ideas for the movement. The section, therefore, is called the *exposition.* The exposition can be diagrammed:

EXPOSITION				
First theme (in tonic key)	Transition	Second theme (in dominant key or relative major)	Transition	Codetta (in dominant key or relative major)

Normally a composer indicates a repeat of the entire exposition. In performances today this sign is frequently ignored, and the music moves right into the next section, the development.

Development. In music, *development* means the manipulation of the themes. It is a demonstration of the composer's ability to present the themes in different and musically satisfying ways. Development means more than variation of a theme, however. Variation is a limited concept, suggesting that a theme is given a new setting—a new set of clothes. Development is a restructuring of the theme.

What does Mozart do in the development section of the first movement of his Symphony No. 40? Basically, he treats the first theme in three ways:

1. The first half of the theme is played three times, each time in a new key. Musical interest is achieved by dividing up and shortening the theme and by frequent modulations.

2. Counterpoint is employed. While the lower strings play the first theme in yet another key, the violins begin a countermelody of rapidly moving notes:

When the lower strings finish the first half of the first theme, they take up the countermelody, while the violins play the theme. A similar exchange occurs two more times, with each key center a note lower than its predecessor—an example of sequence.

3. The theme is fragmented even more. The first few notes are tossed back and forth among the flute, clarinet, and violins. Again new keys are used, but the section is quiet as compared with the busy, vigorous exchange that preceded it. Soon the answer in the woodwinds is shortened again to include only the first three notes of the first theme. Several times the direction of the first two notes is inverted, so that they ascend in pitch rather than descend as in the original theme:

Theme fragmentation appears so much throughout this section that bits of the first theme appear in *all but the first two measures* of the development section. Fragments of the theme also appear in the transition leading from the development into the next main section of the sonata form.

In this particular development section Mozart works with only the first theme. He fragments it, modulates frequently, adds countermelodies, and reverses the direction of melodic intervals. These devices are typical of development sections in sonata form. He could have done more. He could have developed the second theme, or he could have introduced an entirely new one. He might have altered the rhythm of the original theme, written different chords to harmonize it, or combined the two themes in a contrapuntal manner. The means of development are endlessly varied.

In sonata form the composer is challenged to show what he can do, not only in writing melodies but, equally important, in manipulating and developing them.

Recapitulation. The term for the third section of sonata form, *recapitulation,* means literally "return to the top." And sure enough, Mozart comes back to the same theme that began the movement. It is played by exactly the same instruments, with exactly the same accompaniment, and it involves exactly the same notes. The literal repetition is quite short. At first, the changes are small; the bassoon adds a few notes in contrast to the theme. But as the music moves into the transition heading toward the second theme, more changes occur. The transition is longer than it was in the exposition. In fact, for a short time it sounds like another development section. While the second violins play rapidly moving notes, the short fragment heard just briefly in the exposition is exchanged between the first violins and low strings:

There is another difference: The second theme is not in a new key; it stays in the tonic. If the second theme were in a different key, the composer would be caught off base, away from the home key and near the end of the movement. He would need to get back to the tonic in a hurry and make the key change sound convincing—a difficult thing to do. So the second theme stays in the same key as the first in the recapitulation. Following the second theme the transitional music is similar to that found at the comparable place in the exposition.

The movement ends with a *coda.* The coda is like the codetta except that it is longer, which provides the movement with a convincing conclusion. In the coda to this movement Mozart again utilizes a fragment from the first theme. Chords alternate between dominant and tonic as one movement of one symphony concludes.

No two movements in sonata form are exactly alike. Each example contains some deviations from the form. In general, however, sonata form can be diagrammed as shown on page 207. Although this symphony does not have a slow introduction before the exposition, many first movements in sonata form do have this optional feature.

Two more points need to be mentioned about sonata form. One is key. The Classical composers were quite careful in their use of keys. Mozart's Symphony No. 40 is planned around the key of G minor. The first movement is expected to begin, end, and center around its tonic key, and the other movements are planned accordingly. The second movement is in E-flat major, a closely related key because it has only one flat more than the original key of G minor. The third and fourth movements are in G minor. This attention to

EXPOSITION				DEVELOPMENT	RECAPITULATION				
First theme (tonic)	Trans.	Second theme (dominant (or relative major)	Trans. Codetta ....)	Working over of musical ideas. Sometimes new melodies introduced	First theme (tonic	Trans.	Second theme	Trans.	Coda ....)

key may have had an effect on the eighteenth-century listener; it is hard to say how people heard things 200 years ago. Today we are used to music that modulates frequently, so the impact of key change in the Classical symphony is reduced.

The other point that needs to be mentioned is the unity of everything in the form. Sometimes people not familiar with the form assume that only the themes are worthy of attention, while transitions and development are merely "fillers." But a transition does far more than connect themes and provide modulations; it has musical interest in itself, and it contributes to the total impact of the music. A coda has a necessary place in providing a feeling of completeness. Knowing the themes is only the first step in understanding a movement in sonata form.

What do Jefferson's Declaration of Independence, David's *The Oath of the Horatii,* and the first movement of Mozart's Symphony No. 40 have in common? In many ways, not much. One is a political document, another is a painting, and the third is a musical work for orchestra. They do, however, reveal a similar outlook and attitude. They are all rational, planned, and logical. The plan of presenting musical material, working with and manipulating it, and then restating it shows thought and reasoning. Also, the type of musical material put in the sonata-form pattern is reasonable and well thought out.

For this reason, listeners should approach this music in a thinking frame of mind. They should notice the nature of the themes and transitions, how the material is balanced with other material, and how themes are developed. It is in doing this that the enjoyment comes in listening to music from the Classical period. To help in learning to listen in this way, a simplified line score of the first movement of Symphony No. 40 is included in the *Study Guide and Scores* book. Listen while following the score until you don't get lost, and until you have a good sense of the patterning of the musical material.

16

THE CLASSICAL SYMPHONY AND CONCERTO

One of the most significant changes in music from the Baroque to the Classical periods was the establishment of the orchestra and the development of a number of musical forms. Until the Classical period, and to some extent in it, there was little difference between music written for large groups and music intended for small ensembles. Furthermore, a composer often did not specify precisely what instruments he wanted. Being a craftsman-artisan in a patronage system, he had to accept whatever instrumentation was available.

THE SYMPHONY

This was soon to change. About the middle of the eighteenth century Mannheim became the site of an orchestra that was to influence the development of music. The Mannheim orchestra was noted for its excellence and its experimentation with new effects, such as the gradual *crescendo* and *decrescendo,* which are standard techniques today. Inevitably, Mannheim attracted composers who wrote music for the orchestra. The pieces they developed through trial and error were called "symphonies." Although these works seem small and immature when compared to the full-fledged symphonies of Haydn and Mozart, they were nevertheless influential.

Since the Classical period the word *symphony* has come to mean a work for orchestra containing four movements. Bach wrote instrumental works that he called "sinfonias," but these were more on the order of overtures for cantatas.

The first movement of the Classical symphony was introduced in describing sonata form in the preceding chapter. That movement is the most sophisticated of the four in a symphony in terms of its musical content, often the longest (not quite true of Mozart's Symphony No. 40), and frequently preceded by an introduction (again, not true of Mozart's Symphony No. 40). Its tempo is moderately fast to fast, and ten times out of ten it is in sonata form.

Second Movement. The second movement of the Symphony No. 40 by Mozart is also in sonata form, which is somewhat unusual. An *A B A* form is much more common. Traditionally, the second movement is slow and melodious, and a theme is difficult to develop in such music. The slow tempo creates a time problem for composers. The time relationships are stretched out, which means that everything, including development, is slowed down. Furthermore, a graceful melody usually does not adapt well to fragmentation or other devices of development. So in this symphony the development section of the second movement is shorter and less important than it was in the first movement. It consists primarily of a first theme and a pattern of coupled quick notes being exchanged between the woodwinds and the strings, concluding with a new short phrase repeated four times. The codetta and coda are not long.

The first theme starts with six equal soundings of the same pitch—hardly a melodious beginning.

But Mozart makes the music interesting by having the theme enter in another instrument. To balance the evenly spaced opening notes, he concludes the theme with a gentle rocking melody that could easily remind one of a gentleman's graceful eighteenth-century bow. The notes altered by natural signs and flats are typical of Mozart's style:

The quick couplet of notes  is interesting. Essentially, Mozart is suggesting a melodic contour that goes:

There is nothing wrong with the two alternate examples, but Mozart's version is more interesting. The quickness of the notes in contrast to the others around them, the short rest that helps the listener to anticipate the important note with its *sforzando* (sudden emphasis)—all these features transform what would have been ordinary into something worth noticing. A subtle change, yes. But it is such subtleties that have caused Mozart's music to be heard 200 years later.

The two quick notes have another function in this movement. Mozart works them into the transitions and the development. In fact, this pattern of notes becomes a *motive*. In music the word "motive" means a brief fragment (sometimes consisting of only two notes) that acts as a unifying theme throughout a movement.

The second theme, in good sonata-form tradition, contrasts with the first:

Notice how symmetrical the theme is. Each short phrase in the first two measures is played twice; then the entire theme is played again. After the second appearance of the theme, the third measure is more decorated, but this version is clearly related to the first. The key of the second theme, typically, is centered around the dominant, five notes higher than the key center of the first theme. Again, the motive appears between the playings of the theme.

The codetta is only nine measures long. It features the throbbing qualities of the first theme in the low strings. The codetta includes an example typical of Mozart's writing:

There are two chords in the last measure. The first chord has tension and dissonance in it. By contrast, the second chord has little tension and is consonant. The motion from the first to the second chord gives a strong feeling of conclusion, a clearly defined ending to this section of the music.

The aural impression gained from these two chords proves again that composers create a constant state of motion by manipulating sounds in time, and they involve the listeners' memory and anticipation while so doing. Normally, the music would have resolved to the tonic chord in the concluding measure, and normal motion would have been quite acceptable. But if only the expected happened in music, it would be less interesting. In this instance Mozart decided to add some interest, to create musical tension by delaying the normal progression of the music. Of course, there are limits to the number of surprises that a listener can accept. Too many unexpected happenings create confusion and frustration. So Mozart handles the *unexpected* (a delay in chord resolution among some sections of the orchestra) in the *expected* way (resolution to the tonic chord). In doing so he achieves that blend of something old and something new described in Chapter 1.

Third Movement—Minuet and Trio. For the third movement of this symphony, Mozart composed the traditional *minuet and trio* (Record 3, Side 1). Stylized dances, of which the minuet is one, were discussed in Chapter 14. Although Classical composers were not so fond of writing music based on stylized dances as were their Baroque predecessors, the minuet was the expected third movement of works containing four movements.

The movement begins at a moderately fast speed with this melody, in the minor key of the symphony:

It contains an unusual rhythmic pattern for the minuct. Normally, the first beat in each measure is the strongest. Instead of following the normal *1 2 3*, *1* 2 3 pattern, Mozart, in this theme, accents almost every other beat in the first five measures: *3*, *1* 2 *3*, 1 *2* 3, *1* 2 *3*, 1 *2* 3. Metrical freedom is common today, so a change such as this is not as impressive as its must have been to the symphony's first hearers. The short fourteen-measure section containing the theme is then repeated exactly.

Next, a thirteen-measure section occurs that is quite similar to the first, but it is in the relative major key, B-flat. The low strings and woodwinds play a two-measure segment much like the first, with this addition: The violins and bassoon play a downward pattern outlining the tonic chord, B-flat major:

On its reappearance the theme is treated somewhat in imitation. The melodic lines are very similar to the original and to each other, but some liberties are taken with them. In this music one violin section enters, then the other. A contrapuntal device such as canon is not so common in the Classical period as in the Baroque. Its presence here, however, demonstrates the fact that some contrapuntal writing is present in all historical periods, even though homophonic music may be predominant at the time.

The trio section derives its name from the fact that traditionally it contained only three instrumental parts: the continuo part plus two other instruments. By the time Mozart wrote his symphony, custom no longer required such sparse instrumentation for the trio, but the distinct change to a quieter mood and fewer players was retained. The trio contrasts with the minuet not only in style and instrumentation, but also in key. In the Symphony No. 40 the minuet is in G minor, and the trio is in the parallel major key, G major. (Major and minor keys are called "parallel" when they have different key signatures but the same starting note.) The first theme of the trio is:

The form of the trio is the same as that of the minuet with the same sections repeated. Its *B* theme merely outlines a chord *and* is not very memorable. After the trio the minuet is heard again exactly as before, but without repeats.

The third movement is based on a strict formal structure:

MINUET	TRIO	MINUET
A *a a b a' b a'*	*B* *a a b a' b a'*	*A* *a b a'*

Of all the forms in the Classical period, the minuet-and-trio structure was the least variable. It presented the composer with the challenge of following tradition and yet writing interesting music, a challenge that Mozart met admirably in this symphony.

A line score of the third movement of Mozart's Symphony No. 40 is provided in the *Study Guide and Scores* book to help listeners to follow the form better. Be sure to notice where the sections are repeated and to what point the repeat applies.

Fourth Movement. As is typical of symphonies in the Classical era, the last movement of Mozart's Symphony No. 40 is lively and brilliant. It moves at a rapid rate and provides an exhilarating finish to the work. In fact, Mozart marked the movement with the word *"finale"* (fee-*nahl*-ee) in addition to a tempo marking. In composing a lively conclusion to a symphony, a composer does not pour profound musical ideas into it. Instead there is a tendency to fall back on simpler ideas, common patterns, and rapid runs of notes, which is what Mozart did in this movement.

Final movements come in several forms, some of which will be presented later. Mozart on this occasion chooses—you guessed it—sonata form. The first theme is based on the notes of the G minor chord. The theme itself was not completely original with Mozart. Many other Classical composers also used a similar pattern, so many in fact that the theme has acquired a nickname, "the Mannheim rocket." Like the first theme in the first movement, the melody again follows a symmetrical statement-answer scheme:

The transition that follows is longer and of more interest than the transitions found in the other movements of the symphony. Again, the end of the transition is easily heard because of the clearly marked phrase ending followed by a rest.

The second theme, again like that of the first movement, contains many chromatic notes and features the woodwinds. It is in the relative major key, B-flat:

A melodic fragment from the first theme occurs frequently in the codetta that concludes the exposition.

The development is built around the first theme. It begins with harmonies that sound unsettled. Soon the "rocket" is passed back and forth between the violins and bassoon. Then the strings treat the theme in imitation. The appearances of the theme in the various string parts are not identical. They are similar enough, however, to suggest the theme strongly. Throughout the development, especially when lines imitate each other, the music modulates many times. The development concludes with the wood-

---

CRAFTSMANSHIP IN COMPOSING

In the nineteenth and twentieth centuries a certain amount of mystery and individual genius has been ascribed to the composing of music. This was not the view of composers or the musical public prior to that time. Bach, Mozart, Haydn, and their contemporaries thought of themselves as highly skilled in the art of musical composition, which they certainly were, but not as creating musical "monuments" that would live throughout the ages. Their view of composing might be compared to that of a writer for a quality magazine who skillfully writes informative and interesting articles. The writer thinks of the articles as well written and useful, but not anything that people will pour over a year or more after publication.

Sometimes one wonders if the composers before 1800 worried much at all about some of the music they composed. Plagiarism was not illegal, and in fact a composer was flattered to have someone else use his theme. Even the great Mozart employed a theme in the fourth movement of his Symphony No. 40 that several other composers of his day had used previously.

Mozart also prepared an ingenious pamphlet in which one throws dice to compose a little piece of music. The pamphlet went through at least six or seven editions, including one published in London under the title *Mozart's Musical Game, fitted in an elegant box, showing by an Easy System how to compose an unlimited number of Waltzes, Rondos, Hornpipes, and Reels.* Mozart's system was to roll the dice for each measure. The system is described and shown in the accompanying pictures. The music is a complete piece, of which only the first eleven measures are shown here. Only the English translation of the original German is pictured. It is quaint, to say the least. In it the word "times" is used to mean "measure" and "in the notes" to mean "in the music." The "Zahlen Tafel" is the table of numbers. The system quarantees that no matter what one's luck with the dice, the results will be a pleasant Mozart-like country dance.

Other composers tried similar methods for composing dance music, including Carl Philipp Emanuel Bach, Franz Joseph Haydn, and Muzio Clementi. One such system attributed to Haydn claimed to be capable of producing "the astounding number of nearly forty-six thousands of millions of different melodies," a statement which proves that all exaggerated advertising did not begin in the twentieth century.

---

winds and strings trading the theme back and forth, followed by an abrupt stop.

The recapitulation is conventional and faithful to the characteristics of the form. The development and recapitulation are marked to be repeated—a direction that is unusual. The coda is almost identical to the codetta except for being slightly expanded.

This symphony, like others, is both typical and unique. It is an excellent example of the style and one by which all symphonies of this period can be better understood.

Music-Tafel für Contra-Tänze.

Instruction

To compose without the least Knowledge of Music, *Country-Dances*, by throwing a certain Number with two Dice.

1) The letters A — H placed at the head of the 8 Columns of the Number-Tables show the 8 times of each part of the Country-Dance, Viz. A, the first, B, the second, C, the third, etc. and the numbers in the Column under the letters, show the number of the time in the notes.

2) The numbers from 2 to 12 show the sum of the number that can be thrown.

3) For inftance, in throwing for the first time of the first part of the Dance, with two Dice, the number 6, one looks next to that number in the Column A, for the 105th time in the notes. This time is written down, and makes the beginning of the Dance. — For the second time, for instance, the number 8, being thrown, turn to the same table Column B, and the number 81 shall be found. This time is put next to the first, and one continues, in this manner till the eight times shall be thrown, when likewise the first part of the Dance shall be finish'd. — The sign of repetition :|: is further placed and the second part begun.

ZAHLEN TAFEL.

Erster Theil.

	A.	B.	C.	D.	E.	F.	G.	H.
2.	70.	14.	164.	122.	25.	153.	18.	167.
3.	10.	64.	100.	12.	149.	30.	161.	11.
4.	33.	1.	160.	163.	77.	156.	168.	172.
5.	36.	114.	8.	35.	111.	39.	137.	44.
6.	105.	150.	57.	71.	117.	52.	132.	130.
7.	165.	152.	112.	15.	147.	27.	73.	102.
8.	7.	81.	131.	37.	21.	125.	49.	115.
9.	142.	106.	40.	69.	43.	140.	23.	89.
10.	99.	68.	86.	139.	120.	92.	143.	83.
11.	85.	45.	90.	158.	82.	123.	78.	58.
12.	145.	97.	6.	121.	56.	67.	63.	16.

Although the solo concerto existed in the Baroque era, the concerto grosso was the more common type. The Classical period, however, saw a complete reversal in the relative popularity of the two forms. The concerto grosso with its small group disappeared almost entirely, not to be resurrected until the twentieth century. The predominant concerto form became the solo concerto, in which one player was featured. Since the concerto grosso was no longer popular, it was not necessary to retain the word "solo" in designating the other form. So, from the Classical period on, the word "concerto" refers to the solo type.

The concerto of the Classical period instituted another change. No longer did it rely as heavily on the contrast between a large group and a small group or solo instrument. The music for the soloist became more elaborate and more difficult than the music for the large accompanying group.

In many ways the concerto is like the symphony. It is a work of some length and importance. It makes use of the same forms as the symphony, and it is divided into movements that are arranged in the same order of tempo and style. There is one difference, however. Usually concertos contain three movements instead of four. The movement dropped from the four-movement scheme is the third—the minuet and trio.

Mozart and Franz Joseph Haydn wrote many concertos, the majority of which were for the usual concerto instruments such as piano and violin. An often overlooked aspect of their genius are the concertos they wrote for unusual solo instruments: the French horn, flute, clarinet, and bassoon. Particularly noteworthy about these concertos is the fact that after nearly 200 years they are still considered among the best for those instruments. Today if a bassoonist or clarinetist plays a concerto with orchestra, it is likely to be a concerto by Mozart; if a trumpeter plays a concerto, it is likely to be the one by Haydn. Equally impressive is the fact that when Mozart and Haydn wrote these works, instruments such as clarinet, French horn, trumpet, and bassoon were technically undeveloped compared to today's models.

Haydn's Concerto for Trumpet and Orchestra

Haydn's Trumpet Concerto in E-flat was composed in 1796 for a keyed (not valve) trumpet. The keys were added to the sides of the instrument somewhat like keys on clarinets and saxophones today. The valves, which are much superior, replaced the keys about 1813. The work was written for the great trumpet virtuoso of the time, Anton Weidinger. He must have been quite a performer, because Haydn did not hesitate to write difficult passages for him to play.

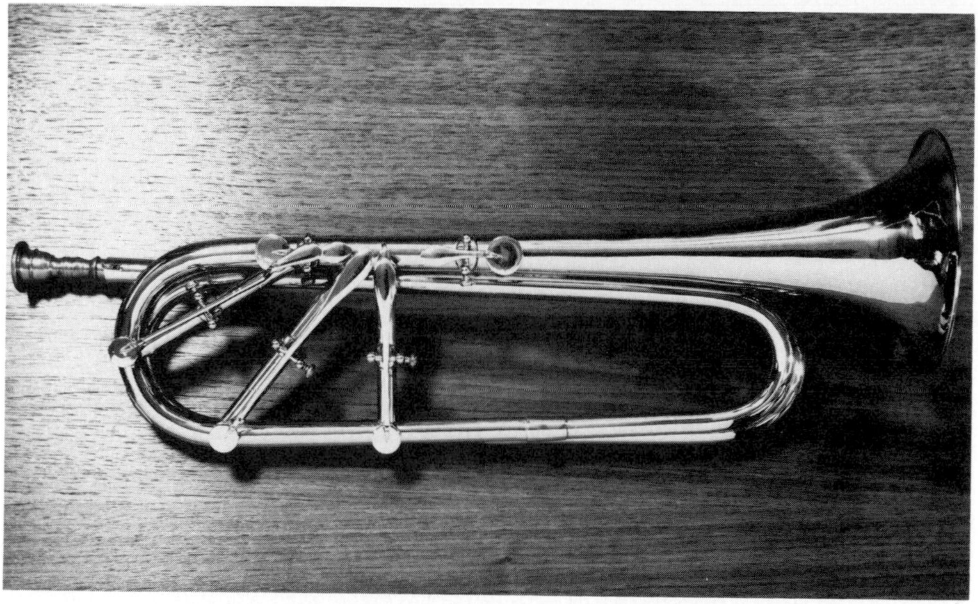

A keyed trumpet.

First Movement. Since the focus of this discussion is on the techniques involved in writing for a soloist and orchestra, and since sonata form has just been presented and, it is hoped, learned, the features of this particular form need not receive detailed attention. Before the soloist begins his main playing efforts, the orchestra presents a shortened version of the exposition. The first and most important theme is:

A second theme is heard soon afterward. It is short and serves as a counterbalance to the first theme.

Toward the middle of the movement the trumpet presents a third theme, one that is derived from the first theme.

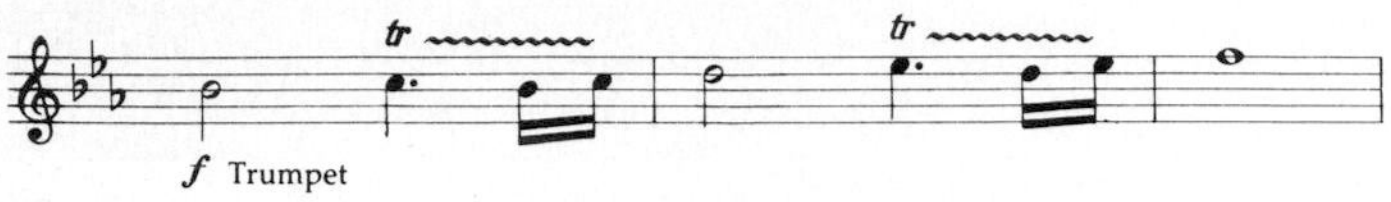

The soloist plays a few short passages before entering on the main theme, which occurs after thirty-six measures have passed. This concerto features the typical *double exposition,* one for the orchestra and one for the soloist. Except for the double exposition, the movement proceeds through the normal sonata form. The development section is shorter and simpler than was its counterpart in the G Minor Symphony. The development section consists more of the addition of different musical ideas than the development of themes.

There is another feature of the concerto that is not found in symphonies. Shortly before the end of the movement, the orchestra comes to a complete stop, and the soloist begins playing alone a freely constructed and often difficult paraphrase of the preceding musical material. Many stops and starts are made, holds and different tempos appear freely, and the rhythm is entirely flexible. This portion of a concerto is called a *cadenza.* During the Classical period it came to be expected in at least one movement of the concerto. The cadenza was conceived as an unabashed opportunity for the performer to show off, both in playing the instrument and in improvising.

Improvisation was a common practice among concert performers in the Classical period. As a part of their piano recitals, both Mozart and Beethoven frequently made up variations on the spot, and were even known to take a theme supplied by someone else and improvise on it immediately. In those days the cadenzas were supposed to be made up by the performers, and theoretically were to be improvised, although one suspects that the performers must have thought out well in advance what would be played in the cadenza. Therefore, Haydn indicated only where the cadenzas were to be inserted in his music; he did not write them out. By the time of the Romantic period, however, composers wrote everything, including the cadenzas.

Second Movement. The second movement is in the style of a pastorale, which is mentioned in conjunction with Corelli's *Christmas Concerto* in Chapter 14. The mood is leisurely and the music melodious. The main theme is played first by the orchestra before the solo trumpet is given a turn at it.

LISTENING GUIDE

HAYDN: CONCERTO FOR TRUMPET AND ORCHESTRA IN E-FLAT MAJOR

Third Movement (Record 3, Side 1)

Rondo

0:00 Main theme *(A)* played by violins rather softly and at a rather fast tempo:

0:10 Main theme repeated by orchestra; louder.

0:22 First contrasting theme *(B)* played by violins:

0:28 Transition leading back to main theme.

0:38 Trumpet enters playing *A* theme.

0:48 Trumpet repeats *A* theme.

0:58 Transition leading to *B* theme.

1:08 Trumpet and violins alternate playing *B* theme in new key.

1:34 Second contrasting theme *(C)* played by violins and trumpet:

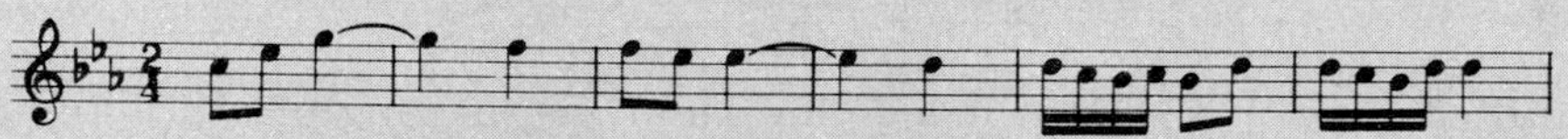

1:49 Trumpet plays *A* theme again.

1:59 Short development of *A* theme by trumpet and orchestra; several changes of key.

2:38 Trumpet plays *A* theme; some imitation of theme by violins.

2:55 Trumpet and violins play *B* theme again.

3:11 Portion of *C* theme played alternately by violins and woodwinds.

3:27 Trumpet plays first portion of *A* theme.

3:36 Portion of *C* theme played by violins and trumpet with trilled notes.

4:05 Coda begins with trumpet playing portion of *A* theme softly.

4:20 Closes after crescendo and full chord.

The middle section of the movement contrasts with the main theme and modulates into a remote key. The overall form of the movement is *A B A*. It does not contain a cadenza.

Third Movement—Rondo Form. For the final movement of the concerto Haydn chose *rondo* form. The basis of the rondo idea is a melody that returns several times, with other musical material interspersed among its various appearances. Symbolically it can be represented *A B A C A D A* and so on. Theoretically there is no limit to the number of sections possible in a rondo, but a minimum of five sections is customary.

The idea of a rondo can best be understood by listening to the third movement of Haydn's Trumpet Concerto while following the Listening Guide on page 219. Remember, the times refer specifically to the recording in the *Record Album;* other recordings will have the same features but the times will vary somewhat.

The *C* portion of the form is a contrasting episode without an easily remembered melody. Often the contrasting sections in a rondo do not have noteworthy themes. Also, occasionally the composer works the material into a short development section, as Haydn does in this concerto. The movement concludes with a coda that contains two brief statements of the main theme.

A rondo contains one musical theme to which it returns alternately between presentations of new musical material. Its sections are not usually long, and there is usually little attempt to develop melodies or deal in complex musical ideas. Since the final movement was traditionally supposed to be light and cheerful, encouraging the listeners to leave in a happy frame of mind, it is especially suitable for the final movement of a large work. The rondo form reached its widest popularity in the Classical period. Soon after that time it fell out of favor with composers, although it is still used occasionally today.

BAROQUE AND CLASSICAL MUSIC COMPARED

The following chart summarizes some of the characteristics of Baroque and Classical music.

MUSICAL ASPECTS	BAROQUE	CLASSICAL
New long musical forms	Opera, oratorio, cantata, sonata (solo), concerto grosso, suite	Symphony, solo concerto, sonata, string quartet
New short musical forms	Chorale, fugue, passacaglia, toccata, prelude, overture, recitative, aria	A few one-movement chamber works
Texture	Homophony and polyphony equally prominent	Homophony predominates
Tonality	Major/minor system with strongly felt center	Major/minor system with strongly felt center
Basso continuo	Usually present	No longer used
Modulation	Moderate amount	Rather frequent to nearly related keys
Harmony	Systematic; chords with roots a fifth apart	Systematic; chords with roots a fifth apart
Meter	Metrical	Metrical
Beat	Steady and strongly felt	Steady and strongly felt
Melody	Many long melodies, sometimes quite ornamented	Often composed of short ideas that are strung together; some ornamentation
Formal patterns	*A B A, A B*	Sonata form, rondo, theme and variation, minuet and trio
Changes of loudness	Terraced and abrupt	Gradual changes introduced
Instruments featured	Organ, harpsichord	Piano, full orchestra
Size of orchestra	20–25	40

17

CLASSICAL OPERA

Because opera is less well known in America (not as in Europe) than symphonic music, it is often not as well liked or understood. Among a small group of devotees, it is considered the summit of musical and artistic expression. To other persons, it smacks of excessive showmanship and exaggerated emotional appeal. They regard it as an unfortunate hybrid, lacking both the dramatic power of the stage or film and the musical appeal of a symphony or concerto. In fairness it should be pointed out that opera does have a loyal following among a portion of the general public. It deserves a wider acceptance, however.

How can a listener approach opera in order to achieve the fullest possible understanding of the medium? Let us begin by looking at what opera aspires to be.

THE ELEMENTS OF OPERA

Opera includes several artistic elements in addition to music. Opera takes place on a stage; therefore, it is a form of theater, requiring eye appeal and action. Thus, the success of opera depends to some extent on its staging—the scenery, costumes, and actors' movements. As drama, it must present a story, delineate the various characters, and project their feelings. Dancing is sometimes integrated into the production. Opera, then, involves many things: literature, drama, vocal and instrumental music, staging, and dancing. It is the great union of the arts. For that very reason, opera presents the composer and performer with more opportunities and difficulties than any other type of music.

Believability is hard to achieve because communication takes place through singing rather than talking. Normally a phrase such as "John will be here at nine o'clock" is spoken. Singing it would cause people to wonder! But suppose the sentence about John's arrival is in an opera. If the singer performs the words with a minimum of musical expressiveness, the music is less interesting. On the other hand, if a composer writes a beautiful melody to these words, then realism and credibility have been sacrificed.

The element of time is a factor, also. Stage action can proceed normally if "John will be here at nine o'clock" is spoken as in real life. If an aria is developed around these words, the forward motion of the plot will have to be suspended for its duration. If interesting music is to be included, therefore, the drama will have to be cut back to accommodate the pressures of time, and it will have to be interrupted occasionally to allow for expressive and interesting music.

A sense of realism has been hampered by the style of singing that has evolved in the operatic tradition. This style was developed in the centuries before recordings and mechanical amplification were available. Above all, a singer had to be heard—clearly—all the way to the last row of the balcony. If the style was somewhat unnatural, it was at least powerful. Nuances and shadings were sometimes sacrificed to the need for sheer projection of the voice, and the style that resulted sometimes "turned off" inexperienced listeners.

The drama-music dilemma has a bearing on the appearance and acting ability of the opera singer. Some outstanding singers of the past were either not talented at acting or not interested in it. Because of the strenuous vocal demands of opera, it is difficult to find persons who can both sing and act with skill. Fortunately, opera companies today are aware of the need for a more natural vocal sound, appropriate appearance, and acting ability, and they are casting accordingly.

It must also be admitted that some opera plots are hardly fascinating. Many of the stories make no attempt to be believable. Others are dated and quaint.

Another distraction in opera is the problem of understanding the words. Even when sung in English, the words are not easily comprehended. The problem is increased by the large number of operas in a foreign language. Operas can be translated and sung in English, but should they be? Although translation is difficult, involving correct number of syllables, natural accents, shades of meaning, and rhyme schemes, the answer is probably "yes."

The public that has followed opera through the years is to be commended for its interest, but it has sometimes shown a lack of understanding of opera's purpose. Some of the audience apparently knew or cared little about music. They cheered the singers' virtuoso efforts and applauded the pomp and color of the staging. Others wanted to associate with the "right" people and be numbered among the elite. So the opening night of an opera season was often a social event, and the music was only incidental.

The repertoire of most opera companies caters to the audience, which means that certain favorite operas are performed year after year, to the exclusion of contemporary works. Financial considerations, as well as audience preference, tend to work against the performance of a new opera. The cost of producing an opera is enormous, and therefore few opera company managers can afford the expense of trying a new work. When they have done so in the past, the public has generally not indicated enough interest to make the venture worthwhile.

APPRECIATING OPERA

What attitudes and knowledge will help you to enjoy opera? First, accept some limitations on realism in terms of time and situations. Accept the fact that commonplace statements are sung and that the stage action differs from the routine of ordinary events. An opera is not intended to be a slice of life; it's bigger than life in its concept and impact. Realize also that the drama will have to be abbreviated. A good story helps make a better opera, but the plot in

Gorgeous Baroque decorations and staging adorn the presentation of the opera La Contesa dei Numi, *presented at the Polignac Palace in Rome in 1729. The painting is by Panini.*

itself does not guarantee a successful opera. Accept the fact that the characterizations will not receive the subtle development found in good drama. It just is not possible to dwell on such nuances and still devote proper attention to the music.

Concentrate first on the music. Because it is associated with specific events in a story, operatic music is very expressive. The drama provides composers with situations that are ripe for musical expression. The emotional impact of the right music at the right place in the drama accounts for much of opera's appeal, especially nineteenth- and twentieth-century operas. Some operatic "I-love-yous" cause in some listeners a sensuous reaction best described as "goosepimply."

Notice opera's nonmusical aspects, remembering that they are intended to enhance the music rather than displace it. The pageantry of the staging can be quite impressive. The combination of the visual and the aural has an impact that neither can achieve alone. A person who hears opera without seeing the action on stage is missing a vital part of the opera experience. It is like listening to a radio broadcast of a basketball game—the sense of involvement is lessened. Opera really must be seen to be appreciated. As with any type of music, the more you know about opera, the greater the chances are that you will like it.

The early development of opera is described on page 229. Classical opera is presented next in conjunction with Mozart's *The Marriage of Figaro.*

Mozart's The Marriage of Figaro

This opera is in Italian, and its original title is *Le Nozze di Figaro.* Although Mozart was Austrian, he wrote operas in a language other than his native German. He had made several journeys to Italy and knew the language. The *libretto* (the text of an opera) was written by the Italian Lorenzo da Ponte, the best librettist of his day. The selection of an Italian text was a good choice because opera was a thoroughly Italian development, and audiences in Vienna were more accustomed to hearing opera in Italian than in their own tongue.

Because of the opera's length, the discussion here is limited to only the first of its four acts. The plot is complex, with each character trying to outwit others, so the music should be heard with libretto in hand.

The overture is full of gaiety to set the appropriate mood for the action that follows. As the curtain rises, Susanna (fiancée of Figaro and maid to Countess Almaviva) and Figaro (valet to Count Almaviva) are in Figaro's unfurnished apartment. Susanna is trying on a hat before a mirror, while Figaro is measuring the room in order to plan its furnishings.

In the recitative that follows (often spoken instead of sung in performances today), Figaro explains that the room will accommodate the bed the

Count has given them for a wedding gift. Susanna objects to using the room as their bedroom. In the duet that follows, Figaro points out that the room is convenient to the Count's apartment on one side and the Countess's on the other. If their employers ring in the night, it would be only two steps to their doors. The music fits Figaro's description of the ringing bell. *But,* Susanna replies, what would happen if Figaro had to be absent for a few days? She then reveals that the Count has been trying to woo her and take advantage of his feudal rights (the right to court a maid in his service before she is married). Susanna leaves to answer the Countess's ring.

Now Figaro knows why he and Susanna have been asked to accompany the Count to London! Figaro has a few tricks of his own in mind.* At this point he sings a short aria (Record 2, Side 2). The words are:

Se vuol ballare, signor Contino	If you want dancing, my lord and master,
il chitarrino le suonerò.	on my guitar I will play the tune.
Se vuol venire nella mia scuola,	Come if you want to into my schoolroom,
la capriola le insegnerò.	all kinds of capers I'll teach to you.
Sapro, ma piano, piano;	I know, but quiet, quiet;
meglio orni arcano dissimulando scoprir potrò.	I'll soon discover every dark secret; I'll find him out.
L'arte schermendo, l'arte adoprando,	Camouflage tactics, crafty deception,
di quà pungendo, di là scherzando,	Knowing the sting that comes from his joking,
totte le macchine rovescierò.	all these sly tricks of his I'll overturn.

In a number of ways the aria is typical of operatic music of the Classical period. It is neat, tasteful, and tuneful. Its form is the three-part *da capo* pattern. The middle section, which begins on the words *"L'arte schermendo"* ("Camouflage tactics"), is very different from the surrounding music. The meter changes from three beats per measure to two, and the tempo is very fast, so fast that you can hardly make out the words. It contains several examples of sequence. The middle section is also performed more softly. The final measures of the short aria seem to send Figaro off the stage, which is what he is supposed to do.

*The theme of a servant's outwitting a member of the aristocracy was a popular one in *opera buffa.* There was a keen awareness of social class in the eighteenth century, and the seeds of rebellion had been planted by 1786. *Opera buffa* was attended largely by people of the merchant class; thus the popularity of the theme.

The plot becomes more complex as Dr. Bartolo and Marcellina enter discussing a contract Figaro has signed. The contract stipulates that he will repay the money he has borrowed from Marcellina or else marry her. Bartolo sings of his determination to do away with Figaro. (In Italian the aria is appropriately named *"La vendetta!"*) Susanna returns. She and Marcellina exchange insults before Marcellina leaves the stage.

Cherubino, the Count's page, enters. He is a teenager who has just discovered women, and he is infatuated with them all.* He explains to Susanna that he has been caught with his arms around Barbarina, the gardener's daughter, and now the Count is going to send him away. And he cannot bear to leave the Countess, his most recent infatuation.

Susanna hears the Count approaching and hides Cherubino behind a chair. The Count sits in that very chair, of course, and proceeds to propose lovemaking to Susanna by trying to arrange a meeting for that night. Basilio is then heard outside. Basilio is a music teacher as well as a sly and devious master of intrigue. The Count goes behind the chair while, shielded by Susanna, Cherubino slips into the chair. Susanna flings one of the Countess's dresses over him.

Basilio is suspicious and asks Susanna if she has seen the Count. He makes some insinuations about the Count's interest in her, and advises her to warn Cherubino to restrain his affections for the Countess. The Count, hearing this, can stand it no longer and leaps out from behind the chair. A delightful trio follows in which the music offers insight into the characters and their various reactions to the situation. Susanna, for example, sings "Oh, how dreadful! I am ruined!"

In this trio there is one of those operatic situations that must be seen to be appreciated. While Cherubino is being discussed, Susanna becomes faint. The two men almost—but not quite—seat her in the chair in which Cherubino is hiding. Throughout this action, the music and libretto unite into a truly enjoyable scene. It is opera at its lighthearted best. The trio concludes as the Count describes how just yesterday he caught the youth in Barbarina's room. Re-enacting the scene, he pulls the dress from the chair, only to find Cherubino again.

Confusion follows. The Count wants to tell Figaro that Susanna has been unfaithful, but then he remembers his proposals of only a few moments before. The scene is interrupted by the entrance of a group of peasants and Figaro himself, all of whom are singing the Count's praises. Figaro explains that the demonstration is in honor of the Count because he has revoked the

---

*The part is written for a soprano and is sung by a woman. The purpose of this operatic tradition is probably to convey the idea of Cherubino's youth. Even his name, which contains the word "cherub," makes fun of him.

In this scene from The Marriage of Figaro, *Susanna becomes faint. The Count and Basilio almost seat her in the chair in which Cherubino is hiding underneath the cloth.*

laws of feudal privilege. Figaro requests that the Count now bless the marriage of Susanna and himself. Aware of Figaro's ruse, the Count shrewdly suggests that the event be postponed until that evening.

After the peasants leave, Cherubino begs for mercy and is supported by Figaro and Susanna. But the Count is unrelenting and orders the youth to a post in his regiment.

As the act closes, Figaro, in the well-known aria *"Non piu andrai,"* offers Cherubino some parting advice about military life. He tells the young man that he must give up his amorous exploits for the stern duties of war, such as marching through mud and snow. It closes with a marchlike section to the words *"Cherubino alla vittoria, alla gloria militar"* ("Cherubino off to victory, to military glory"). The curtain falls.

Mozart was a master composer of opera as well as instrumental forms. In his operas he welds music and drama into an effective whole. His characters have individuality. His melodies are always pleasant and tuneful. He makes a clear-cut distinction between recitative and aria, treating the recitative text with the greatest possible economy. In Mozart's operas the problem of realism has been largely surmounted by the use of a lighthearted story so that listeners are not concerned about reality. They are free to concentrate on the beauty of the music and the amusement the tale provides.

OPERA'S INFANCY AND ADOLESCENCE

Opera is the child of Florence, Italy. Specifically, it was the creation of a group of noblemen, poets, and musicians called the "Camerata," an Italian word meaning "fellowship" or "society." Its membership included Vincenzo Galilei, father of the famous astronomer Galileo, and Count Bardi in whose home the group met. Beginning in about 1575 the Camerata wanted to create a new dramatic vocal style that was modeled on the music of the ancient Greeks. No Greek music was available, of course, since either none had been written or it had been lost. They believed that the Greek dramas were sung in a half-singing style in which the vocal line followed the rhythm and pitch fluctuations of the spoken word. To achieve this artistic goal, the Camerata developed recitative, which has been described earlier in Chapter 11. As you may recall, it is homophonic, accompanied simply, and sung very flexibly to allow for greater expressiveness.

The first opera was probably *Dafne* by Jacopo Peri, with text by Ottavio Rinuccini; it dates from 1597. Unfortunately, the music for it has been lost. The first opera for which music is available is *Euridice,* also by Peri and Rinuccini. It was composed for the gala wedding of King Henri IV of France and Marie de' Medici. (The wealth and power of the Medici family was mentioned in connection with Leonardo da Vinci.) The music was nearly continuous recitative with a few melodic portions, which isn't all that attractive for most listeners.

Opera did not remain an infant for long. The important composer Claudio Monteverdi wrote an opera in 1607, which is based on the Greek myth about Orpheus descending into Hades to bring back his beloved Eurydice, the same story that Peri had used for his opera. By 1637 the first public opera house opened in Venice, and by 1700 there were seventeen opera houses in that city alone.

During the years following Monteverdi, opera entered what might be called its "adolescent" stage. The artistic ideals of the Camerata had been pretty much forgotten. True, the nearly exclusive use of recitative had been abandoned and the music was much more pleasing to hear. The orchestra also had become more important. However, the audiences now wanted to hear virtuoso singing. The notated music became a skeleton on which the singer built a stunning set of embellishments and added runs to show off vocal technique. The singer reigned supreme. Also, the stories contained irrelevant incidents, spectacular scenes, and incongruous episodes.

Christoph Willibald von Gluck (1714–1787) helped opera to "grow out" of this "adolescent" phase. Gluck had written operas himself, so he knew the field and was right in trying to bring back the dramatic integrity by making the music serve the text. According to Gluck, everything in the opera, including ballet, was to be an integral part of the drama. There should be no more unrelated scenes or arias that the singers could do with what they wished. Gluck composed several operas that demonstrated his reforms.

In the decades following the opening of the opera house in Venice, opera evolved into two rather distinct styles. One was *opera seria,* which was of a serious nature. The other was *opera buffa* (*boo*-fa), which was lighter and more comic. Mozart and other composers wrote in both styles, but the buffa type has usually been more successful with the public.

Another important operatic tradition is found in the first act of *The Marriage of Figaro.* Mozart has the ensemble of principal characters sing at the same time, each expressing his or her own thoughts. Often such ensemble numbers conclude with a resounding full finish, and so this device is well suited to end an act.

Mozart's operas represent the Classical style in which the music exhibits good taste. True, the librettos of his comic operas are sometimes spiced with double entendres, and the singers' emotions are exaggerated for comic effect. But the music is handled with a restraint that contrasts nicely with any incongruities of text or action. Even in serious operas he did not allow the music to become bombastic or sentimental. There is about his operatic writing what might be called the "light touch," an awareness that music can be valid even when conceived as entertainment.

18

CHAMBER MUSIC

Until the Classical period most music written for instruments (except for keyboard) did not clearly indicate the size of the group that should play it. In fact, until the Baroque period it was not often clear whether a piece of music was to be sung or played or both. As the orchestra became more standardized, composers began to specify the type of group for which they were writing. Apparently they felt that music for an orchestra might or might not be suitable for a small group of players. There emerged, then, music for large groups (symphonies, concertos) and *chamber music* for small groups (quartets, trios, etc.).

Chamber music thrived in the Classical period, because the social milieu encouraged this type of music. The public concert was only beginning to be a factor. Most performances were still for private audiences of the rich and wellborn. When a host wished to provide after-dinner diversion for guests in his home, he quite naturally thought a small chamber group to be more appropriate than a symphony orchestra.

Musicians to this day have continued to value chamber music, primarily because it permits a refinement and intimacy of expression that cannot be derived from a large musical organization. An orchestra has power and color, while a string quartet provides a sense of involvement and clarity. One medium can be as satisfying as the other in the hands of a skilled composer.

In chamber music there is only one player on each part. When the instrumentation of some chamber groups is considered, this definition may appear to be wrong. For instance, a string quartet consists of two violins, one viola, and one cello. There are, however, two different violin parts. As long as each has a different part, there could be three or more violins and the work would still be considered chamber music.

Voices are not customarily involved in chamber music, although early chamber works were influenced by vocal style. In the Renaissance, madrigals could be either sung or played on string instruments. Such music was described as being "apt for voyces or viols." In the twentieth century Stravinsky, Schoenberg, and others have written for voice in chamber compositions. Since the Renaissance, however, and particularly during the Classical period, chamber music has been understood to be instrumental.

Listening to Chamber Music

The techniques for listening to chamber music are essentially the same as those needed for listening to music of any type. However, since chamber music is performed by a small group, it lacks the tonal power and the lush, colorful sounds of a full orchestra or chorus. Chamber music cannot compete in sheer mass of sound or richness of color. For this reason, it cannot rest its case to any degree on its sensuous qualities, and listeners should not expect it to do so.

Chamber music must instead stand on its musical qualities, so listeners must concentrate on what is happening in the music itself. The composer's musical ideas and his treatment of them in the composition are the warp and woof of chamber music.

The fewer the number of players, the more easily heard are small errors in playing, so the performers must execute their parts with much accuracy and unity. This feeling of oneness in musical performance is called *ensemble,* the French word for "together." Chamber music is traditionally performed without a conductor, so the sensing of tempos, phrasing, and dynamics is the responsibility of each player. Although one person is acknowledged to be the leader (for example, the first violinist in a string quartet), the cues and nods that start and stop the group are so subtle that they can be seen only by watching carefully. That is why the word "ensemble" can refer not only to the sense of unified performance by the players but also to the chamber group itself.

When a chamber music group is heard live in a home or small recital hall, something is added to the listener's enjoyment. Perhaps the closeness of the performers provides a sense of involvement that is essential to chamber music listening. Possibly the fact that the sound comes from a group seated only a few feet away makes for better aural comprehension than when the sound is reproduced mechanically through a loudspeaker. In any case, chamber music is best heard in a live performance at close range.

Concert music is far better known than chamber music, perhaps because more knowledge and attention are required for successful chamber music listening. Since there is a limited audience, few chamber groups can earn a living by means of their performance. Today, chamber ensembles are found in residence at many universities.

FRANZ JOSEPH HAYDN

One man who had much to do with the delineation of chamber and orchestral music was Franz Joseph Haydn (1732–1809). He was born in the same year as George Washington in the town of Rohrau in eastern Austria. His father was a wheelwright. An uncle, with whom Haydn went to live at the age of six, gave him his first musical instruction. At eight he became a choirboy at the Cathedral of St. Stephen in Vienna. When his voice changed, he was dismissed. For the next few years he lived a precarious existence doing odd jobs and teaching, as well as studying music theory on his own initiative. In 1761, at the age of twenty-nine, Haydn was taken into the service of Prince Paul Anton Esterházy (*Es*ter-hahzy), head of one of the richest and most powerful noble families in Hungary.

The next year Nicholas Esterházy succeeded his brother Paul Anton. Nicholas, besides being rich and powerful, was also a connoisseur of music. Most of the time he lived at a country estate that was as sumptuous as the French court at Versailles. On the estate were two beautiful concert halls and

Franz Joseph Haydn. *A portrait by Thomas Hardy.*

two theaters, one for opera and one for marionette plays. The Prince's interest in music aided and influenced Haydn, as the material on page 234 indicates.

Like Bach and other musicians of the time, Haydn not only composed but also conducted the performances, trained the musicians, and kept the instruments in repair. Unlike Bach, Haydn had twenty-five *good* instrumentalists and a dozen or so fine singers.

Haydn's contract was typical. It called on him "to produce at once any composition called for" and to smooth out all difficulties among the musicians. He was expected to present himself twice daily in the antechamber to await orders. For the most part, Haydn's experience with the Esterházy family represented the patronage system at its best. Haydn liked them and they him.

After Haydn had been with the Esterházys for thirty years, Prince Nicholas died. Haydn subsequently made two visits to London in the 1790s. For each trip he composed six symphonies. The twelve are known as the *London Symphonies:* Numbers 92 to 104. They are Haydn's best orchestral music. After the London trips he returned to work for a while for Nicholas Esterházy II, who was not so interested in music as his father had been. Haydn then wrote mainly vocal works, including two oratorios, *The Creation* and *The Seasons.* He gradually retired from his life of composing and died in 1809.

During his lifetime Haydn was recognized as a great composer by the

HAYDN, PRINCE ESTERHÁZY, AND THE BARYTON

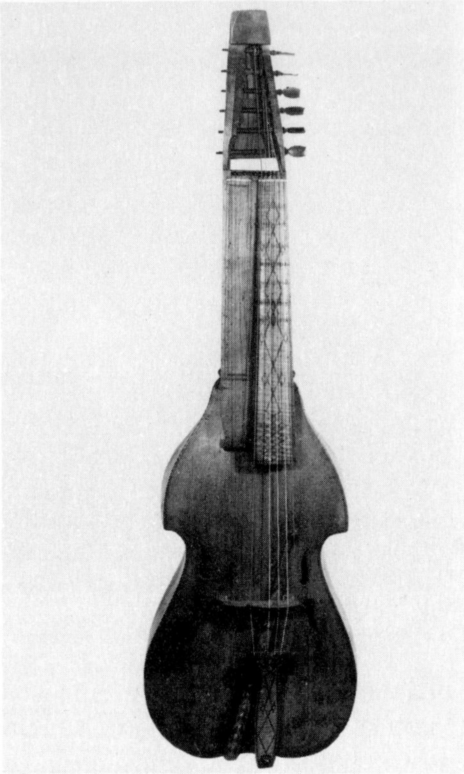

A baryton

The baryton is not an instrument usually found in Europe or America. It looks something like a cello, but its ancestry is from the viol family, which is not the same as the violin, viola, and cello. That fact doesn't mark it as being very different, but the presence of six strings that the player draws the bow across and six more that can be plucked or allowed to vibrate in sympathy with the others does make it unusual. The viols, including the baryton, rather much disappeared from the musical scene by 1800, although there is nothing unpleasant about their gentle tone quality. So why bring the instrument up here?

Mainly because the baryton illustrates well a couple of facts about the Classical times in which Haydn and his patron Prince Nicholas Esterházy lived. It so happens that Nicholas Esterházy enjoyed playing the baryton, and he was a competent though amateur (princes had no need to work at anything, at least princes as rich as the Esterházys) performer on it. Haydn obliged his patron by composing 125 trios for baryton, viola, and cello, 12 short divertimenti for two barytons and bass or cello, and a duet for two barytons. The point illustrated by Haydn's compositions is the influence that the patron had on what a composer wrote. Their job was to compose music—music that their patron-employers liked. Give Haydn an "A" in pleasing his patron.

The 138 chamber works by Haydn including baryton are a lot of music, but only a small portion of the total amount of chamber music that he composed. He also wrote eighty-five string quartets, thirty-one trios for piano, violin, and cello, eighteen trios for two violins and cello, eight sonatas for violin and piano, six duets for violin and viola, and about forty other chamber music works, including a number involving wind instruments. The point is evident here that chamber music was very important during the Classical era. Many situations existed that called for its performance, and for many of these programs new compositions were expected. No wonder Haydn is reported to have worked sixteen hours a day. So give him another "A" for effort.

And while we're at it, give him one more "A" for writing music of quality and interest.

public and other musicians. He and Mozart admired and learned from each other's music. Beethoven also regarded Haydn with esteem.

Haydn is sometimes referred to as the "father" of the symphony, the string quartet, the modern orchestra, and instrumental music in general. Although such claims are exaggerated, they give some indication of his significance. What Haydn did was to work out a better balance for the new forms. For example, he developed the finale of the symphony. Prior to Haydn, the fourth movement had been no more than a frothy little section. Haydn exchanged it for a movement in sonata or rondo form. While it still did not have the scope of the first movement, it was given musical substance and had better overall balance.

THE STRING QUARTET

One of Haydn's contributions to music was the shaping of the string quartet. With its instrumentation of two violins, viola, and cello, the string quartet is probably the most significant chamber music grouping. Early in the eighteenth century, compositions called *divertimenti* were common. As the name implies, they were diversionary, innocuous little pieces. They could be played by either a quartet or a string orchestra. Haydn took the divertimento, deleted one of its two minuets, and gave it more musical substance. He called these new works *quartets* rather than divertimenti. The change did not occur quickly; it was stretched out over much of Haydn's adult life. Over a forty-year span his quartets show an evolution toward a more sophisticated content.

Haydn's String Quartet, Op. 76, No. 3

This work represents the mature development of the string quartet. It was written in 1797, after Haydn's successful journeys to London.

The first movement is in sonata form. The levels of loudness of the first theme show definite contrast as they move from loud to soft to loud. All four instruments have important parts. For instance, in measures five to seven of the example on page 236, the instruments play identical rhythmic figures (dotted sixteenth and thirty-second notes) at different times in an ascending scale pattern. The figure seems to have been influenced by polkalike dance music. The development section presents the viola and cello alternating a dronelike part reminiscent of Scottish music, while the violins play the figure. To provide further interest, Haydn extracts the first two notes of the first theme (circled in the example) and uses them as a motive.

Allegro
Violin I
Violin II
Viola
Cello
f
p
fz

Theme and Variation. For the second movement Haydn revised a melody he had composed some years earlier (Record 2, Side 2). The melody is also sung as a hymn in many churches today under the title "Glorious Things of Thee Are Spoken."* It is constructed of two repeated phrases with contrasting phrases inserted between the two.

Again, the classical ideal of balance is evident. Brackets have been drawn over the two main ideas.

The movement is a *theme and variation,* which is a series of variations on a given melody. Haydn is especially helpful to the listener in this movement because he has one of the instruments continue to play the melody while a variation is played.

Variation I presents the melody in the second violin, while the first violin plays a contrapuntal line that embellishes the melody:

*It is today the Austrian national anthem, although after 1918 the words were changed to eliminate references to the Emperor.

In Variation II the melody is in the cello, supported by the second violin. While this is happening, the first violin plays a countermelody that is quite rhythmic:

The counterpoint becomes increasingly complex.

Variation III presents the melody in the viola, with other instruments playing contrasting parts against it:

Variation IV finds the first violin again playing the melody, sometimes an octave higher than before. The other three instruments play a somewhat intricate chordal accompaniment:

Var. IV

Notice that several accidentals appear in the accompanying instruments. They indicate that the harmony has been changed; different chords were used in the original presentation of the theme. A four-measure concluding section is added to this final variation.

Most examples of theme-and-variation form are not so easy for the listener to follow. Not often does a composer keep the melody intact and sounding. Indeed, a century later composers wrote variations so remotely related to the original theme that it can't even be sensed while one is listening. Haydn, however, treats the theme imaginatively without obscuring it. He employs two devices in doing this: He adds contrapuntal parts, and he changes the harmony. He might also have varied the rhythm or the pitches of the melody itself. Although in this movement Haydn chose not to exploit every possible means of altering the theme, all four possibilities for variation—melody, harmony, counterpoint, and rhythm—are effective and are used frequently by composers. Furthermore, different techniques of variation often appear in combination with one another.

The final two movements of this quartet maintain the standard of excellence that is evident in the first two movements. Typically, the third movement is a minuet and trio, and the fourth movement is a fast finale.

Mozart's Clarinet Quintet

Mozart's Clarinet Quintet in A Major, K. 581 is a relatively late work, written after his Symphony No. 40. It is in the best "polished" style of the eighteenth century. The form is clearly delineated, the parts are well balanced, and everything is neat and enjoyable.

The first movement is in sonata form, of course. The first theme is:

Some runs for the clarinet are inserted after each of the initial appearances of the first theme, and these runs occur extensively in the development section. The second theme of the movement is:

The second movement is in three-part form and is somewhat an aria for instruments. The main theme is:

The contrasting section consists of many scalewise runs and decorative figures in the clarinet and first violin.

The third movement is a minuet and trio.

This minuet is unusual because it has two trios, one for the strings alone and a second one giving the clarinet a chance to show off its wide range.

The fourth movement (Record 3, Side 2) is a theme and variation, the same compositional technique Haydn used for the second movement of his Op. 76, No. 3 String Quartet. The theme is in two-part or binary form: *a b*. The last part of the *b* line is identical with a portion of the *a* line, a not unusual circumstance. Also, the two halves of the *a* line are nearly identical, and this is not unusual either. The similarities in the phrases make the theme easier to remember. The theme is typically Classical in character.

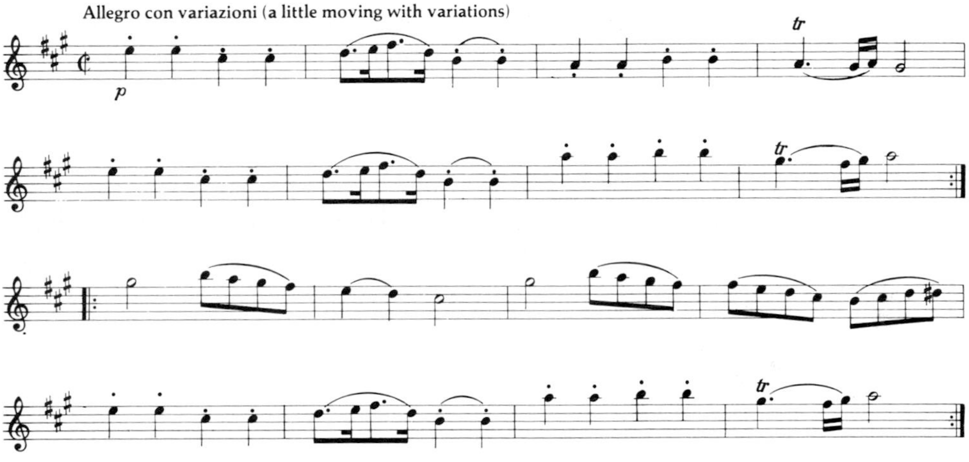

The first variation contains some of the melody in the violin but gives the clarinet a freewheeling countermelody.

In the second variation the viola plays an ornamented version of the melody, while the violins have a counterfigure.

The third variation presents a change of mode from major to minor. The viola "sobs" out this melody.

The second half of the variation on the melody contains many chromatic notes.

The fourth variation returns to major and presents a decorative melodic line in the clarinet and first violin parts.

A very slow variation follows. It features the figure played by the violins in Variation II. The harmony of the theme is preserved, but the original melody is only implied.

The theme is heard again as the coda for the movement.

There is a difference between varying and developing a theme. Recall what Mozart does in developing the themes in his Symphony No. 40, and contrast that with what he does in varying the theme in his Clarinet Quintet or with what Haydn does in Op. 76, No. 3. Development involves fragmenting and remolding a theme. Variation consists of placing the theme in a new setting or giving it a new "costume"—adding a countermelody or altering its rhythmic pattern, for example.

THE SONATA

From the Classical period on, the sonata (not to be confused with sonata form) became a sizable work in three or four movements. The movements correspond to those found in the symphony or concerto, except that the minuet or third movement is often omitted. In tempo, form, and key relationships each movement of the sonata tends to resemble its symphonic counterpart. In this respect the sonata, symphony, string quartet, and concerto all reveal a common ancestry.

Classical sonatas are divided into two categories. The ensemble sonata is usually a composition for two instruments: a piano and one other instrument. The solo sonata is for a single instrument, usually piano. In the ensemble sonata the two parts are considered to be of *equal* importance. In no sense is the piano accompanying the other instrument. As a matter of fact, some of the time the piano part contains the more important musical idea, while the other instrument accompanies. Since the presence of the piano is assumed, the sonata is called by the name of the other instrument. So a violin sonata is for violin and piano.

The players perform an ensemble sonata with the music before them. The custom of memorizing has come to be associated with solo playing, as when a soloist performs a difficult concerto. In chamber music, however, the individual must be subordinate to the ensemble, and so feats of memory seem inappropriate. Furthermore, the complexity of the various parts and the number of players involved (two persons for a sonata, more in other ensembles) make the memorized performance more hazardous and susceptible to error.

One type of sonata is customarily played from memory, and that is the solo sonata. While a few solo sonatas have been written for violin or other instruments, the instrument most commonly associated with the solo sonata is the piano. Music of this type is vast and varied. More will be said about the piano sonata in the next chapter.

OTHER COMMON CHAMBER MUSIC GROUPS

Almost every conceivable combination of instruments has had chamber music written for it. Certain groups are more frequently found, however. The most common have been mentioned: the sonata and the string quartet. Another likely string group involves two violins, two violas, and one or two cellos. The *woodwind quintet* (clarinet, oboe, bassoon, flute, and French horn) was not common in Haydn's time, but it is a standard chamber ensemble today. Brass ensembles have the least standardized instrumentation. Perhaps the quintet (two trumpets, French horn, trombone, and tuba) has most frequently drawn the attention of composers.

It is not unusual to find one nonstring instrument added to a string quartet. For example, Mozart's work for clarinet and string quartet is called a "clarinet quintet," although only one clarinet is present. If a piano plus a string quartet is called for, the work is a "piano quintet." A "piano trio" is a piano plus violin and cello. Apparently, the presence of strings is taken for granted, so the added instrument is mentioned in naming the group.

In one sense opera and chamber music represent the extremes on the continuum running from operatic to symphonies to chamber music. Both Mozart and Haydn, successful in each of these areas, display in their works a similar sense of taste and proportion and high regard for musical craftsmanship.

19

BEETHOVEN: FROM CLASSICISM TO ROMANTICISM

Ludwig van Beethoven is a giant in the world of music. He was a great and distinctive composer who doesn't fit well into grouping. The man and his music merit special attention.

First, his life. Beethoven was born in 1770 into the family of a ne'er-do-well musician in Bonn, Germany. His father, a drunkard, observed the boy's talent and nourished his dreams that he might have sired another prodigy, who like the young Mozart would bring in a good income from his performances. So young Ludwig was pushed into music study, especially piano, viola, and organ. He also sang in the chapel choir. Although talented, he never became the prodigy his father had hoped for. At the age of twenty-two Beethoven set off for Vienna to make his fortune in the world of music.

In Vienna Beethoven studied on and off for about two years with Haydn and with several other teachers. He made a name for himself as a pianist and won friends and admirers among the aristocracy of Vienna. Within a decade he had established himself as a leading composer and performer.

The musical training he received was in the Classical style of the time, which made a lasting impression on him. There were other influences, too.

One was the revolutionary spirit that was awakening in Europe. The spirit of independence was burning not only in Beethoven's music but in the works of other artists as well. Delacroix's painting *Liberty Leading the People* (on this page) is an example of revolutionary art. The American and French revolutions both occurred when Beethoven was still a young man, and so he was aware of these new movements.

Then there was Beethoven's own personality. If he were alive today, he would probably identify himself with humanitarian causes. He would insist on his rights as a person and on those of others. Three instances give support to this view of the man. His Symphony No. 3, entitled *Eroica,* the "heroic symphony," was originally dedicated to Napoleon. When Beethoven heard that Napoleon had declared himself Emperor, the composer, disappointed to learn that his idol was just another ambitious soldier-politician, angrily tore up the dedication. In its place he wrote: "To the memory of a great man." Another example of Beethoven's belief concerns his Ninth Symphony. As early as 1792 he had thought of setting Schiller's *Ode to Joy* to music. The ethical ideals of

Liberty Leading the People, *painted in 1830 by Eugene Delacroix.*

the poem—the universal brotherhood of mankind and its basis in the love of a heavenly Father—and strong appeal to Beethoven. A third instance is described on page 261.

Beethoven is probably the first composer in history to be considered a "personality." His great and independent spirit fills his music. Haydn's music is sometimes difficult to distinguish from Mozart's, and Bach's from Telemann's. Beethoven's mature works sound like no one else's music. His personal life reflected this same desire for independence. He took orders from no one, and he was successful enough at selling his music that he could remain free from worry about publishers' deadlines or patrons.

In appearance he was described as "a short, stout man with a very red face, small piercing eyes, and bushy eyebrows, dressed in a long overcoat which reached nearly to his ankles. . . . Notwithstanding the high color of his cheeks and his general untidiness, there was in those small piercing eyes an expression which no painter could render. It was a feeling of sublimity and melancholy combined."

Beethoven's personality was also affected by a hearing loss that eventually led to complete deafness. The condition was evident by the time he was twenty-eight, and it became progressively worse. After the first performance of his monumental Ninth Symphony, Beethoven did not acknowledge the applause because he could not hear it. His attention was attracted by a tug on the sleeve, whereupon he turned and bowed to the cheering audience.

In 1802 he wrote a letter to his brothers, to be read after his death. In it he describes the anguish caused by his lack of hearing:

> I must live like an exile; if I approach near to people a hot terror seizes me, a fear that I may be subjected to the danger of letting my condition be observed. Thus, it has been during the last half year which I spent in the country . . . what a humiliation when one stood beside me and heard a flute in the distance and I *heard nothing* . . . such incidents brought me to the verge of despair; but little more and I would have put an end to my life. Only art it was that withheld me, it seemed impossible to leave the world until I had produced all that I felt called upon to produce.

His deafness caused him to lose contact with others and to withdraw into himself, becoming more irritable, morose, and suspicious of people. His final compositions were products of this period of his life. They tended to be more personal, meditative, and abstract. His output of new works during the last fifteen years of his life was not large.

How was it possible for the deaf Beethoven to write entire symphonies? People can recall melodies and remember the sounds of voices, even though physically they hear nothing. A trained person can "think out" a sizable amount of music in his mind. And Beethoven was obviously a well-trained musician with more than average abilities!

Ludwig van Beethoven composing his Missa Solemnis. *An 1819 painting by Josef Stieler.*

There is a second reason for his success despite his disability. It has to do with the way he composed. It was his custom to write down themes in a sketchbook. Then he would work over the themes, revising and rewriting them, making slight alterations and trying them out to determine their suitability for the piece he had in mind. This trial-and-error process often continued intermittently over a period of years. So the themes for many of his later compositions had been worked out when he was still able to hear fairly well. The sketchbooks have been preserved, and they are fascinating evidence of the metamorphosis of musical ideas.

Beethoven poured strenuous effort into each measure of his music, for he was not the "natural" that Mozart was. Beethoven is reported to have compared the writing of a particular work, his opera *Fidelio,* with the bearing of a child. The comparison is appropriate. His manuscripts look "like a bloody record of a tremendous inner battle."

Musicologists have assigned three general periods to Beethoven's works. The early period extends to about 1802. In it are included his first three piano sonatas, the Opus 18 string quartets, and the First Symphony—works that resemble the music of the mature Haydn and Mozart. The second period, from approximately 1803 to 1814, was the most productive of his career. It includes seven symphonies (Numbers 2 through 8), his only opera, *Fidelio,* the Opus 59 *(Rasumovsky)* string quartets, a number of piano sonatas, and his last two

This page from Beethoven's manuscript of his Violin Concerto shows the great struggle he went through to put his musical ideas into notation.

piano concertos. The third period encompasses the years from 1815 until his death in 1827. This was a time of personal troubles and deafness, during which he wrote the last five piano sonatas, the *Missa Solemnis,* the Ninth Symphony, and the last quartets.

Beethoven's Pathétique *Sonata*

Although publishers during Beethoven's time often added titles to boost sales, the Piano Sonata No. 8 in C Minor, Op. 13, was named *Pathétique* by Beethoven himself. The "No. 8" comes from the order of the sonata among the thirty-two piano sonatas Beethoven composed. It is a relatively early sonata, dating from 1799.

In Mozart's time, only one generation before Beethoven, the piano was essentially a drawing-room instrument. Its tone was light and delicate, and composers wrote for the instrument accordingly. During Beethoven's lifetime a number of improvements were made in the piano. Probably the most important was the addition of metal braces to the frame across which the strings were strung. (Later the frame was made of cast iron.) These braces permitted heavier strings, since the frame could now withstand the greater tension required to bring such strings up to pitch. In turn the greater tension and heavier strings gave the piano more power. The combination of Beethoven's forceful music and a more powerful instrument enabled the piano to gain a prominent place in the concert hall.

The piano of today has changed only slightly since the beginning of the nineteenth century. The key action has been made a bit more responsive, and a pedal has been added to permit certain sustaining effects, but these improvements are not major ones.

It was probably the introduction to the first movement of Sonata No. 8 that suggested the name *Pathétique* (French for "pathetic" or "melancholy") for the entire work. The introduction is marked "Grave" (solemn) and sounds like a brooding fantasy. Each measure begins with an accented chord that is followed by a dotted rhythm played softly.

Contrary motion can be seen and heard between the treble and bass parts.

The first movement proper is marked to be played fast and vigorously. Essentially the theme is a minor scale that ascends two octaves. It is accompanied by an energetic figure in the left hand that repeats C's at the octave for five measures.

Typically, the second theme contrasts very much with the first.

It is in E-flat minor, which is not a key nearly related to C minor. Notice the *sf* marks under two notes in this theme. The letters are an abbreviation for *sforzando,* which means to emphasize suddenly. The marking is seen often in Beethoven's music. It provides a sense of striking out against something, and this forcefulness is characteristic of some of his music. There is a short third theme and a codetta.

The introduction returns just prior to the development section. In the development Beethoven combines the first theme with the theme from the introduction. Before the end of the movement the slow introduction appears once more, adding a sense of drama to the entire movement.

Although this is one of Beethoven's earlier sonatas, his exploration of the wide tonal and loudness range of the piano has begun. The following example contains pitches spread over several octaves.

The next example shows the extreme and sudden changes of loudness in the final measures of the last movement.

The second movement is songlike. Its main melody opens on middle C over a typical accompaniment figure of the eighteenth century. The melody is repeated one octave higher, and then contrasting sections are heard.

The overall form is *A B A C A*, which gives it the form but not the spirit of a rondo. The *C* section is especially dramatic, with sudden changes in loudness and a triple meter.

The third movement is the final one, which is typical of a sonata. Also typical is its rondo form. Although in minor, the theme is not as somber as the minor theme in the first movement. The form for the entire movement is *A B A C A B A*. This arrangement shows the eighteenth-century fondness for symmetry. There is a codetta after the first *B* section and a coda at the end of the movement, producing a form that combines rondo and sonata—logically called sonata-rondo by some musicians.

A Listening Guide for the third movement appears on pages 252–53.

What characteristics of Beethoven's music can be discovered from a study of the *Pathétique Sonata*? Quite obviously it contains elements of Classicism. Traditional forms are followed, and even when these are altered or expanded, balance and proportion are maintained. But there is also evidence of the forthcoming Romanticism. Beethoven's music has dramatic contrasts of mood; its fiery spirit is often set against tender melodies. (For some reason, he is remembered for the volcanic, eruptive quality of his music, while the calmer beauty is sometimes forgotten.) He exploited the technique of the piano to its fullest, incorporating the range and loudness contrast of the instrument to create effects previously unknown in music.

Beethoven's Symphony No. 5

Beethoven's Fifth Symphony is probably the most popular of any symphony ever composed by anyone. It was written in 1805, only about fifteen years after Mozart's Symphony No. 40, which was discussed earlier. What changes Beethoven made! They are not so much in the technical features of the music, although he made a few modifications, as will be pointed out. The big difference might be described by the word "more." Mozart and Haydn developed themes

LISTENING GUIDE

BEETHOVEN: PIANO SONATA NO. 8, OP. 13, *PATHÉTIQUE*

Third Movement (Record 2, Side 1)

Rondo—A B A C A B A

0:00 Main theme *(A)* in minor played softly in the upper notes:

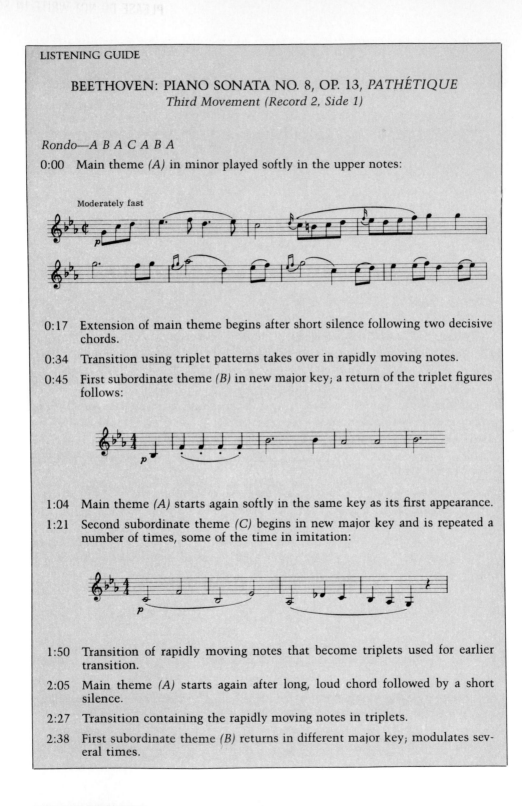

0:17 Extension of main theme begins after short silence following two decisive chords.

0:34 Transition using triplet patterns takes over in rapidly moving notes.

0:45 First subordinate theme *(B)* in new major key; a return of the triplet figures follows:

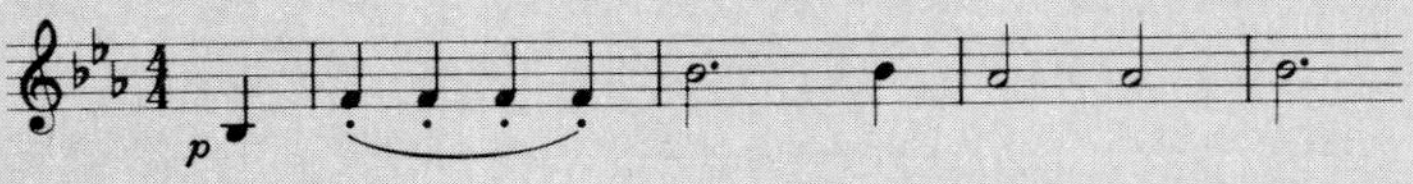

1:04 Main theme *(A)* starts again softly in the same key as its first appearance.

1:21 Second subordinate theme *(C)* begins in new major key and is repeated a number of times, some of the time in imitation:

1:50 Transition of rapidly moving notes that become triplets used for earlier transition.

2:05 Main theme *(A)* starts again after long, loud chord followed by a short silence.

2:27 Transition containing the rapidly moving notes in triplets.

2:38 First subordinate theme *(B)* returns in different major key; modulates several times.

2:58	Main theme *(A)* returns softly in original minor key.
3:10	Coda begins with triplet figures leading up to short "punched out" chords; music increases in intensity.
3:32	First portion of main theme appears softly after long, loud chord.
3:42	Closes with a series of rapidly moving notes and a short chord.

and had some contrast, but Beethoven presents much more development and more contrast of mood and loudness. In some of Beethoven's music, including Symphony No. 5, he seems to want to burst the limits of musical sound. Musical ideas are worked and reworked and reworked again. Some chords are almost hammered in the listener's ear, while at other times a quiet interlude is suddenly ended with a burst of sound.

First movement. The outline of the first movement is presented in the Listening Guide on pages 254–55. It is suggested that you listen several times while following the guide, even if you don't get lost once in a while. Because events occur quite rapidly and because there is much repetition of ideas, the guide is somewhat more difficult to follow than the guides for Mozart and Haydn.

The movement is a premier example of how Beethoven can take what appears to be an ordinary theme and build something monumental out of it. Let's look at a few of the things that he did with that theme. Right away after the theme is presented, it is developed somewhat into a transition to the second theme. It is treated as a germinating idea.

LISTENING GUIDE

BEETHOVEN: SYMPHONY NO. 5 IN C MINOR, OP. 67

First Movement (Record 3, Side 1)

Sonata Form
Exposition

0:00 First theme (form *A* of theme), with fourth note held, played by strings; loud:

0:06 First theme played quietly and repeatedly by strings; leads to held note by violins.

0:20 First theme played loudly by full orchestra; fourth note held.

0:22 Transition beginning with repeated playings of first theme; grows in volume and rises in pitch.

0:44 Vigorous short French horn solo based on first theme (form *B* of theme):

0:47 Second theme, in major key, played softly by violins; followed by other instruments; motive of first theme played softly every fourth measure by cellos and basses:

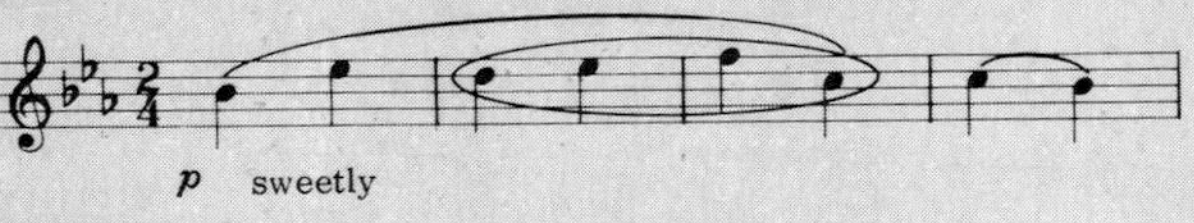

1:08 Codetta starts as smooth phrases of second theme end, and violins take up chord outlines in pattern of first theme; leads to playing of motive loudly by orchestra.

1:18 First theme idea reappears.

Development

1:27 First theme sounded loudly by French horns and then strings; fourth note held; followed by first theme, sometimes inverted, passed among sections of orchestra softly; music slowly increases in volume.

1:56 Full-sounding chords in winds; repeated notes and first theme in strings; followed by silent places.

2:04 Strings sound *B* form of first theme; first theme fragments passed among the woodwinds.

2:14 Two-note motive (circled in example) derived from *B* form of first theme predominates; later reduced to only one note exchanged between winds and strings.

2:37 Vigorous, loud sounding of *B* form of first theme, contrasted with softly played single notes.

2:45 Sudden loud appearance of first theme, form *A*.

Recapitulation

2:59 First theme played loudly by full orchestra; fourth note held.

3:10 Short oboe cadenza.

3:24 Transition growing out of first theme; music increases in volume and pitch.

3:46 French horns play the *B* form of the first theme.

3:50 Second theme, in tonic minor key; played softly by violins; transition based on portion of second theme; first theme sounded occasionally by lower strings.

4:14 Coda begins as smooth phrases of second theme end, and violins take up chord outlines in pattern of first theme.

4:32 Rhythmic pattern of first theme alternated between winds and strings; much repeating of notes; silent places follow.

4:47 *B* form of first theme played by low strings; two-note motive expanded and extended.

5:03 Four-note melodic idea, sometimes inverted, derived from second theme, is played in ascending sequence by violins.

5:14 Woodwinds and strings alternately play four-note idea; fragmented to two notes as music progresses.

5:33 First theme pattern played loudly again by orchestra, leading twice to held notes.

5:48 Quiet appearances of first theme, then suddenly loud.

6:03 Closes with series of brusque chords.

Most of the development section is an outgrowth of the original motive.* He does such things as fill in the interval of the original motive.

To the filled-in interval he adds the inversion—the upside-down version—of the motive.

He reiterates a few simple ideas.

He also fragments themes. The notes circled in the example on page 254 in the Listening Guide are the two middle pitches from the transition played by the horn. The two pitches are echoed between the woodwinds and strings, and then the segment is fragmented further until just one note is echoed.

---

*There have been several attempts to explain the origin of this motive. One proposal suggests that it is Fate knocking at the door; another claims that the three dots and a dash stand for the letter "V" in Morse code. Neither of these theories has been substantiated. The latter is especially doubtful since Morse code was developed after the writing of the symphony.

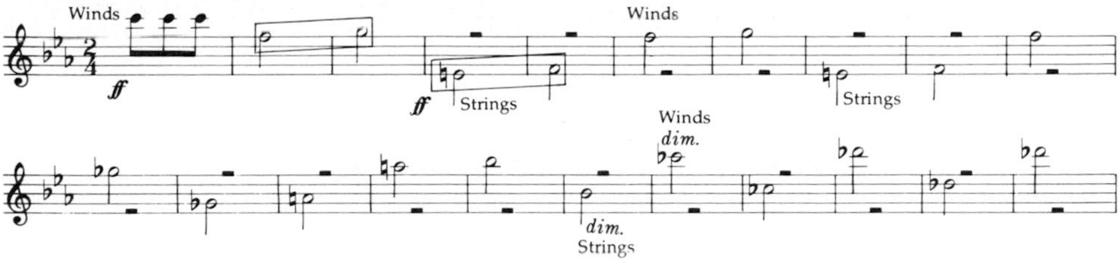

There are also long, gradual crescendos and abrupt changes from loud to soft. After a transition back to the original key of the symphony, the unrelenting rhythm of the motive begins again.

The recapitulation is rather typical, except for a free-sounding oboe solo that provides a momentary respite from the driving quality of the music. The recapitulation is followed by an extended coda. Beethoven made the coda almost as important as the other three parts of the sonata form. He seemed to regard it as a second development section. A synthesis of thematic ideas can be seen in this example.

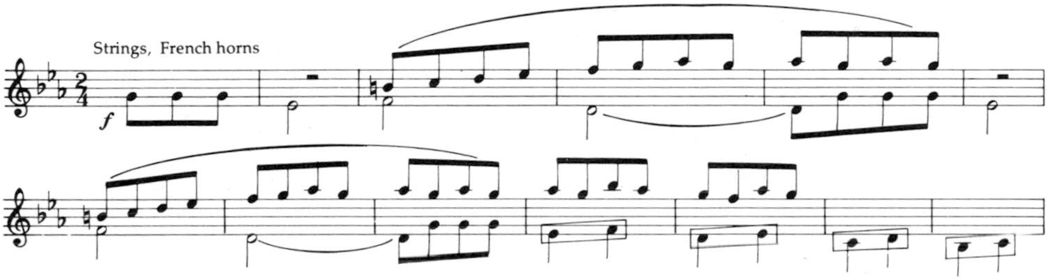

The pitches of the first theme and the rhythmic pattern of the transition are combined. The two-pitch fragment emphasized in the development appears again, this time in a downward sequence.

Second Movement. The second movement shows another side of Beethoven's creative abilities—his skill at writing serene and lovely melodies. The movement is a theme and variations built on two melodic ideas. The first melody is:

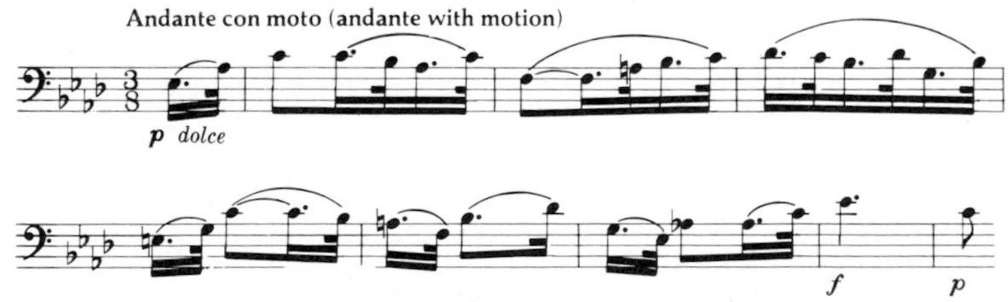

It is played first by the violas and cellos. The second theme is:

As the movement progresses, Beethoven achieves variety in the themes by changing the melody and ornamenting it, and by altering the harmony, rhythm, loudness, tempo, registration, key, and type of accompaniment.

Third Movement. The third movement is quite a change from the traditional minuet and trio of Haydn and Mozart. In its place Beethoven writes what he calls a *scherzo,* which in Italian means "joke." No longer is the music refined and polished; it becomes more rollicking. This is partly achieved by greatly speeding up the tempo. The initial theme is the "Mannheim rocket." This time, however, it is smooth and pitched in the low strings, so that it sounds more appropriate for Halloween than for the concert halls of Austria in the early 1800s.

The French horns introduce the contrasting melody, which is loud and blatant.

The middle section of the scherzo is still called the trio, but it assumes a much more significant place in the movement. The opening figure is a lusty motive of running eighth notes played by the cellos and basses. The theme is played in turn by the violas, second violins, and first violins.

The music starts as though it could be a fugue, but it does not follow through with that idea. The melodies of the trio are repeated at different pitch levels, and the loud French horn melody is now played softly by various woodwind instruments. The form of the minuet is retained as the original opening section, the *A* portion, returns in a modified version but with different orchestration. It is followed by a transition that develops out of the scherzo theme and is started in the timpani. The transition slowly accumulates power until it surges without a break into the fourth movement.

Fourth Movement. The fourth movement is in sonata form and is of massive proportions, a characteristic that lasts for the rest of the nineteenth century among symphony writers. The movement is built around two themes. The opening one is based on the C major chord and scale.

This theme has a second half:

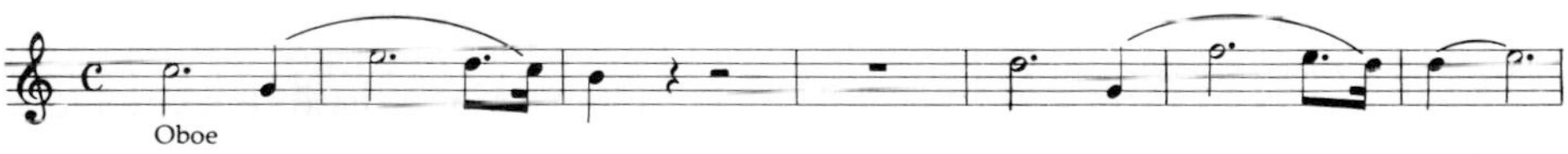

The second main theme is:

Heard in the cellos in the third measure of this theme is a motive that appears prominently in the development section.

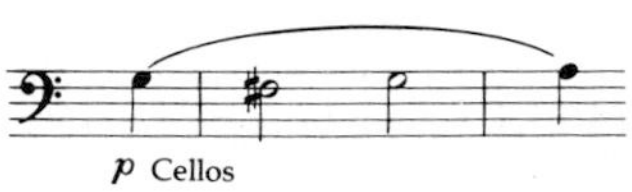

The codetta features a short theme that becomes important later in the coda.

The development section is marked by active rhythm and frequent changes of key. In it Beethoven does something rather unusual for his time—he brings back the second theme from the third movement of the symphony. When themes from one movement are found in other movements, the treatment is referred to as *cyclical.* The recapitulation is followed by an extensive coda, which at times sounds as if Beethoven is having trouble deciding when to stop. The final result, though, is a grand and monumental piece of music.

Beethoven's Egmont Overture

In 1810 Beethoven was commissioned to write an overture and incidental music for a performance of the tragic play *Egmont,* by the German poet and dramatist Goethe (*Gerh*-tuh). (Goethe is presented more fully in the material on page 261.) In Beethoven's day music was often performed incidentally in conjunction with a stage play, as well as before the opening curtain and between acts. Beethoven, von Weber, Mendelssohn, and other composers received commissions to write in this manner for the theater. So there exists a sizable body of music written for use with dramas. Generally, only the overtures are still heard today.

The term "overture" was discussed in Chapter 14, at which time it referred to the introductory movement in a Baroque suite. The overture in those days often had a slow beginning section, which was followed by music of a fugal nature. In many respects Beethoven's overture resembles Bach's. It, too, has a slow introduction followed by a rapidly moving section, although Beethoven's music is less contrapuntal.

In Goethe's drama, Egmont is a nobleman and heroic leader of the Netherlanders. In his fight against Spanish tyranny he is killed, victim of the oppressor's brutality. However, the triumph of liberty appears in a vision to him before he dies. A human and romantic touch is given the drama by Egmont's love for Klärchen, a lovely girl who adores him.

Beethoven may have tried in his *Egmont Overture* to associate the music directly with the events contained in the drama *Egmont;* no one knows for certain. Whatever his intent, the overture now stands on its own musical merit, because the play is seldom performed and is not generally known today.

Egmont Overture begins in a slow tempo. In typical Beethoven style it starts with a loud, commanding sound.

GOETHE AND BEETHOVEN

Few people in contemporary America know much about Johann Wolfgang von Goethe (1749–1832), a situation that scholars and intellectuals of the nineteenth century would have found difficult to understand. A century ago Goethe was a giant of literature, philosophy, and science. In some ways, he seemed to be a reincarnation of Leonardo da Vinci (page 126) in that he was gifted in so many ways. He was an outstanding writer in a variety of styles ranging from fairy tales to drama to psychological prose, including the best-known version of the Faust legend (pages 268–69) and the text for Schubert's *"Der Erlkönig"* (pages 275–76). He was also a critic, statesman, painter, and prolific writer on science. Throughout his adult life he produced a steady stream of brilliant works. Perhaps some of the neglect of Goethe's writings can be attributed to their being in German, which clearly makes them more difficult for English-speaking people to appreciate, even in translations.

It was only natural that Beethoven would admire this intellectual giant of his time. Although the two men had not met at the time, they corresponded about the music Beethoven had composed for Goethe's *Egmont.* Beethoven submitted his composition to Goethe and in a letter wrote: "You will receive the music for *Egmont* . . . that wonderful *Egmont* which I have put to music as warmly as I thought of . . . you. I should very much wish to hear your opinion of it, for even a censure could be but profitable to my art, and would be gladly accepted as the greatest praise." Goethe replied in kind, saying, "I thank you from my heart for the sentiments [expressed in the letter] and I can assure you I most sincerely return them, for I have never heard your works . . . without wishing that I might hear you in person playing the piano, and take delight in your extraordinary talent." Goethe goes on in the letter to praise the music "in the highest terms."

Beethoven finally met Goethe in 1812 at Teplitz. Once when walking with Goethe there, they met the Empress with her entourage. "Keep going as we are," Beethoven muttered. "They must yield to us, and not we to them." Goethe, who was courtly and well mannered, was shocked at the suggestion of disrespect to the Empress, and he stepped aside and held his hat in hand. Beethoven pushed his hat on even harder while the imperial party divided and went around him. When Goethe rejoined him, Beethoven told him, "I have waited for you because I honor and respect you as you well deserve; you did the Empress too much honor," and proceeded to criticize him for stepping aside. It was a small incident, but it reveals quite a bit about the personalities of these two famous men.

Goethe was impressed with Beethoven's talent but not his personality, probably due to incidents such as the one just described. He wrote to a friend: "But I am sorry to say that his is an untamed personality. He is not far wrong in finding the world detestable, but he does not, therefore, make it any the more enjoyable either for himself or for others. He must be excused however, and is greatly to be pitied for the loss of hearing. . . . Since he seems inclined to talk very little, this defect will make him still more so."

After somber chords, the oboe and woodwinds enter with a tender melodic line:

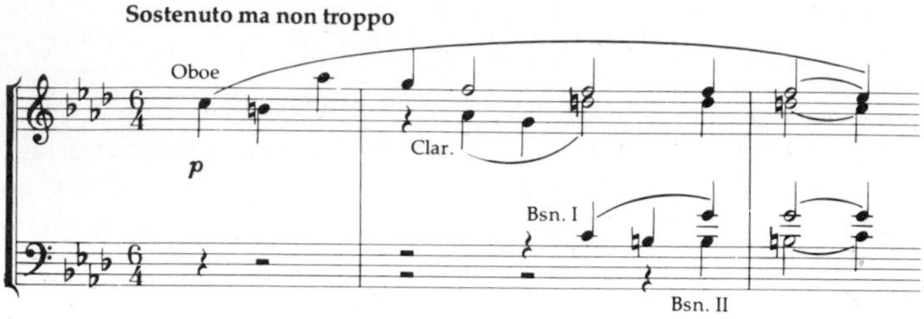

After about two and a half minutes, the tempo becomes more brisk. The theme at this point is typical of Beethoven:

It is built on chordal patterns. Furthermore, it is definitely instrumental in that it wends its way down two octaves—a wider range than is normally practicable in vocal music. The accompaniment for the theme is also characteristic of Beethoven: a row of repeated notes.

After a transition that grows out of the repeated notes, followed by some repetition of the theme itself in the violins, a second theme enters. It is constructed of material found in the slow introduction but this time played at a much faster speed:

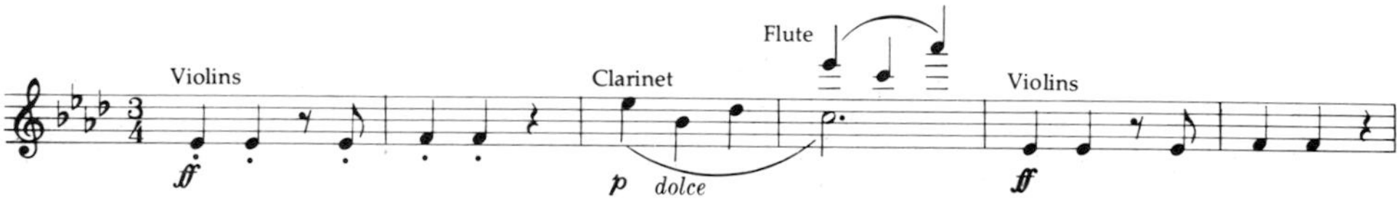

The last example amply illustrates the contrast of power and mood for which Beethoven is so well known. In fact, the music takes on the air of a conversation. The rough sounds of the strings are answered by the lighter tones of the woodwinds. A rather abrupt modulation into a foreign key adds further musical interest.

After some solidly convincing chords, the music proceeds to a short development section. The first five notes of the first theme provide a pattern that is played by the various woodwinds in turn. The lyric quality of the music is suddenly broken at eight-measure intervals by two brusque chords—a characteristic of Beethoven's writing.

The music then moves to a recapitulation. The contrasting second theme is repeated in the coda. This time, the answering violins sound as though they are pleading, possibly a reference to events in the play to follow. Up to this point, the *Egmont Overture* has been in sonata form: introduction, the statement of two contrasting themes, a development, a recapitulation, and a coda built on the previous themes.

But to this structure Beethoven adds a second coda, one that is not related thematically to the remainder of the overture. It contains another favorite technique of Beethoven: the long buildup to a climactic point. The music begins very softly, almost like the rumble of a distantly approaching thunderstorm. Many familiar Beethoven devices are unloosed: the *sforzandi,* the timpani roll, the twisting line in the lower strings. The effect of this coda might be compared to the gradual appearance of a bright vision. Perhaps it is intended to relate to Egmont's vision of the triumph of liberty. Goethe is reported to have wanted the idea of victory when Egmont is executed, and Beethoven tried to fulfill his request.

During his career Beethoven wrote many overtures, seven of which have become part of the standard orchestral repertoire. In addition to *Egmont* they are *Prometheus, Coriolan, Leonore No. 1, Leonore No. 2, Leonore No. 3* (Beethoven's three unsuccessful attempts to find an overture that would not overwhelm his only opera *Fidelio*), and *Fidelio* (the overture he finally accepted). Although Beethoven had a flair for the dramatic, he seemed more at ease when writing instrumental music. His abstract works contain the dramatic elements of suspense, buildup, and surprise. He achieves these elements in sheerly musical terms, without reference to a specific story.

If a man of Beethoven's complexity can be summarized at all, it might be said that he lived at a favorable time in history. He inherited the objective, organized style of the Classical period, but the emerging revolutionary spirit of the times and his own personality provided him with strong Romantic inclinations. Thus, Beethoven stands in the musical world with one foot firmly planted in Classicism and the other in Romanticism. This position gives his music a nearly ideal balance.

PART FOUR

NINETEENTH-CENTURY MUSIC

20

EARLY ROMANTIC MUSIC: SONGS AND CHORAL MUSIC

To most people, the word "romantic" pertains to the emotion of love. To the scholar, however, romantic means much more. It comes from "romance," which originally referred to a medieval poem written in one of the Romance languages (those that developed from Latin) and dealing with a heroic person or event. Later, the word took on the connotation of something far away and strange or something imaginative and full of wonder. Yes, it also includes the idea of love—romantic love.

In Beethoven one can see substantial evidence of Romanticism, especially in his works written after 1800. Romanticism as a musical style started to appear at the beginning of the nineteenth century. By about 1820 or 1825, it had become the predominant style, and it remained so until at least the beginning of the twentieth century.

CHARACTERISTICS OF ROMANTICISM

The Romanticists were fascinated by the unknown and stood in awe of the world. They were impressed by the mystery, not the clarity, of the world and its inhabitants. At times, they were almost mystic. They seemed especially fascinated by the mystery and power of evil in the world, as the popularity of the Faust legend (described on pages 168–69) indicates.

Romanticists tended to rely on emotion and imagination rather than on the rational intellect that had been central to the Classical outlook. Feelings replaced reason, an idea that has received renewed emphasis in America in recent years. Truth became what one *felt* to be true, so it was wrong to deny one's feelings. Keats said in one of his letters: "I am certain of nothing but the holiness of the heart's affections, and the truth of the imagination. What the imagination seizes as beauty must be truth." Inevitably, Romanticism became distrustful of reason and science. To quote Keats again, this time from "Lamia":

Do not all charms fly
At the mere touch of cold philosophy?*

Romanticists were fascinated by the long ago and far away. During the Classical period, intellectuals had thought of medieval times as the Dark Ages; the Romanticists thought of them as heroic. Literature abounds with examples of this attitude, as in Tennyson's *Idylls of the King,* Keats's "Eve of St. Agnes," Coleridge's "Christabel," Scott's *Ivanhoe,* and many more. Eugène Delacroix chose Dante's *Inferno,* an early fourteenth-century masterpiece of literature, as the subject matter for his painting *The Bark of Dante* (plate 10).

Not only were the Romanticists impressed by the unknown forces of the world, they reveled in the struggle against those forces. Coleridge's ancient

*That is, science.

Planting Potatoes *by Jean Francois Millet exemplifies one Romantic painter's admiration for the common people and rural life.*

mariner was "alone on a wide, wide sea." Delacroix's Florentines struggle helplessly against their fate.

The Romanticists resented rules and restraints, another attitude that is very much alive in contemporary American society. They regarded the Classical period as cold and formal and were unimpressed by its rational deductions and universal laws. They felt perfectly capable of making their own rules, and they proceeded to do so in their artistic works. They cherished freedom, limitless expression and passion, and the pursuit of the unattainable. After all, what more glorious struggle could there be than the yearning and seeking after the impossible? This search is perhaps best epitomized in the legend of the Holy

---

THE FAUST LEGEND

The idea of the devil and evil forces fascinated writers and composers in the nineteenth century. It still does to some extent in the twentieth century, as is demonstrated by the popularity of books and films such as *The Exorcist*, the Count Dracula legend, and "Gothic horror" stories. The Faust legend as one form of interest in evil was a special favorite of the Romantic period. Charles Gounod's (1818–1893) most famous work is his opera *Faust*; Liszt wrote a *Faust Symphony* and a piano work titled *Mephisto Waltz**; Berlioz composed *The Damnation of Faust*; Schumann produced *Scenes from Goethe's Faust*; Wagner composed *A Faust Overture*; and a composer named Boito also wrote an opera *Faust*. The most famous writer of a Faust play or story was Goethe, on whose version Gounod's opera is based. At least five or six other writers of importance in the nineteenth century wrote on the Faust legend.

The word "legend" is the correct one for Faust. Apparently there was a magician and charlatan in the sixteenth century who was about as wicked as they come, but parts of the story may have been about a second evil sorcerer of the time. The few accounts of Faust written during his life refer to his indulging in "the most dastardly form of lewdness" with the boys at a school where he worked and call him "the great sodomite and necromancer." (A necromancer is one who conjures up the spirits of the dead.) Faust's fame is the result of a book published in 1587, about forty-five years after his death. This imaginative but fictional account soon caught on throughout Europe. It was translated into several languages and rewritten and adapted by other writers over the next century. Each version changed the original story, so they have little in common except the name of the character Faust and his dealings with the devil.

Gounod's opera involved only a portion of Goethe's drama. In this version Faust is an aged philosopher and pseudochemist who trades the devil his soul for his lost youth. In youthful form he makes love to Marguerite, then betrays and deserts her. Her brother seeks revenge and ends up challenging Faust and the devil. He is killed. In the meantime, Marguerite has murdered her child and is sentenced

*Mephistopheles, in this legend, is the name of the devil in his human form.

Grail, which was a favored theme in Romantic literature and operas (particularly Wagner's *Parsifal*).

Romanticists were also attracted by nature. They had a rural orientation instead of the urban outlook of the Classical period. In Mozart's day the cities—London, Paris, Vienna—were the centers of artistic activity, and so they attracted people of creative and artistic inclinations. To Romanticists, however, nature had more appeal because it represented a world untainted by humans. Sometimes nature was extolled to the point of pantheism—the belief that God and nature are one. The rural interest of the time led to landscape painting, poems on natural phenomena, and works like Beethoven's Symphony No. 6

---

to execution. At that point Faust tries to save her, but it is too late. She rejects Faust, collapses, and is carried aloft by angels.

In an age that was fascinated with the unknowable and prided itself on trusting feelings rather than reason, the Faust legend was a logical topic for exploitation. After all, what could be more irrational than trading one's soul to the devil, and what is less understandable than the power of what most people believe to be wrong and immoral?

In this scene from Ferruccio Busoni's Doktor Faust, *Faust (left) goes to Mephisto's stud, which is equipped with an hourglass and skull.*

(Pastoral Symphony). The latter work is intended to convey the moods evoked on Beethoven's visits to the Vienna countryside. Beginning with Jean Jacques Rousseau and the Earl of Shaftesbury, and continuing through the American Henry David Thoreau to the present time, a group of philosophers have expounded the idea of natural goodness. The "artificialities" of civilization are rejected because they corrupt people. Wordsworth summed up the Romanticists' thinking on nature when he wrote in "The Tables Turned":

> One impulse from a vernal* wood
> May teach you more of man,
> Of moral evil and of good,
> Than all the sages** can.

Because Romanticists were highly subjective and individualistic, it is not surprising that they tended to become egocentric. Works of art were no longer objective examples of a person's craftsmanship; they were considered instead to be a projection of the creator. Romantic artists felt that a bit of their psyche had been given to the world in their poems or preludes. And these personal works were no longer done for a patron. They were now intended for posterity, for an audience that someday, somewhere would appreciate their true value. Some Romanticists were nonsocial, if not antisocial. They withdrew into a world of their own surrounded by a close circle of friends and admirers. Yet, the Romantic era saw the establishment of the concert hall with its large audiences, and some Romanticists thoroughly enjoyed the adulation of the public. In any case, the attitude toward musical creativity changed, and with it came the altered position of the musician and composer in society.

Romantic musicians were generally concerned with the other arts and with philosophy. They were familiar with the writings of Goethe and Lamartine, and they often knew the writers personally. Liszt wrote a number of literary works, including a book on gypsy music and another entitled *Life of Chopin.* (The latter book, unfortunately, contains inaccuracies of fact.) Schumann's literary bent led him to edit his music magazine. Wagner wrote lengthy treatises on music, art, and philosophy. Romantic composers believed strongly in a unity of the arts. This attitude is exemplified in the music dramas of Wagner, which will be discussed in Chapter 23.

These observations provide a brief introduction to the wonderful and turbulent time called the Romantic period. Several less general characteristics will be pointed out as they occur in the presentation of Romantic music.

---

*Springtime.
**Wise men.

Plate 8
Francois Boucher: *Venus Consoling Love.*
(Chester Dale Collection, National Gallery of Art, Washington, D.C.)

Boucher was trained as a decorator by his father who designed embroideries. That influence is evidenced by the exquisite lightness and decorative qualities of his paintings. The aristocracy of the Rococo period demanded a type of art that was light and decorative, even if it was superficial. A wide range of colors was used. Often the subjects of Rococo art were mythological or allegorical. The protagonist almost always appears as a young, elegant, and sensually abandoned woman. Cupids, nymphs, and doves are found in many paintings, and frequently are pictured in beautiful gardens or forests.

Plate 9
Jacques Louis David: *The Oath of the Horatii.*
(Louvre, Paris. Courtesy of Art Reference Bureau, Inc.)

David's painting depicts the three sons of Horatius swearing to their father that they will come home either with their shields or upon them (in other words, dead). Notice how frozen the figures are, like characters on the frieze of a Greek temple. Notice also the symmetry and balance of design—the staged and planned appearance, the focus of interest (the swords) in the center, the group of figures to the left of Horatius (his sons) and the right (the weeping women). The composition of the painting causes one line to lead to another in a balanced way—the spear on the far left with the legs of the sons, the lines of the two women on the far right, and so on. The work reveals the formal, restrained quality that is classicism in the arts.

Plate 10
Eugene Delacroix: *The Bark of Dante.*
(Louvre, Paris. Courtesy of Art Reference Bureau, Inc.)

Delacroix shows the struggling souls of the wicked Florentines trying to escape from Hell by climbing into the boat with Virgil and Dante. The painting depicts the interest among Romantic artists for subjects from ancient times. In the painting the sea and clouds swirl in an awesome way. The twisted and pained bodies are very much involved in the scene, unlike the characters in David's *The Oath of the Horatii.* There is not much symmetry; Dante (in the green cloak) stands about a third of the way to the left. The even planes are gone, too; the bodies of the sinners writhe throughout the scene.

Plate 11
Claude Monet: *Rouen Cathedral, West Facade, Sunlight.*
(Chester Dale Collection, National Gallery of Art, Washington, D.C.)

As is often true of impressionistic painters, Monet was not really trying to represent the Rouen Cathedral. Rather, he was using its lines and shapes as an object for the interplay of light, shadow, and color. The color has a glowing quality, and the blue, gray, and gold colors seem to complement each other. Monet does not attempt to show the entire front of the Cathedral. The tiny figures at the very bottom of the painting are hardly the center of attention, and seem placed there as an afterthought.

FRANZ SCHUBERT

Franz Schubert (1797–1828) is often considered the composer who marks the beginning of the Romantic era. And there is much about his life to justify his reputation as the prototype of the Romantic artist. Born into the family of a school teacher in a Vienna suburb, young Schubert's creative talent was evident while he was still a boy. Upon completing school, he tried to follow in his father's footsteps, but he could not accept the routine involved in teaching. He preferred to spend his time composing.

Schubert never did adjust well to adult life. He never held a real position of employment; indeed, he made only half-hearted attempts to find one. He had a small circle of friends who appreciated his talents. They housed and fed him when he was in need, which was his normal situation. Unlike Beethoven, Schubert was incompetent in dealing with publishers, who made good profits from his music. He sold some pieces, later worth thousands of dollars, to pay for a meal.

As the years passed, he became lonelier and more discouraged. He was even unlucky in love.* His output of compositions never dwindled, however. Finally, he contracted typhus and died at the age of thirty-one, leaving the

*In 1823 he was hospitalized "from a severe venereal illness" and was not in good health for most of the last five years of his life.

Franz Schubert.

world his clothing, his bedding, some manuscripts valued at ten florins—and a vast store of beautiful music.

Schubert was a versatile composer. He wrote piano works, chamber music, and symphonies. Popular legend has falsely assumed that the familiar Symphony No. 8 *(Unfinished)* was left incomplete because of his death or because of his despair over a lost love. The probable reason is less dramatic. The work was left unfinished because Schubert never got around to completing it. In any event, the symphony was *not* cut short by his premature death. He went on to compose and complete the C Major Symphony (the *Great*), which was widely esteemed by composers such as Schumann, who exclaimed over its "heavenly length."

In his instrumental works Schubert tends to be less Romantic than in his vocal works. His vocal music, which includes seven Masses and about fifteen operas, is thoroughly Romantic. His 600 songs do much to assure his place in the world of music.

THE ART SONG

The songs Schubert wrote are of a type called *art songs* or *lieder* (*leeder*). *Lied* is the German word for "song"; *lieder* is its plural. Essentially the art song or *lied* was a musical setting of a poem. The order is important here. Composers first selected a suitable poem and then composed music that would best project the mood and thought of the text. The idea of preserving and amplifying the message of the words is basic to the art song.

Because the setting of the words was so important, the composers were not primarily concerned with a lovely melody. They wanted a good melody, of course; but more than that, they wanted the melody to be expressive of the words. The interest in expression also suggested that the accompanying piano part should be descriptive enough to support the singer's efforts. For instance, in the song *Die Forelle* ("The Trout") the piano gives the impression of a trout darting through the water. At times, the piano is given solo passages of its own.

The singer of such music is expected to project the idea of the song. Sometimes the singer is called on to express different roles. Any mood can prevail in the *lied:* anger, sadness, anxiety, boisterousness, contentment, pity. The demands on the singer who performs art songs are somewhat different from those imposed on the opera singer. In fact, singers tend to specialize in one type or the other. The art song is usually less demanding in a technical sense; the range is narrower and there are few virtuoso passages. But the singer must be versatile in vocal technique and able to project within a brief time span the essence of a character or situation. Because art songs are usually sung in small recital halls, the performer must establish rapport with the audience. In matters of facial expression and gestures, as well as interpretation, a balance between good taste and expressiveness is necessary. The art song might well be compared to its instrumental counterpart, the chamber ensemble: Both are intended to produce a sense of intimacy, refinement, and listener involvement.

A feeling of involvement is more complete if the listener understands the words. Unfortunately for English-speaking persons, many fine art songs are in a foreign language, and this fact hinders their popularity. For reasons pointed out in the discussion of Handel in Chapter 12, the placement of words in the music is a delicate and crucial matter. When a word is translated, the syllable pattern must usually be changed, either in accent or in number of syllables, and this requires an alteration of the original rhythm. There is also a real problem in translation: Many words have shades of meaning that cannot be accurately translated. It is not surprising, then, that most art songs are sung in their original language.

Added to the translation problem is the fact that many poems that Schubert and others set to music are not of high literary quality. Some of them are overly sentimental, almost maudlin. Many of the texts about love seem a trifle silly and unrealistic to contemporary Americans who have grown up with unflowery popular songs.

Despite the obstacle of translation and the quaintness and obscure imagery of some of the texts, art song literature is filled with music that is well worth knowing. A study of Schubert's *lieder* shows the musical possibilities available to the art song composer and reveals Schubert's skill in writing for the combination of solo voice and piano.

Schubert's Die Forelle *("The Trout")*

This song typifies the Romanticist's interest in nature. It is a rather unrealistic type of admiration. (Any trout fisherman knows that stirring up the water will either frighten the fish away or make it more difficult for them to see the fly.) At any rate, the sympathies of the poet are entirely with the trout; the observer is not thinking about how good a trout tastes when properly cooked. The text is:

In einem Bächlein helle,	Within a sparkling stream
Da schoss in froher Eil'	That sang its merry song,
Die launische Forelle	I saw a silver trout
Vorüber wie ein Pfeil,	Like an arrow, speed along.
Ich stand an dem Gestade	Beside the brook I lingered
Und sah in süsser Ruh	And watched the playful trout

Des muntern Fischleins Bade
Im klaren Bächlein zu!
(last two lines repeated)

That all among the shadows
Was darting in and out.

Ein Fischer mit der Ruthe
Wohl an dem Ufer stand,
Und sah's mit kaltem Blute,
Wie sich das Fischlein wand.
So lang' dem Wasser Helle,
So dacht' ich, nicht gebricht,
So fängt er die Forelle
Mit seiner Angel nicht.
(last two lines repeated)

With rod and line there waited
An angler by the brook,
His one intent to capture
The fish upon his hook.
I thought, "There's little danger
When water's flowing clear.
His labor will be fruitless;
The trout can go quite near."

Doch endlich ward dem Diebe
Die Zeit zu lang.
Er macht das Bächlein tückisch trübe,
Und eh' ich es gedacht
So zuckte seine Ruthe
Das Fischlein zappelt d'ran,
Und ich mit regem Blute
Sah die Betrog'ne an.
(last line repeated)

The angler loses patience,
He stirs the stream,
And makes the limpid, shining water
All dull and muddy seem:
"I have him," said the stranger
As swift his line he cast:
And heeding not the danger,
The trout was caught at last.

The piano accompaniment attempts to picture in sound some aspects of the scene—the flowing brook, the leaping fish, and the muddying of the water. The song is enjoyable but not profound.

All the stanzas of the poem are sung to basically the same music. This type of writing is called *strophic,* and it is evident in many of the songs heard today: hymns, popular songs, and many familiar pieces such as "America."

Schubert later took the melody of this song and used it as the theme for a set of variations for the fourth movement of his Piano Quintet, Op. 114, which is logically called the *Trout Quintet:*

Schubert's Der Erlkönig *("The Erl King")*

Schubert wrote this song when he was only eighteen. He chose a text from Goethe. The prevailing mood of the work is one of fear and suspense engendered by the mythical king of elves. According to the legend, whoever is touched by him must die. The singer is required to portray narrator, father, child, and Erl King—quite an assignment.

Before listening to the song (Record 4, Side 1), it is a good idea to go through each group of lines in the text and make a note of which role the singer is presenting. Then, as you listen, notice how Schubert and the singer treat the different roles. For example, be aware of how "My son, it's only a misty cloud" differs from "You lovely child, come . . . robe of gold" and "My father, my father, now don't you hear" differs from "My son, my son, all I can see . . . willow tree."

Wer reitet so spät durch Nacht und Wind?	Who rides so late through night wind wild?
Es ist der Vater mit seinem Kind;	It is a father with his child.
Er hat den Knaben wohl in dem Arm,	He holds the boy within his arm,
Er fasst ihn sicher, er hält ihn warm.	He clasps him tightly, he keeps him warm.
"Mein Sohn, was birgst du so bang dein Gesicht?"	"My son, why do you hide your face in fear?"
"Siehst, Vater, du den Erlkönig nicht?	"See, father, isn't the Erl King near?
Den Erlenkönig mit Kron' und Schweif?"	The Erl King with crown and shroud?"
"Mein Sohn, es ist ein Nebelstreif."	"My son, it's only a misty cloud."
"Du liebes Kind, komm, geh' mit mir!	"You lovely child, come, go with me!
Gar schöne Spiele spiel' ich mit dir;	Such pleasant games I'll play with thee!
Manch' bunte Blumen sind an dem Strand,	The fields have flowers bright to behold,
Meine Mutter hat manch' gülden Gewand."	My mother has many a robe of gold."
"Mein Vater, mein Vater, und hörest du nicht,	"My father, my father, now don't you hear
Was Erlenkönig mir leise verspricht?"	What the Erl King whispers in my ear?"
"Sei ruhig, bleibe ruhig, mein Kind;	"Be calm, be calm and still, my child;

In dürren Blättern säuselt der Wind."

The dry leaves rustle when wind blows wild."

"Willst, feiner Knabe, du mit mir geh'n?
Meine Töchter sollen dich warten schön;
Meine Töchter führen den nächtlichen Reih'n
Und wiegen und tanzen und singen dich ein."

"My lovely boy, won't you go with me?
My daughters all shall wait on thee,
My daughters nightly revels keep,
They'll sing and dance and rock thee to sleep."

"Mein Vater, mein Vater, und siehst du nicht dort
Erlkönigs Töchter am düstern Ort?"
"Mein Sohn, mein Sohn, ich seh' es genau,
Es scheinen die alten Weiden so grau."

"My father, my father, can't you see the face
Of Erl King's daughters in that dark place?"
"My son, my son, all I can see
Is just the old gray willow tree."

"Ich liebe dich, mich reizt deine schöne Gestalt,
Und bist du nicht willig, so brauch' ich Gewalt."
"Mein Vater, mein Vater, jetzt fasst er mich an!
Erlkönig hat mir ein Leid's gethan!"

"I love thee, thy form enflames my sense;
Since thou art not willing, I'll take thee hence!"
"My father, my father, he's grabbing my arm,
The Erl King wants to do me harm!"

Dem Vater grauset's, er reitet geschwind,
Er hält in Armen das ächzende Kind,
Erreicht den Hof mit Müh' und Noth:
In seinen Armen das Kind war tot!

The father shudders, he speeds through the cold,
His arms the moaning child enfold,
He reaches home with pain and dread:
In his arms the child lay dead!

The music, unlike that of "The Trout," does not repeat itself. New lines of melody follow one another until the song ends. The term for this type of song is *through-composed.* The accompaniment adds to the mood with an agitated triplet figure and a foreboding bass pattern:

Dissonance is heard as the child expresses fear, while the father's music has a reassuring quality about it. Notice how effectively Schubert ends the song. The piano stops and the singer declaims, "In his arms the child"—a pause to allow anticipation to build up—"lay dead."

These two songs of Schubert typify the art song of the Romantic period. When Schubert combines text, vocal line, and accompaniment, something of artistic worth is created. That "something" is not duplicated elsewhere in the world of music. Folk songs and operatic arias do not achieve the same kind of expression; they have other virtues. The art song is the acme of the expression of specific ideas in connection with music.

FELIX MENDELSSOHN

Felix Mendelssohn (1809–1847) was born into a famous and wealthy family. His grandfather, Moses Mendelssohn, was a distinguished philosopher. His father was a banker with a knowledgeable interest in art. They were converted to Christianity when Felix was a child, and added the name Bartholdy to the name Mendelssohn to indicate this change.

Felix grew up hearing good music performed in his own home. Occasionally his father employed instrumentalists to play in his home, and so Felix enjoyed a privilege that is rare among composers: the opportunity to hear his instrumental compositions performed at any stage of their development. With all the benefits of a fine education, he became a successful pianist, composer, conductor, and organizer of concerts. Under his direction, the Gewandhaus Orchestra at Leipzig became the finest in Europe. (The custom had been for the orchestral conductor to stand inconspicuously among the players; Mendelssohn was one of the first conductors to stand in front of the orchestra.) It was he who revived the interest in Bach's music by organizing a performance of the *St. Matthew Passion.* He made ten journeys to England to conduct or perform. Like Schumann, he was happily married. However, after the death of a sister to whom he was deeply attached, he died of a stroke at the age of thirty-eight.

Mendelssohn's music is eminently listenable. A movement of his Fourth

Felix Mendelssohn.

Symphony was presented in Chapter 2. His Concerto for Violin and Orchestra is one of the most frequently performed works for the instrument. He wrote for piano, generally in a rather light vein. His vocal works are especially enjoyable to hear. He followed the oratorio tradition of Handel in England by writing *St. Paul* and *Elijah,* the latter being one of his finest works. Both of these oratorios are in English.

Mendelssohn's Elijah

Elijah appears suddenly in the Bible narrative when he causes a drought to fall on Israel because his people are worshipping Baal instead of Jehovah. Hiding from Ahab's anger, Elijah is fed by ravens and given shelter by a widow whose food is miraculously multiplied and whose son is brought back from the dead by Elijah.

Elijah challenges the prophets of Baal to a contest on Mount Carmel (the center of Baal worship) to prove dramatically that their god is false. A bullock is slain, but no fire is put under it. Elijah states the conditions of the test: "And the god who by fire shall answer, let him be God." At Elijah's urging, the chorus of worshipers of Baal confidently invokes Baal to ignite the fire:

Nothing happens. Elijah begins to needle his fellow countrymen who have turned from Jehovah to Baal:

> Call him louder, for he is a god.
> He talketh, or he is pursuing, or he is on a journey;
> Or peradventure, he sleepeth, so awaken him.
> Call him louder, call him louder!

The followers of Baal now implore more anxiously.

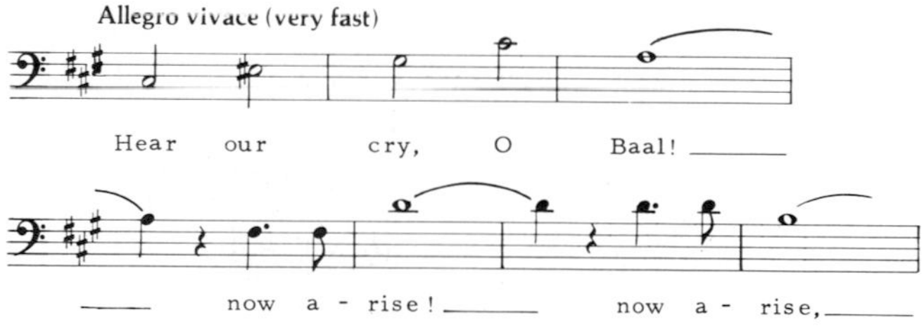

Again, nothing happens. Elijah a third time challenges followers of Baal. This time his remarks are more cutting:

> Call him louder! He heareth not
> With knives and lancets cut yourselves
> after your manner;
> Leap upon the altar ye have made.
> Call him and prophesy.
> Not a voice will answer you.
> None will listen; none heed you.

By now, the Baalites are frantic:

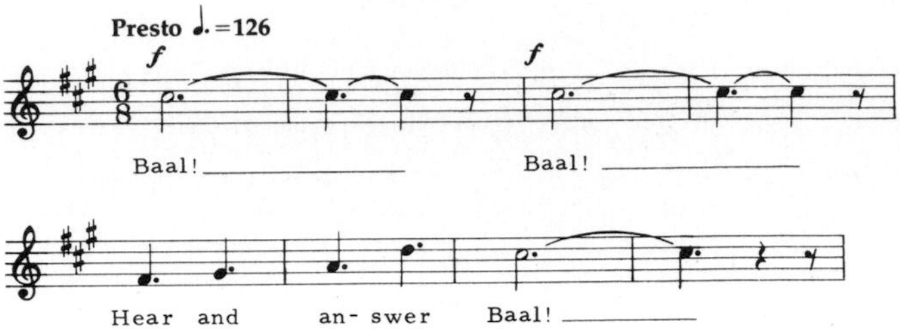

Their pleas of "Hear and answer" become increasingly frenzied. Finally, in a last desperate appeal, the people call twice more and wait for a divine signal. Each time their plea is followed by silence—a silence that adds more drama than could sound at this climactic point.

Then the mood changes completely as Elijah in an aria offers up a prayer to God:

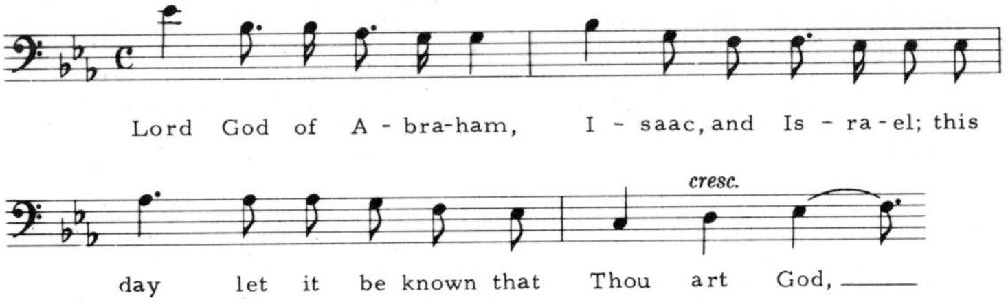

The chorus sings a hymnlike melody, "Cast thy burden upon the Lord." This is followed by a quiet recitative in which Elijah prays:

> O Thou, who makest Thine angels spirits;
> Thou, whose ministers are flaming fires:
> Let them now descend!

The chorus excitedly describes what happens:

> The fire descends from heav'n!
> The flames consume his off'ring!
> Before Him upon your faces fall!

Their statement ends triumphantly with the words "The Lord is God! O Israel, hear! Our God is one Lord; and we will have no other gods before the Lord!"

21

EARLY ROMANTIC MUSIC: PIANO MUSIC

In the early Romantic period there tended to be two different concepts of piano music. They were by no means mutually exclusive, but they were distinctive enough to be noticeable. Composers such as Liszt exploited the powerful sound of the instrument and dazzled the listener with technical display. Others, like Chopin, tended to treat the piano in a more intimate manner. Although Chopin wrote some works in which the piano is called on to roar, most of his piano pieces seek to enchant the listener with their beauty. Chopin—unlike the born showman Liszt—was by nature a shy man. He was not at ease nor at his best before a large audience; he preferred the atmosphere of the drawing room. He seemed to seek in his piano music the same intimacy of expression found in chamber music.

CHARACTER PIECES

Romantic composers did not want to be bound by the strict forms that Mozart and Haydn had used so ably. To replace the rondo, sonata form, and others, the Romanticists created many free, short forms that are called *character pieces*—the ballade, impromptu, fantasie, étude, prelude, berceuse, scherzo, and nocturne.

The *ballade* (bah-*lahd*) and *berceuse* (bair-*soos*) are songlike pieces. The ballade is longer and more sophisticated, and is supposedly reminiscent of the ballade poems of the Middle Ages. An *étude* (*ay*-tood) is a piece that comes to grips with a particular technical problem. Its name is French for "study." In the hands of a composer like Chopin, an étude is far from being a dull exercise, however. It is an attractive piece of music—a melodic study suitable for concert performance. An *impromptu* is supposed to convey the spontaneity its name implies. A *fantasie* is a completely free and imaginative work. The scherzos by Chopin are not as playful as are Beethoven's. Instead, they are longer and more serious, although the typical meter and tempo are retained. The *nocturne* (meaning "night song") was the name given by the Irish composer John Field to piano pieces with a songlike melody. Chopin adopted the title from Field and wrote several works under the designation. Other piano compositions were derived from dance forms—mazurka, polonaise, waltz.

These character pieces were intended to have about them the air of improvisation. They were to sound as though they were an inspiration—a momentary feeling that had been put into sound. The impression of improvisation is an illusion, however, because Chopin and his contemporaries labored carefully over each measure. They worked hard at sounding casual.

There is one feature of Romantic music, and of Chopin's piano works in particular, that cannot be observed in the printed score: the use of *rubato* (roo-*bah*-toh) in playing the music. Rubato is a style of performance in which the player deviates slightly from the exact execution of the rhythm; a fraction of time is "borrowed" from one note in order to lengthen another. In fact, the word originally meant "robbed" in Italian. Chopin was often criticized as a performer for his use of rubato. Some listeners charged that he could not keep a steady beat. Undoubtedly he could, but apparently he preferred not to in much of his playing. He adhered to the Romantic ideal of freedom of expression, and this was manifest in a certain amount of tasteful rubato.

FRÉDÉRIC CHOPIN

Frédéric Chopin (*Show*-pan, 1810–1849) was the son of a French father and Polish mother. He showed much talent at an early age and received his musical education at the Conservatory in Warsaw. Before he was twenty he set out to make his way in the world. Shortly after his departure from Poland, the Poles revolted against the Russians and their czar. In time the Russians crushed the revolt, an event that caused Chopin considerable anguish.

He traveled extensively and then reached Paris, the city that was to become his adopted home. His skill as a pianist and composer made him a sought-after musician. Soon he began to move in a circle of artistic friends—the painter Delacroix, musicians like Liszt and Berlioz, writers like Victor Hugo, Balzac, Lamartine, Alexander Dumas, and Heinrich Heine. Through this group of friends Chopin met George Sand, who is described on pages 284–85. They lived together for several years.

In time his health began to fail, and the relationship with George Sand became strained. Finally they parted in bitterness, and with this event his creative energy seemed to wane. At the age of thirty-nine Chopin died of tuberculosis. Symbolically, his heart was returned to Poland, and the rest of his body stayed in Paris.

Frederic Chopin. A rare daguerreotype made in 1849 shortly before his death.

Bach, Handel, Mozart, Haydn, Beethoven, and Schubert were all extremely versatile composers. They wrote successfully in nearly every medium, vocal and instrumental, solo and ensemble. Chopin was different. He was one of the first "specialist" composers, who tended to limit their writing to one or two areas. Although Chopin attempted a few works for other instruments, the bulk of his effort was directed toward the piano, and through those works he earned his reputation as an outstanding composer.

Chopin's Prelude, Op. 28, No. 4

This Prelude is an extremely simple but moody work, a short piece only twenty-five measures long. The music is strongly homophonic, consisting of a melodic line with throbbing chords for an accompaniment.

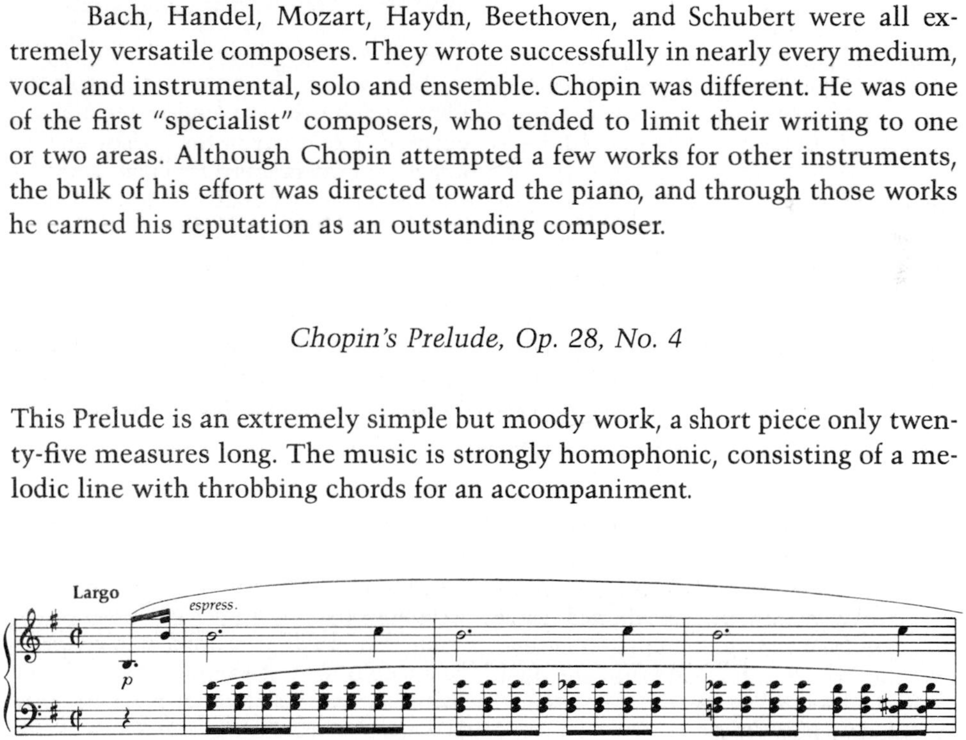

The melody is the epitome of simplicity, and the accompaniment changes little; the entire first measure consists of one chord sounded eight times. But in the handling of such simple elements, Chopin demonstrates his shrewd musical judgment.

Look at the first three measures. The first complete measure has no change until another note is sounded on the fourth beat. As with Mozart's delaying the resolution of a chord (a device discussed in Chapter 16), Chopin heightens interest by withholding any changes as long as possible, but not so long that the effect is overdone. In the second measure the harmony changes after four soundings of one chord. To have sounded the chord eight times would have been too much and would probably have caused listeners to lose interest. In the third measure the harmony again changes after four soundings of a chord and then changes after only two. Melodic interest is created solely by the movement to the quarter note C, which is usually a dissonant pitch in the chord pattern when it appears in this piece.

In measure 2 there is another dissonance—a *suspension*. The top note

---

GEORGE SAND: A ROMANTIC PARADOX

Many of history's famous people can correctly be described as "complex personalities." Certainly this is true of George Sand (1804–1876). Even her name did not come about simply. Originally it was Amandine Aurore Lucile Dudevant, née Dupin. Her mother was of low social status and her father, who died when his daughter was four years old, was an officer born of nobility. Her mother and paternal grandmother struggled for control of the young girl, with the grandmother winning out. As a teenager she was attracted to religion and spent some time in a convent, but she also loved the countryside and the peasant people of Nohant in France where she grew up. After leaving the convent she married and had a son. Within a few years she began to prefer the company of a number of other men. Even her adopted name of George Sand came from one of her lovers, the writer Jules Sandeau; she first wrote under the pseudonym "Jules Sand," but soon changed it.

At the age of twenty-six she moved to Paris, where she became active in the Romantic movement and made the acquaintance of many of the artistic and intellectual leaders there. Probably her most famous liaison was with Frédéric Chopin. When they first met, Chopin, who had always been drawn to attractive women and loved the polished and elegant life, was turned off by her. And with good reason! She had adopted a number of masculine attitudes and habits, including wearing men's clothing and smoking a cigar, and she was not physically very attractive. And yet, in time he was drawn to her, and she to him. She was one of the great writers of her time and was admired by the leading literary figures of the day. Chopin liked this, because he was partial to famous people. But more than that, her strong personality seemed to be a good balance for his not very forceful ways. Finally, she was six years his elder, and perhaps she became for him a sort of sub-

---

in the bass clef part, E, is held after the chords change, so that it is no longer consonant. This dissonance is retained for four playings of the chord, or half a measure. Chopin nurses all he can out of the situation. By manipulating consonance and dissonance over a span of time, he creates some wonderfully attractive but brooding music. This same compositional device also appears later in the Prelude.

The chords demonstrate the color and interest Romantic composers achieved in their harmonies. The development of harmony was, in fact, one of their notable contributions to music. No longer do the three basic chords (tonic, dominant, and subdominant) constitute so great a share of the harmony. All sorts of chromatic alterations appear. Modulations to distant keys become common. Often a basic three-note chord has a fourth note added on top to further extend its alternate-note pattern. (In musical terminology the result is called a *seventh chord,* because the interval between the root and the uppermost chord tone is a seventh.)

The Prelude, Op. 28, No. 4 illustrates several aspects of Chopin's com-

---

Portrait of George Sand painted by Eugene Delacroix. Notice how the artist de-emphasized the cigar in her hand.

stitute mother figure. Although things often were not peaceful between them, they lived together for almost nine years. When they separated, she seemed to have been unaffected; Chopin lived only another two years. Franz Liszt wrote of the effect of the separation on Chopin: ". . . in the breaking this long affection, this powerful bond, he had broken his life."

She was a prolific writer whose collected works fill more than 100 volumes. She seemed to be at her best in novels in which love transcends the obstacles of convention and social class. Often the stories were set in the countryside, and a type of idealism shows through in many of them. In a conversation with Honoré de Balzac, another great French novelist of the nineteenth century, she is reported to have said to him: "You aim at painting and do paint man as he is, but I am inclined to paint him as I wish he were, as I believe he ought to be." Such a view of the human race along with a masterful writing ability earned for George Sand a place in history.

---

posing technique, but none is more impressive than the total effect of this short work. Its notes ooze a kind of pained and moody beauty that is typically Romantic.

Chopin's Polonaise, Op. 53

The *polonaise* was originally a courtly dance somewhat like a promenade. It was developed in a regal Polish court 250 years before Chopin wrote his polonaises. Although other composers wrote such works before Chopin, his name is most often linked to the form. He wrote thirteen in all and considered them to be expressions of his Polish sympathies.

The Opus 53 *Polonaise* (Record 4, Side 1) is a stylized version of the old *polonaises,* just as the dances in the Baroque suite are stylized. It begins with a sizable introduction, followed by this majestic theme:

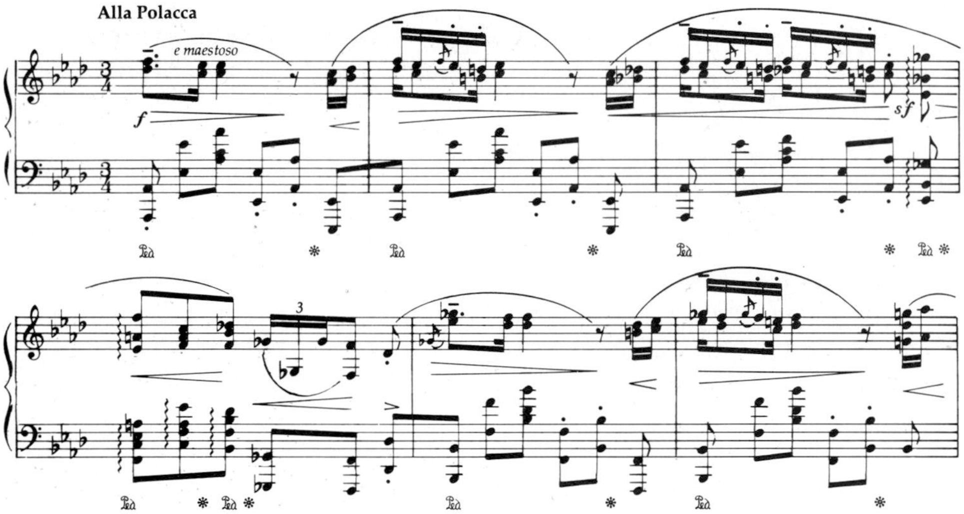

The melody is full of decorative notes and figures. At one point the rhythm seems to stop as a sweeping run is played. The theme is repeated but—as usually happens in Chopin's music—additional notes are added. A short, contrasting section is heard, and the first theme appears again.

At this point the music modulates from A-flat major (four flats) to E major (four sharps), which is a distant modulation by any standard. Then come the rapidly moving notes an octave apart in the bass. The chugging bass line grows over some seventeen measures into a roaring torrent. This piece is one in which Chopin abandons his usual introspective style.

After a repetition of this section, the music takes on a rhapsodic character. Part of the melodic idea used in the section is derived from the contrasting portion. This leads again to the original theme. So the piece has a loose three-part, or *A B A,* form. Even though Chopin follows a scheme, as did Mozart and Haydn, his music does not give the same impression of a planned design.

ROBERT SCHUMANN

Another outstanding Romantic composer was Robert Schumann (1810–1856). He wrote many works for piano, including a widely performed piano concerto. He also composed several symphonies and chamber works and was second only to Schubert as the best song composer of his day. One series of songs with related texts (a *song cycle*), *Frauenliebe und Leben* ("Woman's Love and Life"), is especially melodious and sensitively conceived.

Schumann is remembered not only as a composer but also as the founder and editor of a respected journal, *The New Magazine for Music,* in which he was the first to proclaim the talents of Chopin and Brahms. The journal promoted the concepts of the new Romantic music and was influential in bringing this music to the attention of the public.

Schumann's fame and success were partly attributable to his wife, Clara Wieck Schumann. Clara was herself an outstanding pianist, and she did much to promote his works. Their romance had about it many storybook qualities, including her obstinate father and a nine-year age difference between Robert and the young Clara. Their marriage was a happy one, but Schumann's musical productivity gradually declined. He suffered the tragedy of a mental breakdown and died at the age of forty-six.

FRANZ LISZT

Franz Liszt (1811–1886) was a man as varied and complex as the Romantic period itself. He grew up on a Hungarian estate of the Esterházy family, the son of a steward and a simple Austrian woman. He was sent to Paris to study under a scholarship arrangement provided by a group of Hungarian noblemen.

Paris in the 1830s was enamored with virtuoso music, especially that of the sensational Italian violinist Niccolò Paganini, whose life and musical influence are described on page 290. On March 9, 1831, Franz Liszt attended a recital by Paganini. The dazzling violin virtuoso left an indelible impression on the nineteen-year-old Liszt. He was overwhelmed by the belief that he could do for the piano what Paganini had done for the violin. He could provide it with a new richness of technique and sound. The next morning he canceled all his concerts and began to retrain himself. He spent hours practicing technical maneuvers such as octaves, trills, scales, and arpeggios (playing the notes of a chord successively rather than simultaneously). He returned again and again to hear Paganini's recitals and to take notes on the incredible feats the master violinist could perform. He even imitated some of the visual aspects of Paganini's appearance: the black, tight-fitting clothes, the tossing hair, and the facial expressions.

As Liszt was well aware, the select audience of the eighteenth-century drawing room had been replaced by the public audience of the nineteenth-century concert hall. This new audience demanded spectacular performances by colorful personalities. Liszt seized upon the opportunity by becoming the outstanding piano virtuoso of his day and by writing music that provided abundant opportunity to demonstrate his extraordinary performing talents.

Traditionally the keyboard soloist had performed with his back to the audience. Liszt was one of the first to turn to the sideways position familiar today. In so doing, he provided a visual experience as well as an auditory one. His chiseled profile fascinated the audience, especially the women, as he crouched over the keys, alternately caressing and pounding them.

And speaking of women, Liszt's life was much involved with them. Although he never married, he had many an affair. One musicologist has painstakingly catalogued over thirty such relationships. Liszt lived for one summer with George Sand and for several years with the novelist Countess Marie d'Agoult. Their relationship produced three children, one of whom, Cosima, subsequently became the wife of Richard Wagner. Later, in Weimar, Liszt lived with the Princess Carolyne von Sayn-Wittgenstein, who assisted him in several of his literary efforts.

Behind the image of the sensational artist, which Liszt did not discourage, there was a musician of depth and a man with a generous heart. He had deep admiration for Beethoven and his music. On one occasion he tried

Franz Liszt. Early daguerrotype.

to play an all-Beethoven recital but had to abandon his plan because of the increasing clamor of the audience for flashier numbers. During his thirteen-year stay in Weimar, where he was court conductor to the Grand Duke, he was able to help several musicians, including Wagner and Berlioz, to get their new works performed. He was also a talented and dedicated teacher, often receiving no pay for his teaching. He was strongly religious and wrote a number of compositions for the church. In the last years of his life he took minor orders in the church and was known as Abbé Liszt.

Liszt's La Campanella

Liszt's admiration for Paganini led him to transcribe six of Paganini's violin works for the piano. *La Campanella* ("The Little Bell") is one of these efforts. Liszt retains the bell effect by sounding a high D-sharp repeatedly throughout the piece.

Transcriptions were popular in the early Romantic era. They offered the new public audience the opportunity of hearing technically stunning variations on operatic melodies and other works not originally written for the piano.

PAGANINI—A VIRTUOSO'S VIRTUOSO

Portrait of Paganini by Ingres, dated Rome, 1818.

Even in an age when musical "personalities" were plentiful, Niccolò Paganini stands out. Part of his fame was the result of his appearance and personality. He had a pale, long face with hollow cheeks and thin lips that seemed to curl in an evil smile and his eyes had a piercing quality. At a time when people were fascinated with the notion of the devil, Paganini was a prime candidate for suspicion. He was once forced to publish letters of his mother to prove that he had human parents! On another occasion he had to issue a written denial that the devil stood at his elbow telling him what to do when he played. One rumor had it that the lowest string on his violin was made from the dried intestines of a murdered mistress!

His violin playing was phenomenal. Schubert exclaimed after hearing Paganini, "I have heard an angel sing," and Liszt changed his whole approach to the piano after attending a Paganini concert. Paganini spared nothing to astound and impress the audience with his great ability. He reportedly put old strings on his violin so that one or more would break during the performance; he would then successfully finish the concert on the remaining strings. He developed a repertoire of violin tricks and technical maneuvers which he guarded so jealously that he refused to have much of his music published for fear that others might find out exactly what he was doing.

Born in 1782 in Genoa, Italy, Paganini had a difficult childhood. His father recognized young Niccolò's talent and did not spare the rod in requiring him to practice incessantly. By the age of thirteen he was an experienced and recognized performer. By the age of seventeen he was able to be independent from his father and free to pursue his two great passions: women and gambling. Women were fascinated by him, and he enjoyed many of them. His gambling brought him gains (he won his Stradivarius violin in a wager) and disappointment (he lost part of his large fortune in an investment in a Paris gambling house named "Casino Paganini").

Although in poor health much of his life and somewhat limited in travel, he amassed a fortune. By the late 1830s, however, cancer was afflicting his throat, and he died in 1840. Because he had refused the final sacrament of the Church, for a long time his body was refused burial in holy ground. Some of the townspeople claimed that at night they heard sounds of a ghostly violin coming from his coffin. The legend of Paganini had outlived his body.

Since there were no recordings in those days, and few orchestras (none that traveled), a piano recital was often the listener's only contact with art music.

La Campanella is a typically Romantic composition. First, it is virtuoso music through and through. Even a good professional pianist does not undertake it lightly. Second, it demands of the player the full range of techniques developed in the Romantic period, a period that has properly been called the "golden age of the piano." Third, it is an attempt to make the piano more orchestral in sound and concept. The very name of the piece suggests that the piano is to be descriptive of something more than the piano.

While the piece is technically awesome, it is musically rather simple. It is a set of scintillating variations on a simple melody in which the opening two-measure phrase is stated and then repeated twice with a concluding phrase. After the main theme is presented again, there is a contrasting section. It, too, is composed of short, repeated phrases. The entire theme, then, has a formal pattern of *a a b*.

The work can be followed rather easily by the use of the Listening Guide on page 292, where the music for the theme is presented.

The technical devices employed are too numerous to cover fully here. A few will suffice to provide examples of the virtuoso techniques found in the piece. When nonpianists hear rapidly repeated notes played on a piano, they assume that the player is rapping his finger on the key with tremendous speed. Strange as it may seem, however, it is easier to repeat notes in rapid succession if the fingers are changed with each sounding. Liszt calls for this technique in one variation:

He also calls for an extremely fast execution of the chromatic scale:

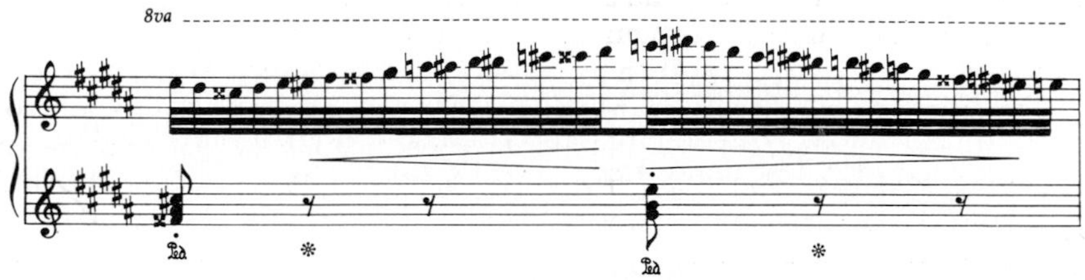

The use of alternate hands gives the player more speed and power:

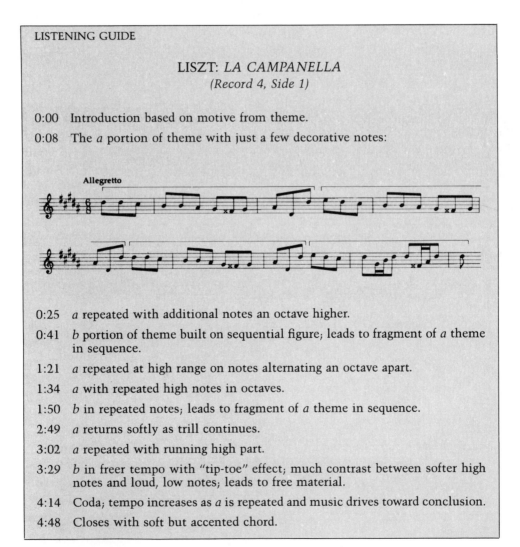

LISTENING GUIDE

LISZT: *LA CAMPANELLA*
(Record 4, Side 1)

0:00 Introduction based on motive from theme.

0:08 The *a* portion of theme with just a few decorative notes:

0:25 *a* repeated with additional notes an octave higher.

0:41 *b* portion of theme built on sequential figure; leads to fragment of *a* theme in sequence.

1:21 *a* repeated at high range on notes alternating an octave apart.

1:34 *a* with repeated high notes in octaves.

1:50 *b* in repeated notes; leads to fragment of *a* theme in sequence.

2:49 *a* returns softly as trill continues.

3:02 *a* repeated with running high part.

3:29 *b* in freer tempo with "tip-toe" effect; much contrast between softer high notes and loud, low notes; leads to free material.

4:14 Coda; tempo increases as *a* is repeated and music drives toward conclusion.

4:48 Closes with soft but accented chord.

Liszt's exploitation of the range of the piano can be heard in the long trill on the high D-sharp, only a few notes from the top of the keyboard.

From time to time the artistic worth of virtuoso compositions like *La Campanella* is questioned. True, sometimes the construction is superficial and the harmonies repetitious. But not all virtuoso works are sparse in musical content. The bell idea in *La Campanella* is handled imaginatively, and most of the variations are attractive and fresh in sound. Furthermore, virtuoso works offer the listener aural pleasures that are not possible in nonvirtuoso music. The high notes of the piano are used in *La Campanella* in a way that is not heard in a Mozart sonata. Also, it is a pleasure to see or hear someone who does something exceptionally well, whether it is a champion figure skater or a fine pianist. This is especially true if you have tried some skating or piano playing and have some appreciation of the skill demanded.

ROMANTIC AND CLASSICAL STYLES COMPARED

The following chart summarizes the main similarities and differences between the Romantic and Classical styles.

MUSICAL ASPECT	CLASSICAL	ROMANTIC
New short types of music	Some one-movement works	Character pieces; Art song
Texture	Homophony predominates	Homophony predominates
Tonality	Major/minor system with strongly felt center	Major/minor system with weakened feeling of center
Modulation	Rather frequent; to closely related keys	Frequent; to diverse keys

(continued)

MUSICAL ASPECT	CLASSICAL	ROMANTIC
Harmony	Functional; a few chords predominate	Often rich and beautiful; more types of chords
Beat	Steady and strongly felt	Somewhat flexible
Rhythm	Metrical	Metrical
Melody	Often composed of short ideas that are strung together; some ornamentation	Often broad, flowing; expressive, some ornamentation
Level of loudness	Gradual changes	Undulating changes; more use of very soft and very loud
Formal patterns	Followed extensively	Followed loosely
Virtuoso performance	Some in solo vocal music	Developed greatly for several instruments, especially piano and violin
Instruments	Piano; full orchestra	Piano; larger orchestra
Concerts	Usually for private audience	Public concerts common

22

PROGRAM MUSIC AND BALLET

Program music is instrumental music that the composer associates with some nonmusical idea. The particular associations are often indicated in the title, or in some cases by an explanatory note—the "program." It is the composer who supplies the information about these nonmusical associations. Works that have been named by publishers merely as a means of identification are not really program music. When there is no suggestion of a program, the music is called *absolute.* Most of the instrumental music of the Baroque and Classical periods is absolute music.

Program music is a special feature of the nineteenth century. It provided composers of that time with a means of organizing a musical work without following the forms that had been so prevalent in the eighteenth century. A nonmusical association acted as a stimulus for musical ideas and a "form" of sorts for a musical composition. However, some program works actually reveal an established form. In other cases, music with a title such as Symphony No. 3 may have been stimulated by nonmusical associations that the composer does not care to identify or admit.

Musical sounds cannot "tell a story" in and of themselves. Only a song with its words can provide a specific message. Music can convey an atmosphere or feeling and can give listeners a general idea. They may hear some massive chords and assume it is the coronation of a king, when in fact the composer had in mind the walking motion of a large animal. The idea of size or importance is there, but a specific association through music alone is impossible. One can make up a story to accompany a program work, but that story will often bear little resemblance to what the composer had in mind.

Good program music has substance in and of itself; it can stand without being associated with a story. Its musical qualities, not its program, determine its success or failure.

TYPES OF PROGRAM MUSIC

Concert Overture. An overture to an opera is an instrumental introduction that incorporates programmatic ideas from the story that follows it. A concert overture is similar, but it is not associated with an opera. It is an independent concert piece whose program is self-contained. Often it follows sonata form. Several overtures of this type were composed in the nineteenth century. Examples include Mendelssohn's seascape *Hebrides (Fingal's Cave)* and Tchaikovsky's *Festival Overture "1812."*

Incidental Music. Early in the nineteenth century, composers were often asked to write music for a drama, not an opera. They would write an overture and five or six other pieces to be performed at a play. Although strictly instrumental music, these works are associated with a particular drama at least by title. Beethoven wrote incidental music, including some of his better-known overtures such as *Egmont* and *Coriolan.* Mendelssohn wrote incidental music for Shakespeare's *A Midsummer Night's Dream.* George Bizet composed his *L'Arlesienne* for a drama, as did Edvard Grieg for Ibsen's drama *Peer Gynt.*

Tone Poem. The most important type of program music is the *tone poem,* also called a *symphonic poem.* It is a rather long, complex orchestral work that resembles a symphony but may not have clearly delineated movements. The contrasting sections of these long orchestral works are developed along the lines suggested by the nonmusical program being followed. The form was developed by Franz Liszt and Hector Berlioz and was expanded by Richard Strauss.

HECTOR BERLIOZ

Hector Berlioz (1803–1869) was born in a small town near Grenoble, France. His father was a well-to-do physician and expected his son to follow in his footsteps. Young Berlioz was even sent off to Paris to go to medical school, but he was much more interested in the musical life of the city, so he decided to give up medicine for music.

Berlioz soon found himself part of a group of other artists and writers such as Eugène Delacroix and Victor Hugo. His parents cut off his funds, so he gave lessons, sang in a theater chorus, and did other odd jobs of a musical nature. He became fascinated with the music of Beethoven and the dramas of Shakespeare. It was in observing one of these dramas in 1827 that he first saw the actress Harriet Smithson and became obsessed with her. He made no attempt to meet her, but was content to visit a rehearsal of one of her plays (during which, seeing her in the arms of a stage lover, he gave a loud shriek

Hector Berlioz.

and ran from the theater), to take solitary midnight walks around Paris, and write letters with phrases like, "Trust me, Smithson and Berlioz will be reunited in the oblivion of the tomb."

In 1830 Berlioz was awarded the coveted Prix de Rome, which gave him an allowance and an opportunity to work in Rome. It was in that year that he turned out his famous *Symphonie fantastique.* When he returned from Rome, after the breakup of his engagement to another woman, a hectic courtship of Harriet Smithson followed. Both families objected, and after much excitement they were finally married. Their marriage turned out to be a stormy one. It ended in 1841 when Hector left to live with an Italian opera singer.

Like several other composers of the nineteenth century, Berlioz wrote reviews and articles. His literary efforts earned him income and allowed him to promote his ideas about music. His music achieved success in his lifetime, although some of his compositions have since been largely forgotten. He tried his hand at several operas and wrote a gigantic Requiem.

Berlioz's Symphonie fantastique

Berlioz's *Symphonie fantastique* is an example of a symphony that is built around a program. And what a program it is! Berlioz had fallen in love with Harriet Smithson. To ease his pain and to indulge his fantasies, Berlioz decided to compose a symphony. Berlioz wrote this about the music: "A young musician of morbid sensibility and ardent imagination in a fit of lovesick despair has poisoned himself with opium. The drug, too weak to kill, plunges him into a heavy sleep accompanied by strange visions. The sensations, feelings, and memories are translated in his sick brain into musical images and ideas. The beloved one herself becomes for him a melody, a recurrent theme that haunts him everywhere."

This recurrent theme is a "fixed idea" (in French, an *idée fixe)* that becomes a melodic fragment associated with a particular person or object. The fixed idea, then, is subject to changes in rhythm, harmony, tempo, meter, and elaboration with other tones. This technique is called *theme transformation.* It should not be confused with theme development or theme and variation. Variation involves keeping the theme intact to some extent (perhaps only its harmony and rhythm) through a series of musical treatments. Development involves retaining the themes but treating them in a variety of ways, including breaking them up. Transformation is a freer concept in which only a few characteristic intervals are preserved, sometimes interspersed with new material. Theme transformation provides the music with some degree of unity, although the listener may not be aware of it. Since program works often lack traditional formal structure, the employment of elements of a theme in several guises helps provide a sense of organization. Composers other than Berlioz have exploited this technique; Brahms was masterful in its use.

Symphonie fantastique is in five rather long movements, and it has little relationship to the traditional eighteenth-century symphony. Berlioz provides a program of images to be associated with each movement.

I. Reveries, Passions. "He remembers the weariness of the soul, the indefinable yearning he knew before meeting his beloved. Then, the volcanic love with which she at once inspired him, his delirious suffering." There is a slow introduction that establishes the atmosphere of a reverie. Soon the *idée fixe* (marked by brackets in these examples) is heard.

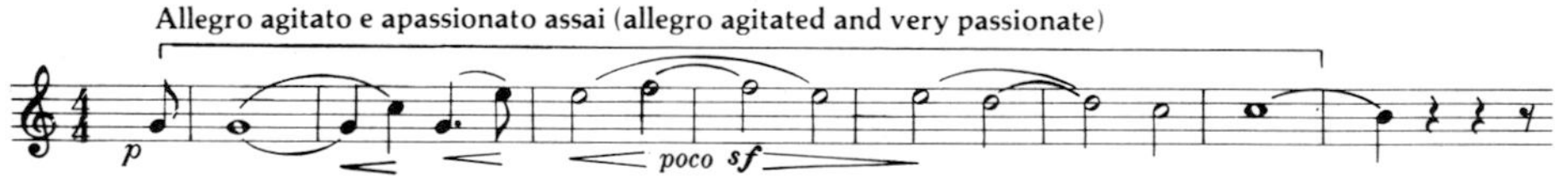

Characteristically, Berlioz has the orchestra wind up to mighty climaxes of sound.

II. A Ball. "Amid the tumult and excitement of a brilliant ball he glimpses the loved one again." This movement of the symphony is a waltz. The introduction presents arpeggios played on the harp against rapidly repeated notes in the strings. A waltz is marked to be played sweetly and tenderly.

The movement is in three-part form. The middle section contains the "fixed idea."

III. Scene in the Fields. "On a summer evening in the country, he hears two shepherds piping. The pastoral duet, the quiet surroundings . . . all unite to fill his heart with a long absent calm. But *she* appears again. His heart contracts. Painful forebodings fill his soul. The sun sets—solitude—silence." The movement starts slowly. In it Berlioz shows his unusual ability to orchestrate—to write skillfully for the instruments of the orchestra. The movement features the English horn, which was only a recent addition to the orchestra when he composed the music. The "fixed idea" appears in the middle section of this movement, which is in three-part form. Before the movement closes there is a distant rumble of thunder, which can be heard in the timpani, while the English horn plays a melancholy melody.

IV. March to the Scaffold. "He dreams that he has killed his beloved, that he has been condemned to die and is being led to the scaffold. The procession moves to the sound of a march somber and wild, now brilliant and solemn . . . at the very end the 'fixed idea' appears for an instant like the last thought of love interrupted by the fall of the ax." The movement is basically a march.

The movement demonstrates the imagination of Berlioz. In it he takes a common type of music, a march, and creates a colorful and novel piece of music. The last two movements of *Symphonie fantastique* demonstrate also his outstanding ability to manipulate the instrumental timbres. The music of the fourth movement can be studied more carefully through the use of the Listening Guide on pages 300–301. In spite of Berlioz's desire to write program music, this movement is essentially in sonata form.

V. Dream of a Witches' Sabbath. "He sees himself at a witches' sabbath surrounded by a host of fearsome specters who have gathered at his funeral. Unearthly sounds, groans, shrieks of laughter . . . the melody of his beloved is heard, but it has lost its noble and reserved character. It has become a vulgar tune, trivial and grotesque. It is she who comes to the infernal orgy. A howl of joy greets her arrival. She joins the diabolical dance. Bells toll for the dead. A burlesque of the *Dies irae.* Dance of the witches. The dance and the *Dies irae* combined."

The movement opens at a slow tempo. There are flickering scales, played softly on muted violins and violas. In the allegro portion that follows, the

LISTENING GUIDE

BERLIOZ: *SYMPHONIE FANTASTIQUE*, "MARCH TO THE SCAFFOLD"

Fourth Movement (Record 4, Side 1)

Sonata Form: Exposition

0:00 Timpani and French horns open playing fragment of *B* theme very softly.

0:34 First theme *(A)*, a descending minor scale, is played forcefully by low strings.

0:50 Bassoon adds counterpoint based on fragment of *B* as *A* is repeated by low strings.

1:06 Violins play *A* theme, now in a major key, while low strings have a line of counterpoint.

1:22 Violins repeat *A* with low strings playing counterpoint.

1:38 *A* theme returns in minor key in low strings while violins play the theme upside down in inversion by plucking (pizzicato); bassoon has line of counterpoint.

2:01 *B* theme enters in full played loudly by the brasses; theme is in major.

2:17 *B* theme repeated by brasses and woodwinds; music leads up to short codetta composed of dotted-note figure.

Development

2:33 Brasses continue a marchlike theme at loud level in contrast to woodwinds and strings playing rapidly moving notes.

2:41 *A* theme played softly pizzicato by strings and woodwinds.

2:53	Brasses return with marchlike theme played over "busy" string accompaniment.
3:09	*B* theme returns in brasses and woodwinds at loud level; "busy" string accompaniment continues.
3:24	Brasses return to marchlike material that opened development section; alternate melody with woodwinds at loud level.
3:33	Strings play *A* theme softly, pizzicato.
3:42	First portion of *A* theme played loudly several times by trombones against "busy" notes in woodwinds and strings; music increases in intensity.

Recapitulation

4:01	*A* theme returns in minor key played very loudly by full orchestra.
4:16	*A* theme repeated loudly by orchestra in inversion; figure from theme is fragmented and used as transition to coda.
4:37	Coda begins with dotted-note pattern in strings repeated many times.
5:04	Dotted-note pattern exchanged with woodwinds; music grows softer.
5:14	Very loud chord by orchestra and descending scale leading to clarinet solo.
5:24	Solo clarinet plays the *idée fixe.*
5:34	Loud, abrupt chord (head falling off?) followed by stern, forceful chords played over a drumroll.
6:01	Closes with very full chord.

theme of the beloved is transformed into a grotesque dance played on the clarinet.

The traditional religious *Dies irae* ("Day of Wrath") theme, taken from the medieval Mass for the Dead, is played by the bassoons and tubas.

In the *Ronde du sabbat* ("Witches' Dance") a driving rhythm is heard in the cellos and basses, after which it is taken up by other instruments. The combining of the various lines creates an intricate sound. Toward the conclusion of the movement Berlioz combines the dance theme and the *Dies irae.* The symphony closes in a rousing theatrical manner.

RICHARD STRAUSS

Richard Strauss (*Ree*-kard Strouse, 1864–1949) was born of a musical family but was related neither to the Johann Strauss family of waltz fame nor to Oskar Straus, composer of operettas. Richard's father was a horn player in the orchestra at Munich, and his mother was the daughter of a wealthy brewer. From his parents he apparently inherited a love of music and a good business sense.

From childhood Strauss displayed unusual musical talent. In his early twenties he was already writing his famous tone poems, and he soon established himself as an outstanding musician. In those days he was considered a radical, an "angry young man." His works were in the general style of Wagner, who had been dead over five years when Strauss wrote *Don Juan,* his first successful tone poem. His music is highly colorful and expressive, sometimes almost blatantly so. Probably it was this quality, rather than any musical

Richard Strauss at the age of twenty-four, when he was appointed to a position in the Munich Court Opera and composed Don Juan.

innovations, that earned him his early reputation. Until 1900, Strauss confined his compositions largely to tone poems. Six are standard orchestral fare today: *Don Juan, Death and Transfiguration, Till Eulenspiegel's Merry Pranks, Also sprach Zarathustra, Don Quixote,* and *Ein Heldenleben.*

After 1900 Strauss turned to opera. His first successful opera, *Salome* (1906), was a German setting of Oscar Wilde's version of the biblical story. Strauss's next opera, *Elektra,* is based on a version of Sophocles' play by a Viennese dramatist named Hugo von Hofmannsthal, with whom Strauss collaborated on several operas. Since the opera dwells on the emotions of hatred and revenge, Strauss seized the opportunity to experiment with bold and innovative harmonies. For his next opera, *Der Rosenkavalier* ("The Cavalier of the Rose"), he switched style completely. The story is poignantly humorous, centering about the decadent elegance of the powder-and-wig world of the eighteenth century

By the end of the First World War, Strauss's creative career was largely behind him. He continued to live in his villa in the Bavarian Alps and write operas until his death in 1949, but he never again enjoyed much success. He was regarded no longer as a daring radical but as a wealthy and outmoded conservative.

Strauss's Don Juan

Strauss wrote *Don Juan* in 1888 when he was twenty-four years old. The literary work that inspired Strauss was a poem by Nicholaus Lenau. Don Juan is the legendary hero whose life has become the prototype of irresponsible sensuality as he bounds from one mistress to another. In Lenau's version of the story, Don Juan's escapades are part of his idealistic search for the perfect woman, an explanation that seems hardly credible in light of his actions. Nevertheless, the harm he has brought to others begins to weigh on him, and his concern for the pleasure of the moment leaves him more and more dissatisfied and bored with life. Finally he is challenged to a duel by Don Pedro, the son of a nobleman whom Don Juan has killed. Don Juan battles gloriously and has Don Pedro at his mercy. At that moment he realizes that victory is worthless and that defeat would relieve him of the tedium of living. He allows Don Pedro to kill him.

Strauss included only three excerpts from Lenau's poem at the front of the score. Nothing else is indicated about the program. So listeners can fill out the details to suit themselves. Like all good program music, however, it can stand very well without literary association.

Despite the fact that *Don Juan* is a tone poem, it is in a rather loose sonata form. The most important theme, which might be called the "Don Juan" theme, is a composite of motives that are developed later in the work.

The melodic ideas are in themselves a commentary on Don Juan's nature—impatient for adventure, full of vitality and power, lusting for love and life. The music in the examples moves rapidly because it is in two moderately fast beats per measure.

The vigorous quality of the music continues:

The first amorous episode suggests lighthearted flirtation:

Soon comes the first true love scene. The winds sound a radiant chord, the solo violin plays sweetly, and this lovely theme appears:

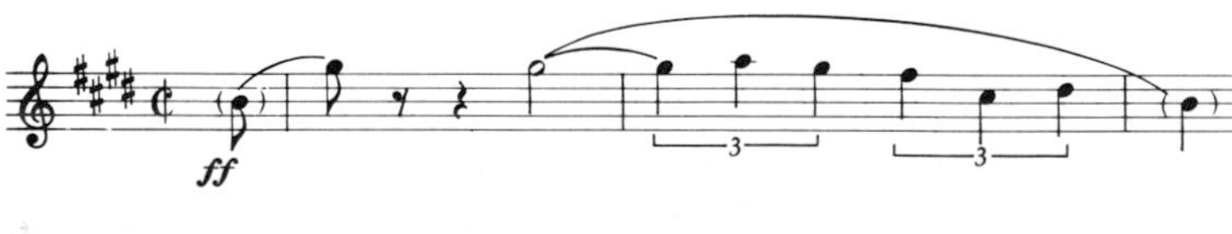

It grows more passionate as the music progresses. The "Don Juan" theme is heard again as the hero awakens from the oblivion of this love and sets out for new adventures.

His next conquest is less willing. Don Juan pleads with her, and the gasping tones of the flute seem to indicate her half-hearted resistance. She soon weakens, and a second beautiful love theme is heard:

This theme has about it an air of sadness and regret, and there follows the feeling of boredom. The music reaches a soft, quiet climax, ending with a touch of hopelessness.

Here another "Don Juan" theme appears, played by the four horns:

Presently Don Juan runs to a carnival (in Lenau's version it is a masked ball). The section juggles a theme of its own with motives from the original "Don Juan" theme. After a while the music becomes increasingly solemn, reflecting Don Juan's feelings of depression. In this condition he sees the ghosts of his previous mistresses, and their melodies reappear.

Then comes the challenge of the duel. Don Juan responds, and the music grows ever stronger, reinforced by the second "Don Juan" theme played again by the horns. The pitch level is three notes higher than it was in its first appearance, and this change adds to the exhilaration of the music. There is a short return of the opening music, which gains in driving force.

Suddenly there is a deathly halt—apparently the moment in which Don Juan decides to give up. The music shifts to minor and the trumpet jabs out a dissonant note. In shuddering sounds Don Juan's life is ended.

In this tone poem Strauss associates motives and themes with specific ideas and characters. What was begun with Liszt and Berlioz has been refined and further adapted. Wagner exploited this technique to its fullest in his operas, which will be discussed in Chapter 23.

Strauss wrote for a large orchestra. Not only are many instruments required, but most of them play most of the time. This scoring gives the music a thick, heavy sound. Early in *Don Juan* when the solo violin plays, the listener can't help wondering if the orchestra won't soon overwhelm the single instrument. It doesn't; Strauss manages to make the important lines come through.

Strauss's favorite instrument seemed to be the French horn, his father's instrument. He wrote concertos for it and featured it prominently in most of his compositions. Throughout his writing for French horn, he showed its capabilities and thereby promoted the instrument.

PETER ILICH TCHAIKOVSKY

Until early adulthood Tchaikovsky (Chy-*koff*-skee, 1840–1893) seemed destined to follow his father's footsteps by working in a governmental position. At the age of twenty-three, however, he decided to become a musician, so he resigned his job and entered the newly founded Conservatory of St. Petersburg (now Leningrad). He did well, and in three years he had finished his course and was recommended for a teaching position in the new Conservatory of Moscow. He taught harmony there for twelve years.

Throughout his life, Tchaikovsky was plagued by the fact that he was a homosexual. He once described his existence as "regretting the past, hoping for the future, without ever being satisfied with the present." He married a Conservatory student, a rather unstable girl who was madly in love with him. He could feel only pity for her and despair for himself. The marriage was a disaster. Finally, on the verge of a complete mental breakdown, he went to live with his brothers in St. Petersburg.

Peter Ilich Tchaikovsky.

At this point in his life entered Nadezhda von Meck, a wealthy widow who, though a recluse, successfully ran her inherited business empire and the lives of her eleven children. She was impressed by the beauty of Tchaikovsky's music and decided to support him financially. There was, however, one unusual twist to the arrangement. So that she could be sure she was supporting a composer and not a personal friend, she stipulated that they should never meet. And so it was. For thirteen years Mme. von Meck and Tchaikovsky carried on intense and devoted contact—all by letter.

In 1891 he accepted an invitation to America, where he participated in the opening of Carnegie Hall in New York. According to his letters, he liked Americans and was gratified by the fact that they appreciated his music. In 1893, while in St. Petersburg to conduct his Sixth Symphony, he contracted cholera and died at the age of fifty-three.

BALLET

Classical ballet began in the courts of Europe, especially France, about 300 years ago. Its main goal was grace and courtliness, not artistic expression. Deportment and etiquette were supreme virtues among the aristocracy. In the court of Louis XIV of France, for example, *everyone* took dancing lessons, and not a type of dancing in which you just shuffle around. One point learned in such dancing was the proper ballet posture; another was a balance of footwork and elevation—the ability to rise on the toes and to leap gracefully. The posture was based on a straight and quiet spine, a stiffened, straight knee, and a level hip line; the hips were not to lift, thrust out, or rotate, and the shoulders were not to ripple.

From such principles and practices there developed a systemized set of positions and steps that are basic in classical ballet. From these and other positions and movements, which often carry French names, the *choreographer* (designer of dances) plans routines and sequences for a complete scene. These movements are carefully planned to fit with the music and its story, if any. (Not all ballets have a story.)

The art of ballet remained relatively unchanged until the twentieth century. It was (and is) a beautiful art form, but it was also artificial. The first reaction to these artificialities occurred at about the turn of the century, when Isadora Duncan threw off her corset and shoes and danced barefoot throughout Europe. She believed that dancing should be harmonious and simple, with no ornaments. Although she devised no new techniques, she gave ballet a more natural look. Her ideas were adopted by Michael Fokine, Ruth St. Dennis, Martha Graham, Agnes de Mille, and others. To some extent the separation between classical ballet and modern dance still exists, with dancers usually strongly promoting one type or the other. Both types appear to have much artistic quality when danced well.

Photographs by Richard Pflum, Bloomington, Indiana

Tchaikovsky's Swan Lake

Swan Lake was given its premiere performance at the Bolshoi Theater in Moscow in March of 1877. Tchaikovsky's interest in the story began in 1871 when he was visiting his sister's children in the country. He composed for them some pieces based on a legend from *A Thousand and One Nights.* The tale involves a woman who magically becomes a bird. Four years later Tchaikovsky was commissioned to create a ballet on the story. Its initial reception was rather discouraging. The merits of the ballet were not fully appreciated until the production was presented in St. Petersburg in 1895. Since that time it has remained one of the most beloved ballets in the repertoire. George Balanchine, one of the great choreographers of the twentieth century, has written: "To succeed in *Swan Lake* is to become overnight a ballerina. All leading dancers want to dance *Swan Lake* at least once in their careers."

The story is pure magic. Prince Siegfried is approaching his twenty-first birthday. His mother plans to hold a great ball at which he will select the most attractive young woman to be his bride. On the day before the ball the prince and some of his friends go into the country to hunt swans. They come upon these glorious white birds, and the prince notices one that is obviously their Queen. (In the ballet she usually wears a diamondlike crown.) She is a ravishing creature, but is she a swan or a girl? Siegfried finally soothes the creature into telling him that a sorcerer named von Rothbart has transformed her into Odette, Queen of the Swans, and that she must remain that way forever—except between midnight and dawn. The spell can be broken only by a man who loves her, marries her, and never loves another. Siegfried immediately wants Odette to come to tomorrow's ball.

The third act of the ballet takes place at the ball. Siegfried is melancholy because he is afraid he has lost Odette. Six of the most beautiful girls in the kingdom dance for Siegfried, but he refuses to marry any of them because he loves another. Soon the lights dim and a dark beauty is led forward by the Knight of the Black Swan. She is Odile, but Siegfried knows only that she is the image of Odette. Odile's dancing enchants Siegfried and she leads him into the garden. In the meantime the guests are honored by dances from foreign lands—Spain, Hungary, Poland. Odile reappears to do the final dance. With the Prince she performs the brilliant Black Swan *pas de deux* (dance for two). Siegfried is so taken with her that he swears eternal faithfulness to her, still believing her to be Odette. Now the spell cannot be broken; von Rothbart has tricked Siegfried.

In the fourth act the Queen of the Swans appears, sobbing and insisting that she must die. The Prince arrives, swears his eternal love, and embraces her. She believes him, but tells him that only death will break the dreadful spell. Odette and Siegfried, wishing to drown, fling themselves into the lake.

Love triumphs, von Rothbart dies, and the spell is broken. Odette and Siegfried glide on a jeweled ship into the ever-after.

Tchaikovsky arranged a suite from the music that he composed for *Swan Lake*. He did the same with his other well-known ballets, *The Nutcracker* and *The Sleeping Beauty*. The music in the suite does not appear in the same order as in the ballet, because in the suite Tchaikovsky does not need to follow the story line. Also, the suite contains only a portion of the music that appears in the ballet. The first movement of the suite contains the most prominent theme from the ballet. It appears at various times in both major and minor.

The second movement is built around the waltz.

The third movement contains the theme for the dance of the swans.

The fourth movement features a harp cadenza followed by a violin solo. A Hungarian dance called the czardas (*char*-dash) appears in the fifth movement. The czardas has a slow beginning, followed by furiously paced music. Traditionally the dancers move as fast as possible. The two themes associated with this movement are:

A sixth movement provides a brilliant ending to the suite.

Tchaikovsky's style of music is especially well suited to ballet. His music has a lilting quality that seems to inspire graceful movement.

Other style periods have had program music and music for ballet, true. But there was something consonant between these two types of music and the music of the nineteenth century. Perhaps it was the imaginative type of story or association that attracted the composers of the Romantic period, or perhaps it was the desire to break away from the previous century's preoccupation with form. In any case, many colorful and beautiful musical works based on programmatic associations and stories for ballets were written in the Romantic century.

23

ROMANTIC OPERA

At the time Mozart died in the last decade of the eighteenth century, Italian opera was predominant. In fact, it might be argued that it was the *only* type of opera at that time. That situation was to change in the Romantic period. There appeared a distinctly German kind of opera and later in the nineteenth century a French style and a Russian one. Italian opera itself was also to change, but only gradually.

ITALIAN ROMANTIC OPERA

At the beginning of the nineteenth century, Italian opera was in the style of Mozart's *The Marriage of Figaro.* Gioacchino Rossini (1792–1868) even based his opera *The Barber of Seville* on the same characters found in Mozart's opera. However, Mozart's *The Marriage of Figaro* should not be confused with Rossini's *The Barber of Seville,* which was written some thirty years later. Both are based on plays from a trilogy by Beaumarchais. The principal characters appear in both operas, but some differences are apparent. For example, Figaro is a valet in Mozart's opera, not a barber.

With Vincenzo Bellini (1801–1835) Italian opera reached a high point of interest in melody. The arias in his operas, such as *Norma,* emphasize beautiful singing (*bel canto* in Italian) through technically demanding melodic lines, cadenzas, and ornamentation. Gaetano Donizetti (1797–1848) also contributed to the *bel canto* style of opera. Although these early operas often lacked convincing dramatic qualities, the brilliance of the soloists' lines and the beauty of the melodies make for highly enjoyable listening.

Italian opera composers seem not to have been influenced by Wagner. They adopted almost none of his compositional or philosophical ideas. Perhaps the German and Italian temperaments are too dissimilar to embrace the same styles. Or perhaps the reason was more political in its basis: The period was one during which northern Italy was trying to achieve liberation from Austria. It is doubtful if anything Germanic would have been welcome in Italy during that time. Whatever the reason, Italian opera maintained its own flavor and style.

GIUSEPPE VERDI

The chief name associated with Italian Romantic opera is that of Giuseppe Verdi (*Vair*-dee, 1813–1901). Verdi brought about significant changes. His characters are neither stock roles, as had been found in the Classical period, nor symbols, which they tended to be in Wagner's music dramas. They are more like real persons who react to situations as average people would. Verdi also improved the quality of music in the recitative. No longer was recitative merely the necessary filler between arias or ensembles. His recitatives are melodious and expressive, more like the ideal formulated by the founders of opera. And Verdi lets the orchestra contribute to the mood of the words.

Verdi made another contribution to Italian opera: He insisted on having a good libretto. The usual libretto for earlier operas had been a not-too-carefully prepared version of a mediocre story. Verdi selected the finest literature—Schiller, Victor Hugo, Dumas, Shakespeare. Then he collaborated with the librettist whenever possible to ensure maximum quality.

Verdi's career was long and magnificent, spanning more than fifty years. His last opera, *Falstaff,* was completed when he was seventy-nine! Of the twenty-seven operas he composed, the following are perennial favorites with operagoers: *Rigoletto* (1851), *Il Trovatore* ("The Troubador") (1853), *La Traviata* ("The Fallen Woman") (1853), *Un Ballo in Maschera* ("The Masked Ball") (1859), *La*

Forza del Destino ("The Force of Destiny") (1862), *Aida* (1871), *Otello* (1887), and *Falstaff* (1893).

GIACOMO PUCCINI

Giacomo Puccini (Poo-*chee*-nee, 1858–1924) was not so sophisticated a composer as Verdi. He did possess, however, a wonderful gift of melody and an instinct for what would be successful on stage. These abilities have won for his operas a popularity equal to that accorded the works of Verdi.

Puccini belonged to a group of opera composers who stressed *verismo* (realism). Therefore, he drew material from everyday life, rejecting heroic or exalted themes from mythology and history. He was fond of parallel chord movement, and he selected chords for their particular sound as well as for their harmonic function.

Giacomo Puccini.

Puccini's best-known operas include *La Bohème* (1896), *Tosca* (1900), *Madame Butterfly* (1904), which is a story about the marriage of an American naval lieutenant and a Japanese girl, and *Turandot* (1926), which was completed by a friend after Puccini's death.

Puccini's La Bohème

In true *verismo* style, *La Bohème* ("The Bohemians") is a story of hippie life on the Left Bank of the Seine in Paris. The setting provides the composer with ample opportunities to inject emotion into the music.

The curtain rises on the ramshackle garret in which live four young bohemians: the poet Rodolfo, the painter Marcello, the philosopher Colline, and the musician Schaunard. Rodolfo and Marcello try to work but can think of little except the bitter cold. It is Christmas Eve, and they can't afford fuel for a decent fire. Colline and Schaunard come home shortly and flourish some of that rare item—money. The landlord, evidently aware of their good fortune, soon comes asking for the rent. By the use of a little chicanery, they are able to get rid of him. They decide to celebrate at the Café Momus, so they leave in high spirits,—all except Rodolfo who is finishing some writing and plans to join them shortly.

There is a knock at the door. It is Mimi, who at the time has not met Rodolfo. Her candle has gone out, and she can't see to get up the stairs to her apartment. She is also weak and out of breath, so Rodolfo gives her a little wine and offers her a chair. As he helps her search for the key she has dropped on the floor, a draft of wind blows out their candles. They grope in the dark for her key. He finds it and, thinking quickly, slips it into his pocket without telling her. As they continue feeling along the floor, Rodolfo's hand meets hers and he exclaims, *"Che gelida manina!"* ("How cold your little hand is!") Then begins one of those glorious arias and a duet that exemplify Romantic opera at its best (Record 4, Side 2). First, Rodolfo tells Mimi about himself and his lonely life as a poet. In the aria he joins with the orchestra in a luscious Puccini melody:

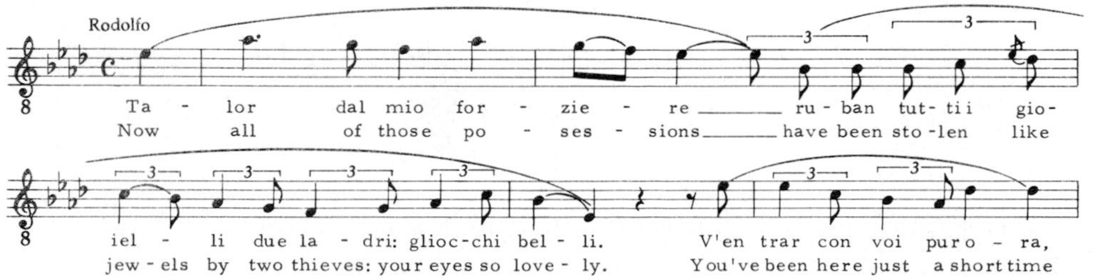

In this scene from Act 1 of La Boheme *Benoit, the landlord, is boasting about his virility. His boasts provide Rodolfo and his companions with an excuse to get Benoit out of the apartment without his collecting the rent due him.*

Mimi responds with an equally beautiful aria, *"Mi chiamano Mimi"* ("I'm always called Mimi"). In it she describes her simple life and her flower embroidery:

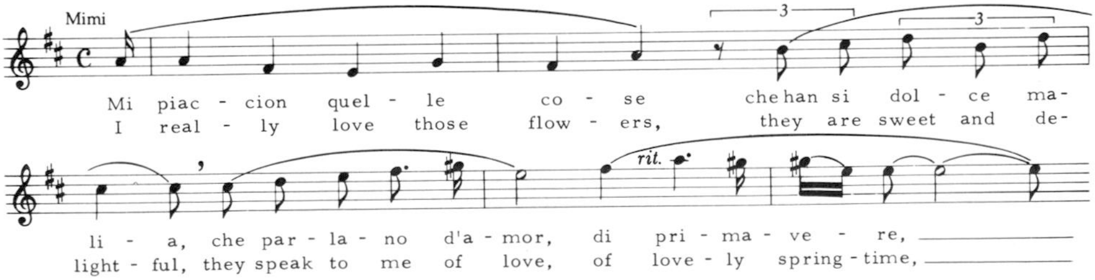

The aria continues with another lovely melody, some of which appears later in the opera:

ma quan-do vien lo sge - lo il pri - mo so - lee mi - o,
but when the frost is o - ver, sun - shine's first rays are mine,
allarg.
il pri - mo ba - cio del - l'a - pri - le e mi - o!
then comes the first sweet kiss of Ap - ril, to me!

Rodolfo's friends return to the courtyard outside, urging him to hurry. He goes to the window and tells them to return to Momus and reserve a table. As the friends leave, Mimi and Rodolfo break into a duet in which they speak of the new love that binds them together. Some of the melodies previously introduced in the arias are heard again. The curtain falls with Mimi and Rodolfo embracing as they sing "Amor."

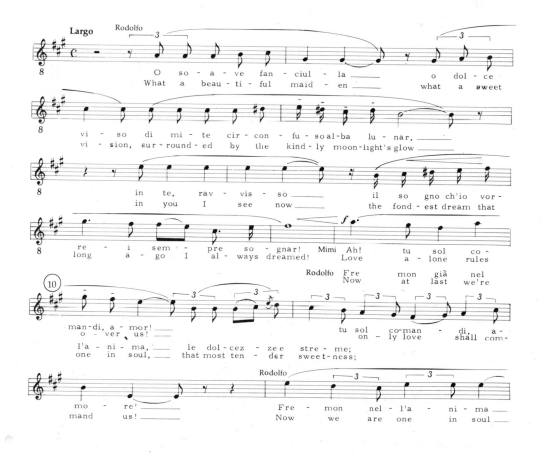

Ah! tu sol co -
Love a - lone rules

Fre mon già nel
Now at last we're
10
man-di, a - mor!
o - ver us!
tu sol co-man - di, a -
on - ly love shall com -
l'a - ni - ma, le dol - cez - ze e stre - me;
one in soul, that most ten - der sweet - ness;
mo - re!
mand us!

Fre - mon nel - l'a - ni - ma
Now we are one in soul

Largo

O so - a - ve fan - ciul - la o dol - ce
What a beau - ti - ful maid - en what a sweet
vi - so di mi - te cir - con - fu - so al - ba lu - nar,
vi - sion, sur - round - ed by the kind - ly moon - light's glow
in te, rav - vis - so il so gno ch'io vor -
in you I see now the fond - est dream that
re - i sem - pre so - gnar!
long a - go I al - ways dreamed!

Mimi: Oh! co-me dol - ci scen - do-no le sue lu-sin - ghe al co - re . . . tu
Oh! how the pow'r of love's sweet joy has filled my heart with glad ness . . . our
Rodolfo:
dol - cez - ze es-tre - me, fre-mon dol-cez-ze es-tre-me, nel
Most ten - der sweet - ness there is such ten-der sweet-ness, in
sol co-man-di, a - mor!
on - ly mas-ter is love!
Mimi
No, per pie-tà!
No, please do not!
Rodolfo
Sei
Be
(kisses Mimi)
ba - cio fre-me a - mor!
this, our first kiss of love!
20
Mimi
Rodolfo
mi - a! V'a - spet - tan gli a - mi - ci. Già mi man - di
my own! Your friends are still wait - ing. Are you send - ing
Mimi
Rodolfo
Mimi
vi - a? Vor-rei dir . . . ma non o - so.. Di'! Se ve-nis - si con
me out? I would say . . . but I don't dare.. Say it! Could-n't I come with
Rodolfo
voi? Che? Mi-mi! Sa reb-be co - si dol-ce re-star qui. C'è fred-do
you? What? Mi-mi! It would be much more plea-sant to stay here. Out-side it's
Mimi
Rodolfo
fuo - ri. Vi sta - rò vi - ci - na! E al ri -
freez - ing. I'll stay close be - side you! When we
30
Mimi (mischievously)
Rodolfo
Mimi
tor - no? Cu-rio - so! Dam-mi il brac-cio, mia pic-ci-na. Ob-be-di-sco, si -
come back? I can't guess! Take my arm my lit - tle dar-ling. I o-bey you, kind
Rodolfo
pp
Mimi
(they leave)
gnor! Che m'a - mi di', lo t'a mo!
sir! Say you love me, I love you!
Strings, harp, flute
Rodolfo and Mimi
(off stage)
A - mor, a - mor!
My love, my love!
40
pp
Orchestra
3
A - mor.
My love.
dying away (curtain)

The realism problem mentioned in Chapter 17 is always present, even in *verismo* opera. Rodolfo and Mimi tell about themselves briefly, they are interrupted for a few moments, and then—suddenly—they are proclaiming their love for each other. Musically, the course of events is well conceived: an aria by the tenor, an aria by the soprano, a short break, and a duet in which they join forces. The scene would not be good opera if the love between the two were allowed to grow more naturally over several hours.

The scene between Rodolfo and Mimi also illustrates the smooth transition between recitative and aria. No longer is there a clear demarcation, particularly now that the recitative has assumed melodic and expressive interest.

For a small, frail girl dying of tuberculosis, Mimi engages in some rather robust singing. Again there is a break with reality that listeners must accept if they are to enjoy the opera. The full, vibrant singing style associated with opera is a musical necessity. The characters in most operas, including Puccini's, react to their environment and emotions on a grand scale. Their responses are exaggerated. Although ordinary persons are reluctant to make declarations of love, especially to people they don't know well, the characters in an opera proclaim their feelings promptly and with magnified intensity. Such a telescoping of emotions and actions is good theater. Ordinary individuals do feel deeply, but they are unlikely to express their feelings with the openness and force of Rodolfo and Mimi. The typical listener, then, responds to opera because of having experienced emotions similar to those depicted on stage, but the timing, degree, and manner of expression are different.

To convey the necessary power and intensity of expression, the singer must produce an "operatic" tone. Anything less will leave listeners unmoved. The vocal style of popular-song artists, even good ones, is inappropriate and inadequate for opera. Most of the currently popular singers lack tonal power, a fact that is usually covered up by amplification systems and recording devices. Then there is the matter of sheer singing ability. Opera singers certainly outclass popular singers when it comes to breath control and endurance, wide pitch range, richness of tone, control of dynamic level, and technical know-how. If a popular singer were to attempt Rodolfo's role, it would be comparable to putting a twelve-year-old boy into the starting lineup of a professional football team.

Opera has acquired some traditions regarding the type of voice and the character to be portrayed. The heroine is almost always a soprano. In most stories she is young and beautiful, so the higher, lighter voice is more suitable. The leading male role is usually sung by a tenor. He is young and frequently sings duets with the soprano, often doubling her pitches one octave lower. This puts his pitches near the top of the male range, and gives the voice quality greater intensity. If there are older people or villains in the plot, the female

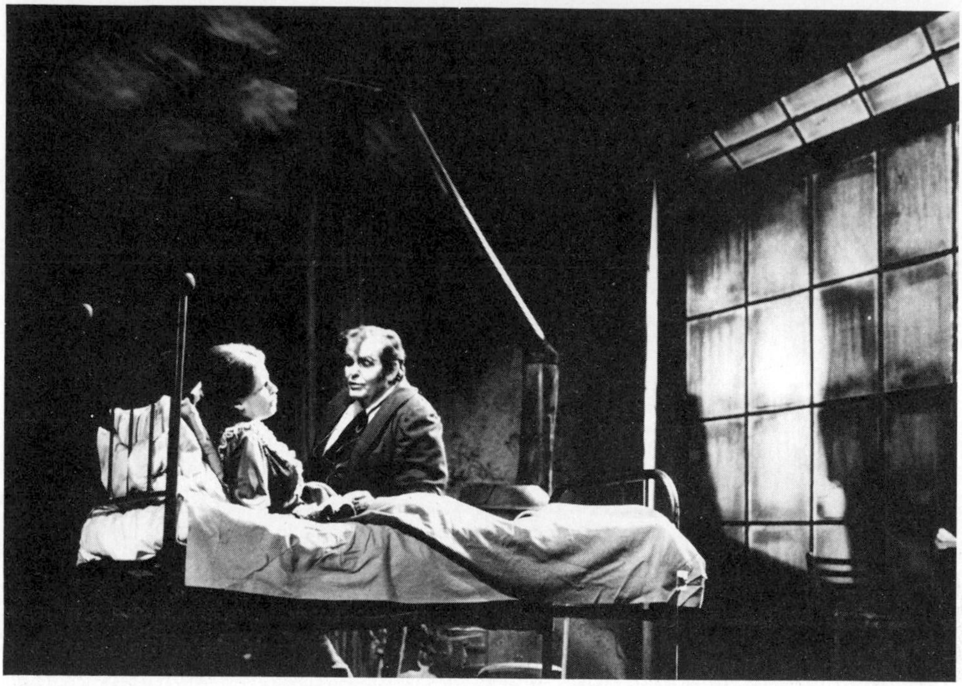

Rodolfo consoles Mimi shortly before she dies.

parts are usually written for mezzo-sopranos or contraltos, the male roles for baritones or basses. Often they are supposed to sound ugly; Madame Flora in *The Medium,* an opera presented in Chapter 28, is an example of this.

The rest of *La Bohème* is equally beautiful and not long. The second act is a delightful scene at the Café Momus in which Musetta, Marcello's former love and notorious flirt, sings a bewitching waltz. In Act III, Mimi and Rodolfo have broken apart. There is a hint of impending doom because of Mimi's worsening tubercular condition.

In Act IV the setting is again the garret, and there are several musical and dramatic parallels to the first act. This time Musetta enters, saying that Mimi is downstairs, too weak to climb them—an ironic parallel to events of the earlier act. Mimi is helped into the room, and the friends leave quickly to get medicine and a doctor. Rodolfo and Mimi recall their first meeting. The old themes are heard, but the music is no longer robust. It is pathetic and shattered. The friends return. They talk quietly among themselves, hoping Mimi can sleep. Suddenly they realize she is dead. "Mimi! Mimi!" Rodolfo cries. The orchestra strikes the same chords heard in the love music of the first act. This time the music is weighted with grief. The curtain falls.

GEORGES BIZET

Georges Bizet (Bee-*zay*, 1838–1875) was born in Paris and lived most of his life there. Young Georges wanted to become a musician, and his parents supported the idea—quite a change from the situations of Handel, Berlioz, and others. He won the Prix de Rome, which afforded him a three-year stay in Rome. He composed a symphony and a few other works, but opera seemed to be his primary interest. *The Pearl Fishers,* written in 1863, is a drama of love and life in Ceylon. Four years later he wrote another opera, *The Fair Maid of Perth,* and later an opera named *Djanileh,* which is set in Cairo. None of these operas was successful, and they are rarely performed today. One of Bizet's better works is the incidental music to the drama *L'Arlesienne* ("The Woman of Arles"), which was written in 1872.

Most of Bizet's fame is the result of his opera *Carmen.* Its initial performances were largely failures. (One critic wrote: "If the devil were to write an opera, it would probably come out sounding very much like *Carmen.*") Bizet had poured enormous effort into its writing and production. Worn out by months of rehearsal and tension, he was not prepared to take the blow of its failure. He died at the age of thirty-seven, exactly three months after the premiere of the opera. Today *Carmen* is perhaps the best-known and best-loved opera in the world.

GERMAN ROMANTIC OPERA

German Romantic opera began with Carl Maria von Weber (*Vay*-ber, 1786–1826). In 1821 he wrote *Der Freischütz* ("The Free-Shooter"), an opera based on German folklore and Romantic ideals. The story is about a marksman who receives from the black huntsman (that is, the devil) seven magic bullets, six of which do as he wills but the seventh as the devil wills. The devil also gets the soul of the one who receives that bullet. Besides mysticism, the opera features peasants, rustic scenes, and hunting horns. Weber completed two more operas before his early death. Although they are seldom performed today, they had a significant influence on Richard Wagner, one of the musical giants of the Romantic era.

RICHARD WAGNER

Richard Wagner (*Ree*-kard *Vahg*-ner, 1813–1883) was an artistic phenomenon. Born in Leipzig, he was the son of a minor police official who died when Richard

Richard Wagner.

was still an infant. His mother married a talented actor and playwright, who encouraged his stepson along similar lines. For most of his career Wagner was largely self-taught. At the age of twenty he obtained a post as chorus master in a small opera house in Leipzig and produced his first operas.

Success was slow, and for the next ten years it looked as though Wagner would spend his life hovering on the edge of poverty. His first successful opera was *Rienzi,* which earned him a position as conductor for the king of Saxony. Other successful operas followed in the 1840s: *The Flying Dutchman, Tannhäuser,* and *Lohengrin.* The latter two operas derive their subjects from medieval German epic stories, which emphasize supernatural elements and glorification of the German people.*

In 1848 Wagner became associated with the political uprisings that were taking place in Europe. He even published two articles in a magazine that advocated anarchy. A revolution broke out in Dresden in 1849, and the king and his court fled. Wagner was forced to escape to the home of his friend Franz Liszt at Weimar. Since there was a warrant out for his arrest, Wagner soon fled on over the border into Switzerland. At that point he seemed a ruined man, but he was helped by some willing patrons, and the years in Switzerland were some of his most productive. It was during this time that he began work on *The Ring of the Nibelung.*

*Adolf Hitler was very familiar with Wagner's music dramas and was extremely fond of them.

In the 1850s he composed *Tristan and Isolde,* and in the early 1860s *The Meistersingers of Nuremberg.* Wagner became estranged from his wife, who had grown unsympathetic to his artistic aims and desires. He became involved with a succession of women who appreciated him but whose husbands did not. In 1864 again all seemed lost.

At this point fate seemed to step in. A nineteen-year-old who was an admirer of Wagner's music ascended to the throne in Bavaria. He was Ludwig II, known as "Mad Ludwig." He summoned Wagner to Munich, where the composer resumed work on *The Ring of the Nibelung.* In time he married Cosima, the daughter of Franz Liszt. Unfortunately, at the time their affair began, Cosima was already married to Hans von Bülow, the most famous conductor of the nineteenth century.

By 1876 Wagner had reached the top of the artistic world. It was during that year that he opened his first Bayreuth (*By*-royt) festival. Later he built an opera house there, and the Bayreuth festivals continue today. It is the only theater in the world that is devoted exclusively to the music of one person. His last opera was *Parsifal,* which is a legend based on the Holy Grail. He is buried at Bayreuth, which in a sense is his monument.

Wagner's Music Dramas

It is hard to know where to begin or end in discussing the music of Wagner. Entire books have been written on one or another of his operas. In fact, each of his operas has a score the size of a large book. His music is awe-inspiring, profound and pompous, fantastic and forceful. He was a complex musician and a complex personality, with one of history's most massive egos.

As no opera composer before him, Wagner consciously tackled the dilemma of balance between music and drama. In his lengthy philosophical discourses, he often indicated his belief that poetry and music should be one. To meet his artistic goals, he set about creating a vastly different kind of opera, one that he called *music drama* instead of opera.

The music drama required a new and different approach to the concept of libretto. And so Wagner wrote his own texts. The topics were mythological because he felt that such stories best appealed to the emotions. For poetry he revived an old German alliterative form, of which the following is an example:

Die *L*iebe bringt *L*ust und *L*eid Doch in ihr *W*eh auch *w*ebt sie *W*onne.	Thus *l*ove doth *l*ighten *l*oss, For 'tis from *w*oe she *w*eaves her *w*onder.

Wagner's favorite libretto themes were not only mythological. They were also rich with philosophical overtones: the struggle between good and evil, the contest between the physical and spiritual, and the idea of redemption through love. Because these themes are present, the characters in the music dramas are not personalities but more nearly symbols or pawns being pushed about by forces beyond their control. In this respect Wagner approaches the drama of the ancient Greeks.

In addition, Wagner refined a technique developed by Weber and used later by Richard Strauss in *Don Juan.* The technique is to associate a musical motive with a particular character, emotion, or idea, and the concept is called *leitmotiv* or "leading motive." As soon as various motives are established, Wagner weaves them in and out of the music at appropriate times to enhance the plot and provide unity. Such use of motives also permits the orchestra to assume a more vital role in the music drama.

Since the division of music into recitatives, arias, and choruses breaks into the forward motion of the drama, Wagner eliminated these forms as independent sections. Instead he created a flowing, melodious vocal line to serve as an unending melody. The vocal line emphasizes the expression of the words being sung. With its continuous interweaving of motives, the orchestra contributes to the impression of never-ending motion. It is incorrect to say that there are no arias in Wagner's music dramas. There are, but they are woven into the continuously flowing music.

To heighten the impression that a musical work is "seamless," Wagner uses much chromatic harmony. That is, by making half-step alterations of chords, he weakens the "magnetic pull" of chords toward a tonic. The absence of a strong tonic means that the music seldom arrives at a feeling of conclusion, which results in a weakened feeling of key.

Wagner does not treat the orchestra as mere accompaniment for the singers on stage. The orchestra equals, if not exceeds, the importance of the singers. In a real sense his orchestra is symphonic both in its size and in its ability to stand virtually without the vocal parts. In fact, many portions of his operas are performed today as concert pieces without singers. Probably Wagner's greatest genius was his ability to exploit the full resources of the orchestra. He made it produce effects that had previously never been dreamed of—brilliant light as well as dark, somber colors; overwhelming force and sensuous intimacy.

Siegfried's Rhine Journey

Wagner's most ambitious achievement was a cycle of four complete operas entitled *Der Ring des Nibelungen* ("The Ring of the Nibelung"). The four operas in the cycle are *Das Rheingold* ("The Gold of the Rhine"), *Die Walküre*

("The Valkyries"), *Siegfried,* and *Götterdämmerung* ("The Twilight of the Gods"). The story of the cycle of operas is built around some gold supposedly guarded by the Rhine maidens in the Rhine river. The gold is stolen and a curse put on it. (In Romantic operas the direction of events often hinged on curses and magic potions.) The curse states that if the possessor will renounce love, he will rule the world. The result is a chain of misfortunes affecting all the characters in the drama. The story inspired American Albert Pinkham Ryder's murky painting *Siegfried and the Rhine Maidens,* which appears on this page.

In the Prologue to *Götterdämmerung* the three Fates or Norns (weavers of destiny) are spinning. When their thread breaks, a terrible catastrophe is predicted. The Fates vanish. At this point, a section of the opera called *Siegfried's Rhine Journey* begins. It is often performed as a concert orchestral number without singers. A Listening Guide for *Siegfried's Rhine Journey* (concert version) appears on pages 326–28. Each of the *leitmotivs* is identified and the accompanying scene is indicated.

Siegfried and the Rhine Maidens, *painted by Albert Pinkham Ryder (1847–1917).*

LISTENING GUIDE

WAGNER: *SIEGFRIED'S RHINE JOURNEY*

(Record 2, Side 1)

Dawn

0:00 Timpani roll played very softly.

0:04 Fate motive played by trombones, soft and slow; followed by cellos playing a melodic line:

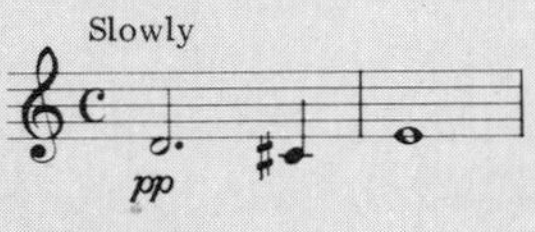

0:42 Siegfried motive played by horns softly; cellos again answer with melodic line at higher pitch than first time:

1:43 Siegfried motive played by French horns more strongly.

1:54 Brünnhilde motive played by clarinet; answered by bass clarinet; music is still soft and slow:

2:21 Violins take up Brünnhilde motive; answered by cellos; music begins to grow in power, and tempo slowly increases.

Parting of Siegfried and Brünnhilde

3:09 Siegfried motive played powerfully by trumpets and woodwinds; portion of Walküre's motive from earlier opera played by trombone.

3:28 Brünnhilde motive returns, played by violins; followed by clarinet and oboe.

3:47 "Desire to travel" motive played by violins:

4:11 Music slowly builds, using the travel motive.

4:42 Siegfried motive played more impetuously and loud by trumpets.

5:09 Brünnhilde motive played by violins; followed by French horns as music slowly becomes calmer.

5:55 "Adventure" motive (a transformed version of Siegfried motive) played by solo French horn:

6:10 Bass clarinet answers with Brünnhilde motive.

6:25 Motive for Brünnhilde love played by strings:

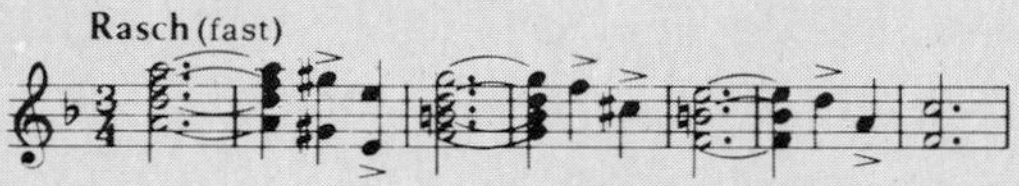

6:42 Motive called "Love's resolve" from earlier opera *Siegfried* is played by strings and woodwinds.

6:56 Adventure motive played quietly by French horn; oboe takes up motive shortly.

Siegfried's Journey to the Rhine

7:16 French horns play a short extension of adventure motive; violins play a decorated version of that motive.

7:37 Orchestra takes up extension of adventure motive; many changes of pitch by half step are heard.

8:08 Rhine motive played strongly by brasses; later joined by woodwinds and French horns:

(continued)

9:12 Portion of Siegfried motive played rapidly by trombone; later by woodwinds.

9:36 Motive for Rhine maidens and Rhine gold:

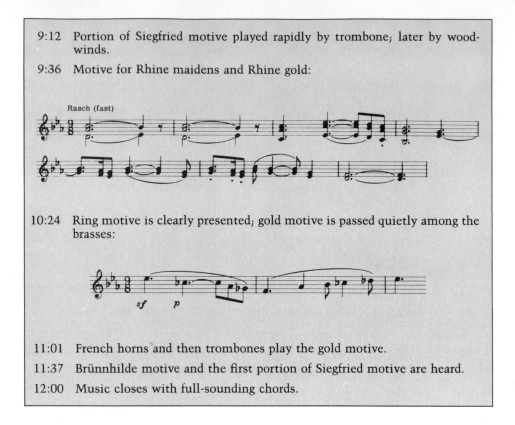

10:24 Ring motive is clearly presented; gold motive is passed quietly among the brasses:

11:01 French horns and then trombones play the gold motive.

11:37 Brünnhilde motive and the first portion of Siegfried motive are heard.

12:00 Music closes with full-sounding chords.

Siegfried's Rhine Journey is only one small portion of one opera, and that opera is only one of four in *The Ring of the Nibelung.* Still, it does offer some insights into Wagner's style.

It is hard to assess his music. Sometimes it is brilliant and superbly imaginative. At other times, it is slow-moving and repetitive. The sheer length of his productions makes the task of evaluation difficult. For instance, the *Ring* cycle requires over twelve hours for performance, and it contains more than ninety motives, the exact number depending on how one chooses to count them. For the listener who is unfamiliar with Wagner, the best way to learn about his music is to concentrate on specific short sections, like *Siegfried's Rhine Journey.* Attention to the motives will make the music more meaningful.

By the end of the nineteenth century opera had come a long way from its founding in Florence 300 years earlier. Everything about opera now was bigger and grander—its length, the size of the cast, orchestra, and chorus, the scope of the staging, and so on. The plots no longer involved characters from

Greek mythology or even the elegant aristocrats of Mozart's operas. The continuous recitative of Peri's *Euridice* had been abandoned long before the Romantic age, only to be partly reincarnated in Wagner's music dramas. When all is said and done, however, the same obstacles and opportunities existed in both early and Romantic operas. It was still an immensely fascinating and expressive combination of art forms.

24

LATE ROMANTIC MUSIC

The Romantic composers of the second half of the nineteenth century tended to be more sophisticated and less colorful than the generation that had preceded them. Late Romanticists like Brahms and Strauss were able to build on the work of Liszt and Schubert. No longer was there a concern with new departures or a turning away from the Classical past. Since the later composers were more distant in time from the Classical period, they did not feel the need to prove that their compositions were different from the earlier style. They employed some features of both the Baroque and Classical periods and yet introduced innovations of their own.

The late Romantic composers were generally less able performers than their predecessors. Tchaikovsky did not perform publicly and was a poor conductor, almost ruining the first performance of his Sixth Symphony. Richard Strauss and Brahms did not concentrate on public performance either, although both were skilled conductors, and Brahms was a fine pianist. Late Romantic composers thought of themselves as composers first of all; other skills were secondary.

JOHANNES BRAHMS

Johannes Brahms (1833–1897) was the son of a musician, a somewhat shiftless double bass player in Hamburg, Germany. Young Brahms got his start by playing piano in the dance halls in the poorer sections of town. He demonstrated considerable talent, and by the age of twenty he was serving as piano accompanist to the best violinist of the day. He showed talent in composition as well and soon went to study with Robert Schumann. The Schumanns took the shy young man into their home. In his magazine Schumann spoke highly of Brahms's work, and before long Brahms was known throughout the musical world. He was a great help to the family when Schumann suffered a mental [illegible]pse and had to be hospitalized.

At first Brahms admired and then grew to love Clara Schumann, who [illegible] ourteen years older than he and the mother of seven children. Because he [illegible] he highest regard for her husband, his ailing benefactor, the situation [illegible] d him much conflict. After Schumann died Brahms should have felt free [illegible] ow through on his love for Clara and marry her; she was no longer the [illegible] inable ideal. But somehow he could not bring himself to take a step that [illegible] have obligated him and limited his freedom.

Brahms reacted in a similar way to employment. He never accepted a [illegible] n that made heavy demands on him. The one position Brahms coveted—[illegible] torship of the orchestra in his native Hamburg—eluded him throughout his life. Apparently the directors of the orchestra could not forget that he started out as a waterfront musician. Most of his adult life, therefore, was spent in Vienna, where for short periods of time he directed various choral groups and a music society.

Brahms was every bit a human being. A bachelor, he scrimped on buying food for himself but never failed to eat heartily if invited to someone's home for dinner. He was brusque, especially as he grew older, but he was also fond of children and enjoyed a good laugh. He had a caustic wit.

Brahms was aware that he had extraordinary talent as a composer, and this was partially the reason for his wanting to be as uncommitted as possible. Unlike Beethoven, he left no rejected versions of his music for posterity to find. He wanted the world to know only his best work, so his rough sketches were carefully destroyed. It is said that he burned as many of his compositions as he allowed to be published.

Brahms composed almost every type of music, and wrote with consistently high quality—symphonies, concertos, chamber music, piano works, songs, and choral music. One of his greatest compositions, *A German Requiem,* was written early in his career. This work for chorus, orchestra, and soprano and baritone soloists is one of the most moving in all music literature.

In spite of his demonstrated skill in writing for both the choral and

Johannes Brahms as a young man.

strictly instrumental idioms, Brahms was not attracted to either opera or tone poems. His coolness toward opera may have been partly due to the excessive competition raging between his followers and those of Richard Wagner. In the second half of the nineteenth century music lovers evidently felt obligated to choose sides between the two men. The division concerned artistic philosophy as much as it did personalities. The Wagnerites held that music was a medium for the communication of emotions and ideas. Brahms promoted the idea that music was an end in itself. Since there is some truth in both views, the dispute has never been resolved to everyone's satisfaction. Brahms handled the matter quite sensibly: He ignored it as best he could and went about his composing.

Brahms's Symphony No. 4, Op. 98

Brahms wrote only four symphonies, but each has a prominent place in the orchestral repertoire and is frequently performed today. He approached the writing of a symphony with utmost seriousness. After some labor on what was to have been his first symphony, he decided that the material was not properly symphonic, so he reworked it as his First Piano Concerto. Finally, at the age of forty-three he did bring out his First Symphony. He completed his Fourth Symphony nine years later, in the summer of 1885. By this time his reputation as a composer was firmly established, and there was much demand for his music.

Before Brahms finally released a work, it was his custom to invite a few close friends, especially Clara Schumann, to look it over and offer suggestions. The Fourth Symphony underwent similar scrutiny before Brahms deemed it ready for presentation to the public. Hans von Bülow, the most famous conductor of his time, referred to Brahms's drive for perfection in a letter to a concert agent: "J. Brahms proposes to rehearse a new Symphony round about October. If he is satisfied with it—you know how he repolishes and no amount of revision is too much for him—then I am sure he would not be adverse to take it on the Rhine and to Holland with us." When the symphony was first performed, Brahms himself conducted it. The work was a great success on the tour, although later audiences in Vienna received it more coolly.

First Movement. The first theme of this sonata-form movement has a sweep that is typical of Brahms:

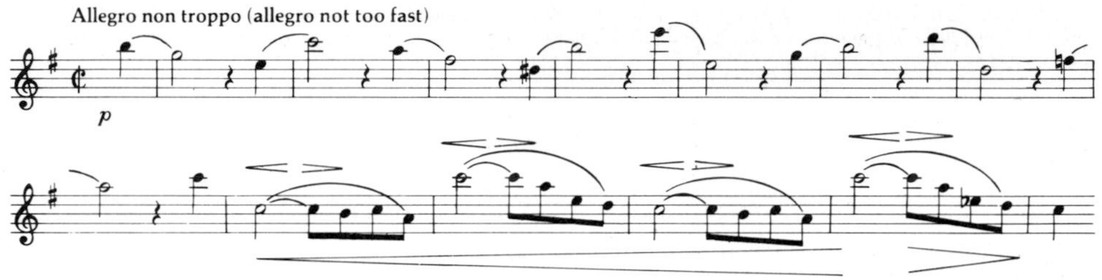

This theme is developed and transformed throughout much of the movement. For instance, in the next few measures the same idea appears at *twice* its original speed. This technique of shortening all the note values proportionately is called *diminution.* Usually the pitch relationships in the new phrase closely resemble those in the original phrase. Here Brahms chooses to alter the melody somewhat as he presents the rhythm in diminution:

At the end of the development section the same idea appears at *half* its original speed; the note values have been lengthened to produce *augmentation.* At this point Brahms retains the melodic line but alters the rhythmic relationships. Despite that alteration, the phrase strongly resembles the opening theme:

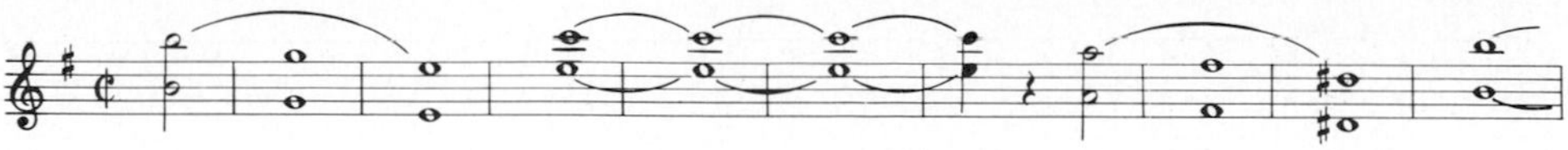

At another place the theme is varied and exchanged between the first and second violins:

Elsewhere it is exchanged between strings and woodwinds:

One could go on for pages showing the countless ways Brahms varies, develops, and transforms the theme. The movement is filled with fragments and suggestions of it. Almost from the time the theme appears, he is developing it and blending it into the structure of the music in such a way as to create a symphonic masterpiece. Perhaps most noteworthy is the fact that throughout the symphony he maintains the melodious sounds of the Romantic era. His music displays much intellectual content without becoming pedantic.

The second theme combines two melodic ideas. One is played by the horns and a few of the woodwinds. It sounds somewhat like introductory music, and perhaps it is, because soon a highly romantic melody starts in the cellos and horns:

The short, martial notes of the woodwinds appear extensively from this point on.

A third theme appears later in the movement but is not quite so pervasive:

The first movement continues along the familiar plan of sonata form.

If you can remember the first movement of Mozart's Symphony No. 40, you can realize how the symphony grew over the years from 1789 to 1885. Not only is Brahms's first movement much longer, it is much larger in concept. Its themes are longer and more complex, and there is even one more of them. The transitions now grow smoothly out of the themes; gone are the neat, clear-cut cadences that marked the conclusions of sections in the Classical period. Also, the orchestra is much bigger, nearly twice as large. These differences do *not* mean that one style of symphony is superior; rather they mean only that they are different.

Second Movement. The techniques of theme transformation, variation, and elaboration that Brahms handles so ably are especially well suited to slow movements. Each second movement of Brahms's four symphonies seems incomparably beautiful.

This movement shows the gradual weakening of key center that took place in the late Romantic period. The two horns that begin the movement seem to be playing in C major, when in fact those few measures are centered around a mode—one of the tonal patterns that had seldom been employed since the Renaissance. When the strings repeat the theme, they place it squarely in E major. Such momentary vagueness about the key provides some inkling of the abandonment of key center that occurred in some music within twenty-five years after the writing of this symphony.

The theme is:

Brahms's inventiveness is shown in the fact that the second four notes are the inversion of the first four. The melody is well suited for development because the group of four notes seems ready-made to serve as a motive.

The strings start out by playing it pizzicato. While they are sounding the melody, the clarinet is playing a smooth version of the same line. The theme is developed a bit and varied before a new theme is introduced.

The second theme is another romantic, passionate melody played by the cellos. Notice that it is high in the range of the cello, to provide more intensity:

Both first and second themes are heard again before the first theme returns to close the movement.

Third Movement. The spirit of this movement is one of heartiness and vigor. In one respect at least Brahms might be compared with Robert Browning: Both men displayed a sturdy nineteenth-century optimism. For example, Browning says in "Rabbi Ben Ezra":

Grow old along with me!
The best is yet to be,

The last of life, for which the first was made:
Our times are in His hand.
Who saith, "A whole I planned,
Youth shows but half; trust God:
See all, nor be afraid!"

Brahms indicates the tempo as *allegro giocoso.* In the opening measures two themes are presented simultaneously, one of which is nearly the inversion of the other:

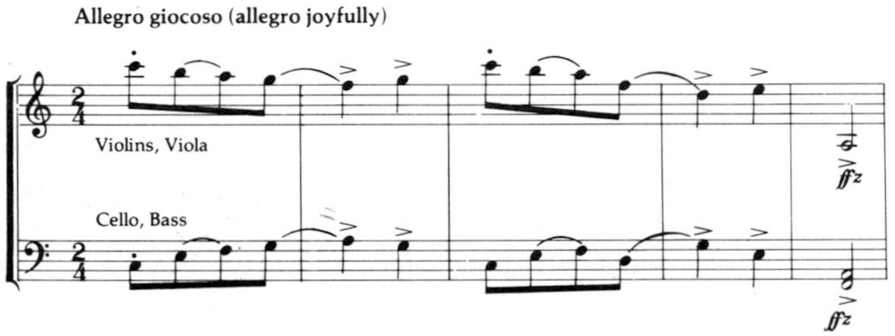

Notice that the slur marks cause the rhythmic emphasis to fall off the beat in measures 1 and 3. This adds to the playfulness of the music. The rhythmic figure  appears throughout the movement and contributes to the overall heavy, robust German sound.

This movement differs from a Beethoven or Mendelssohn scherzo in that it has two-beat rather than three-beat meter, but it is similar in style and spirit.

Fourth Movement. The form of the fourth movement is called a *passacaglia* or *chaconne.* Scholars have never quite agreed on which it is, and Brahms did not say what he thought about the matter. The passacaglia was mentioned in Chapter 13 in connection with Bach's outstanding organ work in that form. The word "chaconne" (shah-*cone*) denotes a similar structure. The forms are most often found in Baroque music. Both are based on the principle of variation in which a melody or harmonic progression, usually about eight measures long, is repeated many times and a new variation occurs simultaneously with each appearance. Both types are in a moderate three-beat meter and begin with a clear statement of the theme or chord progression on which the work is to be based. If there is a difference between them, it is that a passacaglia consists of variations on a melody or theme, and a chaconne consists of variations on a certain prescribed harmonic progression. The principle of both techniques is to provide unity through the use of the theme or chord pattern and to sustain interest through the use of continuous variation.

The theme of the fourth movement of Brahms's Fourth Symphony (Record 4, Side 2) is a solid melody of eight measures, with one note per measure:

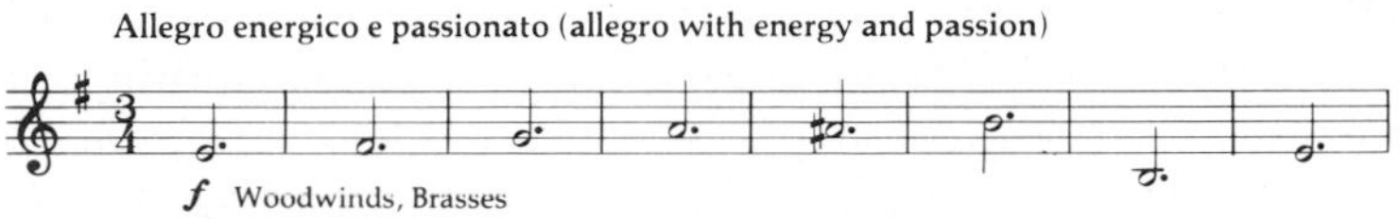

There are some thirty-five variations and a coda. An examination of the first few variations will show how the music is organized.

In the second variation the theme is played pizzicato by the strings and by the trombones on the second beat of each measure, following a pedal-tone chord that occurs on the beat and is sounded by the horns.

The third variation continues the theme on the second beat of the measure in the low strings but adds smooth contrapuntal lines in the woodwinds:

In the fourth variation the strings sound the theme on the first beat of the measure, still in pizzicato style. The winds play a contrapuntal part in an abrupt, biting manner:

The character of the fifth variation is quite different. The cellos and double basses play the theme with the bow, while the violins contribute a broad, romantic countermelody:

At the beginning of the thirteenth variation, the speed at which the notes of the theme are sounded is slowed to one-half the original tempo. This augmentation is achieved by a change of meter. The theme is only implied in the harmony, which serves as accompaniment to a free-sounding flute solo. The fourteenth variation consists of melodious lines in the woodwinds, while both the fifteenth and sixteenth variations are in chorale style.

The return of the theme to its regular tempo is easily heard, because it is the same clear-cut statement that occurred at the beginning of the movement. This return indicates that the music is actually a combination of two forms. First, it is a passacaglia/chaconne. Second, it is a large three-part form with a slower middle section based on the pattern of chords. Following the slow center section are another sixteen variations. Generally these are a bit more difficult to follow than those in the first portion of the movement. Included among them are rescorings of variations heard earlier (no. 28 is in the style of no. 6, and no. 29 is no. 7 rescored). Pedal point is used extensively in variation no. 27, and no. 31 is a canon.

The coda consists of another four settings of the theme. The number of measures becomes irregular and the theme is more disguised, but the listener can sense the relationship of the coda to the theme.

The fourth movement is not quite as complex as the description of Brahms's techniques might lead you to think. It is, however, a sophisticated and beautiful piece of music. For this reason, it is strongly suggested that you listen to it several times while following the simplified score in the *Study Guide and Scores* book. Each variation is marked by its number in a triangular-shaped box.

Brahms was fortunate to be able to please both the public and the trained musician. Because of its beautiful sounds, his music can be enjoyed in blissful ignorance of the compositional techniques being employed. On the other hand, because of his skill at writing, his music offers much reward to the listener who seeks to know *why* it sounds good. Perhaps these are the traits that make his music timeless in its appeal.

CÉSAR FRANCK

Franck was born at Liège, Belgium, in 1822, and died in Paris in 1890. His father was a banker who had a keen love of music. He gave his two sons, Joseph and César, a good musical education. To make sure it was adequate, the family moved to Paris so that the boys could finish studying at the Conservatory there. César won a number of prizes for his music abilities. He was a quiet, unassuming man who spent most of his adult life as the organist at St. Clotilde. At the age of fifty he was appointed organ professor at the Conservatory, but his music was not understood much by his colleagues. His compositions received only modest acclaim during his lifetime. What success and recognition he did achieve came in the last few years of his life, and his best compositions were written after the age of fifty-seven: a piano quintet, a string quartet, his only symphony (which is performed frequently today), a set of variations for piano and orchestra, and the violin sonata discussed next in this chapter. Most of his music consists of compositions for organ and sacred choral works. Several of his techniques influenced later composers, especially Debussy.

Franck's Violin Sonata

One of the best-known sonatas for violin and piano is Franck's Violin Sonata in A Major. The first movement of the sonata is in moderate tempo and presents two themes. The first theme has no distinct ending. Franck keeps the elements of a thematic idea going for quite a while, and in so doing he transforms them into transitional material. He gives the impression of a brief development shortly after each presentation.

The second theme appears almost exclusively in the piano part. The movement is in a loose sonata form, but there is little actual development.

The second movement is a dazzling allegro. A difficult and dynamic piano solo opens the movement. The piano is soon joined by the violin.

The second theme is far more lyric and smooth.

Again the music is in a loose sonata form.

The third movement is marked "Recitativo-Fantasia." The word "recitative" refers to a free declamatory style that is featured in sections of operas and oratorios. Here Franck adapts that style for the solo violin. "Fantasy" indicates a free piece with no particular form. The second theme that appears in the fantasy is of interest because it appears again in the fourth movement.

For the final movement Franck combines a flowing melody with one of the oldest techniques in music, a *canon.* One part enters after another in strict imitation. The word "canon" literally means "rule." It has fascinated composers since at least the year 1200.

The fourth movement is presented in a Listening Guide on page 341.

ANTONÍN DVOŘÁK

Dvořák (pronounced D'*vor*-zhock) was born in 1841 into the family of a Bohemian innkeeper and amateur musician. Young Antonín grew up listening to the folk music of his native land. After several years of conflict between his music teacher, who wanted his talented pupil to go to Prague to study, and his father, who wanted him to become an innkeeper, an uncle provided Antonín the necessary funds for a year of music study in Prague. When the money ran out, he earned his living for the next fifteen years by playing in café bands and the National Opera orchestra.

As he grew older Dvořák became less satisfied with the prevailing German style and more determined to write Bohemian music. At about the age of forty his fortunes changed. He submitted a composition to the Austrian Commission. Although the prize he won was small in monetary value, it gained him the devoted friendship and unsparing help of committee-member Johannes Brahms. Brahms opened many doors to publishers, performers, and conductors for Dvořák, who was humble and grateful. He once wrote Brahms, ". . . all my life [I] owe you the deepest gratitude for your good and noble intentions toward me, which are worthy of a truly great artist and man."

By 1885 Dvořák was esteemed throughout the world. A few years later he accepted the directorship of the National Conservatory of Music in New York at a salary over twenty times what he was earning in Prague. He became homesick for his native land while he was living in New York. To ease this feeling, he spent his summers in Spillville, Iowa, which was populated by Bohemians. During his stays in Spillville he wrote some of his best works, including the *New World Symphony* (formerly No. 5 but more recently designated as No. 9) and the Cello Concerto. He was introduced to the music of

LISTENING GUIDE

FRANCK: SONATA FOR VIOLIN AND PIANO

Fourth Movement (Record 5, Side 1)

0:00 Main theme *(A)* begins in piano, followed in strict imitation by violin four beats later and an octave higher:

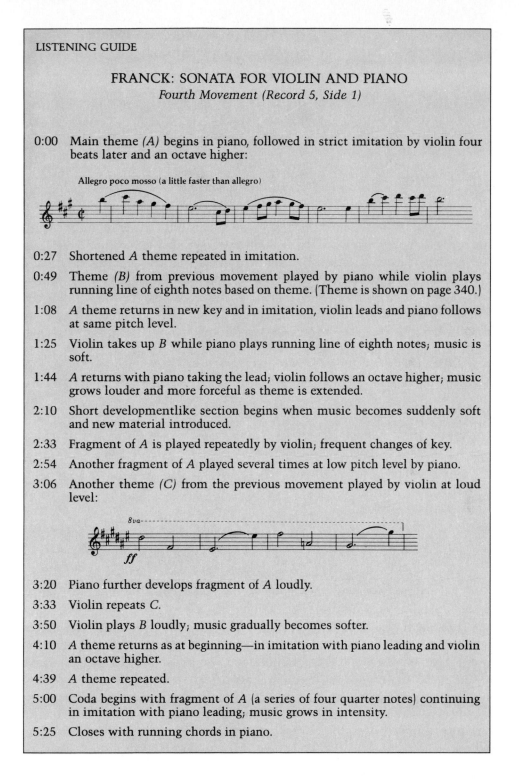

0:27 Shortened *A* theme repeated in imitation.

0:49 Theme *(B)* from previous movement played by piano while violin plays running line of eighth notes based on theme. (Theme is shown on page 340.)

1:08 *A* theme returns in new key and in imitation, violin leads and piano follows at same pitch level.

1:25 Violin takes up *B* while piano plays running line of eighth notes; music is soft.

1:44 *A* returns with piano taking the lead; violin follows an octave higher; music grows louder and more forceful as theme is extended.

2:10 Short developmentlike section begins when music becomes suddenly soft and new material introduced.

2:33 Fragment of *A* is played repeatedly by violin; frequent changes of key.

2:54 Another fragment of *A* played several times at low pitch level by piano.

3:06 Another theme *(C)* from the previous movement played by violin at loud level:

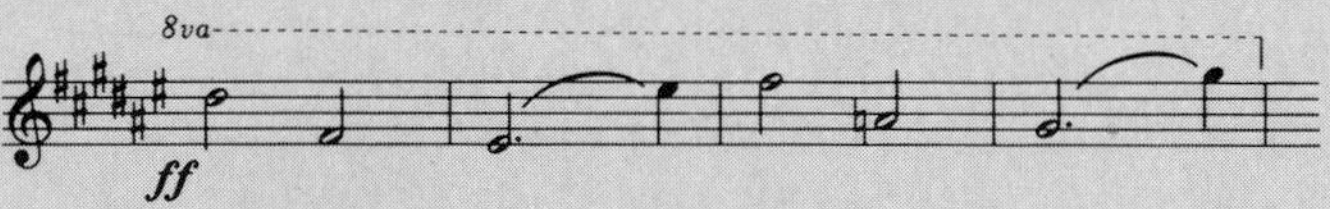

3:20 Piano further develops fragment of *A* loudly.

3:33 Violin repeats *C*.

3:50 Violin plays *B* loudly; music gradually becomes softer.

4:10 *A* theme returns as at beginning—in imitation with piano leading and violin an octave higher.

4:39 *A* theme repeated.

5:00 Coda begins with fragment of *A* (a series of four quarter notes) continuing in imitation with piano leading; music grows in intensity.

5:25 Closes with running chords in piano.

the American black people by Harry T. Burleigh, who was a pupil of his. He also became acquainted with the music of the American Indians. He was the first composer, native or foreign-born, to recognize these great musical resources.

After three years in America he returned to Bohemia, where he became director of the Prague Conservatory. In 1904 he collapsed and died of a stroke, and a national day of mourning was declared in his honor.

Dvořák's Cello Concerto

Dvořák wrote his only cello concerto while he was living in the United States. The music is Bohemian-Czechoslovakian in character, however, not American. The concerto was first performed in 1896 in London, and it has remained a standard in the cello repertoire since its first performance.

The first movement reveals the now-familiar sonata form, including the double exposition in which the first presentation of the themes is made by the orchestra. The opening theme is a vigorous melody in which the second measure is almost an inversion of the first.

The second theme is a flowing songlike melody:

The development section is built around the first theme, including a presentation in augmentation.

Part of the cello solo is accompanied by a flute, making an interesting duet. Dvořák includes four other cello-flute duets in the concerto, indicating an apparent fondness for the combination. The most unusual aspect of the movement is that in the recapitulation the themes are presented in reverse order from their appearance in the exposition. In other words, the recapitulation opens with the lyric second theme instead of the more rousing first theme. Apparently Dvořák wanted to give the movement a more vigorous ending.

The second movement is in a large three-part form, or *A B A*. For several decades in the twentieth century, musicians reacted strongly against what they considered to be the sentimentality of nineteenth-century music. Perhaps that feeling is not quite so strong today as it was in the 1930s and 1940s. In any case, this particular movement is one of the more sentimental pieces of music written in the nineteenth century. It is based on two song melodies, the second of which is a paraphrase of a song that Dvořák wrote, "Lead Me Along" from *Four Songs*, Op. 82.

The first theme is:

The second theme, the one that is a paraphrase of Dvořák's song, is:

The third movement is lively and happy, and it contains about four themes. In a sense it is a rondo, but the form is quite free. The first main theme is:

The second important theme is:

Of special interest is the fact that Dvořák brings back in this movement the opening theme of the first movement—cyclical form. This technique helps give a multimovement work a sense of unity. The coda of the third movement presents the opening theme of the first movement and contributes to a sense of fulfillment for the entire concerto.

The cello has a wide range and a rich, almost passionate tone when it is played well. It presents the flowing romantic melodies, such as are found in the second movement, in an especially suitable manner.

OTHER LATE ROMANTIC COMPOSERS

Anton Bruckner

Anton Bruckner (1824–1896) was born in the small Austrian town of Ansfelden. By nature he was a shy, almost mystical man. He was employed as a church organist, and he did not compose his first major work until he was past forty. A few years later he joined the faculty of the Vienna Conservatory. He wrote Masses, a Requiem, and other religious choral music. Like Beethoven, he composed nine symphonies, and all of them are mighty works. His body, according to his wishes, is buried under the organ at the monastery of St. Florian, where he had spent much time as a young man.

Camille Saint-Saëns

Camille Saint-Saëns (Sans-Sawns, 1835–1921) was a gifted, intelligent man who could converse authoritatively on many subjects other than music. His outlook toward music was more in the Haydn-Mozart Classical tradition than in the Romantic spirit of his time. In this respect he was like Brahms. Unfortunately, in Saint-Saëns's case, his attitude led to music that a times seems to lack conviction. He tried little that was unique or innovative.

He did write some interesting works, however. The well-known *Danse Macabre* is one of them. The program that inspired the music is a postmidnight dance of the skeletons and spirits in a graveyard; the event ends with the crow of a rooster. Other quality works are *Introduction and Rondo Capriccioso* for violin, the opera *Samson and Delilah,* and *Carnival of the Animals* for two pianos and orchestra.

Gabriel Fauré

Gabriel Fauré (For-*ay,* 1845–1924) was for many years not fully appreciated outside his native France. Like Franck, he was masterful in his handling of harmony, and his music is subtle and melodious. He wrote many songs and a Requiem that is frequently performed. He also composed for piano, orchestra, and chamber ensembles, especially those including strings.

25

NATIONALISM

Nationalism, when associated with the arts, refers to a deliberate, conscious attempt to develop artworks that are characteristic of a particular country or region. Often it involves specific subject matter such as a painting of a national event or an opera about a historical character. During the nineteenth century this search for nationalistic expression was largely an attempt to break away from the prevailing German-Austrian style. Bach, Mozart, Beethoven, Schubert, Liszt, Schumann, Brahms, and Wagner had long ruled the musical world. To men like Mussorgsky in Russia, Debussy in France, and Grieg in Norway, it was time for something different. They knew that Russians and Frenchmen and Norwegians were as capable of composing music as were the Germans! And they set about proving it.

Several factors in the nineteenth century encouraged nationalism. One was Romanticism. It exalted individual feelings and the inherent goodness of humankind in its natural state. Eighteenth-century intellectuals had considered common folk to be untutored and rough; Romanticists admired them. They thought of their way of life as good because it was so uncorrupted by civilization. (It should be noted that almost no Romantic musician *lived* as a peasant. They admired the simple life from a distance.) Furthermore, the life of the common people was a source of subject matter that composers and artists had seldom tapped before.

There was another reason for nationalistic art. The nineteenth century was a time of rising political nationalism. Italy and Germany were finally formed. Wars were pathetically frequent. In such conflicts a nation's efforts involved the average citizen to a degree that was unknown in previous centuries. No longer was a war fought by professional soldiers; most of the young men of the nation were involved in one way or another. Nor were sacrifices made for a king who may not have been particularly popular. Now the effort was for one's country—France or Germany or Italy. Nationalistic movements in music would probably have occurred even if there had been no political struggles, but the political atmosphere encouraged such music.

In their effort to assert their independence from foreign influences, nationalistic composers often wrote the tempo markings and other musical indications in their native language instead of in the more internationally accepted Italian. So Debussy wrote "Vif" instead of "Vivace," Wagner wrote "Schnell," and some Americans, even today, write "Lively" or "Fast." Such manuscript notation does not affect the sound of the music, of course, but it provides some insight into the composers' thinking and the temper of the times.

THE RUSSIAN FIVE

Until well into the nineteenth century, Russia had little musical tradition of its own. The czars imported French and Italian opera as well as French ballet. Mikhail Glinka (1804–1857) was the first Russian composer to write an opera on a Russian theme. Today he is generally considered the father of Russian music.

More important to the emergence of Russian music was a group of five composers who lived in the latter half of the Romantic period. Their leader was Mily Balakirev (Bah-*lah*-ke-ref, 1837–1910). He himself was not a talented composer, but his contribution was significant. He persuaded the others—César Cui (1835–1918), Alexander Borodin (*Bor*-oh-deen, 1833–1887), Modest Mussorgsky (1839–1881), and Nikolai Rimsky-Korsakov (1844–1908)—that they need not ape the German style in order to compose great music. He urged them to draw on the musical resources of their native Russia.

Generally the "Five" had little formal training. Balakirev was self-taught, and Cui, an engineer, was not a particularly successful composer. Borodin was a celebrated chemist and an excellent composer. Had he been able to devote more time to composing, his name would be far better known than it is today. His Second Symphony is still performed, as are *In the Steppes of Central Asia* and String Quartet No. 2, from which the *Nocturne* presented in Chapter 3 is taken. His greatest work was an opera, *Prince Igor,* which was completed after his death by Rimsky-Korsakov and Alexander Glazounov (1865–1936). Excerpts from Borodin's works furnished the music for the Broadway musical *Kismet.*

Rimsky-Korsakov represents a phase of Romanticism called "exoticism." Like many other Romantic composers, he felt drawn by the mystery and splendor of Eastern cultures. For example, his best-known work is *Scheherazade,* a tone poem based on the Persian legends in *A Thousand and One Nights.* His "Song of India" from the opera *Sadko* and "Hymn to the Sun" from the opera *Le Coq d'Or* ("The Golden Cockerel") are other works that reveal his keen interest in the Orient. Rimsky-Korsakov also wrote nationalistic music and worked avidly to advance the cause of Russian music.

Modest Mussorgsky.

Mussorgsky's Boris Godunov

Of the "Five," the most original was Mussorgsky. He chose an army career and later became a clerk in the engineering department. He was perhaps the most technically inept of the "Russian Five," but he is the one whose music best represents the Russian character.

His most significant work, the opera *Boris Godunov* (*Goh*-duh-noff), is derived from a play by Pushkin. It does not follow a sequential plot, as do most operas. Pushkin's play contained twenty-four scenes. Mussorgsky adapted the libretto himself, using only seven scenes and changing them extensively. The story concerns Czar Boris, who ruled from 1598 to 1605. For many years it was believed that he had instigated the young Prince Dmitri's murder in order to gain the throne. Although recent scholarly research has indicated that Boris was innocent of this crime, the murder is presumed to have taken place before the action of Mussorgsky's opera begins, and it is central to the plot. The opera describes Boris's mental torment (stemming from his feelings of guilt) and finally his death. There is a scheming Polish princess, who seeks, with an ambitious pretender to the throne, to capture the Kremlin. The real losers are the people, who suffer from the greed and ambition of those who would be czar.

The monk, Pimen, tells about a dream a shepherd told him in which a vision of the murdered Dimitri has returned in spirit to work miracles. Boris, seated on the throne, becomes more and more disturbed with what is being described.

The music reveals Mussorgsky's musicianship and his flair for the dramatic. The Prologue features the people of Russia. Afraid for the future after the death of a czar, they pray for a ruler for their land. To encourage a greater public clamor for himself, Boris sends one of his lieutenants to tell the crowd that Boris still refuses to become the czar. A chorus of religious pilgrims approaches and sings before the curtain falls on the Prologue.

The Coronation Scene, which follows, is one of the most famous scenes in all opera (Record 5, Side 1). It takes place in a courtyard of the Kremlin. The Cathedrals of the Assumption and the Archangels flank the stage. The music is best studied while you follow the simplified score in the *Study Guide and Scores.* The orchestra opens with moody and ponderous music, containing dissonant intervals and distant modulations. In music one of the most dissonant and awkward intervals occurs when an octave is divided into two equal segments, each containing three *whole* steps (six half steps). The orchestra alternates between a chord built on A-flat and another on D, two notes that are themselves a distance of three whole steps apart. How unconventional and nationalistic in its sound; how unlike the music of Germany! A few measures later the higher-pitched instruments present an imaginative contrapuntal line.

From a porch on the Cathedral comes the cry "Long life to thee, Czar Boris Feodorovich!" The crowd then shouts its praises to him, singing this Russian folk song in a stirring manner:

The text is: "Like unto the bright sun in the sky, Glory! Glory! Is the glory of Russia's Czar Boris! Glory! Long may you live and reign, O Czar, our father!"

Mussorgsky's innovative ideas can be observed in this passage, which is built out of the first five notes of the folksong theme.

The notes of each part on the syllables "our fa-" (marked by an X in the example) form a scale: A-flat B-flat C D E F-sharp A-flat. Unlike all major and minor scales, this scale has no half steps. It contains only whole steps. So it is called, logically, a *whole-tone scale.* In 1872, when Mussorgsky was writing this opera, whole-tone scales had seldom been encountered in musical compositions. Twenty years later Claude Debussy, who lived in Russia for a year and heard Mussorgsky's music there, would use whole-tone scales quite extensively.

When Boris finally appears in the opera, he is clearly a troubled man. Already the feelings of guilt for ordering the murder of the youthful heir are gnawing at his soul. The text of his solo is:

> My soul is sad!
> Strange, dark forebodings and evil feelings
> Oppress my spirit.
> Oh, Holy Saint, oh my Almighty Father!
> Look down from heaven on the tears of thy sinful servant,
> And send down thy holy blessing upon my reign!
> May I be honest and merciful as Thou,
> And reign in glory over my people.

Finally Boris agrees to order the coronation celebration. As he sings the words of invitation to the traditional coronation feast, the quality of the music changes.

> Now let us go to kneel
> Before the tombs of Russia's former monarchs.
> Then all the people are summoned to a feast;
> All, from the boyars to the blind beggars,
> All are invited, all shall be my honored guests.

"Glory! Glory! Glory!" shout the people. "Long may you live and reign, O Czar, our father!" At this point the bells of the Moscow cathedrals begin to peal. Mussorgsky calls for a period of silence in the music, so that each conductor may direct the sounding of all the bells available for as long as desired. The chorus then repeats the words and music with which they began the scene.

Throughout the Coronation Scene a virile, masculine quality is evident. Mussorgsky's admiration for the vigor and strength of his people has found its way into his music. The role of Boris must be sung by a deep bass voice to give the impression of a mighty man, the leader of all Russia. The best singer for the role of Boris is the one who gives the impression that he is six and a half feet tall, weighs at least 225 pounds, and can bend steel with his bare hands.

Boris's solo is expressive and flexible. It suggests both an aria and a recitative because the union of words and music seems perfect. For example, his prayer sounds almost like chant, which is completely natural and appropriate since chant is a feature of Russian Orthodox worship.

The chorus parts illustrate another aspect of Russian music: rhythmic flexibility. As was demonstrated in the African children's song in Chapter 8, the metrical pattern is broken when the text calls for it. This practice of Mussorgsky's forecasts the metrical freedom that would be exploited in twentieth-century Western music.

At the end of the scene, Mussorgsky anticipates the use of rhythmic technique in twentieth-century music.

The bass clef orchestral parts sound as though they are in 2/4 meter because alternate beats are emphasized. But the 3/4 meter signature is retained, and the choral parts follow it. So the effect is that of two different meters occurring simultaneously. This technique is called *polymeter.* It is closely related to polyrhythm, which was described in Chapter 8, and both techniques appear frequently in twentieth-century music.

The innovations in harmony and the freer rhythms made Mussorgsky's music fresh and different. In fact, in 1872 it was so innovative that it was looked on with suspicion. Even Mussorgsky's friends and admirers had trouble understanding everything he did. *Boris Godunov* was twice rejected for performance by the Imperial Opera. Only after two reworkings and a performance of three scenes at a benefit concert was all of it performed and published. After Mussorgsky's death in 1881, Rimsky-Korsakov served as musical executor of his estate. He had the bulk of Mussorgsky's music published, but only after he had made many "improvements"; that is, he rewrote the orchestrations and harmony to sound more conventional.

Mussorgsky wrote in other mediums in addition to opera. He was an especially good art song composer. One of his most unusual songs is entitled "The Flea." His tone poem *Night on Bald Mountain* is somewhat eerie. *Pictures at an Exhibition,* originally for solo piano, was orchestrated by Maurice Ravel. It is an exciting work in either form, a musical description of a series of paintings created by Victor Hartmann, an artist friend of Mussorgsky's. The music ranges in mood from the twittering "Ballet of the Chickens in Their Shells" to the massive finale, "The Great Gate of Kiev."

OTHER NATIONALISTIC COMPOSERS

Hungary-Bohemia. Franz Liszt was affected by the spirit of nationalism. His interest in such music is apparent in twenty *Hungarian Rhapsodies* and several shorter works.

Bohemia, which is today part of Czechoslovakia, produced two nationalistic composers in Antonín Dvořák and Bedřich Smetana. Throughout most of the nineteenth century, Bohemia was part of the Austrian empire. So the style of Dvořák and Smetana does not differ substantially from the prevailing Romantic style of the time. Bohemia was too steeped in the German-Austrian culture to create new styles. Bohemian nationalism, therefore, had to assert itself in folk melodies and native subject matter. Music from Smetana's opera *The Bartered Bride* is frequently performed today. Dvořák, whose Cello Concerto is discussed in Chapter 24, also arranged native dances and wrote several operas. His Symphony No. 8 makes skillful and charming use of folklike melodies.

Bedřich Smetana

Bedřich Smetana was born in 1824 in a little town in Bohemia, the seventh child of a music-loving brewer. Family activities included string quartet performances at home. Bedřich studied for a while in Prague, served as music master for a rich family, and later became pianist for Kaiser Ferdinand, who had abdicated his throne and was living in Prague. After about ten years Smetana moved to Gothenburg, Sweden. He earned a good living there, but the climate was bad for his wife's failing health, and he moved back to Prague some years later. Like Beethoven, Smetana became deaf toward the end of his life. Some of his best compositions were written after this affliction. Among them were *Má vlast* ("My Country"), operas, a string quartet, and some songs and choruses. He died in 1884 after suffering from a nervous breakdown a year earlier.

Smetana's Moldau

Typical of Bohemian nationalism is a cycle of six symphonic poems entitled *Má vlast* ("My Country"), which Smetana wrote between 1874 and 1879; so these nationalistic works are also program music. The best known of these tone poems is the second, *Vltava* (the river Moldau). The program that Smetana placed in the score reads: "Two springs pour forth in the shade of the Bohemian forest, one warm and gushing, the other cold and peaceful." These two springs join together to form the river Moldau. "Coursing through Bohemia's valleys, it grows into a mighty stream. Through thick woods it flows as the gay sounds of the hunt and the notes of the hunter's horn are heard ever closer. It flows through grass-grown pastures and lowlands where a wedding feast is being celebrated with song and dance. At night, wood and water nymphs revel in its sparkling waves. Reflected on its surface are fortresses and castles—witnesses of bygone days of knightly splendor and the vanished glory of martial times." The stream races through the Rapids of St. John, "finally flowing on in majestic peace toward Prague and welcomed by historic Vysehrad," the legendary castle of ancient Bohemian kings. "Then it vanishes far beyond the poet's gaze."

The opening of the music is a rippling dialogue between two flutes. Next is heard the broad, flowing melody that is associated with the river. The melody is an adaptation of a Czech folk song.

The river passes a wedding feast, where a rustic dance of the peasants is heard.

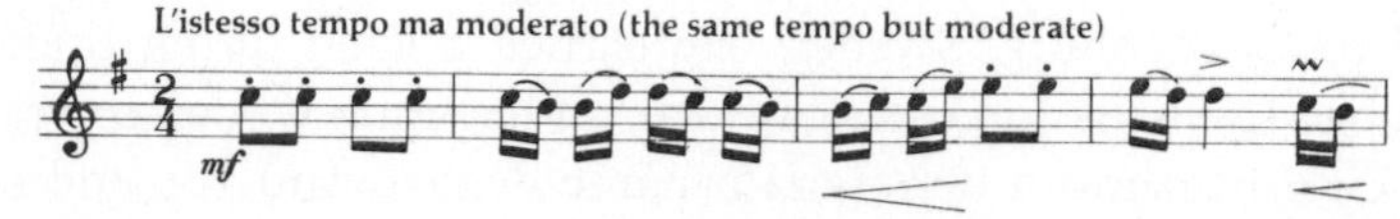

Where the score is marked "Moonlight—nymphs' revels," the mood changes to one of mystery. An atmosphere of enchantment is produced by muted strings and woodwinds.

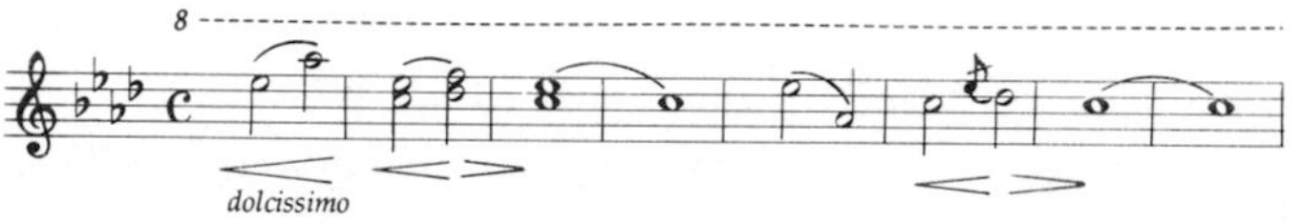

A gradual crescendo leads to a return of the Moldau theme. The music grows faster and depicts the Rapids of St. John. As the river approaches the site of the royal castle, the melody comes back with certain of its tones altered to give it a more exuberant sound. The effect is aided by a change from minor to major. Next is heard a triumphant brass chorale.

The music fades away, in accordance with the program Smetana has supplied. Smetana once said that he simply could not write absolute music. Perhaps his feelings of nationalism were too strong to allow him to think of music in absolute terms.

Scandinavia. Edvard Grieg (1843–1907) of Norway was the leading proponent of Scandinavian music. Among his well-known works are the *Peer Gynt Suites,* which were originally written as incidental music for Ibsen's play. He also wrote a highly successful and melodious piano concerto, as well as many shorter piano pieces and chamber works.

To Italians living in northern Italy at about the time of the Civil War in America (1860 and thereabouts), "Verdi" referred not only to a popular opera composer; the initials of the name also formed an acronym, Vittorio Emmanuele Re D'Italia, which translated means simply Victor Emmanuel, King of Italy. Northern Italy was struggling to break free of the Austro-Hungarian Empire and to join the rest of what is today Italy. The deed was accomplished under the leadership of Garibaldi and Cavour, and Victor Emmanuel became the first king of Italy.

Although not particularly drawn to politics and participation in revolutions, Verdi was strongly associated with Italian nationalism, not only because of the letters in his last name but also because of his music. Opera was an extremely popular form of entertainment in Italy at that time, something comparable to football in the United States today. The stories in Verdi operas often involved oppressed people suffering under tyrants. Usually they were somewhat veiled references to Italy's current fate under the Austrians, but were not explicit enough to bother the censors. In his opera *Nabucco* ("Nebuchadnezzar") Verdi composed some music for the Israelite slaves to sing. The music became the unofficial hymn of the Italian struggle for independence, something like "We Shall Overcome" becoming the song of the civil rights marchers in the United States in the 1960s. A line in another Verdi opera always brought a great response from Italian audiences: It is in an opera heard little today, *Attila* ("Attila, the Hun")— "Give me Italy, and you can have the world!"

For his contributions to Italy Verdi was made an honorary deputy in the first Italian Parliament, something that has happened to no other composer.

Patriotic Italians, intent on establishing their country, scribble "Viva Verdi" on the walls of buildings.

Finland's Jean Sibelius, mentioned later in the next chapter, also exhibited nationalistic tendencies, especially in the early part of his career. One of the themes from his *Finlandia* was made the national anthem of Finland. He also used native themes as the basis for program works such as *The Swan of Tuonela* and *Pohjola's Daughter.*

England. The music of Edward Elgar (1857–1934) enjoys perennial popularity with English audiences and in the musical world at large. His music is not conspicuously different from that of other Romantic composers, nor is it particularly nationalistic. Elgar, incidentally, is the composer of *Pomp and Circumstance,* the stately march that is heard at many graduation exercises. More typical of his writing, and more worthy of attention, is his *Enigma Variations* for orchestra. On the score before each variation he has inscribed anagrams, initials, and other clues to indicate which family member or friend is being represented in each variation. Guessing the intended identities is the puzzle or "enigma" for which the work is named. This composition would be little more than a clever gimmick if the music were not so listenable and well constructed.

Italy. Nationalism in Italy was evident primarily in its operatic tradition, as is described on page 312. Italian nationalism in instrumental music did not come to the fore until the twentieth century, with the works of Ottorino Respighi (Res-*peeg*-ee, 1879–1936). His familiar *Pines of Rome* and *Fountains of Rome* are decidedly nationalistic, and his handling of coloristic effects is typically Romantic.

Spain. Nationalism in Spain was evidenced by composers such as Isaac Albeniz (Al-*bay*-neez, 1860–1909), Enrique Granados (1867–1916), and Manuel de Falla (de *Fy*-ya, 1876–1946), all of whom exploited the rhythm of Spanish dances. Although their careers extended into the twentieth century, their works are essentially Romantic in character.

In other countries, too, the tide of nationalism has been prominent in the twentieth century. The United States is one such country. Its music will be discussed in Chapters 32 and 33.

26

IMPRESSIONISM AND POST-ROMANTICISM

The predominant style of French music at the end of the nineteenth century and the beginning of the twentieth was *impressionism.* In one sense it represented French nationalism because it was a conscious attempt to break away from the influence of German music. French composers also wrote program works based on French stories. But impressionism was more significant than just a manifestation of French nationalism.

As is true of most artistic movements, impressionism did not spring up overnight. For much of the nineteenth century, painters had been getting away from grandiose scenes and traditional subject matter. They were becoming more concerned with commonplace scenes and informality, and less interested that the painting carry a moral or message.

Impressionism probably owes its name to Claude Monet (1840–1926), who in 1874 exhibited a picture called *Impression—Sunrise.* Critics used the term "impressionism" to poke fun at the new movement, but the word is somewhat accurate in describing what the impressionistic painters were trying to achieve: something not fully finished, incomplete, of the moment, a sensation rather than objective analysis.

Impressionistic painters were primarily interested in light and color. They believed that things are not so much seen as objects but rather as agents for the absorption and refraction of light. Hard outlines, therefore, were avoided. They maintained that shadows are not black or gray but tend to take on a color complementary to the other objects in the scene. Impressionistic painters achieved brightness in their works through the fusion of the primary colors. For example, to achieve a green, the painter placed small daubs of yellow and blue close together instead of mixing them on the palette. Seen up close, as if you were looking at a newspaper photo through a magnifying glass, the picture is a confusing pattern of dots, but at a short distance these dots and daubs seem to blend. This technique contributes to the luminous quality of light found in impressionistic paintings. Nor were impressionistic painters concerned about posing their subjects or arranging the objects in an orderly manner. Their passion for catching the atmosphere of a particular time and place led them to make rough sketches of the same scene at two or three different times during the day, because the impression of the scene changes with the light conditions. The painting would then be finished in the studio.

Claude Monet's *Rouen Cathedral, West Facade, Sunlight* (plate 11) is an excellent example of impressionistic painting.

The impressionistic movement in poetry and drama was highly symbol-oriented. Its leader was Stéphane Mallarmé, whose poem is the program idea for Debussy's *Prelude to the Afternoon of a Faun.* As with their painter compatriots, the symbolist writers tried to capture the fleeting moment by presenting a sequence of images in words. They intentionally left their poems in an inconclusive and fragmented condition; it was up to readers to determine the meaning for themselves. At times they advocated a synaesthesia by exploring the notion of listening to colors, looking at sounds, and tasting perfumes. They hovered, as one writer states, "in a twilight zone where sensation ends and ideation begins." The symbolist writer Maurice Maeterlinck, on whose drama *Pelléas et Mélisande* Debussy developed his opera of the same name, wrote in one of his essays, "Beneath all human thoughts . . . there lies the vast ocean of the Unconscious. All that we know, think, feel, see and will are but bubbles on the surface of this vast sea."

While impressionism seemed to exhaust itself in painting, poetry, and music in about twenty or twenty-five years, it was a fresh and different view of the arts. Some very interesting and beautiful works were created according to its principles.

The impressionistic movement was unusual in the extent to which writers, artists, and musicians were united by common attitudes. Many of them knew and admired one another's work. The impressionistic view of time was the underlying viewpoint among the arts: The painter wanted to capture a fleeting moment on canvas, the author in the printed and spoken word, and the composer in the transitory world of sound. And so they shared in common the subtle nuances of light and shadow, the vague contours, and the veiled thoughts that mark impressionism.

CLAUDE DEBUSSY

Claude Debussy (Deb-yew-see, 1862–1918) was born in a small town near Paris, and at the age of eleven he entered the Paris Conservatory. He often revolted against the rules of composition his professors tried to teach him, a trait that lasted throughout his life. When he was twenty-two, one of his compositions

Claude Debussy.

won him the Prix de Rome, a coveted award that included a period of study in Rome.

Debussy loved the gaiety and bustle of Paris, and he also valued the company of painters and writers such as Mallarmé, in whose home they often gathered. His early admiration for Wagner faded after a second visit to Bayreuth in 1889, and he developed a strong dislike for German Romantic music and philosophy. Being a writer of articles on music, he articulated his sentiments well. Of that beloved German tradition, sonata form, he wrote that it is "a legacy of clumsy, falsely imposed traditions." He considered thematic development to be a type of dull "musical mathematics." Debussy stated his views more seriously in this way: "Extreme complication is contrary to art. Beauty must appeal to the senses, must provide us with immediate enjoyment, must impress or insinuate itself into us without any effort on our part." He offered another observation to fellow Frenchmen who were tempted to imitate Wagner: "The French forget too easily the qualities of clarity and elegance peculiar to themselves and allow themselves to be influenced by the tedious and ponderous Teuton."

Debussy, predictably, cast his own opera, *Pelléas et Mélisande,* from a completely different mold. Built on a story by Maeterlinck, it is dreamlike and restrained. In one scene with her lover Pelléas, Mélisande unbinds her hair while doves fly about. The text is elusive; nothing is stated clearly. Mélisande's words exemplify the effect: "Neither do I understand each thing that I say, do you see . . . I do not know what I have said . . . I do not know what I know

. . . I say no longer what I mean." The opera has not won a place in the hearts of a majority of the opera-going public, but many critics consider it a masterpiece, and it did establish Debussy as a first-rate composer during his lifetime.

World War I profoundly affected Debussy. For a while it caused him to lose all interest in music. The war was not his only torment, however, for he was slowly dying of cancer. In March 1918, during the bombardment of Paris, he died.

Debussy was a careful workman, and his piano works are held in high regard, perhaps because they reveal a free and sensitive style that is reminiscent of Chopin. Debussy added much that was his own, however: parallel chord movement (forbidden in conventional harmonic writing), chords with added notes, and new colors. He wanted the patterns of his piano works to merge, in performance, into a "sonorous halo"—an apt description of impressionism. His *Clair de Lune* ("Moonlight") is widely known. Other works representative of his piano writing are *La Cathédrale Engloutie* ("The Sunken Cathedral"), *Reflets dans l'Eau* ("Reflections in the Water"), and several preludes.

His orchestral works, too, are impressionistic. There are three nocturnes, each conveying a distinctive mood: *Nuages* ("Clouds"), *Fêtes* ("Festivals"), and *Sirènes* ("Sirens"). In *La Mer* ("The Sea"), Debussy writes his impressions of the sea as it might be observed on three different occasions. Also frequently performed are *Ibéria* and the perennial favorite *Prélude à l'après-midi d'un Faune* ("Prelude to the Afternoon of a Faun").

Debussy's Prelude to the Afternoon of a Faun

As a literary springboard for this work, Debussy turned to a poem by his friend Stéphane Mallarmé. The faun referred to in the poem is not a deer but a mystical creature, half-man and half-goat, who dwells in the forest. His interests are simple and sensual. The faun awakens from a wine-induced sleep with vague visions of having been visited by three lovely nymphs. Is he recalling a dream or reality? He'll never know. The afternoon is balmy and restful, so he decides to fall asleep again.

This work in some ways resembles a tone poem, but its scope is considerably smaller. The pattern is only loosely *A B A*, and Debussy does not attempt to relate to Mallarmé's tale specifically. He tries only to convey the mood of the poem—the impression of a lazy afternoon and an idyllic existence. Accordingly, the music has a dreamy, relaxed beginning and conclusion and a voluptuous center section. A simplified score is available in the *Study Guide and Scores,* and it is on Record 5, Side 1 in the *Record Album.*

The orchestration of the music contributes to its impressionistic "feel." The flute opens the work with a solo line:

The harp answers with a shimmering effect called a *glissando,* in which the strings are sounded consecutively in rapid, scalewise fashion. The effect is that of nebulous waves of sound rather than individual notes.

Debussy does not call for many full chords from the brasses in his music. The *Prélude* does not even require a tuba, trumpets, or trombones. There are no drums, either. (Such instruments would never be lacking in Wagner's works!) Furthermore, Debussy is economical in his writing for particular instruments. Unlike the individual lines in music of Strauss and Brahms, many of Debussy's instrumental parts have lengthy passages with nothing but rests.

Debussy knew how to write to get the desired sounds out of the instruments. He does not ask the flute to play its opening solo in its high, brilliant range. Instead he writes the passage in the lower portion of the flute range, where the tone quality is soft and warm. Near the beginning he writes a violin accompaniment for the flute solo:

What he wants is a quiet, shimmering sound, and so he directs the violinists to play with the bow over the fingerboard *(sur la touche),* to make the tone mellower in quality and softer. At the same time he calls for *tremolo*—a rustling sound produced by rapid agitation of the bow back and forth across the string. A similar quivering effect by the violins is required later in the piece. This time it is produced by the fingers of the left hand as they play two alternating pitches in quick succession in a pattern lasting several moments. The French horns are not given a noble melody, such as was found in *Don Juan*; instead they play a mellow and melodious part. Frequently they are directed to *mute* the sound by inserting the right hand tightly into thc bell of the horn. At the close of the piece Debussy requests the harpist to touch the strings lightly (in addition to plucking them) to produce a crystalline, bell-like sound called a *harmonic.*

Debussy heard Javanese and other Eastern music performed at the International Exposition in Paris in 1889. (The Eiffel Tower was built for that exposition.) The sounds fascinated him, so he incorporated some of these tonal effects in his compositions. The *Prélude* calls for antique cymbals: tiny metal discs fastened to the thumb and fingers and valued for the bell-like sound emitted when they are tapped against one another.

Debussy emphasizes chords and scales that contribute to the nebulous, impressionistic character of his music. The whole-tone scale, for example, is found in the clarinet and flute solos occurring about three minutes from the start of the piece. Instead of simple chords containing three different pitches, Debussy employs chords of four and even five different pitches. The music modulates freely.

The rhythm is blurred and the beat is not easily felt. Never in the piece are you tempted to tap your foot. A heavy beat would destroy the dreamy, smooth quality of the music, just as sharp lines would change the character of an impressionistic painting.

The principal melody of the center portion has been marked in the following example to indicate where the beats occur. (When two notes *of the same pitch* are connected by a curved line with no other notes between—that is, a *tie*—they are played as one note lasting for the combined duration of both. In this example the dots below the tied notes in the lower line indicate a gentle articulation of each note.)

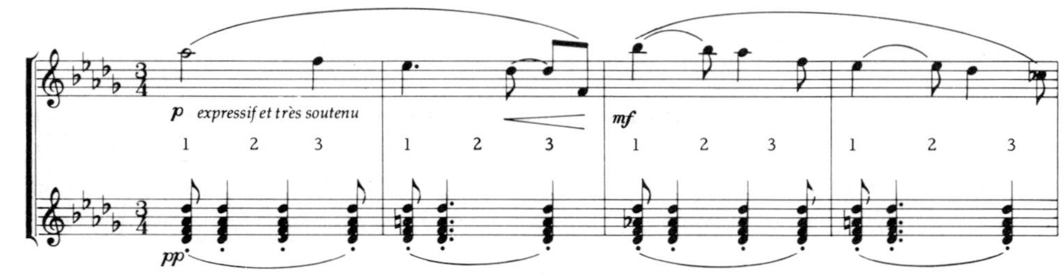

Many notes in the melody and even more in the accompanying strings (bottom line of the example) do not occur on the beat. Furthermore, on only a limited number of beats do the notes of the melody and accompaniment coincide. When the strings take up the melody a few measures later, the rhythm becomes even more intricate. The woodwinds play a figure built out of triplets, the two harps maintain a steady three beats per measure, and the strings present the syncopated rhythm of the melody.

Debussy tried to break with the past. He wanted to write music that differed substantially from the prevailing Romanticism. In some ways he succeeded. His use of parallel chords, free treatment of dissonance, and handling of modes and the whole-tone scale mark his music as being different. No one can for long confuse it with the music of Brahms or Wagner. In other ways, however, he fell short of his goal. His music is still basically Romantic. This is not surprising since Romanticism and impressionism are similar in outlook: the emphasis on subjective feeling, the fondness for mystery, and the desire to recreate a mood. By breaking with rules of the past, Debussy pointed to the new paths that composers after him have pursued.

To understand impressionistic music, one must realize that its appeal is delicate, refined, and sensual. Debussy and Ravel were marvelously skilled, not at developing themes, but at creating beautiful sounds, luscious chords, and elegant nuance. Its beauty does, in Debussy's words, "appeal to the senses."

MAURICE RAVEL

The fact that Maurice Ravel (1875–1937) followed Debussy both chronologically and stylistically has tended to place him in the background despite his many fine compositions. He did have the good fortune to be born into the family of a mining engineer who had once aspired to be a musician himself. Like Debussy, Ravel studied at the Paris Conservatory. Although he was a composer of some merit, the professors at the Conservatory four times denied him the Prix de Rome, an award for which he was highly qualified. The arbitrary nature of these decisions caused a public furor that eventually led to the resignation of the Conservatory's director.

A French patriot, Ravel drove an ambulance along the front lines during the First World War. After the war he was recognized as France's leading composer, and he toured the United States in 1928. Eventually his polished post-impressionistic compositions became dated in a world whose tastes had changed since the turn of the century. As he grew older, he became more despondent and depressed. At about the age of sixty, he acquired a rare disease of the brain and slowly lost his speech and motor coordination. In desperation he agreed to a dangerous operation from which he never regained consciousness.

One of Ravel's best-known orchestral works is his *Bolero,* which draws its rhythm and spirit from the Spanish dance of the same name. He wrote it in 1928, and its fame derives from its hypnotic melody, its gradual crescendo that proceeds uninterrupted from beginning to end, and its two-measure rhythmic pattern that is reiterated without pause throughout the entire seventeen-minute work. Recently it was featured in the film *10.* Other works include the Concerto in G Major for Piano, *Concerto for the Left Hand, Daphnis et Chloé, La Valse, Rapsodie Espagnole* ("Spanish Rhapsody"), and *Ma Mère l'Oye* ("Mother Goose")—a ballet from which he compiled music for a suite.

POST-ROMANTICISM

The influence of the Romantic period was so pervasive that it was felt through the early years of the twentieth century. In fact, elements of Romanticism can still be found in music written today, and they will probably always be evident to some degree in many works of the future. As might be expected, therefore, a number of composers continued to explore the musical possibilities of the nineteenth-century style even after it had been supplanted by other trends. Three of these men, by dint of their musical keenness, merit a place in any list of outstanding composers.

One is Jean Sibelius (Yon Sih-*bay*-leeus, 1865–1957), who was mentioned in Chapter 25 for his nationalistic compositions. His reputation among musicians stems primarily from his symphonies and a violin concerto. In his compositions he develops and combines a number of melodic fragments, often accompanied by ostinatos—those persistent, repeated figures. He exploits this device to help build toward climactic musical moments.

Sibelius's symphonies are often cyclical, and they tend to depart from traditional forms. The music has a free sound, with many stops and starts and changes of tempo.

In 1914 Sibelius visited the United States, where he conducted some concerts and received an honorary doctorate from Yale University. Although he lived until 1957, almost all of his works were written before 1925. The last years of his life were spent teaching.

Jean Sibelius.

Sibelius's Symphony No. 2

Sibelius's Symphony No. 2 in D Major, Op. 43, is a majestic work written in 1901. The first movement is in a loose sonata form and utilizes about six or seven short melodic ideas that are woven in and out of the music. The most important are the throbbing introductory phrases:

the first theme, which has two parts:

and this theme:

The second movement also employs a sonata form and free-sounding, almost fantasylike sections.

The third movement is a scherzo in style, which begins with a machine gunlike figure.

The oboe plays a smooth, slow melody in the contrasting sections.

The third movement is attached to the fourth movement without a break.

The fourth movement is in sonata form and is built almost entirely around four themes. There are only a few moments during which one of the themes in not being played. The first and most important theme starts out like this:

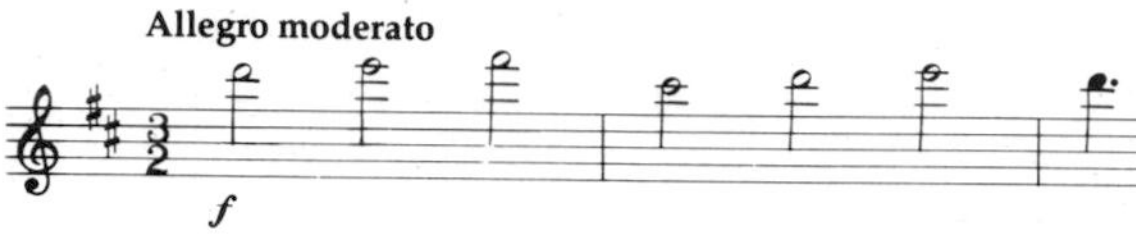

There is a short, contrasting center section followed by a repetition of the first phrase. Twice when the theme is heard Sibelius suspends all forward motion while he interjects an exciting passage for the trumpets and an answer in the French horns—all while the listener waits for the melody to resume. The delay not only holds the listener's attention but tends to prove the adage "Absence makes the heart grow fonder" by making the theme seem especially satisfying when it resumes.

After some minutes Sibelius shifts almost abruptly to another theme that is transitional in character. That is, it gives the impression not of being important in itself but rather of leading to other musical ideas.

Then begins the second main theme. First it is heard in the oboe part and then in the clarinet. When performing this work, most professional orchestras delay the sounding of the second note of the theme for a split second and also give that note a little more emphasis.

Sibelius slowly builds to tremendous climaxes using this theme, sometimes in a slightly varied form.

The fourth melody is found in the codetta. It is more like a melodic motive.

Sibelius freely uses fragments from the different themes and has them sounded in contrast to other themes. The coda, which sounds as though it is the culmination of the nineteenth century, uses the first phrase of the first theme in augmentation. The brasses play the theme against a vibrating accompaniment sounded by the rest of the orchestra.

MAHLER AND RACHMANINOFF

Sergei Rachmaninoff (1873–1943) was famous as a composer and pianist during his lifetime. Like several post-Romantic composers, he tended to be in the shadow of someone else's musical style. In Rachmaninoff's case it was Tchaikovsky. Rachmaninoff at times equaled his predecessor in the writing of lovely, sentimental melodies, although his composing techniques were perhaps not so imagnative. His best works are for piano, with the Second Piano Concerto being the most popular. Like Brahms and Liszt, he drew on a violin caprice by Paganini for his *Rhapsody on a Theme of Paganini*. His solo piano works include two frequently performed preludes, one in C-sharp minor and another in G minor.

Gustav Mahler (1860–1911) was a successful conductor as well as an excellent composer. He had a strongly vocal outlook on music. Not only did he write many songs, but he even conceived his instrumental music in a style that is more vocal than instrumental. He followed Beethoven's lead by combining voices and orchestra in several concert works. Mahler believed in the unity of the arts and often combined music, poetry, and philosophical ideas into his compositions. He abandoned traditional forms. Instead, his symphonies contain many songlike melodies that are woven together, often contrapuntally, in an intriguing manner. The music sounds so effortless that the listener can easily miss the expertise in his handling of the musical ideas.

Mahler and Anton Bruckner, his teacher, both exhibit one of the traits of Romanticism: a tendency toward musical elephantiasis. Mahler's Symphony No. 3 holds the dubious distinction of being the longest ever written. It consumes about one hour and thirty-four minutes, with its first movement alone requiring nearly forty-five minutes of performance time. His Eighth Symphony is sometimes called "the Symphony of a Thousand" because it requires so many people to perform it: a gigantic orchestra, additional brass, and male, female, and children's choirs. Amazingly, Mahler does not allow the music to be engulfed; he handles the vast resources with skill and discretion.

Perhaps the length and bulk of these symphonies are omens of the frustration that composers were beginning to feel with the Romantic style. How far can one go in giving vent to feelings without becoming "sticky sentimental" or bombastic? How much longer than one hour and thirty-four minutes can a symphony be without becoming an intolerable bore? If a thousand performers are augmented, will the music be any better? Sibelius and Mahler were able to develop some individuality within the post-Romantic style. However, its resources were fast being consumed. A mood of change was in the air even as the post-Romanticists were composing.

PART FIVE
TWENTIETH-CENTURY MUSIC

27

TWENTIETH-CENTURY MUSIC: MAINSTREAM INSTRUMENTAL

We are so close to the events going on around us that it is hard to see them in perspective. Furthermore, most of us seldom consider how the changes in society affect the creative artist. For these reasons, it is worthwhile to take a closer look at the character of the present time and assess the ways in which it is influencing the fine arts.

CONTEMPORARY SOCIETY AND THE CREATIVE ARTIST

The twentieth-century world is increasingly shaped by technology. Just about every civilized human activity is involved in some way with technology. Not only does this fact have far-reaching economic implications; it affects people's values and thinking as well. The vast array of goods made possible by technology and mass production in an affluent society has encouraged an attitude of materialism—the placing of primary value on material goods. Materialism usually means that nonmaterial items such as learning, truth, and beauty usually come out second to a vacation in the Caribbean and a sports car.

Twentieth-century society is becoming increasingly urban in its orientation. More and more people live in metropolitan areas, and the comforts and conveniences of the city are also enjoyed by residents of the country. Existence no longer seems to depend directly upon an adequate rainfall or sunlight; fields can be irrigated and lights turned on by which to work.

Any place in the world is accessible in a few hours by jet; communication via radio and television is instantaneous. Even the moon has been explored. These advances have made human beings think and act in international terms. Except in newly emerging nations, the ardor of nationalism has decreased somewhat. Many of the nations of Europe, which were at war with one another so frequently during the nineteenth century, have now joined into the European Common Market.

The intellectual climate of the twentieth century is different, too. It is more objective and concerned with scientific inquiry. Evidence of this can be seen in paintings such as Mondrian's *Broadway Boogie-Woogie* (plate 13). Intellectuals feel they have outgrown the slushy sentimentality and emotionalism of the Romantic period, although some second thoughts have surfaced recently about the emphasis on intellectual activity. Neither is the Romantic fascination with the unknown as common as it was in the nineteenth century. Scientists are exploring the outermost reaches of space and the inmost realms of the mind.

However, despite material comforts and scientific achievements, people seem to be less clear about the meaning of life than were their predecessors; consequently, they seem no happier. Many old beliefs have been rejected, but new understandings and beliefs have not appeared. The result is often a feeling of confusion, a desire to escape from reality, or a sense of being hopelessly trapped in the tangle of life. Twentieth-century drama illustrates these points well. In Jean-Paul Sartre's *No Exit* the three characters are trapped in their private hell, which is largely of their own making. In Samuel Beckett's *Waiting for Godot* two characters symbolizing mankind wait for Godot, who will take care of their problems. Godot never shows up.

Coupled with the difficulty of finding meaning in life is the change that contemporary people see all about them. But change to what, and for what reason? Sometimes change seems to be valued for its own sake, yet a few of the older values persist. Some nineteenth-century ideas, specifically those of Thoreau (who in turn drew upon the ideas of Jean Jacques Rousseau), have received renewed attention in recent years. Some of the tenets of Renaissance humanism are still espoused, too. However, there is little consensus on what is really important in life or how life should be lived.

The creative artists are especially sensitive to what they see about them. They often mirror the feelings of the times in which they live. They react to circumstances and give expression to prevailing attitudes. Creative artists do not, of course, all react alike. Some become cynical and discouraged; others withdraw along an escapist route that ignores society; others reflect the conflict and confusion of the times. Still others become "commercial," bowing to mass taste in order to get a fair share of society's material comforts.

With advances in transportation and communication, creative artists are usually internationally minded. They know the work of other writers, painters, and composers, and this exchange encourages international styles in architecture, art, and music.

On July 18, 1877, Thomas Alva Edison wrote in his diary, "The speaking vibrations indented nicely and there's no doubt I shall be able to store up and reproduce at any time the human voice perfectly." As he wrote, Edison had no way of knowing the musical revolution his invention would cause. In fact, what Edison had spoken, not sung, into the new instrument was the rhyme "Mary had a little lamb." He thought the phonograph (as he was later to name it) might be useful as a dictaphone, and he put it aside while he worked on other projects.

About ten years after the invention of the phonograph Emile Berliner discovered that the disc was a better shape for the reproduction of sound than Edison's cylinder. However, even then music was not the most common offering available on recordings, many of which included speeches, jokes, bird songs, and other sound curiosities.

It wasn't until about the turn of the twentieth century that music really caught on as recorded material. In 1902 an Italian tenor named Enrico Caruso was signed to record several operatic arias. In one afternoon he was paid about $300 for making ten records. (Later his recordings made him famous and a millionaire.) In those days, making records was hard work. One performance of a song would be recorded on 5 master cylinders; from each of these masters 25 copies could be made before the master copy wore out, which meant that only 125 copies could be made of each performance. So, the artist recorded the same music again and again.

Recording limitations favored the human voice. The piano was in competition with pianos that could be played mechanically, and early attempts at recording an entire orchestra were truly crude. The first orchestral recording wasn't attempted until 1909, and in 1915 a seven-minute version (!) of Richard Strauss's fourteen-minute long *Till Eulenspiegel* was released. Strange as it may seem to us today, popular music was slow in taking advantage of recordings. By 1910 about three-fourths of all recordings were of non-popular music. It wasn't until the 1920s that popular music surpassed art music in sales. It was also in the 1920s that electrical recordings replaced the horns and microphones of the earlier years, and the industry began to flourish. In 1921 a piece called "The Japanese Sandman" became the first record to sell over one million copies; today that mark is achieved about 150 times each year.

The introduction of the long-playing record in 1948 was another significant breakthrough for art music. No longer was it necessary to interrupt the music every three to five minutes to change discs. Also, storage and handling were made much easier, and the quality of sound reproduction continued to improve.

The magnetic tape recorder opened a new era in recording techniques. A "perfect" uninterrupted performance was no longer required; the best of several performances could be pieced together. Also, sound engineers could alter and enrich the original sound, a practice that is virtually standard in recordings of popular music. The tape recorder also made possible the recording of sixteen or more tracks at one time, which are then combined into the two normally used today in records and tapes sold for home use.

Millions of records are sold each year in the United States, to say nothing of the hundreds of thousands of pieces of music played over radio and television stations and in airports, restaurants, and stores. From a rare commodity in 1877 Edison's invention has made music almost superabundant today.

An 1878 portrait by Mathew Brady of Thomas Alva Edison with his phonograph.

An early recording session, with Rosario Bourdon conducting the Victor Orchestra. Notice the use of risers to get some of the players closer to the pick-up horn.

TWENTIETH-CENTURY MUSICAL CHARACTERISTICS

Virtually every aspect of music has been altered in the twentieth century, but not by everyone, and not in a unified manner. One characteristic of twentieth-century music is its diversity, its pluralism. Subsequent chapters in this book look at the more significant types of music this century has brought forth. There is, however, a sizable carry-over into the twentieth century from the music of preceding centuries. Although some composers have created music that bears little relationship to previous music, most composers have been evolutionaries, not revolutionaries. The twentieth century has retained some of the old, while adding much that is new in music.

Rhythm

The element of rhythm has become more prominent in twentieth-century music. Although melody and harmony are present, they are less important than they were in the nineteenth century. Composers have become much more interested in rhythmic effects.

The twentieth century has moved away somewhat from metrical patterns based on the regular recurrence of an accented beat. Most composers in this century have preferred freer concepts of rhythm. One of these concepts is the use of mixed meters. Composers shift the metrical pattern to suit the music, rather than making the music conform to a regular meter. For example, in a portion of one of his works Stravinsky changes the meter signature with each measure: 3/16, 5/16, 3/16, 4/16, 5/16, 3/16, and so on. The effect, when done in the right musical circumstances, can be quite exhilarating.

Another feature of rhythm in this century is the presence of polyrhythm and polymeter, which were discussed in Chapter 8. These words imply the use of more than one rhythmic pattern or metric pattern simultaneously. Polyrhythms are frequent in African and Latin American music. Small amounts of polyrhythm can also be found in compositions of Western composers in the nineteenth century, but twentieth-century composers have exploited these rhythmic devices as never before in art music. A similar feature of contemporary music is the rhythmic ostinato—the persistent repetition of a short rhythmic pattern.

The percussion section is featured more prominently. Timpani rolls and an occasional cymbal crash are heard in music of previous centuries, but today a great variety of percussion sounds is called for, and these sounds are more important in the music. Complete works have been composed for percussion ensembles.

Melody

The twentieth century has witnessed a return to the modes that flourished before 1600. Modal scales reappeared in art music early in the century, and began to surpass major and minor keys in popular music in the 1960s.

Composers in the twentieth century have broken away from the idea of balanced phrase design. In the Baroque and Classical eras, phrases seemed to run in multiples of four. Four measures were answered by another four measures, and these eight measures added up to a logical unit of musical thought. With increasing frequency composers in the nineteenth century began to favor phrases of irregular length, and this trend continued extensively into the twentieth century. Gone is the idea of statement and answer, the symmetrical design that is so prevalent in the music of previous centuries.

Many twentieth-century melodies have moved away from the idea of melody as a beautiful, singable series of pitches. Instead, melodies have become far more angular and instrumental in concept. Their range is wider, their intervals are greater and more awkward to sing, and some of the patterns must be executed too rapidly to be singable.

Harmony

By the end of the nineteenth century, composers had "stacked" more pitches onto the triad and the seventh chord. Such procedures weaken the feeling of a root or fundamental pitch in the chord, because the total sound contains the pitches of two or more triads.

In this example the ninth chord contains three complete triads: C E G, E G B-flat, and G B-flat D. Depending on how the composer treats this chord and how the listener hears it, the sound can be interpreted in several different ways. The logical consequence of an increase in chord size is *polychordal* and *polytonal* music in which two or more key centers occur simultaneously. The effect is almost always more dissonant, but it can also be quite interesting.

Some twentieth-century composers, beginning with Arnold Schoenberg, felt that the tonal system of the eighteenth and nineteenth centuries had been pumped dry of its possibilities. So they discarded it entirely, including the idea of a tonal center, and replaced it with a type of music that is called *atonal*—

music with no feeling of key. Such music may still contain harmony, but it is not related to any tonal system.

A third development of twentieth-century harmony is the practice of *pandiatonicism.* Instead of adhering to a particular tonal system, with its implication of a key and particular chords to go with that key, composers are free to harmonize a melody according to their intuitive instincts. Pitches appear in a chord because the composer likes the particular sound at that point in the music rather than following systematic harmony with its progressions.

A fourth development affecting harmony in the twentieth century is the exploration of different chord structures as an alternative to the "every-other" pattern of thirds that prevailed from about 1650 to at least 1900. Composers have experimented with chords built in fourths (C F B-flat), in fifths (C G D), and in seconds (C D E F). Seldom do composers rely on a nontraditional chord structure for an entire piece, but they do intersperse the new chords among the more traditional chords that are based on the every-other pattern.

A fifth influence on contemporary harmony is the return of modes. If two similar chord progressions are played, one major and one modal, the listener hears two different musical effects.

Sixth, more and more composers are breaking away from the traditional chord progressions found in eighteenth- and nineteenth-century music.

Dissonance

The history of music shows a steady trend toward increasing dissonance. It is as though the temperature were creeping up from 0 degrees to 99 degrees on a thermometer. Of course, the amount of dissonance is a relative matter. There is little that is purely dissonant, except perhaps a chord in which every note on the keyboard is sounding, and little that is purely consonant, except possibly the octave. In any case the twentieth century has moved about as close to complete dissonance as is possible. One composer calls for the pianist to take a stick that is $14^2/_3$ inches long and push it down on the keyboard. Obviously all notes under the stick will sound. Another composer asks the performer to push an elbow down on the keyboard. Although most composers do not go to this extreme, it is clear that dissonance is more of a factor in twentieth-century music than it has been in any other century.

Some current dissonances do not create tension, which was their usual purpose in previous centuries, but rather offer a certain "color" or tonal effect. Whether the dissonant chord is perceived as tension or as a coloristic effect depends on the listener's inclination and the structure of the music.

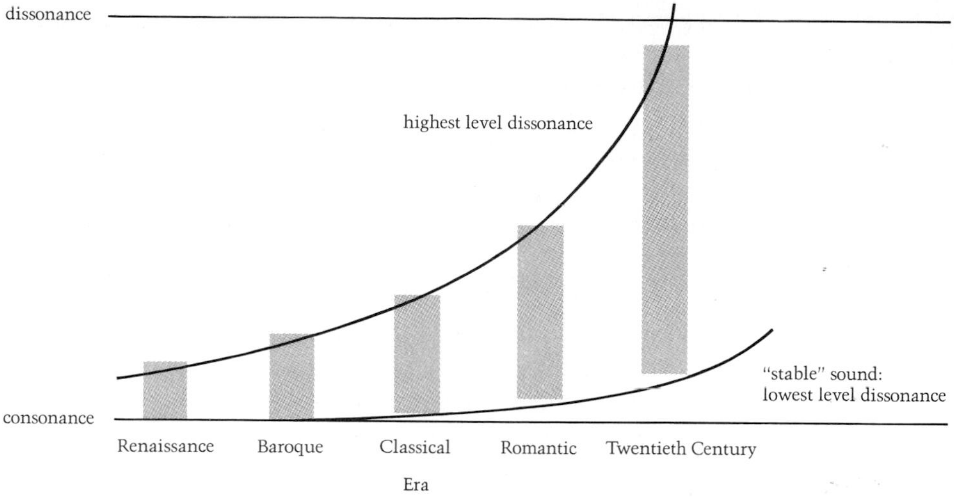

Counterpoint

After the Baroque period counterpoint was used less frequently than homophony. This situation has changed in the twentieth century. The line-against-line writing of the Renaissance and the Baroque has interested composers again, and today counterpoint and homophony exist as equals. Contemporary counterpoint differs, of course, from the counterpoint of the sixteenth century. Now the pitches and intervals can be as free as any found in lines of melody, so the lines of counterpoint are often quite dissonant.

Orchestration

The orchestra reached its maximum size at the beginning of the twentieth century. A few post-Romantic composers wrote gigantic works, like Mahler's "Symphony of a Thousand," which is scored for hundreds of singers and orchestra players and includes such uncommon instruments as chains and euphoniums. Stravinsky's *The Rite of Spring,* discussed in a later chapter, also requires a large orchestra. Around 1920, however, there was a swing away from the large orchestra and the monumental composition and a renewed interest in the smaller orchestra and chamber music. Instead of striving for an impressive mass of sound, composers tried to achieve greater clarity in their writing. Chamber music has increased in importance. Even when a full-sized orchestra is present, many of the players do not play much of the time. Gone are the rich sounds of the nineteenth century. There is new interest in the concerted style that characterized the concerto grosso, and new effects are achieved by balancing different timbres and sections of the orchestra.

Timbre

A most significant development in twentieth-century music is the interest musicians have taken in sounds and tonal effects. Every conceivable sound has been milked from conventional instruments and the human voice—shrieks, babbling, teeth-clicking, tongue-clucking, banging, rasping, squeaking, buzzing, and other noises. In addition, since 1950 composers have moved on to unconventional sounds created by synthesizers and recorded on tape. The timbres heard in the twentieth century are far more varied than those occurring in any other century.

Varied Sources

Twentieth-century musicians have been influenced by music from every geographical and historical source. Although nationalism is still alive, with evidences of ethnocentrism (the belief in the superiority of one's own culture), composers display a wide-ranging musical interest. Twentieth-century music is pan-cultural and pan-historical as no other music has been.

Composers also feel free to change styles, as Stravinsky did, and to seek out new directions for their compositions. For example, Karlheinz Stockhausen changed his orientation from highly controlled, intellectual electronic music to a farcical stage work in which the performers do partly what they want to do.

THE MAINSTREAM OF TWENTIETH-CENTURY MUSIC

Twentieth-century music is highly diversified. Some of it is new and experimental, deliberately rejecting the influence of other times and places. Some of it is subjective or expressionistic, while other works are cerebral, intellectual, and academic; both types of music are presented in a later chapter. If the experimental, expressionistic, and intellectual music were somehow to be removed from the body of music composed in this century, probably more than half of all twentieth-century music would still be left. Much of it is a logical evolution of trends observable in the nineteenth century. Some of it utilizes ideas and practices from folk-ethnic music.

It is hard to know what to call this body of "conventional" music. Some writers have coined the word "folkloric," because the music is partly derived from folk or ethnic sources. But folk influences are found in only a portion of this music, so folkloric is not an adequate term. "Traditional" or "conservative" are not accurate words, because most twentieth-century composers broke with nineteenth-century traditions to some extent. "Cosmopolitan" or "eclectic" are not ideal descriptions, because many composers did not attempt to integrate a variety of musical styles in their music. "Mainstream" seems to say it best; it refers to music that is neither experimental nor committed to a particular compositional outlook.

One feature of twentieth-century music is its lack of a clearly dominant style. Although the music of the past seventy-five years is quite pluralistic, these works exhibit similarities so that they can be grouped logically in the same chapter.

BÉLA BARTÓK

Béla Bartók (1881–1945) composed works that are essentially within the mainstream of music. Although thoroughly familiar with the music of his contemporaries, he was influenced by them to only a small degree.

Bartók's father was director of an agricultural school in Hungary, and his mother was the boy's first music teacher. After she was widowed, she became a schoolteacher, moving frequently with her son. Finally they settled in Pressburg (today called Bratislava), where he began serious study of piano and composition. In 1899 he enrolled as a student at the Royal Conservatory in Budapest. He became an excellent pianist and gave concerts throughout Europe. During much of his life, piano teaching was his main source of income.

Bartók first became noted throughout the world, however, not as a pianist or composer but as a collector of Hungarian folk songs. He and another important Hungarian composer, Zoltán Kodály, made a significant contribution to musicology through their compilations and analyses of the folk music of their native land and other countries.

In 1907 Bartók became a professor of piano at the Royal Conservatory and spent most of the next thirty years in Budapest. He received little recognition until the late twenties, when his works began to earn attention outside of Hungary.

After the rise of Hitler and the subsequent collaboration of Hungary with Nazi Germany, Bartók felt impelled to leave his homeland. In 1940 he came to the United States to live. He had to leave most of his worldly goods behind and his health was failing. He was appointed to a position at Columbia University, primarily to continue his folk-music research. He did receive a few

Béla Bartók.

commissions for compositions. ASCAP (American Society of Composers, Authors, and Publishers) provided him with medical care, and jazz clarinetist Benny Goodman also aided him. In 1945 he died of leukemia, with his true stature as a composer still not fully appreciated.

Bartók displays in his early works an admiration for Richard Strauss and Debussy. In 1911, two years before Stravinsky wrote *The Rite of Spring,* Bartók began composing rude, barbaric works. In his piano compositions written during this period, he treats the instrument percussively. Instead of the rolling, luscious sounds found in Chopin, he has the pianist bang out thick, dissonant chords.

Bartók composed his greatest music between 1926 and 1937. His *Mikrokosmos* is a set of 153 piano pieces in six volumes, arranged so that the music progresses from simple pieces for the beginner to works of awesome difficulty. In this collection he employs nearly every pianistic device and displays a wide variety of composing techniques. *Music for Strings, Percussion, and Celesta* also stems from this period.

Most significant, however, are his string quartets Nos. 3, 4, and 5. In them he achieves a striking union of twentieth-century and traditional elements. They are particularly well designed. Their harmonies are usually dissonant, and the rhythm tends to be violent and pounding, making the character of the music rather wild even though traditional forms appear in it. There is much counterpoint and Bartók includes several modal melodies, probably a result of his study of folk music. Although some of the melodies are folklike, Bartók did not normally draw on folk tunes for his compositions.

During the latter years of his life Bartók's mood appeared to mellow. His music became less dissonant. Besides those already mentioned, his most frequently performed compositions include String Quartet No. 6, the well-known Concerto for Orchestra, and the Piano Concerto No. 3.

Bartók's Concerto No. 3 for Piano

Bartók completed the Concerto No. 3 in 1945, just before his death. It was in one sense an insurance policy for his wife. He wanted to compose a work that would be easily accepted by concert audiences so that she might receive some income through its performances.

First Movement. The first movement is in conventional sonata form. The first theme, vigorous and rhythmic, begins immediately in the piano:

Instead of rich, full chords Bartók has the pianist play a single line doubled at the octave. The effect is clear and concise. The jogging, syncopated rhythm is easily heard because there is no thick accompaniment to obscure it.

After a transition featuring a variety of scale and rhythmic patterns, the second theme enters:

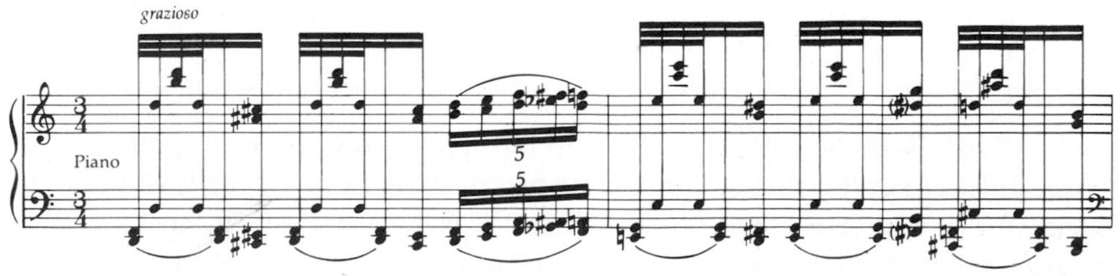

It is thoroughly pianistic and would be inappropriate for another instrument or for voice. The theme suggests a series of tonal clusters, and it has several subordinate melodic figures.

There is a codetta in which the music achieves a climax of sound and then tapers down into a two-note figure that sounds like a cuckoo call.

The development presents new material. The piano has a florid part while the woodwinds play a songlike melody. The effect would be romantic if it were not for the fact that Bartók's orchestration and harmonization retain that certain coolness associated with twentieth-century music. Fragments of the first theme are worked into the latter half of the development section.

The first theme is treated dissonantly in the recapitulation. Bartók seems to be seeking dissonance of tonal color rather than tension, however. Because of the dissonance, the theme in the recapitulation gives a different impression than it did in the exposition.

The coda embodies the same ideas as the codetta. After the series of "cuckoos," it ends quietly with a colorful figure in the piano. As is true of many works of this century, the movement concludes without need of a flashy romantic ending. The music just stops when the composer is finished.

Second Movement. The second movement is presented in the Listening Guide on pages 385–86. It opens with an introductory section primarily for strings. The music is constructed with such extreme simplicity that it seems to succeed by deliberate understatement. The piano answers with a choralelike melody. With each exchange between strings and piano, the intensity of the music increases.

In the middle section the music shifts radically in tempo and mood. It begins to sound like a summer night in the woods! There are twittering and chirping noises that sound like insects. Aside from a few muted horn effects and some piano runs, the musical ideas are carried by the high woodwinds, including the piccolo, with a little help from the xylophone. This section is evidence of twentieth-century composers' fascination with timbre.

It is tempting for a writer to spend paragraph after paragraph describing the many brilliant features of Bartók's compositions. That will be avoided here, but a few examples should be mentioned. The second movement of the Third Piano Concerto has a slow tempo, so it is somewhat easier to hear features and therefore is a good one to use for pointing out examples. One of Bartók's capabilities as a composer can be discovered from following the Listening Guide and noticing the timings on the left-hand margin. Each of the three portions of the movement begins quietly and works up to a climactic point of intensity. Not only does the music become louder and more dissonant, the exchanges between piano and orchestra become more frequent. The times reveal the progressively shorter lengths for statements as the music gains in force.

The opening phrases played by the strings may sound very simple, but a close examination reveals that they are carefully planned and imaginative. The five string parts enter in imitation one after another at a time distance of two beats. Three of the five parts in the descending opening phrase imitate each other exactly, but the other two play the pattern upside-down in inversion. The amount of inversion increases until finally all five parts ascend near the end of the opening minutes of the movement.

The choralelike melody played by the piano may also sound very simple, but it too contains a number of interesting uses of pitch and rhythm. The opening two measures are a pair of ascending pairs of notes four pitches apart; the second phrase has descending pairs of notes a fourth apart. The rhythmic pattern of the first four measures of the first four piano passages is the same: five half notes followed by four quarter notes, and then another half note. Such techniques give the music a great deal of unity and cohesiveness without becoming boring.

One final feature among the many that could be mentioned about this movement. In the *B* and *A′* sections the piano often has free-sounding runs that precede reappearances of melody. It is as though Bartók were clearly delineating the phrases of music for the listener.

Bartók's treatment of dissonance is worth mentioning. The final piano solo is shown on this page. The music achieves a peak of tension (circled in the upper staff), some of it caused by dissonance, and then gracefully becomes more consonant chord by chord. Although Bartók is using a greater degree of

LISTENING GUIDE

BARTÓK: PIANO CONCERTO NO. 3

Second Movement (Record 5, Side 2)

A section

0:00 Strings play a soft, slow, smooth figure in imitation (some in inversion); five phrases.

1:13 Piano enters in solo passage playing choralelike melody; melody is played softly and smoothly.

1:51 Strings repeat portion of opening material.

2:13 Piano playing alone continues choralelike melody.

2:31 Strings play portion of opening material.

2:48 Piano continues melody; music increases in intensity and more dissonance is heard.

3:04 Strings answer with phrase from opening material.

3:16 Piano continues alone on choralelike melody; increasing intensity in music.

3:49 Strings play phrase from opening material.

3:57 Piano reaches climactic portion of *A* part of movement; quite a bit of dissonance at points.

4:23 Strings quictly play a portion of opening material.

B section

4:45 Woodwinds and piano play coloristic figures while strings play a shimmering background (tremolo); interest of music lies in its timbres.

5:14 Piano plays short, brilliant interlude.

5:23 Woodwinds, xylophone, and piano play melodic fragments with an oriental quality as strings continue tremolo.

5:36 Piano has a short interlude.

(continued)

5:44	Woodwinds and muted trumpet play colorful figures while piano plays rapidly moving runs; music grows in intensity.
6:04	Piano leads transition back to opening material.
A' section	
6:18	Oboes and bassoons play the choralelike melody while the piano plays contrapuntal line, almost Bach-like in style.
6:35	Piano plays short, free-sounding passage.
6:46	Woodwinds continue with melody while piano plays counterpoint.
7:03	Piano plays another free-sounding passage.
7:16	Woodwinds continue with melody as piano plays counterpoint; music becomes more intense.
7:33	Piano has another free-sounding passage.
7:44	Woodwinds play choralelike melody and piano continues counterpoint as music continues to work up to climactic point.
8:24	Strings enter forcefully, playing a portion of melody.
8:34	Woodwinds answer with another phrase of the melody.
8:41	Woodwinds answer with another phrase of the melody; leads to piano solo that works up to much dissonance and then down to little dissonance.
9:21	Strings play portion of opening material very softly and smoothly.
9:32	Piano quietly joins in on opening material.
9:51	Movement closes very softly.

dissonance than did Bach or Brahms, he is adhering to the same principle that guided his predecessors in their handling of it: greater dissonance resolves to lesser dissonance. The final chord (circled in the second staff) contains only two notes, C and G, a fifth apart. Such a combination is less dissonant than the complete chords encountered in Classical or Romantic music.

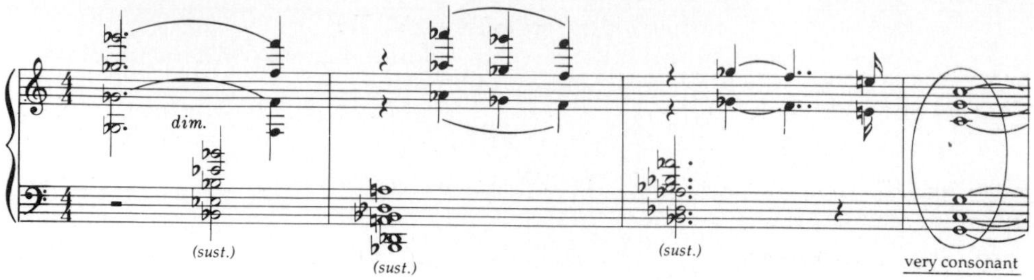

Third Movement. The third movement is in rondo form, a favorite last-movement form in the Classical period. The *A* theme is:

A rhythmic pattern played by the timpani serves as a transition to the *B* section, which is fugal in character:

This section leads directly back to a short statement of *A*. Another timpani transition introduces the *C* portion of the rondo, which is also highly contrapuntal.

The return of *A* is its longest appearance yet encountered because it is treated to some development. The movement ends with a brilliant coda.

Dmitri Shostakovich (1906–1975) received all of his musical training in Russia, and he spent very little time outside the country. He was born in St. Petersburg (Leningrad), and his mother, like Bartók's, was a well-trained pianist. At thirteen he entered the Conservatory at St. Petersburg. In 1925, at the age of nineteen, he finished his First Symphony, which is a mature work that has become a part of the repertoire of most symphony orchestras. His career was off to an auspicious start.

In 1934 he ran into trouble with the Communist Party over an opera entitled *Lady Macbeth of Mzensk*. It was accused of being "formalistic," a vague charge meaning that the music was not sufficiently political or that it was too much like music of the Western world. He publicly promised to do better in the future. In 1937 he brought out his Fifth Symphony, an outstanding work that is discussed in this chapter.

During World War II Shostakovich was not permitted to serve in the armed forces because he was considered so valuable a citizen. He spent the war years in Leningrad, where he remained through the long seige of that city, writing his Seventh Symphony and serving as a volunteer fireman. He had another falling out with the Party in 1948 when he was again accused of

Dmitri Shostakovich.

"musical formalism." A public apology and a new opera extricated him from the predicament. Before his death in 1975 he completed his Fifteenth Symphony, making him the first important composer since Beethoven to accomplish more than nine.

Shostakovich's Symphony No. 5

This symphony is probably Shostakovich's most representative work. Its first movement is in sonata form and begins with a violent-sounding theme treated in imitation:

A second portion of the first theme soon appears:

The next theme has a wide range and is presented over a throbbing rhythmic background:

Throughout the movement these themes are varied and combined with each other. The first movement is long by twentieth-century standards.

The second movement is intriguing, filled with humor and occasional satire. The cellos and double basses begin it in waltz tempo, but what they play is too jovial, too fat to be a waltz in the graceful Viennese tradition. It reminds one of music for a dancing bear in a circus. The tiny E-flat clarinet wheezes out a little tune as though it were trying to take itself seriously. The bassoons burp out notes of the shortest possible length, and the solo violinist slides around on a glissando. A peculiar march starts up in the horns; instead of conventional two-beat meter, however, there is an extra beat in each measure, so that the music hobbles along with an uneven gait. At the very end, when the heavy chords suggest that something important is about to happen, a meek and plaintive oboe is heard, sounding as though it were apologizing for being there. The whole movement is filled with ideas, instrumentation, and rhythms that are incongruous when combined. Some writers have attempted to draw a relationship between this satirical movement and Shostakovich's feelings toward the authorities after his public censure. Shostakovich publicly denied any such connection.

The third movement is impressive. Like Bartók's Third Piano Concerto, it begins slowly with warm romantic sounds from the strings. The themes have a chantlike quality about them:

The third theme is introduced by the oboe:

Throughout this portion of the music the extremely transparent nature of Shostakovich's writing is evident. At times, only one instrument is playing. After a while, the first two themes are heard from the strings. The music then winds up to a tremendous climax of intensity, and the strings move higher and higher with an excited tremolo. At the climactic point the second part of the first theme is heard coming through the orchestra, its notes doubled by the xylophone. The cellos come in full force on the third theme. The movement closes with the same music that began it.

The fourth movement (Record 3, Side 2) opens with savage fury. After a pounding passage in the timpani, the brasses blare out this theme:

It is followed by an excited, dancelike melody:

The music continues at a torrid pace. One of its many exciting moments is when the trumpets sound this counterpattern against a melody played by the rest of the orchestra:

The center section introduces the element of contrast by presenting a solo horn playing in augmentation the theme indicated for the violins in the musical example above. Then other melodies are played, some of them over ostinatolike accompaniments. The second theme (second musical example for the fourth movement) appears in the violins in notes four times the length of the original, or in double augmentation:

The longer notes and the different accompaniment give the melody an entirely new character.

The opening theme is heard again, rounding out the three-part form of the movement. Shostakovich's fondness for pedal point can be seen in the coda. The first three notes of the first theme are retained as a sort of motive:

While the brasses sound the closing notes (which are reminiscent of the musical phrase "How Dry I Am"), the rest of the orchestra continues to drive home a single note.

Shostakovich's music is not as modern as that of the many twentieth-century composers. (Serial compositions and other newer styles of music are not permitted by the Soviet government because it does not want to create a musical elite that is out of touch with the common people.) The ending of the Fifth Symphony, for example, is too heroic to suit most twentieth-century composers. Nevertheless it is a fine work, not because of innovative or advanced ideas but because of the composer's obvious skill in manipulating sounds and his strong gift of melody.

This chapter has devoted attention to two instrumental works by two different composers. A lot of vocal music has also been written in the twentieth century, some of it by Bartók and Shostakovich. Some of that music is examined in the next chapter.

28

TWENTIETH-CENTURY MUSIC: MAINSTREAM VOCAL

The fact that twentieth-century music is often a mixture of old and new is especially evident in vocal music. Instruments change over the years, and new ones are developed. The human voice hasn't undergone any major model changes over the centuries, although the things that composers have asked it to sing are somewhat different.

BENJAMIN BRITTEN

An outstanding twentieth-century English composer was a man with the wonderfully appropriate name of Benjamin Britten (1913–1976). His natural musical ability has been compared to Mozart's. Britten began composing at an early age and was remarkably facile at working out music in his mind. He wrote for every medium and for varied levels of musical sophistication. *The Young Person's Guide to the Orchestra* was presented in Chapter 5.

Britten's forte was the composition of vocal works, especially operas. Among his successful operas are *Peter Grimes* (1945), *The Rape of Lucretia* (1946), *Let's Make an Opera* (1948), *Billy Budd* (1951), *The Turn of the Screw* (1954), *Noye's Fludde* ("Noah's Flood," 1957), and *A Midsummer Night's Dream* (1960). He also wrote for voices and instruments: Serenade for Tenor, Horn, and Strings (1943), *Nocturne,* for tenor and small orchestra (1958), *A Ceremony of Carols* (1942), and the *War Requiem* (1962).

Britten's A Ceremony of Carols

A Ceremony of Carols demonstrates the marriage of traditional and new ideas found in many twentieth-century works. The work consists of nine carols plus a processional, recessional, and a harp interlude. The texts of most of the carols are in either Latin or old English—*"Deo Gracias"* and *"Wolcum Yole!"* are examples of each language. Many of the texts are anonymous. The original

Benjamin Britten.

version of *A Ceremony of Carols* was composed for three treble voices and harp. The boy choir tradition is strong in the Anglican Church, so Britten probably had unchanged boys' voices in mind when he composed the music. In America the work is often heard in a four-part choir arrangement accompanied by piano or organ instead of harp.

The term "carol" originally meant any joyful devotional song, so there are carols for Easter and May as well as for Christmas. Carols date from medieval times, and only in the sixteenth century did the subject emphasis begin to center on Christmas. Britten retains the medieval flavor associated with the heritage of the carol.

The "Procession" is in the style of Gregorian chant and the text is in Latin. The words begin *"Hodie Christus natus est"* ("Today Christ is born"). It is to be sung without accompaniment.

"Wolcum Yole!" is in a brisk tempo. It contains points of imitation, a compositional device found in Renaissance music, but the harmonies are more in the twentieth-century style. The opening music returns after a contrasting section, giving the song an overall three-part form.

"There is no Rose" intersperses Latin responsive phrases sung in chanting style among its old English text. For example, the opening words are: "There is no rose of such vertu (virtue) as is the rose that bare (bore) Jesu. Alleluia, Alleluia." Other Latin phrases include *"Res miranda"* ("Wonderful thing"), *"Pares forma"* ("Formed equal"—referring to the Trinity), *"Gloria in excelsis Deo"* ("Glory to God in the highest"), *"Gaudeamus"* ("We rejoice"), and *"Transeamus"* ("We cross over"—referring to becoming a follower of Christ).

To understand better what Britten has done to express the ideas of the text of "There is no Rose," select one or two of the Latin words for careful listening analysis. For example, listen to the two times the word *"Transeamus"* appears. Notice that it is sung in octaves instead of chords. This gives a hollow, medieval effect. The melody on the word is florid, or in musical terms *melismatic.* In plain English that means that many notes are sung to one vowel sound. While *"Transeamus"* is being sung, the harp plays contrasting material. "Text painting" technique is likely on the word in that the music tries to give the idea of bridging over or crossing over, which is the meaning of the word in Latin.

"That yönge child," a solo in a free style like a recitative, is heard next. It is followed by a lullaby, "Bululalow." "As dew in Aprille" is a carol of praise to Mary. The three voice parts often imitate one another, and the middle portion of the music tends to alternate between major chords a third apart.

"This little Babe" is a militant song:

This little Babe so few days old,
Is come to rifle Satan's fold;
All hell doth at his presence quake,
Though he himself for cold do shake;
For in this weak unarmed wise
The gates of hell he will surprise.

The first verse is in unison, the second verse is a two-part round, and the third verse is a three-part round that ends with a solid coda.

"In freezing winter night" appears after a harp interlude. In it Britten uses an ostinato—an old device—to create some twentieth-century dissonance and to contribute to the feeling of freezing discomfort expressed in the text.

Notice the meter signature of 5/4, something seldom found in the music of previous centuries. When the words change to "This stable is a Prince's court," the music changes from minor to major to give the carol a brighter feeling.

The "Spring Carol" is a duet like the pastorale music of the Baroque era, such as is found in Corelli's Concerto Grosso, Op. 8, No. 6 discussed in Chapter 14. The song praises nature in the spring.

"Deo Gracias" alternates its Latin title phrase with the story of Adam related in old English. The carol concludes brilliantly with the *"Deo Gracias"* figure being tossed about from one voice part to another. *A Ceremony of Carols* closes with the same chantlike music with which it began.

Charles Ives's "Serenity"

Although the Romantic era of the nineteenth century is known for its contributions to the art song repertoire, a great many songs were also composed in the twentieth century. Charles Ives (1874–1954) was an important American composer, and as such he is discussed more fully in Chapter 32. Among his many works are included 116 songs.

For the text of "Serenity" (Record 5, Side 1) Ives selected words from a religious poem by the American writer John Greenleaf Whittier (1807–1892), who is sometimes referred to as "the Quaker poet." It is not a love song, as so often was true in the nineteenth century. Ives adapted the text of the song in 1919. The directions to the performers are very specific: "Very slowly, quietly and sustained, with little or no change in tempo or volume throughout." The piano part consists largely of alternation between two chords, both of which contain four different notes. The loudness level is indicated at *pppp,* which must mean to play as soft as is humanly possible. There is some dissonance in the chords.

The voice part is almost chantlike. It moves almost entirely by step and its entire range is only seven notes. Some of the time the singer is required to sing a note that is dissonant with what the piano is playing. The song is somewhat strophic, but the last several phrases are one step higher than they were in the first part. The rhythm is not simple, even if it doesn't sound very complex. As can be seen in the example, the singer's part makes many subtle deviations from the usual pattern found for music in 6/8 meter. The total effect of the song is one of a brief, dreamlike vision of peace and serenity, which means that Ives accomplished the main objective of a song by providing an appropriate and enhancing setting of the text.

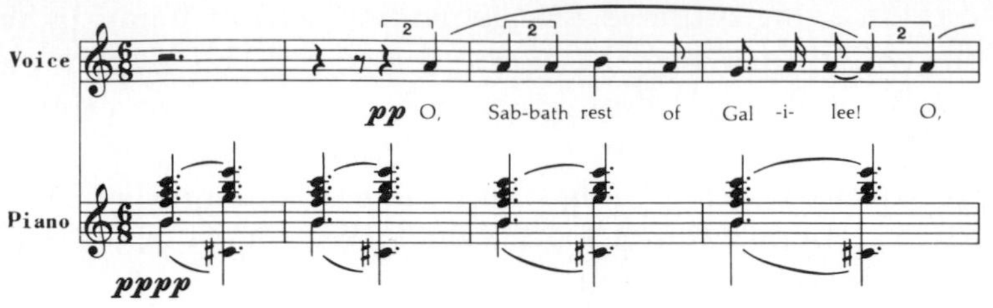

HEITOR VILLA-LOBOS

The Brazilian composer Heitor Villa-Lobos (1887–1959) was encouraged by Milhaud in 1915 while the latter composer was with the embassy in Brazil. Villa-Lobos was a man of tremendous energy who adopted ideas from many sources. His greatest inspiration was the music of the Brazilian people. Although his 2,000 works are of uneven quality, many are fascinating. His *Bachianas Brasileiras* and *Choros* are filled with rich sound that alternates between being romantic and blatant.

Villa-Lobos's Bachianas Brasileiras No. 5, *"Aria"*

Villa-Lobos composed nine *Bachianas Brasileiras,* in which he tried to combine Bach with Brazilian music. The influence of folk or ethnic music in works of art music is referred to by some writers as "folkloric," and such elements comprise one aspect of mainstream twentieth-century music. Villa-Lobos wrote: "This is a special kind of musical composition based on an intimate knowledge of J. S. Bach and also on the composer's affinity with the harmonic, contrapuntal, and melodic atmosphere of the folklore of the northern region of Brazil." The "Aria" of *Bachianas Brasileiras No. 5* was composed in 1938. In 1945 a second movement was added.

The "Aria" (Record 6, Side 1) is for a soprano accompanied by eight cellos—hardly a typical scoring. The music is not typical either. During much of the work the singer just vocalizes on "ah." The melody is luscious:

Heitor Villa-Lobos.

The middle section is somewhat like a Brazilian popular song with syncopation and frequent changes of tempo. The soloist's line sounds improvised. The text is a poem praising the beauties of nature. When the opening theme returns, the singer hums it.

TWENTIETH-CENTURY OPERA

Several twentieth-century opera composers, including Menotti, have had to face the economic problems of opera production. Their operas are smaller in scope, and the trappings of the stage are sparse. These composers know that there is little chance for a *new* opera with a huge cast and extensive scenery to be produced; it is just too expensive. Opera companies can hardly meet expenses even when they confine themselves to the standard repertoire. Besides, opera composers today are not at all sure that the grandiose opera is what they want to write or what the public wants to hear. They think that perhaps opera comes across best in a more intimate situation, in a setting more closely resembling the chamber-music environment. Although a few operas on a large scale are still being written and produced with varying degrees of success, there is a trend toward the smaller, more down-to-earth opera. A study of one opera can include an examination of features that are shared by some other twentieth-century operas.

Menotti's The Medium

The Medium by Gian-Carlo Menotti was first performed in 1946 in New York. It was commissioned by and premiered at Columbia University; it was not at first affiliated with a commercial opera house.

Menotti was born in 1911 in Italy, but he has lived in America since the age of sixteen. His many successful operas include *The Old Maid and the Thief, The Telephone* (a short comic opera that is often coupled with *The Medium* on the same program), *The Consul, The Saint of Bleecker Street,* and *Amahl and the Night Visitors,* the latter work having been commissioned for television. His most recent opera is *Tamu Tamu,* composed in 1973 for the Congress of Anthropological and Ethnological Sciences. He writes the librettos as well as the music for his operas.

The cast of *The Medium* is small. There are only six characters, one of whom is a mute, and three have rather minor roles. There is no chorus. The presentation, then, contrasts sharply with the large casts and choruses found in most romantic operas. Other differences can be observed. Only one stage setting is required for the opera's two acts. Furthermore, the entire opera encompasses less than one hour of performance time. This length is a distinct reversal of romantic tendencies, since three hours is not an unusual length for a romantic opera. (*La Bohème* is an exception.)

Menotti's orchestra is also much smaller. The piano is given a prominent part in the accompaniment; formerly it had only a limited use in the orchestra. Gone are the lush sounds of the past, although the orchestra does provide coloristic effects to augment the meaning of the singer's words. For instance, at one point in this opera Madame Flora is sick with fear. As she wails out the word "afraid," the strings sound rapidly repeating notes to suggest trembling.

The story, which takes place in New York, is about a devious old lady (Madame Flora, known to her family as Baba) who dupes bereaved people into thinking that she can serve as a medium between themselves and the dead. She is assisted in this hoax by her daughter Monica, a sheltered girl of seventeen, and by a mute orphan, Toby, whom she once picked off the streets of Budapest.

The curtain opens on Madame Flora's weird and shabby parlor. The apartment is arranged according to the stage sketch shown. Monica sings to Toby as they indulge in one of their fantasy games, in which he is an oriental king. Madame Flora enters, irked that nothing is ready for the evening séance. Quickly all is made ready—the wires that move the table, the lights, and the curtain behind which Monica imitates the voices of the dead loved ones. Mr.

Gian-Carlo Menotti on the set of his television opera Amahl and the Night Visitors.

and Mrs. Gobineau enter; they have been attending séances for two years. Soon Mrs. Nolan arrives. It is her first experience with Madame Flora, and she is understandably nervous. The Gobineaus and Mrs. Nolan exchange information about the tragedies that have brought them there.

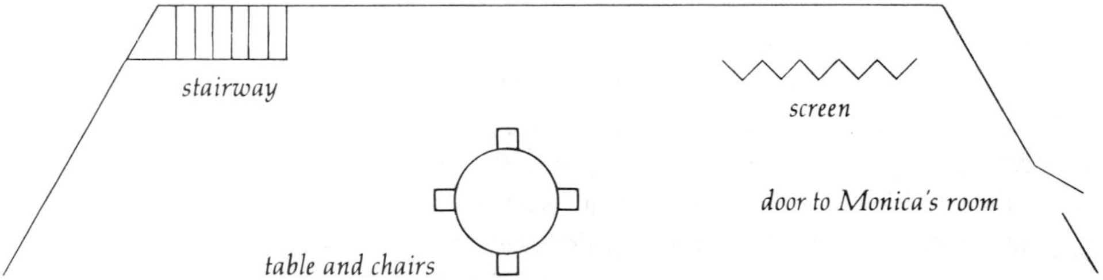

Finally the séance begins (Record 6, Side 1). The lights are dimmed and an eerie wailing is evident. Soon a haunting motive ("Mother, Mother, are you there?") is heard coming from behind the screen, where Monica is impersonating Mrs. Nolan's daughter:

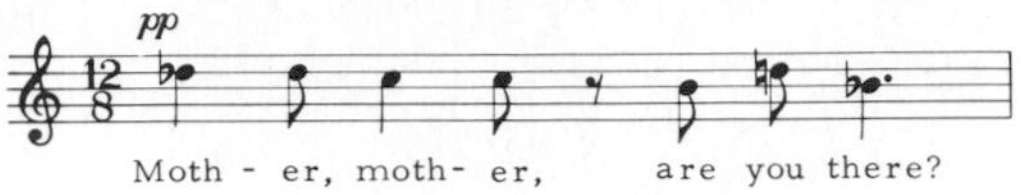
pp
Moth - er, moth- er, are you there?

Monica and Mrs. Nolan converse for a while, and Monica sings some wonderfully warm, reassuring melodies:

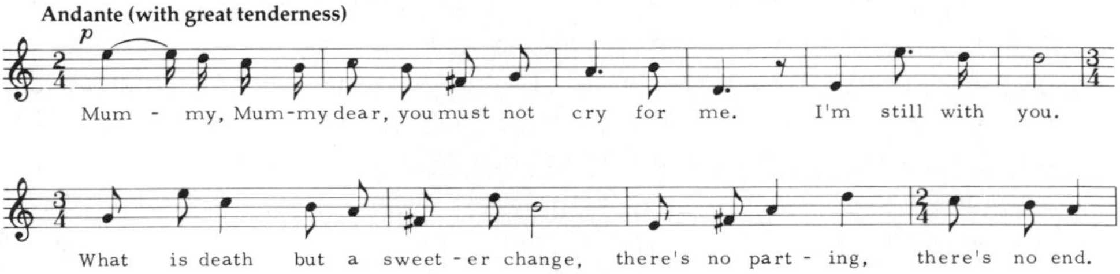
Andante (with great tenderness)
p
Mum - my, Mum-my dear, you must not cry for me. I'm still with you.
What is death but a sweet - er change, there's no part - ing, there's no end.

She encourages Mrs. Nolan to give away her daughter's personal effects, no doubt mostly to Madame Flora. She mentions a locket. "I have no locket," says Mrs. Nolan. The image behind the curtain begins to disappear, and Mrs. Nolan runs to the screen. She is stopped and calmed down.

Next it is the Gobineaus' turn. They talk with their two-year-old son and take comfort from his happy laughter. Suddenly Madame Flora gasps. A cold hand has touched her throat! But who or what? The persons involved in the séance were touching hands at all times. Toby and Monica were behind the screen. Madame Flora abruptly ends the séance and rudely dismisses the customers. As they slowly climb the stairs, bewildered and accusing, they sing a chantlike melody to her: "Why be afraid of our dead?" As the act closes, Monica is trying to calm her mother by singing an old gypsy ballad. Madame Flora, terribly shaken, mumbles superstitiously and whispers her rosary in a distracted manner.

The actions of the second act parallel the events of the first. So does some of the music. A week has passed. Monica sings an aria and improvises a dance for Toby. Suddenly the game is no longer childish. Monica asks, "Toby, what is it you want to tell me?" Toby, the mute, doesn't need a tongue; the orchestra answers for him with intense, impassioned chords that can only mean love. As Monica's aria continues, she sings both Toby's role and her own.

Throughout the scene much tenderness is added by Monica's gentle caressing of Toby's head. Her lines end, "Why, Toby! You're not crying are you? Toby, I want you to know that you have the most beautiful voice in the world!"

The mood changes abruptly when Madame Flora enters, disheveled and carrying a bottle; she is obviously still tormented by the memory of the hand that touched her throat at the séance. She pulls every known trick—emotional blackmail, bribes, threats, and love—to get Toby to admit that he did it. Toby's inability to answer only frustrates her further. Toby can neither admit nor deny any guilt, and his silence contributes to the rising tension of the opera. Madame Flora sings, "Toby, you know that I love you," but the orchestral accompaniment is tense and dissonant. It seems to comment on the falseness of her words. Before she is through with Toby, she loses her temper and begins whipping him.

The doorbell rings. Still breathless, Madame Flora answers. It is the Gobineaus and Mrs. Nolan arriving for their weekly séance. To ease her conscience, she offers to return their money and explains how she tricked them. But they refuse to believe her! Mrs. Nolan has even found the locket! They plead for another séance, but in a rage Madame Flora orders them out. Then, despite Monica's pleadings to the contrary, her mother orders Toby out into the streets and sends Monica to her room and locks her in.

Madame Flora seats herself at the table, laying a bottle and a pistol on it. The haunting "Mother, Mother" motive is heard. Her shouting cannot seem to stop it. She tries to reassure herself: She has seen many horrors in her lifetime, and they never bothered her before. She prays. She laughs at her fears. She prays again. Finally, she becomes drowsy and lays her head on the table.

Silently Toby re-enters the apartment. He tries Monica's door but it is locked. He opens a trunk but the lid drops, making a noise. Madame Flora wakens as Toby scampers behind the screen. "Who's there?" she cries, picking up the gun. "Speak out or I'll shoot!" Toby cannot answer, of course. Madame Flora fires. Silence. Then blood begins running down the white curtain. Finally Toby's body falls headlong into the room. Madame Flora unlocks Monica's door, exclaiming, "I've killed the ghost!" Monica, horrified, sees what has happened. She cries for help as she runs out into the night. Madame Flora kneels over Toby's lifeless form, still demanding an answer: "Was it you? Was it you?"

Here the opera ends, with its tensions unresolved. The audience has looked on the tangled emotions of people under stress. As in other twentieth-century operas, considerable psychological depth is imparted to the characters. People are seen to be complex mixtures of fear, gullibility, tenderness, guilt, and childishness. No longer are their emotions single ones like love or anger. Their feelings are sometimes mixed and their motives uncertain. Freudian thinking has, in effect, moved onto the opera stage. *The Medium* might be described as a "psychological opera." Madame Flora, it can be said, is suffering from hallucinations caused by extreme feelings of guilt. Menotti treats her tortured existence with insight.

OTHER MAINSTREAM TWENTIETH-CENTURY COMPOSERS

Russia

The Revolution in 1917 shook Russian music as well as all other phases of national life. Stravinsky left Russia, never to return except for an occasional visit.

Another fine composer, Serge Prokofiev (Pro-*ko*-fee-eff, 1891–1953), left Russia on a tour as a concert pianist immediately after 1917. He traveled and lived in Paris until 1932, when he returned to Russia and accepted the restraints imposed on his work by the Soviet government. As a young man, he wrote violent works in an effort to reject the romantic style. His best compositions were written after his return to Russia. They are numerous and embrace a wide variety of styles. In addition to the purely patriotic works not heard outside of Russia, his compositions include the delightful *Peter and the Wolf,* the film music for *Lieutenant Kijé,* the ballets *Cinderella,* and *Romeo and Juliet,* and the opera *War and Peace,* plus many symphonies, concertos, and chamber works. These latter compositions are lyric and quite listenable. Like Shostakovich's music, they are modern but often contain strongly romantic overtones.

England

The twentieth century has produced several first-rate English composers. One is Ralph Vaughan Williams (1872–1958). Vaughan Williams helped revive interest in English folk music and also contributed to the improvement of music in the Church of England. For vocal texts he drew on the works of England's finest poets. He also incorporated themes from Elizabethan composers into such works as *Fantasia on a Theme by Tallis.* In short, he wrote English music, thereby shaking off the domination of the German romantic style. As he grew older—he composed well into his eighties—his music became more modern and more complex in character. His Sixth Symphony, an important work, is very different in its style from his early folklike compositions such as *Fantasia on "Greensleeves."*

France

Following World War I, France went through a violently anti-romantic reaction. The informal spokesmen for the new music were a poet, Jean Cocteau, and an eccentric musician, Erik Satie (Sah-*tee*, 1866–1925). Satie reacted to past music in his own inimitable way by writing little compositions entitled *Three Pieces in the Shape of a Pear, Three Flabby Preludes for a Dog,* and *Dried Embryos.* He filled his scores with sly directions: "Play like a nightingale with a toothache" and "With astonishment." The purpose of such titles and directions was to satirize the seriousness with which romantic and impressionistic composers had approached their craft.

From this stream of irreverent thought came a group of French composers known as "The Six," so named by a critic who likened them to the Russian "Five." The most important of these composers were Darius Milhaud (Mee-yo, 1892–1974), Arthur Honegger (On-eh-gair, 1892–1955), and Francis Poulenc (Poo-lahnk, 1899–1963). These men progressed beyond the Cocteau-Satie phase into mature composers in their own right.

In 1914 Milhaud went to Brazil to serve as secretary to the French ambassador. His acquaintance with Latin American music made a lasting impression on him. He returned to Paris after the war by way of the United States. On this trip another world of music was opened up to him—jazz. He wrote of his visits to nightclubs in Harlem:

> The music I heard was absolutely different from anything I had ever heard before and was a revelation to me. Against the beat of the drums the melodic lines criss-crossed in a breathless pattern of broken and twisted rhythms . . . Its effect on me was so overwhelming that I could not tear myself away.

Milhaud was a prolific composer. His opus numbers reached 300 by the time he was sixty. He wrote in every medium. Most of his music is characterized by a French lightness and charm with frequent use of bitonality—two tonalities at the same time. Some of his works show the influence of the jazz he heard in Harlem, especially his ballet *La Création du Monde* ("The Creation of the World") written in 1923. Its story is similar to Stravinsky's *The Rite of Spring.* The similarities stop there, however. Instead of a huge orchestra, Milhaud wrote for a seventeen-piece jazz band.

Honegger was more conservative than Milhaud. While Milhaud was writing his early irreverent works, Honegger was writing the tone poem *Pacific 231,* which is descriptive of a train. By that time, 1922, tone poems had become passé. Throughout his life he proceeded to write as he wished, without being unduly influenced by changing compositional fashions. His most successful works are of large scope, involving chorus, soloists, and orchestra. *Le Roi David*

"The Six." Jean Cocteau (seated); left to right: Milhaud, Auric, Honegger, Tailleferre, Poulenc, and Durey.

("King David," 1921) is the best known of these. Later he wrote more purely instrumental numbers, including symphonies and chamber works.

Poulenc's music more nearly expresses the Cocteau-Satie attitude. Most of his works are intended to be charming and pleasant, even gauche in a well-mannered way. He wrote nothing for full orchestra, preferring instead to write songs, vocal works, and some chamber music. He also wrote two operas: *Mamelles de Tirésias* (1947) and *Les Dialogues des Carmélites* (1953). The two operas are very different. *Mamelles* is a surrealistic farce in which people change sex and babies are born in incubators. It also spoofs some well-known composers and old-fashioned music. *Les Dialogues* is serious and devout—the story of a Carmelite nun who chooses death rather than return to the outside world.

Latin America

Villa-Lobos and his music were mentioned earlier in this chapter. Carlos Chávez (1899–1978) was Mexico's leading composer. His *Symphonia India* is based on genuine Inca music, and his *Toccata for Percussion Instruments* is an exciting, rhythmic work.

Alberto Ginastera (Hee-nah-*stair*-ah, b. 1916) is an Argentine composer who has achieved fame for his instrumental and vocal works. Like the music of Villa-Lobos, his music sparkles with Latin American color. Two of his operas are *Bomarzo* and *Don Rodrigo.*

This chapter has presented three works that are representative of vocal music in this century. As mentioned early in this chapter, however, twentieth-century music is pluralistic. Several significant types have not been discussed yet, and they are the basis for subsequent chapters.

29

EXPRESSIONISM AND PRIMITIVISM

Existing side-by-side with the mainstream twentieth-century music discussed in the two preceding chapters are the musical "isms" or styles of this century: expressionism, primitivism, Neoclassicism, serialism, and anti-intellectualism. Each of these types of music made a significant contribution to the world of music, and each had its advocates and practitioners. This chapter examines the first two of these "isms."

EXPRESSIONISM

One writer has described *expressionism* as "a particular attitude of hedonistic pessimism, joyful skepticism touching on morbid sophistication." Its center was Vienna, the home of Sigmund Freud—a circumstance that may or may not be related. Vienna was also the home of the painters Wassily Kandinsky (1866–1944), Paul Klee (1879–1940), Oskar Kokoschka (1886–1980), Franz Marc (1880–1916), and Marc Chagall (b. 1887), whose painting *Snowing* is plate 14.

These painters distorted images on their canvases and probed into the realm of the unconscious. They depicted hallucinations that defied conventional ideas of beauty in an effort to achieve maximum expression. Their colors are often blatant and unreal with emphasis on intensity of experience and grotesque subjects. Expressionism takes special interest in the demonic forces hidden within the human personality. The painting by Munch, *The Cry,* on page 407, indicates the nature of art during this time. Many paintings are completely abstract, especially those by Kandinsky. Elements of expressionism found their way to America in the writings of Franz Kafka (1883–1924). In a sense, the writers James Joyce, William Faulkner, and Tennessee Williams are descendents of this tradition.

The musical leader of expressionism was Arnold Schoenberg (Shu(r)nbairg), whose life is described more fully in the next chapter. Beginning with his *Three Pieces for Piano,* Op. 11, written in 1909, he began composing atonal music—music with no tonal center. To musicians of the time, eliminating the tonal center was almost as traumatic as eliminating gravity from the universe. It was just that unimaginable. To fill the void left by the lack of tonality, Schoenberg concentrated on changes in orchestral color. Instead of changing the key center, he altered the timbre.

Schoenberg's one-character opera *Erwartung* is typical of the expressionists' fascination with the macabre. The opera portrays the actions and thoughts of a woman who goes at night in search of her lover in the forest. In her overemotional state, her moods range from joy to fear to anguish and hysteria. She can't find him. Exhausted, she sits down on a bench. She feels something at her foot, and discovers that it is the body of her lover. She lies down beside it and kisses it. Her mood changes as she reviles her dead lover for having been unfaithful to her (Death being the "other woman"). She kicks the body. Later she caresses it again, and as the sun rises she sings her irrational goodbyes.

Schoenberg's Pierrot Lunaire

In 1912 Schoenberg wrote one of his most controversial works, although it has not proved popular with audiences. *Pierrot Lunaire* ("Moonstruck Pierrot") is a song cycle containing twenty-one poems that are grouped into seven groups of three poems. A minor Belgian symbolist poet named Albert Giraud (1860–1929) wrote the original poetry, but Schoenberg used an unrhymed German translation. The poems abruptly shift between romantic and sordid images and contain references to the torment and joy of the poet. There is little design or plan in the poems, only contrasts in mood.

Schoenberg's settings add to the feeling of the poems. He calls for five

The Cry *by Munch. (Courtesy of Vaerihg, Art Reference Bureau.)*

instrumentalists, three of whom play a second instrument, to bring the total number of instruments to eight—flute and piccolo, clarinet and bass clarinet, violin and viola, cello, and piano. Except for a few notes, the singer must not sing, but rather employ a singsong style called *sprechstimme.* The rhythms, dynamics, and inflections are carefully indicated by the composer. The pitches, however, are to be only approximated and no sustained pitches are to be produced. The effect is eerie and spooky, but it projects the message of the poems most effectively.

The text of the seventh song is typical. It is entitled "The Sick Moon" and can be translated:

You nocturnal, deathly sick moon,
Up there in the heavens' dark pillow,
Your look too full with fever
Captivates me like a strange melody.

An unquenchable love song will consume you
With longing, deep inside,
You nocturnal, deathly sick moon
Up there in the heavens' dark pillow.

The lover, who intoxicated thoughtlessly goes to his love,
Enjoys the play of your beams,
Your pale, tormented blood,
You nocturnal, deathly sick moon!

Closely associated with Schoenberg were Alban Berg and Anton Webern. Although both men moved on in their mature years to individual styles, they followed the expressionistic tendency to some extent.

ALBAN BERG

Alban Berg, the son of a shopkeeper, was born in 1885 in Vienna. At the age of fourteen he took up composing, an interest that kept him occupied when he was confined by asthma and poor health. After graduation from school he took a position as an accountant for the government. He answered Schoenberg's newspaper advertisement for composition students and was his student for about seven years.

Berg's early compositions were in the Wagnerian, nineteenth-century tradition. But by 1911, the last year he studied with Schoenberg, Berg had changed to atonal, expressionistic works. Most of his instrumental music is for chamber groups, except for *Three Orchestral Pieces.* A *Chamber Concerto* and his esteemed Violin Concerto are among works that he wrote in the tone-row idiom, which is explained in the next chapter.

Berg's place in music history is largely the result of his opera *Wozzeck* (*Vot*-tsec), which he composed in 1921. The plot is pure expressionistic theater.

A soldier, Wozzeck, offers himself to a doctor for medical experiments in an effort to support his mistress and her child. She is unfaithful despite Wozzeck's devotion, and he slits her throat. He throws the knife into a pond; then, afraid that it might be found, he wades into the water after it and drowns. The opera is carefully planned in terms of its musical forms. Its three acts each contain five scenes and each scene is structured to a form: passacaglia, fugue, suite, sonata, scherzo, and so on.

Berg died in 1935 of blood poisoning that resulted from a bee sting and a subsequent infection.

PRIMITIVISM

A second trend in the early twentieth century was an interest in the art and music of non-Western and nonliterate civilizations. African sculpture and masks began to interest the artistic world, as did Gauguin's paintings of Polynesian culture. Although it was written in the nineteenth century, James Fenimore Cooper's phrase "the magnificent savage" did not catch on until the twentieth century.

The high point of primitivism in music was probably reached in 1913 with the premiere of Igor Stravinsky's ballet *Le Sacre du Printemps* ("The Rite of Spring"). For the controversial nature of the premiere, see page 411. The music was written for a production conceived by Sergei Diaghilev, impresario of the Ballet Russe. Each year he brought a new and stunning ballet production to Paris. With keen artistic judgment and calculated showmanship, he decided to capitalize on the Parisians' interest in primitive art. He chose to depict prehistoric rites culminating in the sacrifice of a human being—hardly typical of the lovely stories usually associated with classical ballet.

How could any serious work written in good faith cause such unmannerly behavior as is described on page 411? Probably no one on that famous evening in 1913 thought about it at the time, but the disagreement involved the purpose of the fine arts. The audience was accustomed to ballets that presented pleasant music amid beautiful scenery. Their main expectation of art, music, or ballet was that it be lovely. *The Rite of Spring* had neither lovely dancing nor music. The very basis of artistic integrity was being assaulted, or so it may have seemed.

The Rite of Spring opens with an orchestral "Introduction" (Record 5, Side 2). The scene is a primitive forest in which strange and eerie sounds are heard, buzzing and bubbling. The bassoon begins in its highest range with a haunting, hooting quality. Its melody is not very tuneful. The pitches are confined to a narrow range and the rhythmic pattern is irregular, with frequent stops and starts.

In the "Dance of the Adolescents" that follows, Stravinsky unleashes the potent power of rhythm. The effect resembles the wild beating of savage drums. The strings achieve this by playing a dissonant chord with short bow strokes, each punctuated by a rest. Suddenly eight horns (four more than the normal number) enter to add to the barbaric sound. This sensational new effect is produced by an irregular pattern of accents.

Between the accented chords there is sometimes one chord, sometimes two, three, four, or five. Gone is the underlying regular beat that had prevailed for 300 years. In its place are irregular rhythms that have their roots in nonliterate cultures.

As the chords bump along in their irregular way, several short primitive-sounding melodies are heard:

The melodies encompass only a few pitches and sound as though they are being played on a crude flute or pipe with a limited number of pitches.

The "Dance of Abduction" is even wilder. A scampering tune is played by the woodwinds and answered by a horn call. The timpani have a prominent part that contributes to the violent mood. The meter signatures change with dizzying frequency. At one point they appear in this order: 7/8, 3/4, 6/8, 2/4, 6/8, 3/4. Polyrhythm—the superimposing of two or more rhythms—can also be heard.

"Round Dances of Spring" brings some relief from the frenzy that pre-

---

A MEMORABLE PREMIERE

Igor Stravinsky's *The Rite of Spring* was given its premiere performance at the Théâtre des Champs Elysées in Paris on May 29, 1913. Stravinsky had written two previous ballets for the great impresario Sergei Diaghilev and the Ballet Russe; since the ballets had been performed in Paris, both men were already well known there. Therefore, the premiere of a new ballet by Stravinsky and the Ballet Russe was an event of importance among Parisian society. The theater was filled with dignitaries, royalty, and renowned musicians.

None of them could have anticipated what would happen that May evening. Instead of the expected lovely music, beautiful costumes, and dancing on the toes, the audience was subjected to some harsh-sounding chords and dancers in dark brown burlap making angular, rough motions. No one knows what set off the audience more, the dancing or the music, but the audience reacted—to an extreme. One writer states: "A certain part of the audience, thrilled by what it considered to be a blasphemous attempt to destroy music as an art, and swept away with wrath, began very soon after the rise of the curtain to whistle, to make catcalls, and to offer audible suggestions as to how the performance should proceed. . . . The orchestra played on unheard. . . . The figures on the stage danced in time to music that they had to imagine they heard."

Hardly had the performance started when the composer Camille Saint-Saëns left the theater after saying some caustic remark about the music. One critic yelled as loud as he could, "The music is a colossal fraud." The ambassador from Austria laughed derisively. One lady reached out into the adjoining box to slap the face of a man who was hissing; her escort felt compelled to exchange cards with the slapped man and a duel was arranged. Another lady rose majestically in her seat and spat in the face of one of the disapproving audience. The eminent French composer Maurice Ravel shouted, "Genius!" Backstage, Stravinsky held on to the choreographer Nijinsky to prevent him from going into the audience and fighting with the noise makers.

Much happened in the following years to the people involved in the premiere of *The Rite of Spring*. Many of the countries whose ambassadors were in the audience were soon at war. Diaghilev and his Ballet Russe severed ties with Russia and toured Europe and America season after season. Saint-Saëns's career was behind him and he lived only eight more years, but Ravel was at the height of his career. Both Stravinsky and the conductor, Pierre Montreux, were early in careers that stretched another fifty years! Nijinsky's mental health broke down within a few years and his work ceased. *The Rite of Spring* survived very well. Today it is considered one of the masterpieces of twentieth-century music.

---

cedes it. The tempo is slower and the flutes and other woodwinds play a clearer, sweeter melody that resembles an American Indian tune in its simplicity:

Later the orchestra takes up the melody.

The music becomes energetic again in the scene entitled "Games of the Rival Tribes." Stravinsky expresses the idea of competition musically by pitting one section of the orchestra against another, each with its own distinctive music. Then, in the manner of a contest or debate, the "tribes" answer each other. The music is often bitonal—occurring in two keys at once.

The "Entrance of the Sage" brings back the main thematic material with a thick orchestration.

Act I ends with "Dance of the Earth." It, too, suggests violence and upheaval. The low-pitched instruments play an ostinato line, but, because of

A scene from The Rite of Spring. *Photo by David Schrieber, Bloomington, Indiana.*

the dense quality of the music, the individual lines tend to become lost. The ballet must be seen with this portion of the music if the music is to be fully appreciated.

It hardly needs to be pointed out that *The Rite of Spring* is a complex musical work. For this reason, the use of the simplified score in the *Study Guide and Scores* is strongly recommended. Some portions of the music move extremely fast—the "Dance of Abduction" at measure 248, the "Games of the Rival Tribes" at measure 377, and the "Dance of the Earth" at measure 476. At these places each measure will seem to receive one beat. To keep from getting lost, the first few times try to notice some more easily heard feature such as the trumpet parts in the "Dance of the Earth." If you learn to follow the line score, you will gain a much greater understanding of the music.

The second and final act of the ballet, which is not performed as a concert work, depicts the sacrifice of a young maiden to the Chosen One so that the God of Spring may be satisfied. It is similar in style to the first act.

To the listener hearing it for the first time, *The Rite of Spring* may sound like a jumble of random notes. It may even seem that the instrumentalists can play anything they want, and no one will know the difference. Such an idea is, of course, incorrect. Stravinsky carefully planned everything in the score, and he writes detailed directions for the playing of each part. He even goes so far as to tell the timpani player when to change from hard to soft sticks, the French horn players when to tilt the bells of their instruments in an upward direction, and the cellists when to retune a string so that a chord can be played on open strings to achieve a more raucous effect.

IGOR STRAVINSKY

Igor Stravinsky was born in 1882. His father was the leading bass at the Imperial Opera in St. Petersburg (Leningrad). The boy studied piano, but not intensively because his parents wanted him to become a lawyer. He studied law at the University of St. Petersburg and simultaneously studied music with Rimsky-Korsakov.

Stravinsky soon became associated with Sergei Diaghilev, manager of the Ballet Russe. In 1910, after hearing only one of Stravinsky's compositions, he assigned the twenty-five-year-old composer to write a new ballet. It was *The Firebird,* which is usually heard today in a suite that Stravinsky himself arranged. *The Firebird* was so successful that it earned for the young composer the chance to write a second new ballet, *Petrouchka,* for the next season. Like *The Firebird, Petrouchka* is based on a Russian legend. Stravinsky was given another commission, and this time his creation was the startling *The Rite of Spring.*

Igor Stravinsky. This photograph was taken when he was eighty-four years old.

The year 1913 was the last before World War I, which seriously curtailed artistic activity in Europe. During the war Stravinsky moved to neutral Switzerland. The revolution in Russia cut off his income, and the ballet company had disbanded. He lived quietly in Switzerland for five years, recovering from a serious illness.

After the armistice, he settled in France. At that time, Paris was rich with artists and writers—Picasso, Valéry, Gide—who expressed Neoclassical sentiments in their works. Stravinsky became a French citizen and traveled widely as a conductor and pianist. In 1931 he came to the United States to lecture at Harvard University. When World War II prevented his return to Europe, he settled in Hollywood and became an American citizen in 1945. Although none of Stravinsky's later compositions caused riotous premieres, he has retained his esteemed position as one of the greatest composers of this century. On his eightieth birthday he was the honored guest of President Kennedy at the White House, and on another occasion he was the subject of a special one-hour program presented on a national television network. He died in 1971.

Despite superficial changes of style, Stravinsky remained true to his objective conception of music: Since a piece of music is something a composer makes, it is essentially an object rather than a representation of his soul. Therefore, a person's compositions need not be in a consistent personal style.

The skill of composition is paramount; the composer's personality is irrelevant.

Primitivism appealed to other composers in the years just before World War I. Béla Bartók wrote *Allegro Barbaro* in 1911, and several of his other works are wild and rhapsodic. Some of Serge Prokofiev's early works have driving rhythms and blatant melodies. Ernest Bloch's Violin Sonata, written in the 1920s, has a violent character. But, like expressionism, primitivism seemed to burn itself out within a decade. Stravinsky would lead the way to another style, Neoclassicism, which is the subject of the next chapter.

30

NEOCLASSICISM AND SERIALISM

Stylistic periods seem to move in either of two directions: toward emotional and subjective expression or toward intellectual objectivity. The Baroque period was more dramatic than the Renaissance, and it was followed by the objectivity of the Classical period. Then came the most subjective style of all, the romantic. The inevitable direction of music after Wagner and Debussy was a swing back to more objectivity. And so there evolved an attitude called *Neoclassicism.* It sought to duplicate the rational approach of the Classical period. Neoclassicism is exemplified in the sensitive painting *The Lovers* by Picasso (page 416).

On this matter Stravinsky's position was straightforward and consistent: "What is important for the clear ordering of the work, for its crystallization, is that all the . . . elements . . . should be properly subjugated and finally subjected to the rule of law before they intoxicate us. . . ." In this Neoclassical view writing a musical composition is like solving a problem; it is a task to be done by applying the intellect. Therefore, music is meant to express nothing

The Lovers, by Pablo Picasso, a painting that demonstrates the balance and restraint typical of the Neoclassical style.

except the composer's ability to contrive interesting tonal and rhythmic patterns. This Neoclassical position is one that Stravinsky followed after the 1920s. His intellectually oriented music earned him a reputation as leader of a trend euphoniously named the "Back-to-Bach" movement. Several Baroque forms such as the concerto grosso were revived during this time, and there was a renewed emphasis on counterpoint and the linear aspect of music. So the allusion to Bach is justifiable.

PAUL HINDEMITH

Paul Hindemith was born in Hanau, Germany, in 1895. When he was eleven and his father objected to a musical career for him, he ran away from home.

Paul Hindemith.

He earned his living by playing violin in dance orchestras and movie theaters. (Those were the days of silent pictures.) He later enrolled in the Conservatory at Frankfurt. There he won a prize for one of his compositions, a string quartet. After another successful string quartet he became interested in jazz, and this musical interest is evident in his Concerto for Piano and Twelve Instruments.

In 1927 Hindemith was appointed professor at the Hochschule in Berlin. He encouraged his students to learn several different instruments and to participate in a variety of musical activities. At that time he was much interested in practical, "usable" music. The term *Gebrauchsmusik,* which means literally "use-music," was applied to these compositions. They were not technically difficult and were intended for everyday use. Between 1936 and 1955 he composed a sonata for almost every orchestral instrument, including the tuba.

When the Nazis came to power, German culture was purged of anything more modern than the music of Wagner. Shortly before the outbreak of World War II, Hindemith escaped and emigrated to the United States, where he later became a citizen. He accepted an appointment to the faculty at Yale University and continued to teach there until 1953. He retired to live in Zurich, Switzerland, and died in 1963.

Hindemith's best-known works are two operas: *Mathis der Maler* ("Matthias the Painter"), which is based on the life of the painter Matthias Grünewald, and *Die Harmonie der Welt,* which is based on the life of the sixteenth-century astronomer Johannes Kepler. Hindemith arranged symphonic poems that bear the same names as the operas.

Hindemith was influential not only for his compositions, but also through his writings on music theory and harmony. He was also a leader in the "Back-to-Bach" movement.

Hindemith's Kleine Kammermusik für fünf Bläser, *Op. 24, No. 2*

Translated, the title means "Little chamber music for five winds." The work is for woodwind quintet: flute, oboe, clarinet, bassoon, and French horn. It was composed in 1922 and represents Hindemith at his exuberant best. Like Stravinsky's mature works, it shows strong Neoclassical tendencies in its sparse scoring and in the short, concise format of its movements. There is no attempt to impress the listener with lush sonorities.

The first movement is marked *Lustig* (cheerful). Its first theme is clearly presented by the clarinet and then the oboe.

The accompanying rhythmic figure is taken from the first four notes of the theme. The second theme in the movement is more songlike and is first played by the oboe.

The second movement is a subdued and graceful waltz. The sections are rather short, and their pattern is *A A B C B A.*

The third movement is marked *Ruhig und einfach* (quiet and simple). It is an elegant slow movement with long melodic lines. There are several ostinato accompanying patterns. One feature of the movement is the imaginative manner in which Hindemith writes for the instruments. In one place the flute plays notes lower than those of the clarinet and horn, an unusual arrangement that gives an interesting tonal effect.

The fourth movement is short and quite fast. It is built around a short, pounding theme that alternates periodically with free-sounding solos for each instrument.

The fifth movement is very fast, with an "arch" form that is *A B C D B A*. The differences among the themes are as much rhythmic as melodic. The first theme has accents falling logically on the beat. In the second theme the accents occur off the beat, while a bass line in regular rhythm is sounded. Both themes are presented in the Listening Guide on page 420–21. When the pitches in the second theme ascend, the bass line descends, and vice versa. In other words, the two lines appear in contrary motion. Also, the themes are not the billowy melodies of the romantic period, but are cohesive fragments that remind one of the melodies and themes of the Classical period. The irregular meter of twentieth-century music can be seen in the first two themes. Notice that there is no meter signature. Hindemith didn't write one because the meter changes so often.

The center portion of the "arch" form contrasts with the surrounding portions by being more songlike. Before the movement concludes the second theme is sounded in a dissonant manner, also a characteristic of twentieth-century music. The coda uses fragments of both themes.

ARNOLD SCHOENBERG

Arnold Schoenberg (1874–1951) was born in Vienna. He began studying violin at the age of eight and was an avid participant in amateur chamber music performances. He also attended concerts frequently. After his father's early death, he went to work as a bank clerk. He had little formal music training at an advanced level, but had for many years exhibited an interest in composing. This interest increased, and he decided to make music his lifework. First, he spent two years in Berlin as a music director in a cabaret, and then he returned

LISTENING GUIDE

HINDEMITH: KLEINE KAMMERMUSIK FÜR FÜNF BLÄSER, OP. 24, NO. 2

Fifth Movement (Record 3, Side 2)

0:00 Flute, oboe, and clarinet solidly play *A* theme.

0:12 Oboe softly plays the off-the-beat *B* theme while bassoon sounds accompanying line moving in contrary motion.

0:18 Flute joins oboe on *B* theme as music gets louder; theme is extended and grows quieter with clarinet passage.

0:35 All except French horn play a varied version that develops first three notes of the *B* theme; music is rather soft.

0:47 Short, concluding melodic idea *(C)* begins in the oboe.

1:02 Flute introduces *D* theme, which is more lyric and smooth than preceding themes.

1:21	*D* is repeated by flute, while more rhythmic interest is added to accompaniment.
1:35	*B* theme returns; played rather softly.
1:41	Flute joins oboe in repeating of *B*; music increases in intensity.
1:55	*A* theme returns played forcefully as in beginning by flute, oboe, and clarinet.
2:07	*C* melodic idea returns; played by oboe.
2:17	Coda begins with clarinet playing melodic fragment from *A*.
2:25	*B* played loudly with much dissonance.
2:46	Closes with three low chords.

to Vienna as a teacher, theorist, and composer. His career was interrupted for two years while he served in the Austrian army in World War I.

In 1925 he was appointed professor of composition at the Berlin Academy of Arts. His stay in Berlin ended when Hitler came to power. Although Schoenberg had been converted from Judaism to Catholicism, he left Germany and came to the United States, becoming an American citizen in 1940. He taught at the University of California at Los Angeles until his retirement. His musical activities continued until his death in 1951.

Prior to 1908 his music stood firmly in the tradition of Wagner and Mahler. His best-known composition of this period is *Verklärte Nacht* ("Transfigured Night"), a tone poem for string orchestra. The literary work that inspired the music is pure romanticism. As a couple walks through the woods, the woman confesses that she has been unfaithful. The man assures her that he still loves her, and her gratitude transfigures the night.

Around 1908 Schoenberg began to turn toward smaller groups of instruments. He started to write more contrapuntally and to employ much more chromaticism. Slowly he developed an atonal style. Such a step meant breaking away from the foundations that had undergirded the music of previous centuries. One of his atonal, expressionistic works, *Pierrot Lunaire,* was discussed in an earlier chapter.

About 1923 he devised the tone-row system that will be described shortly. He followed tone-row principles for most of his compositions from that time until the end of his life, departing from that style occasionally in some of his later works. Schoenberg is as much remembered for his influence on twentieth-century music as for his compositions. One of his best-known tone-row works, Variations for Orchestra, is discussed on page 423.

Arnold Schoenberg.

SERIALISM: TONE-ROW MUSIC

If composers throw out tonality, with what do they replace it? Schoenberg tried several ideas but slowly arrived at what is variously called *twelve-tone, tone-row, dodecaphonic,* or *serial music.* The principle is relatively simple. The composer arranges the twelve notes of the chromatic scale in any order. This is the "row"—a series of intervals that form a unique melody. It is not a chromatic scale because the notes are not lined up so as to progress by equidistant half steps. The pitches in the row need not all appear within the range of a single octave, either, and so wide interval leaps are sometimes encountered. No tone in the basic row can be repeated until all the twelve pitches have been heard, because such repeating would emphasize one particular note. There is no special importance attached to any note in the row, and so all are equally significant; there can be no tonal center.

While the tone-row technique may appear limited at first glance, it has been calculated that there are 479,001,600 different tone rows available. And each row can be treated in countless ways. It can appear vertically in chords as well as horizontally in melodies. The row can be transposed, or it can be moved to a different octave. It can be subdivided into phrases of different lengths.

Most of Schoenberg's serial works are for piano or chamber groups. The Variations for Orchestra is his only composition for full orchestra in this style. It is perhaps the most accessible work in the serial idiom for the listener who is unaccustomed to the sound of such music.

Schoenberg's Variations for Orchestra, Op. 31

The introduction to the work is very soft, with violin tremolos and nebulous notes in the woodwinds. The fluttering sound of the flute is actually called "flutter tonguing." Like Stravinsky, Schoenberg employs frequent meter changes and polyrhythm.

After a restrained climax, the music quiets down. The flute plays a graceful line, while the lower instruments sound the notes B-flat A C B-natural, which in German is written B A C H.* Bach elaborated on these notes in his last great work, *The Art of Fugue,* and other composers have used the figure since. The B A C H notes appear later in Schoenberg's Variations. The opening melodic figures return, a rather conventional compositional device. Up to this point, all the music has been based upon the row, although the row itself has not been presented as a melody.

Here are the pitches of the basic row for this piece:

There are four basic ways in which a row can be presented: (1) the original, (2) retrograde (backwards), (3) inversion (upside down), and (4) retrograde inversion (upside down and backwards).

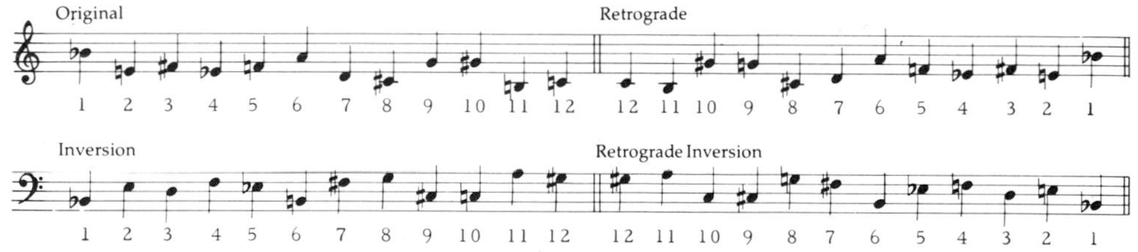

*In German music, the letter B indicates the note B-flat, while B-natural is written as the letter H. This system stems from an old tradition of avoiding the awkward interval of the augmented fourth (see the discussion of Mussorgsky in Chapter 25).

Here is the row with its rhythmic element as it first appears in the cello part (Record 6, Side 1):

Then it is heard in retrograde inversion and transposed upward. Next the retrograde appears, and the inversion is transposed. When put together, the melodic line is:

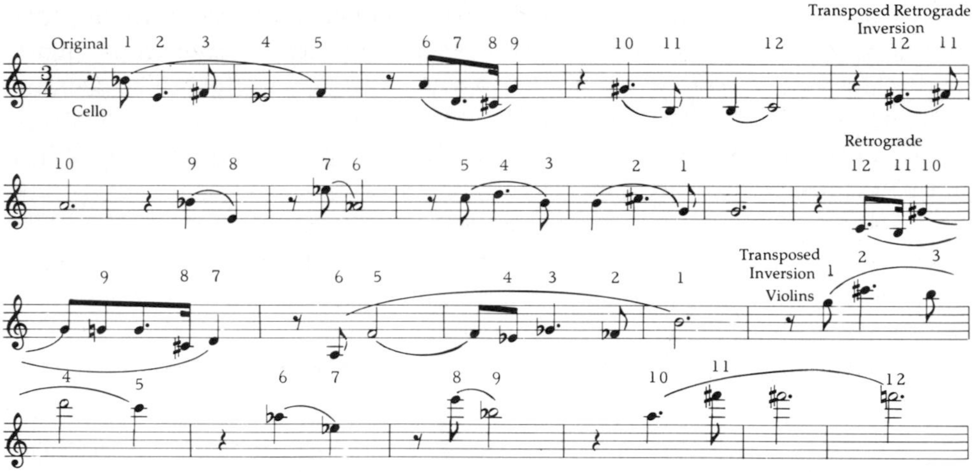

The structure of the music is very carefully planned. For example, the chords are derived from one version of the row. The number of notes in the melodic phrases corresponds to the number of notes in the chord.

In the first variation, which is only twenty-three measures long, the theme in its original form begins in the bass clarinet and then proceeds to other instruments. The accompanying parts are not chords but dashing, short, and colorful lines.

The second variation, again twenty-three measures long, is muted in quality and contrapuntal in texture. There is some imitation between various instruments. Toward the end the trombone sounds the B A C H motive.

The third variation is filled with busy notes that are superimposed over a rugged, vigorous rhythmic figure played by the four horns.

The fourth variation is longer and more graceful. As in the second variation, only solo instruments are playing; that is, there is only one instrument per part. The quality is appealing and not harsh. The theme is treated in a shimmering way by the harp, celeste, and mandolin, while being accompanied by new countermelodies.

The row is almost hidden in the double bass part in the fifth variation. The music seems to be a struggle between opposing melodic and rhythmic patterns. The B A C H motive can be heard popping in and out of the music.

The sixth variation is quiet in character. The solo cello plays the row, while the flute, English horn, and bassoon have significant melodies that are derived from a transposed inversion of the row.

The seventh variation is the softest of all. The row is almost obscured again, being sounded by the piccolo and glockenspiel in single notes in conjunction with a short figure in the solo violin.

The eighth variation is active and strident in character. It has a persistent rhythmic pattern in eighth notes in the bass and an aggressive pattern superimposed above it. The row is heard near the end in the flute, clarinet, and violin parts.

The ninth variation opens with the piccolo playing the theme. The row is in its original form, but the rhythmic pattern is new.

The finale is far longer than any of the variations. It tends to divide into three parts. One has the flutter tonguing and is in the character of the beginning of the entire work. A graceful center section follows. The fast tempo resumes, and the work closes after a final statement of the B A C H motive, which is heard often in the movement. The final chord contains all twelve pitches of the row.

It must be admitted that serial compositions present problems for many listeners. The concept of the row itself is easy to understand, but it isn't easily heard in a composition. When the row is inverted or set in retrograde, it is more sensed than heard. Actually, the row is mainly a compositional technique or approach for the composer, so it isn't necessary that the listener hear it as such. To people not used to the syntax of tone-row music, the sounds often seem disorganized in spite of the highly structured method of composition. Several hearings of the same piece are needed to overcome this.

In addition to tone rows, the idea of manipulating timbre fascinated Schoenberg. He devised a technique for doing this that he called by the wonderful German word *Klangfarbenmelodie* (literally, "tone color melody"). It involves changing the timbre along with the pitch changes. Schoenberg was influenced by contemporary art and was himself a good painter. He even exhibited works with his friend Wassily Kandinsky as well as with Paul Klee, another artist. Schoenberg attempted to adapt some of their ideas in his music. In turn, Kandinsky may have tried to emulate the abstract nature of music in giving his works such general titles as *Composition No. 4* and *Improvisation No. 30.* Many twentieth-century painters were fascinated with the technique of forming art works out of blocks of color and the bold use of color. Picasso's *Three Musicians* (plate 12) employs colors in a style called *cubism,* while Mondrian in *Broadway Boogie-Woogie* (plate 13) uses it in an intellectual, abstract way.

Schoenberg vigorously denied that his music is cold and intellectual. He considered it to be packed with emotion. In view of the rigid intellectual nature of serial composing, his claims may seem to be inaccurate. His music does contain a great amount of activity within a short span. It appears that he has compressed the dimension of time, causing the sounds to be much more concentrated. What took Schubert perhaps one minute, Schoenberg packs into a few seconds. Certainly he was not conceiving of music in the rambling dimensions of the romantic period.

SERIALISM: BEYOND TONE ROWS

Since 1950 an increasing number of important composers (Stravinsky, Copland, and others) have turned to the tone-row principles developed by Schoenberg. This trend can be attributed primarily to the influence of a quiet student of his: Anton Webern (*Vay*-burn, 1883–1945). He wrote in the same compositional idiom as Schoenberg, but his music is more austere and economical. Of his thirty-one compositions, the longest is ten minutes, and his complete works can be performed in less than three hours. His dynamics are usually the softest imaginable, and his frail tone-row melodies are passed note by note from one instrument to another in the subtlest kind of interplay. The principle of economy in composing was carried to its limit by Webern. If he had written more sparsely, one feels, the music would disappear completely.

A parallel to Webern's music can be found in the art of a twentieth-century Russian painter named Kasimir Malevich. About 1918 he painted *White on White* (page 427). Malevich's painting may be an idea carried to an extreme point, but the principle of a calm, objective, abstract art form holds artistic appeal.

On first hearing, Webern's music sounds like muted chaos. Little blobs of sound appear and disappear apparently at random between gaps of silence. But intensive listening discloses that what at first seems disorganized is actually organization of an intense and compact nature. The musical ideas are trimmed mercilessly to exclude every bit of waste or decoration. Only the absolute essentials remain.

White on White *(1918?)* *by Kasimir Malevich.*

ANTON WEBERN

Webern was born "Anton von Webern," but he dropped the royal *von* from his name after the 1918 revolution in Austria. He was born in 1883, the son of a mining engineer in southern Austria. While in school young Webern took lessons in cello, piano, and music theory. When he was eighteen, his family gave him a trip to the Wagner Festival at Bayreuth. This trip inspired a youthful effort at a large-scale work entitled *Young Siegfried.* Webern's style began to change after he met Arnold Schoenberg in 1904. He studied with Schoenberg for a little over two years, but they maintained a lifelong friendship even after Schoenberg had moved to Berlin and then on to the United States.

Webern began his professional career in 1908 as a conductor. Except for a tour of military service during World War I, he conducted orchestras in various Austrian cities. In 1920 his attention shifted to private music teaching. He also came in contact with the activities of the Social Democratic Party and took up duties as conductor of a workers' chorus.

Webern's atonal style began to emerge shortly before the First World War, but his better-known works were written after that time, especially during the 1920s. In 1927, he was appointed conductor and advisor for Radio Austria,

Anton Webern.

a job he held until his political party went out of power. He continued to compose throughout World War II, during which his son was killed in battle and his home was destroyed by bombing. As the last days of the war approached, his future looked brighter. He had received official letters from Vienna asking him to play a leadership role in reconstructing the cultural life of his country. He was shot in 1945 in an unfortunate accident as he lit a cigarette during a time of strict curfew. He died widely esteemed by a few other composers, including Stravinsky, but largely unknown to the general public.

Webern's Concerto for Nine Instruments

Among Webern's more interesting works is a composition that is only nine minutes long: Concerto for Nine Instruments. It carries the idea of serialism to a further level of development. The Concerto is based on the following row:

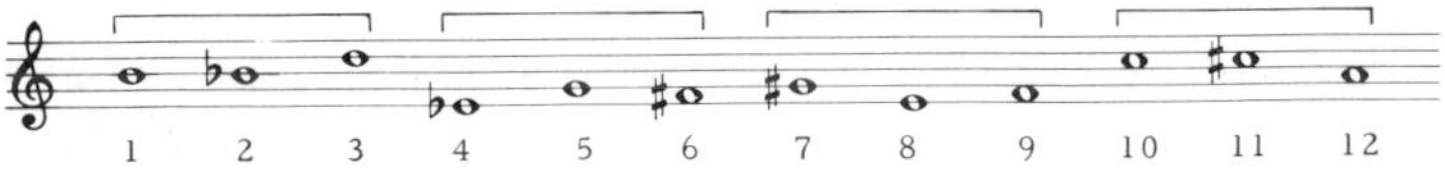

The brackets over the row indicate that it can be divided into four three-note segments, each consisting of two adjacent notes and one that is either a line or space further away. The first three notes can be considered a miniature row, followed by its retrograde-inversion, retrograde, and inversion. So the row itself is highly organized.

The composition starts:

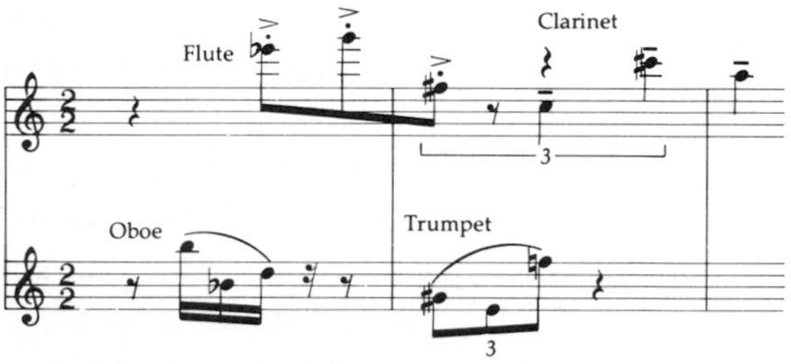

In this example the groups of three notes are retained, although with *octave displacement*—a technique by which a pitch is sounded in a different octave. The first group is played by the oboe, the second by the flute, the third by the trumpet, and the fourth by the clarinet. Notice also that a different rhythm is associated with each three-note group and that different articulations (slurring and tonguing) are specified.

The original three-note groups appear again in the Concerto, but the order of their appearance is varied, as are the rhythmic values and timbres. In the following excerpt the three-note figures have the interval sequence varied, the time values and articulations reversed, and the timbre changed.

Webern's composition has no actual themes. It is held together by the row and the three-note motives. The composition is generated from a principle of composing that presents the same ingredients continuously but in ever-changing ways. "It is always something different and yet always the same,"

Webern said of his music. In any case, his intellectual control over the music seems to be complete.

ANTI-INTELLECTUALISM

Following World War I French artists, musicians, and writers grew increasingly anti-romantic in their reaction against the seriousness and overinflated character (they thought) of recent styles in art and music. The informal spokesmen for the new music were the poet Jean Cocteau and the musician Erik Satie, both of whom are mentioned in Chapter 28. On one occasion Satie created some music that he asked the audience *not* to notice. He instructed them to talk or wander about the room as it was being played. When the audience did not follow his suggestion, he became extremely irritated and walked around urging individuals to talk and otherwise ignore his music.

Elements of this irreverent approach found their way into the music of other composers, especially Francis Poulenc and Darius Milhaud. When balanced with a skilled composing technique, anti-intellectualism was in some ways a refreshing change from the heaviness of nineteenth-century music.

ALEATORY MUSIC: THE "UNCOMPOSITION"

While Satie and Cocteau were anti-intellectual, the American John Cage (b. 1912) is purposely nonintellectual. He has been a prime promoter of chance or *aleatory* music. In such music the sounds are determined partly by chance and are therefore unpredictable. A clarinet player, for example, may be instructed to play anything he wishes for six beats or to rest during that time if he chooses. Or the selection of notes may depend on throwing dice. One of Cage's piano pieces is written on several disconnected sheets of paper. The player is told to drop the sheets, pick them up at random, and then play the pages in the new order. Cage has also written a composition for twenty-four radios and twelve "performers." The performers switch stations according to directions involving the use of a stopwatch. The resulting sounds are clearly a product of chance.

To understand what Cage is trying to achieve, you need to know his underlying philosophy, even if you don't agree with it. For centuries Western civilization believed in progress, the idea of working toward goals. Through increased knowledge, which in turn led to such practical outcomes as improved medical care, more food, a shorter work week, etc., it was held that the human race was progressing. The idea of progress has come under attack in the twentieth century from proponents of existential philosophy and from advocates

Plate 12
Pablo Picasso: *Three Musicians.*
(Collection, The Museum of Modern Art, New York.
Mrs. Simon Guggenheim Fund.)

As the twentieth century saw the return to certain devices used in musical compositions written in earlier centuries, painters also returned to take a look at techniques of artists centuries earlier. One of the techniques artists and painters tried was to forgo the third dimension and to experiment with lines and colors on flat planes or cubes. *Three Musicians* is a type of cubism called "collage cubism" in which the impression is given that the portions of the painting are pasted-up like pieces of paper, which is what the word "collage" means in French. The separate pieces are fitted together firmly as architectural blocks. More than pattern concerned Picasso in the painting, however. He tried to project the image of the musicians as traditional figures of the comedy stage. Their humanness is sensed behind the screen of costumes and masks.

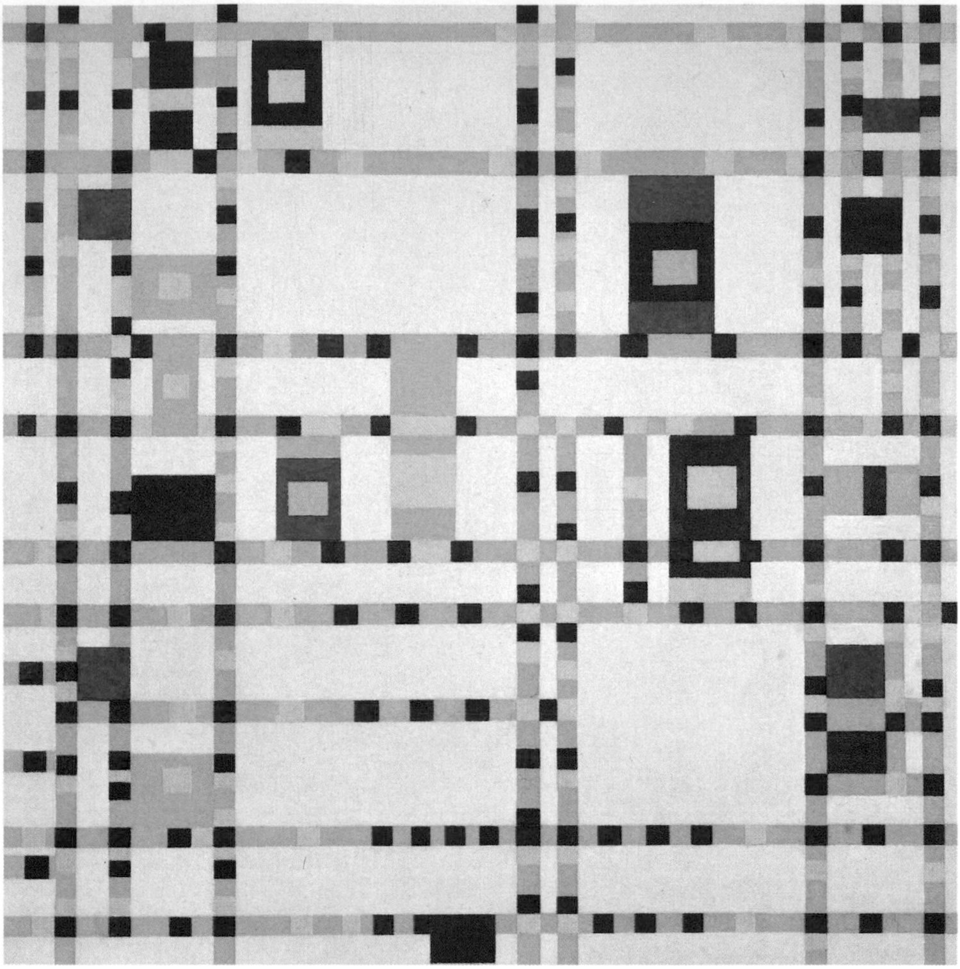

Plate 13
Piet Mondrian: *Broadway Boogie Woogie.*
(Collection, The Museum of Modern Art, New York.)

In spite of its title, *Broadway Boogie Woogie* is not an attempt to represent Manhattan. Mondrian developed a completely nonrepresentational, abstract style. The picture is the picture, and that's all. He restricted himself to horizontals and verticals and only a few simple colors. In this way it would be virtually impossible to paint a picture of an object or scene. At first glance, it may appear easy to imitate Mondrian's style successfully. Actually, the limitations make it very difficult.

Plate 14
Marc Chagall: *Snowing.*
(The St. Louis Art Museum.)

An important current in twentieth-century painting is fantasy. Many painters have become more concerned with "the inner eye," the introspective look at imagination and feeling. Such a view seems to be an artistic counterpart to Freudian psychology and its interest in dreams. Marc Chagall appeared never to lose the memories and dreams of his childhood in a Jewish community in Russia. *Snowing* depicts some of that personal mystery and fantasy. Is it shades of *Fiddler on the Roof*?

Plate 15
Grant Wood: *American Gothic.*
(Courtesy of The Art Institute of Chicago.)

Grant Wood's *American Gothic* is one of the most famous American paintings, found even in cereal commercials and on T-shirts. It depicts something very American in its matter-of-fact representation of life. It celebrates the homely, simple virtues of rural life, of America as it once was. The use of the term "Gothic" is intended to be an ironic comparison with the massive and complex structures found in the European Gothic tradition. The pointed-arch window of the dwelling in the background is an example of the so-called *Carpenter Gothic*, the American version of a European style carved ornately in stone.

of Oriental religious beliefs. The idea of progress is false, they claim; there is only change, not progress. The implications of the only-change, no-goal-toward-which-to-progress position are enormous. It is a little like removing the goal lines and uprights on the football field and ceasing to keep score or time; the game just happens. About the only assumption that one can make is that the players will eventually tire and stop playing.

This view rejects the idea that art must have meaning. As the poet Archibald MacLeish says:

> A poem should not mean
> But be.

Depicting a Campbell's soup can or comic strip character in a painting is not, as some people believe, a comment on the vulgarity of contemporary civilization. The content of such works is so obvious that it no longer invites interpretation, which is the way the artist wants it. A picture is a picture, and that's all. In his book *Silence* Cage urges the composer to "give up the desire to control sound, clear his mind of music [in the usual sense] and set about discovering means to let sounds be themselves rather than vehicles for manmade theories or expressions of human sentiments." Relying on chance devices is one way in which Cage and others try to get listeners to consider sound rather than to seek relationships among the sounds. While at first glance it may seem foolish to determine musical sequence by dropping pages on the floor, such a procedure comes from the consistent application of a philosophical position.

Cage's musical practices and philosophy have been adopted and adapted by composers such as Karlheinz Stockhausen. In a complete switch from his electronic works of the 1950s, Stockhausen's *Originale* (written in 1961) is based on a scheme of simultaneous, incoherent "happenings." The whole effect is something like the clowns taking over the circus. In one scene the directions are:

> Pianist and percussionist put on clothes brought in by cloakroom attendant. The pianist takes off his cultic robes and puts on Oriental female costume. . . . When he is ready, he begins to brew up tea at the piano.

It is difficult to predict much of a future for chance music. Although any object can be contemplated for what it is, the trouble with pop art and chance music is that they lack the evidence of skillful creativity and elegance required to make the works artistically interesting. Very little talent and devotion are exhibited in a painting of a soup can or in a musical work calling on the performer to manipulate a dial on a radio. Things that nearly everyone can do are not valued very much artistically.

TWENTIETH-CENTURY AND ROMANTIC STYLES COMPARED

The following chart summarizes the main differences and similarities between the musical style of the romantic period and that of the first half of the twentieth century.

MUSICAL ASPECTS	ROMANTIC	TWENTIETH CENTURY
New compositional techniques	Expansion of previously existing techniques	Serial composing; aleatory music
Texture	Homophony predominates	Counterpoint and homophony exist equally
Tonality	Major/minor system with tonal center	Modes and major/minor system; some works retain tonality; others are atonal
Harmony	Rich and beautiful; chords built in thirds	Some chords in nontraditional patterns; some pandiatonicism
Dissonance	Occasionally encountered	Increased levels of dissonance
Rhythm	Conventional; not as important as harmony or melody	Sometimes complex; becomes most important element in some works
Meters	Regular	Frequent mixing of meters
Melody	Often broad, flowing; expressive; some ornamentation	Often angular and not "tuneful"; often a combination of short melodic ideas
Loudness	Undulating changes; some contrast between very soft and very loud levels	Extreme contrasts in some works
Timbre	Rich, warm, and colorful	Much changing and exploitation of timbre; sometimes the most important element

Formal patterns	Followed loosely; program utilized	Renewed interest in forms from Renaissance, Baroque, and Classical periods
Instruments	Piano; large orchestra	Trend toward small ensembles
Virtuoso music	Highly developed and important	Some virtuoso passages in concertos; reduced interest in such music

31

ART MUSIC SINCE 1945

With the end of World War II in 1945 the world moved into a new era. In a faltering manner the nations and peoples of the world started to rebuild in both a physical and emotional sense. Webern also died in 1945, and his influence was soon felt on the world of music. Partly because of him, composers such as Stravinsky began writing serial music. Also, a new generation of composers was soon to appear, and with them an interest in the new and improved means of producing sound electronically.

From about 1945 to 1960 the struggle for musical predominance was between those who favored strict controls on music in terms of tone-row principles and those who favored few controls—chance music and improvisation. The most prominent person promoting controlled composition was the Frenchman Pierre Boulez (Boo-lez, b. 1925). In addition to a row of pitches one of his compositions contains this rhythmic row:

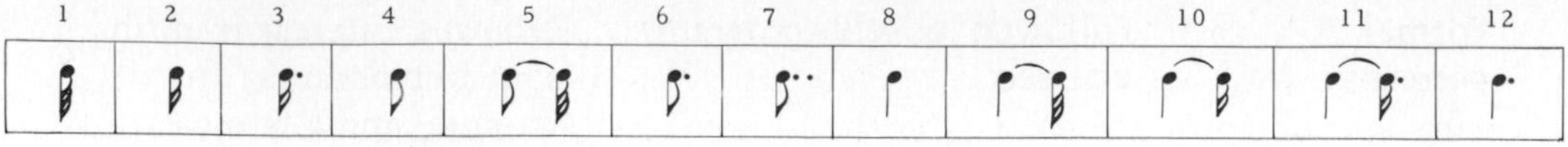

this row of articulations:

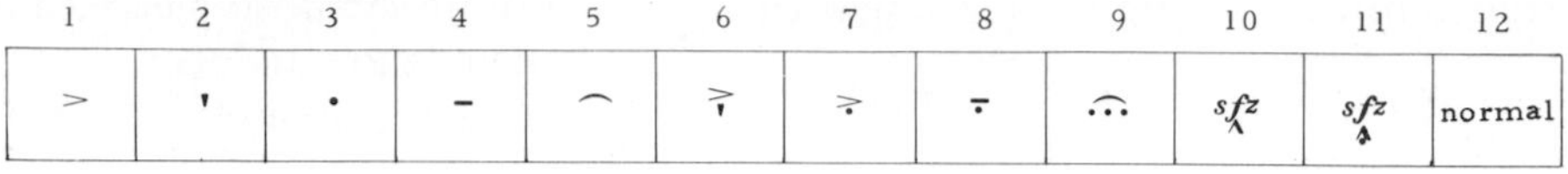

and this row of loudness levels:

1	2	3	4	5	6	7	8	9	10	11	12
pppp	*ppp*	*pp*	*p*	*meno p*	*mp*	*mf*	*più f*	*f*	*ff*	*fff*	*ffff*

So a series of sounds is controlled in four of its aspects: pitch, rhythm, articulation, and loudness. Other composers also control timbre. Compositions with three or four aspects controlled are usually frighteningly difficult to perform.

Other serial composers in addition to Boulez are Karlheinz Stockhausen in Germany, and Luciano Berio and Luigi Nono in Italy. An earlier version of controlled music was created by the Frenchman Olivier Messiaen (Mess-yun, b. 1908). In some of his music he uses one series for melody, another for loudness, another for timbre, and another for rhythm. Each of his four series is of a different length.

THREE ASPECTS OF MUSIC

Although the control and noncontrol advocates dominated the musical scene, three other somewhat experimental developments in twentieth-century music should be mentioned.

Microtonal music. One development is microtonal music—the use of intervals smaller than the usual half step found on the keyboard. Attempts, some as early as 1906, have been made to develop new systems of tuning. Generally, these efforts have involved dividing the present half step into quarter steps. Other intervals have been attempted, too.

To date, microtonal music has not caught on very well. There are several reasons that might explain the negligible response. Many instruments—all the woodwinds, all brasses except trombone, all keyboard instruments, and the harp—cannot play microtones without engaging in some inconvenient technique such as closing a hole halfway. Widespread adoption of microtonal music, then, would require redesigning of instruments, revision of music notation, and retraining of musicians. Furthermore, there is the question of how subtle a pitch difference is useful in music. Unless handled carefully, the use of microtones can make the music sound worse.

Some music created for electronic instruments produces pitches that are arbitrarily established by the composer. Several of these works reject any kind of scale in which the steps are equidistant from one another. Instead, the proportions of acoustical ratios or a mathematical formula are likely to be employed.

Mathematics. Another movement in music today is the use of mathematics to help determine aspects of a work. Historically, music and mathematics have been closely connected. Since the time of the ancient Greeks, the ratios of vibration frequency and rhythms have been a source of philosophical discourse. The analysis of systems of composing and the calculation of probabilities in the arrangement of musical sounds have also received attention.

Yannis Xenakis (Zeh-*nock*-iss, b. 1922) was born in Athens. He studied architecture and then composition in Paris. He believes that musical compositions should be based on the calculus of probabilities. In his music, which he calls "stochastic," it does not matter if a particular note is played or not, since the ear cannot perceive every individual sound.

Timbres. In the twentieth century, interest in timbres has increased even more. There has been further exploitation of the possibilities offered by conventional instruments, as evidenced by Schoenberg's and Webern's *Klangfarbenmelodie*—the changing of timbre rather than pitch. The "nature" or "night" sounds heard in the second movement of Bartók's Third Piano Concerto are another example, as are some of the effects in Stravinsky's *The Rite of Spring.* Concern for timbre as well as intricate contrapuntal relationships has been a mark of the tone-row composers.

Even more advanced has been the experimentation with sources other than musical instruments. One example of this experimentation is the "prepared piano" devised primarily by the American John Cage. To produce distinctive timbres, sundry items are placed on the hammers and strings of the piano according to the specifications of the composer. Necessary equipment can include tape, chewing gum, thumb tacks, coins, cloth, and paper. New timbres are indeed the result. The pianist is sometimes instructed to reach into the top of the piano and strum the strings with the hand.

Not surprisingly, most nonconventional instruments are allied with the

Variation No. 7: Full Moon *(1949–50) by Richard Lippold. This work is made from brass rods and nickel-chromium and stainless steel wires. It stands ten feet high.*

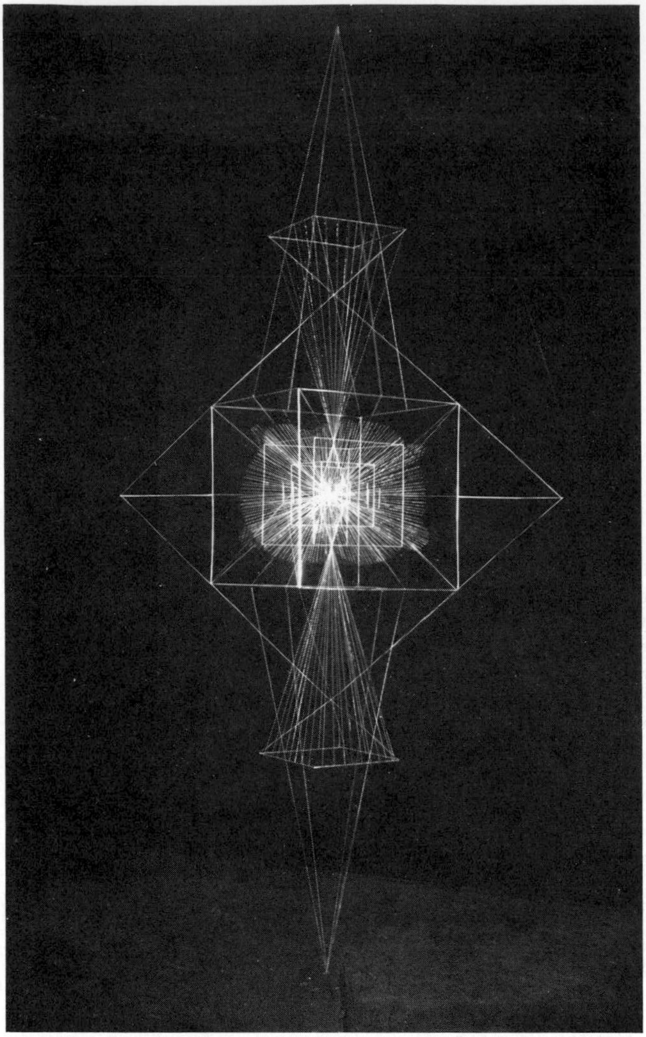

percussion section. In fact, the percussion ensemble is a twentieth-century phenomenon. One of the first composers to write for percussion ensemble was Edgard Varèse (Vah-*rez,* 1883–1965), who was born in France but lived in America after 1916. His *Ionisation* (1931) calls for an orchestra of forty-one percussion instruments and two sirens. The result is rhythm and timbre freed from conventional melody and harmony. Another American leader in developing music around timbres was Harry Partch (1901–1974).

An even more advanced manipulation of sounds and noises was advocated more than sixty years ago by an Italian named Luigi Russolo (1885–1942). He wrote, "We must break out of this narrow circle of pure musical sounds and conquer the infinite variety of noise sounds." He went on to suggest an "instrumentation" of sounds according to six families or types:

1. Booms, thunderclaps, explosions, crashes, slashes, roars.

2. Whistles, hisses, snorts.

3. Whispers, murmurs, mutterings, bustling noises, gurgles.

4. Screams, screeches, rustlings, buzzes, crackling sounds obtained by friction.

5. Noises obtained by percussion on metals, wood, stone, terra-cotta, etc.

6. Voices of animals and humans, shouts, shrieks, groans, howls, laughs, wheezes, sobs.

If his ideas seem futuristic today, imagine how startling they must have been in 1913 when he first propounded them!

ELECTRONIC MUSIC

As music moved into the 1960s, both the serial and chance music began to give way to a third type: electronic music. Today it is the most prominent technique for the creation of art music. Even advocates of other types of composition—John Cage, for example—have gravitated toward electronic music.

There are two types of electronic music. *Musique concrète* is one. Recordings are made of natural sounds and voices—parts of human speech, a fly buzzing, the wind, a motor roaring, a whistle. Then the tape is manipulated by the composer. It can be speeded up or slowed down. It can be spliced. It can be recorded through a second or third recorder and the sounds then combined. The composition in *musique concrète* is a segment of tape that contains selected and manipulated sounds in a planned sequence.

An American advocate of *musique concrète* is Vladimir Ussachevsky (b. 1911). He combines natural sounds and sounds from musical instruments, usually percussion, on tape. For instance, from the ring of a gong, he may salvage only the last portion or "afterglow" of the sound. Then he may treat the taped portion in any of the ways previously described. One such work is "Dramatic Pantomime." A part of the score is shown on page 438.

Musique concrète has functioned successfully as background for movies, plays, and ballet scenes, especially when eerie and unearthly music is required.

The other type of electronic music consists of sounds produced on electronic equipment (synthesizers and oscillators) and then recorded on tape. This

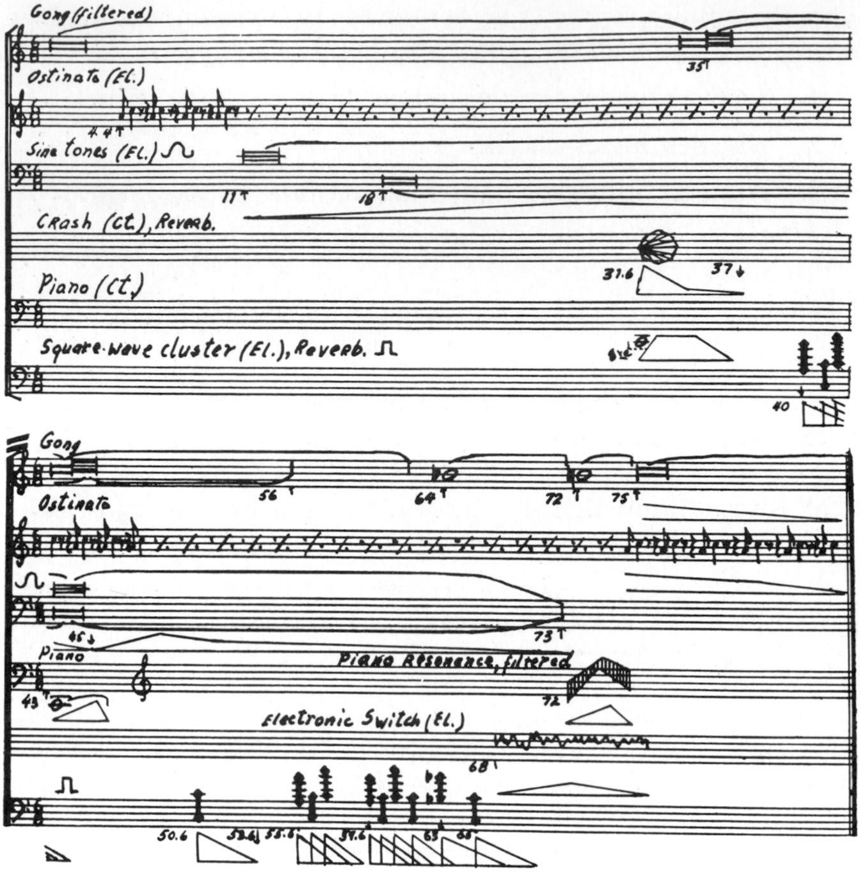

Score for "Dramatic Pantomime," part three of the four-part suite, Four Miniatures *by Vladimir Ussachevsky. "This score combines musical notation with a few specially designed symbols representing either nonpitch sounds or clusters covering delimited pitch areas. As used, such note values are generalizations rather than exact indications of durations. Arabic numerals specify the time in seconds at which each sound enters or is terminated. Triangular symbols below the staff lines are dynamic indications describing the envelope of a given sound or sound pattern. Origins of the sound materials are indicated and further categorized as electronic (El.) or concrete (Cr.)." Vladimir Ussachevsky.*

music had its beginnings in the Studio for Electronic Music of the West German Radio in the 1950s. All sounds within the limits of human hearing are possible, even those too high or low to be identifiable as musical pitches. This range is considerably wider than the customary eighty-eight pitches available on the piano keyboard. Furthermore, every level of loudness and timbre can be reproduced. Also possible are machine rhythms, which are more complex and more accurately executed than those produced by humans.

Electronic music is not performed in the usual sense of the word. A button is pushed to start the machine. If the technician who prepared the tape has followed the directions accurately, the listener hears *exactly* the sounds the composer intended. The need for a performer is completely eliminated. The idea seems revolutionary at first, and yet in the visual arts no one expects to watch a painting being repainted by a "performing" artist. We see just what the original artist painted. The same principle prevails in electronic music.

A computer is not essential for electronic music, although it is often involved. The computer can "create" a musical composition from a prescribed program. The computer program can direct a synthesizer to produce whatever type of music is desired—Mozart-like compositions, popular songs, or psychedelic synthesized sounds. Also, the music the computer specifies can be printed in notation. Currently, the computer holds more promise as a research tool than as an aid to musical composition.

Creating complex electronic compositions is a highly specialized skill; simple electronic works are not difficult, and in fact are developed in some junior high school music classes. Instruction in electronic composition has only recently been offered in European and American music schools.

The potential of electronic music has barely been tapped. There are vast possibilities for sound manipulation, and composers today are exploring the new area in search of musical riches.

Subotnik's Until Spring

Californian Morton Subotnik (b. 1933) thinks of working with electronic sounds as "sculpting." He writes:

> Sculpting with sound . . . placing sound into an imaginary "space canvas" in front of me . . . molding the color of a sound . . . transforming the harmonic content . . . to begin to shape it like the beginnings of some strange visceral language . . . shaping the sounds into contours of pitch . . . blending pulsating points along an imaginary time line . . . increasing and decreasing their occurrences . . . like elastic bands stretching to their original form or let go to snap into a chaotic pattern like a balloon full of air suddenly released.

The essential idea of Subotnik's *Until Spring,* composed in 1976, is a programmatic one (Record 6, Side 1). It deals with three qualities: thrusting out, becoming, and being. Each of the three parts that make up the thirty-minute work is further divided. "Thrusting out" begins with an upward glissando rising out of a plucked-like note, then there is a gradual increase of pulse

Morton Subotnik at the Electronic Music Box.

rates and also an increase of loudness. The idea of emergence from one point in space to another is then represented in sound, and there is an increase of harmonic content. Since the work was created as a composition to be played from a tape or disc, there was consciousness of the placement of tracks, which can be clearly heard as certain portions of the music bounce from one loudspeaker to another.

The materials for *Until Spring* were worked out both on paper and directly on the synthesizer. The sketch for the overall composition can be seen in the diagram on the next page. The instrument used is a synthesizer with console that Subotnik calls the "Electronic Music Box."

If you are going to get anything out of listening to *Until Spring* and other electronic works, you will need to clear your mind of music as you have previously known it. No longer are there melodies with chords; nor is there a metrical, steady beat pattern or the usual timbres of instruments or voices. Instead, the attention must be on the "sculpting" of sounds, of how the composer has manipulated them. That makes the music potentially as fascinating as an example of human ingenuity.

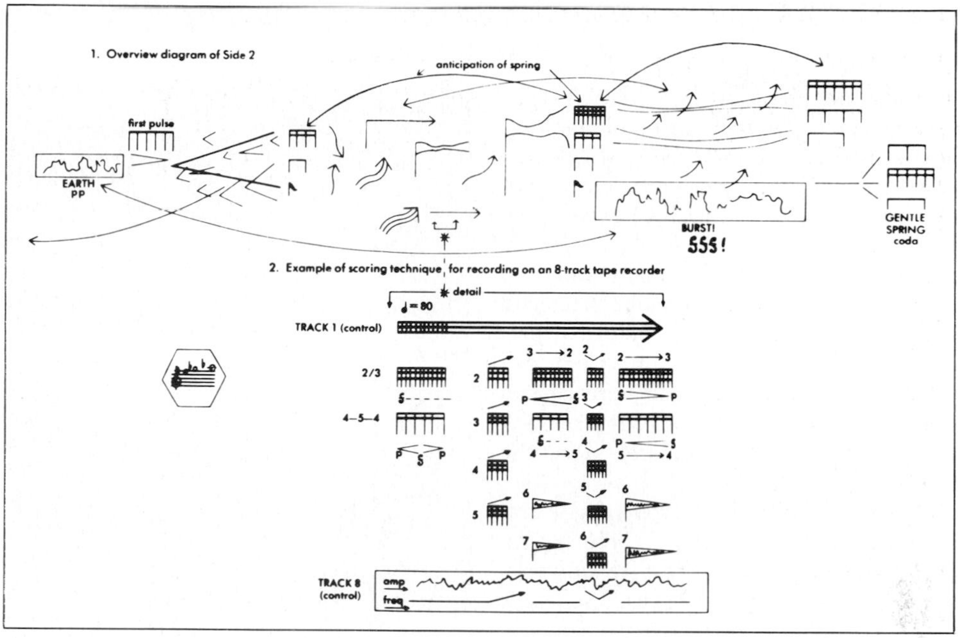

ECLECTICISM—CONSOLIDATION

Although contemporary art music is pluralistic, with composers writing in widely divergent styles, there are some composers who use what they believe is the best of each style. They owe allegiance to no musical system or philosophy, and their compositions cannot be classified in any of the categories previously mentioned in this book.

In the opinion of many musicians, the leading composer today is Krzysztof Penderecki (Pen-der-*et*-ski), who was born in 1933 near Cracow, Poland. He is most interested in timbre and tonal effect, but he also uses the tape recorder in some of his compositions. His best-known works are *The Passion According to St. Luke* and *Threnody to the Victims of Hiroshima.*

Other eclectic, experimental composers include the Italian Luigi Dallapiccola (1904–1975), the Pole Witold Lutoslawski (b. 1913), and the German Hans Werner Henze (b. 1926).

Crumb's Night of the Four Moons

Deciding on representative works to include in a book is difficult, and this is especially so in the case of very recent music. However, George Crumb's series

MUSIC AND SPACE

Probably no event in the twentieth century captured the imagination of mankind as that night of July 20, 1969, when Neil Armstrong climbed down the ladder from the space capsule and walked on the face of the moon. For thousands of years people had wondered about the moon, sun, and stars. Poets penned lines about them and astronomers had tried to calculate their orbits and size. Hundreds of writers had fictionalized about travel in outer space; even comic book characters such as Buck Rogers visited there regularly since the 1930s.

Now it was really happening. A human being was walking on the moon. Some people saw it as a great step forward, as Neil Armstrong said in his first words upon setting foot on the surface, but others felt a tinge of sadness, as did the composer George Crumb, who composed his *Night of the Four Moons* partly in reaction to the event. An old era had ended and a new one had begun.

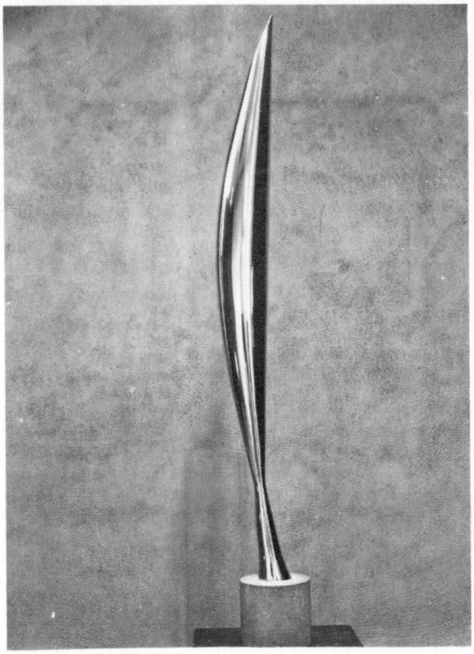

Constantin Brancusi. Bird in Space *(1919). Bronze, height 54". The Museum of Modern Art, New York (Anonymous Gift).*

Few composers reacted as directly as did George Crumb, but many felt the mood of the times and a desire to break out of old earthbound limits. Whether it was the sounds of the electronic radio communication and equipment or the notion of the total feeling of freedom of weightlessness, some composers seemed to reach out for new expanses, new space. For example, Yannis Xenakis's *Metastasis* uses sixty-three instruments with very little of the time more than one instrument on a part. The sounds consist of many *glissandi* (slides) with only the upper and lower pitch limits specified. The effect is not discord or dissonance, as you might expect, but rather of a "haze" of sounds.

In some ways, electronic instruments represent a new space for composers. With such instruments virtually any type of sound and rhythm can be carefully prepared. There are no boundaries of twelve semitones in the octave, ranges of instruments or voices, a restricted number of timbres, or human frailties in the performance of the music. In one sense, with electronic music the composer is completely free—"weightless." Some electronic music composers have associated works of music with space. One such composer is Otto Luening (b. 1900), who created his *Space Fantasy* on tape from the manipulated sounds of the flute. It reverberates and chirps along with no traditional rhythms or timbres.

Whatever else may be said of space exploration and "music exploration" in terms of searching out new types of music, they are a tribute to the inventiveness and restlessness of the human race to try, learn, explore, and accomplish.

of four songs entitled *Night of the Four Moons* appears to demonstrate well a number of the trends in art music today. It was composed during the Apollo 11 moon flight July 16–24, 1969. Crumb writes of the work:

> I suppose that *Night of the Four Moons* is really an "occasional" work, since its inception was an artistic response to an external event. The texts—extracts drawn from the poems of Federico García Lorca—symbolize my own rather ambivalent feelings *vis-à-vis* Apollo 11.

It was commissioned by the Philadelphia Chamber Players and involves a chamber ensemble consisting of an alto singer, alto flute (doubling on piccolo), banjo, "electric" cello (that is, amplified through a speaker), and one percussion player playing a number of instruments: a large drum, crotales (metal shells struck together), cymbals, tambourine, Japanese Kabuki blocks, bongo drums, Chinese gong, Tibetan prayer stones, vibraphone, and African thumb piano (Mbira). The singer's part requires *sprechstimme,* unvoiced singing, and whispering, in addition to normal singing.

The score is preceded by two pages of lengthy instructions to the performers. These directions include specifications regarding placement on stage, stage lighting, the dress of the singer (a Spanish cabaret costume), and stage entrance and exit ("should be solemn and suggest a somnambulistic, trance-like quality").

The text of the work consists of fragments of poems by Federico García Lorca, which are in Spanish. The text for the first song is (Record 6, Side 1):

La luna está muerta, muerta;	The moon is dead, dead;
pero resucita en la primavera.	but it is reborn in the springtime.

The other three songs are: *Cuando sale la luna* . . . (When the moon rises . . .), *Otro Adán oscura está soñando* . . . (Another obscure Adam dreams . . .), and ¡*Huje luna, luna, luna!* . . (Run away moon, moon, moon! . .).

The music has some of the sparse quality developed by Webern, some elements of theater, and quite a bit of interest in timbres. The first two lines of the first song appear on page 444. The unifying element in these lines is the figure circled in the example. The figure is inverted, or turned upside down, freely. Crumb writes of this song:

> "The moon is dead, dead . . ." is primarily an instrumental piece in a primitive rhythmical style, with the Spanish words stated almost parenthetically by the singer. The conclusion of the text is whispered by the flutist over the mouthpiece of his instrument.

The music has notated rhythm, but no metrical, steady beat. Dynamic markings and varied timbres add much to its effect, which seems to be a combination of intellectualism and mysticism.

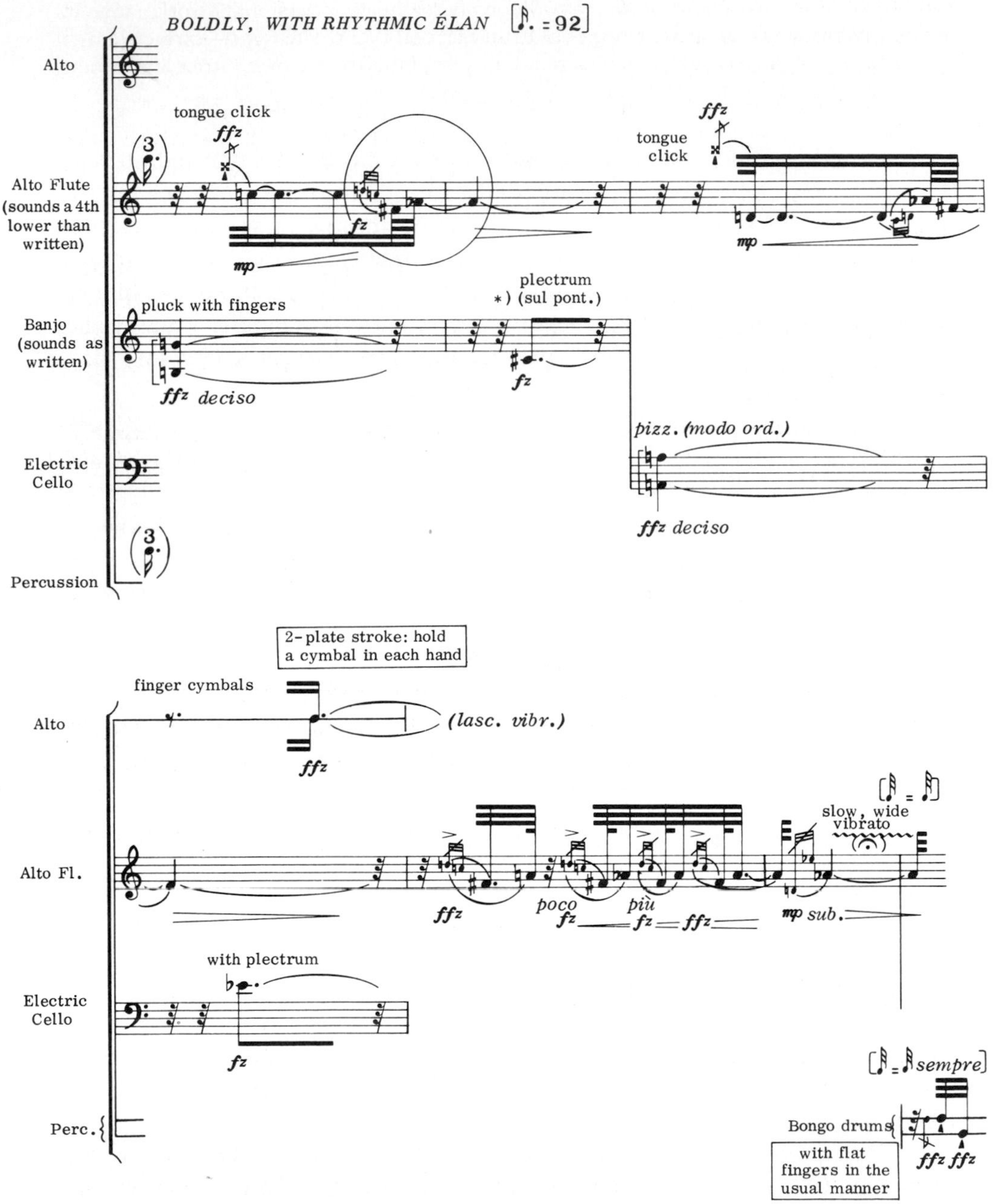

THE FUTURE OF MUSIC

More music is being written today than at any time in the world's history. The population has increased tremendously since Bach's time, and many more persons have been educated to write music. The "composition explosion" makes it even more difficult for anyone to become knowledgeable about the myriad styles and composers of today's music.

As Chapter 30 pointed out, Schoenberg was a composer who lived primarily on income from university teaching rather than from the sale of his music. A similar situation holds true for many contemporary art music composers. In some respects this situation is beneficial. The universities have the services of skilled composers-teachers, and the composers are freed from financial worries and concern about whether their patron and public will like the new work. But the situation also has its minus side. The separation between the composer and the public has too often widened into a gulf. As a result, the composer appears to be increasingly elitist and aloof, and the public responds with little interest.

The new and relatively secure position of the composer of art music is not the only reason for a lack of understanding between public and composer. The twentieth century is an age of specialization. While there have been specialists in performance and composition in the past, the trend toward increased specialization is unmistakable. Some compositions written in this century are so complex and their musical intentions so obscure that one almost has to be a composer in the particular style of the work in order to understand them. This is not a criticism of thc artistic worth of complex works, but it is a possible explanation of the inaccessibility of some new music to people who are not well-schooled musicians. Even trained musicians cannot spend many hours studying scores, listening carefully to themes or tone rows, and reading the composer's explanation of every work. There is little doubt, then, that the specialization of many composers has contributed to the lack of understanding between themselves and much of their potential audience.

Although Bach and Haydn wrote excellent music "on order," no one wants to return to a situation in which the composer must please the audience or else. The gap in understanding is a situation that is often talked about, but, like the weather, no one seems able to do much about it. An upgrading of school music curricula will help, of course. But it is simply not possible for school courses, under present conditions, to teach all the myriad styles of music in the necessary depth. To do so would require devoting most of the school day to music instruction, a most unlikely possibility.

Perhaps the solution to audience acceptance is not a solution at all but rather a realization that for the foreseeable future there will be good art music for the majority of the concert audience *and* more complex, innovative works for a limited, specialized clientele. This view would relieve the conscientious layman of the feeling that all styles and works should be learned, no matter how difficult and unrewarding they might seem. No listener should feel musically delinquent because Copland and Bartók seem more understandable and enjoyable than Webern and Crumb. Perhaps Webern and Crumb will become most meaningful eventually if Copland and Bartók have been grasped first.

Only two predictions can be made with confidence about music in the future. (1) There will be music. Mankind has found sound and its manipulation too fascinating, too satisfying to abandon it completely. In fact, the indications are that music and other fine arts will mean more, not less, in the years to come. (2) Music of the future will differ from music of the past. The creative mind is restless and forever unsatisfied with previous accomplishments. It wants to experiment with new ways, new materials. The truly creative person is constitutionally unable to make imitations or be content with the efforts of others.

By definition, creativity involves the bringing forth of something new and unique. And so in the art of music, as in any creative endeavor, there will always be something new. Music, when it is the product of an imaginative and skilled musician, will always be a fascination to hear and a joy to understand.

PART SIX
AMERICAN MUSIC

32

AMERICAN MUSIC BEFORE WORLD WAR I

Music in America had a slow start, for several reasons. The nation began as a loose confederation of small, struggling settlements, isolated from the mainstream of European life by 3,000 miles of ocean. Physical survival was the most important concern. The stimulation of contact with recent artistic creations was lacking. Furthermore, there could be no truly American music in those days because the settlers came from other lands and were steeped in the traditions of English, Dutch, or German music. The Puritan influence, too, was strong in the colonies. Rightly or wrongly, these devout people thought that art and theater were wicked. At best, art and music were mere diversion; at worst, they were products of the devil. The only music permitted in church was the unaccompanied singing of psalms and hymns. Not surprisingly, then, the first book published in America was the *Bay Psalm Book,* in 1640. The first edition had no music, and none was added until the ninth edition in 1698.

THE EIGHTEENTH CENTURY

The most sophisticated music written in America before the Revolutionary War was the product of the Moravian communities around Bethlehem, Pennsylvania. These people had come from what is today part of Czechoslovakia, bringing with them a rich musical heritage. Besides music for church services, they also wrote chamber works. Musicologists are still discovering some of this fine music. There were several active composers in the Moravian community, but John Frederick Peter (1746–1813) was the most skilled. He came to America in 1770.

Probably the first native-born American composer was an amateur, Francis Hopkinson (1737–1791), a friend of George Washington and a signer of the Declaration of Independence. His most famous song was "My Days Have Been So Wondrous Free." In 1788 he published some songs, for which he also wrote the words. He dedicated the book to Washington, whose reply was humble, especially with regard to his own musical ability: "I can neither sing one of the songs, nor raise a single note on any instrument to convince the unbelieving. But I have, however, one argument which will prevail with persons of true estate (at least in America)—I can tell them that *it is the production of Mr. Hopkinson."*

If Francis Hopkinson's compositions did not sound particularly different from English music at the time, the works of William Billings (1746–1800) did. Billings was a tanner by trade, but he had an insatiable drive to write music. And he was a firm believer in American music for Americans! He explained in his first collection, *The New England Psalm Singer* (1770), that he would follow his own rules for composition. One of the techniques he used in his hymns was "fuguing," which was a high-class name for simple imitation. Billings was not particularly modest in making claims: "[Fuguing] is twenty times as powerful as the old slow tunes. Each part striving for mastery and victory. The audience entertained and delighted. Now the solemn bass demands their attention; next the manly tenor. Now here, now there, now here again! O ecstatic! Rush on, you sons of harmony."

Whatever Billings lacked in training was offset by his native musical ability. Despite some crudities, his music has a quality that has fascinated many musicians and lay people, especially in this century. The tune "Chester" is one of his best known. A version of it from Billings's *Singing Master's Assistant* is shown on this page. The melody is in the tenor part, which is the third line from the top. The music is plain and unadorned. "Chester" was destined to reappear in the annals of American music, specifically in *New England Triptych* by William Schuman.

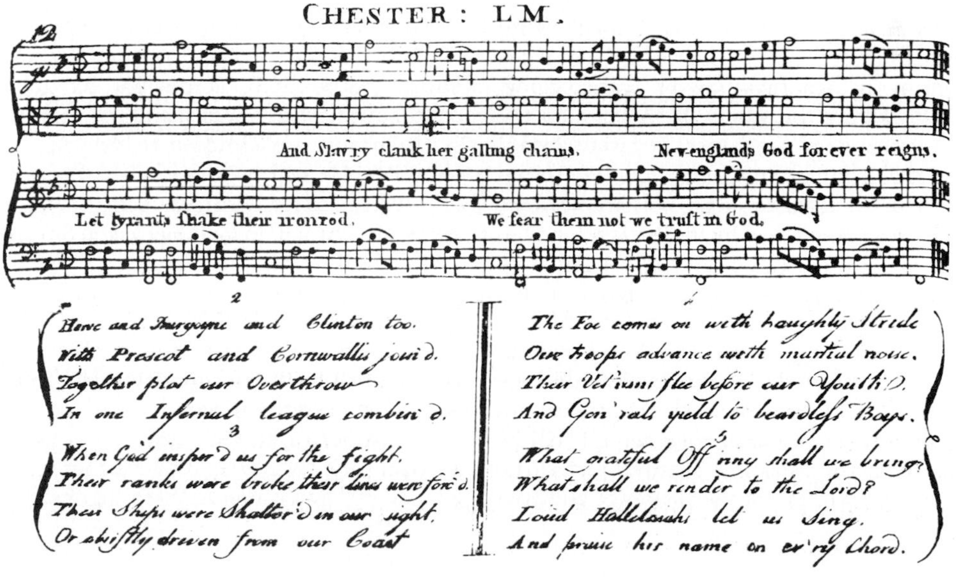

CHESTER : L.M.
And Slav'ry clank her galling chains.
New-englands God forever reigns.
Let tyrants shake their iron rod,
We fear them not we trust in God.
2
Howe and Burgoyne and Clinton too.
With Prescot and Cornwallis join'd.
Together plot our Overthrow
In one Infernal league combin'd.
3
When God inspir'd us for the fight.
Their ranks were broke their lines were forc'd.
Their Ships were Shatter'd in our sight.
Or swiftly driven from our Coast
4
The Foe comes on with haughty Stride
Our troops advance with martial noise.
Their Vet'rans flee before our Youth.
And Gen'rals yield to beardless Boys.
5
What grateful Off'ring shall we bring?
What shall we render to the Lord?
Loud Hallelujahs let us Sing.
And praise his name on ev'ry Chord.

Billings was the only ray of American light to appear in a long night of European-dominated music. Even our national songs had their roots in Europe, as you can see below.

THE NINETEENTH CENTURY

The name Mason is an important one in American music. Lowell Mason (1792–1872) wrote many hymns, including "Nearer, My God, to Thee," and

---

AMERICA'S PATRIOTIC SONGS

As is true of so much of America's culture, most of its patriotic music consists of songs with European roots. The origin of "Yankee Doodle" is unknown, but it was introduced in the colonies by a British army doctor named Shackburg about twenty years before the Revolutionary War began. It was first sung by the British to ridicule the New Englanders, who promptly took it over as their own song by adding new verses.

The melody of "The Star-Spangled Banner" was adapted from a popular English drinking song "To Anacreon in Heaven." This song to an ancient Greek poet was probably composed by John Stafford Smith (1750–1836). The words were written by an American lawyer, Francis Scott Key. During the War of 1812 between the Americans and the British, Key went aboard a British frigate in Chesapeake Bay to negotiate the release of a Dr. William Beames, who was being held by the British. On September 13, 1814, the British fleet sailed up the Bay to bombard Fort McHenry, which guarded Baltimore Harbor. Before the battle began, Key, Beames, and a companion were transferred to a small boat behind the fleet. All night Key paced the deck wondering if the American flag would still be there in the morning, signifying that the Fort had withstood the challenge and that Baltimore had been saved. "By the dawn's early light" Key could see the Stars and Stripes still flying, and he was moved to begin the poem that is sung today. By that afternoon he had finished it, and a week later it appeared in the *Baltimore American.* The words were sung for the first time by an actor in Baltimore. It was not officially made the national anthem until 1931.

"My Country 'Tis of Thee" ("America") is sung to the same tune as the British national anthem "God Save the King," which was written by the English composer Henry Carey (1685–1743). The words as sung in this country were written in 1832 by the American Samuel Francis Smith (1808–1895), somewhat by accident. Lowell Mason was searching for music to arrange for children to sing in the churches. He had been given a collection of songs used in German schools. Not knowing German, Mason had asked Smith, a student at Andover Theological Seminary, to set English words to them in his spare time. It took Smith only half an hour one February day to write his words to the tune, which he did not realize at the time was "God Save the King."

"America, the Beautiful" is sung to a hymn tune "Materna" ("O Mother, dear Jerusalem") by Samuel A. Ward, an obscure

---

conducted the Handel and Haydn Society in Boston. His most significant achievement was the establishment of music in the curriculum of the public schools in 1838. He also spread the idea of music for the masses by organizing "conventions" for the training of music teachers. He made several lengthy trips to Europe to study. Two of his sons founded the piano-manufacturing company of Mason and Hamlin, and a third son became a famous music teacher. Mason led a campaign against the "gospel song," which came into being after the decline of Billings's "fuguing tunes." As part of this effort, Mason published a large number of music collections.

---

organist in Newark, New Jersey. The words were the creation of Katherine Lee Bates (1859–1929). Bates was a professor of English at Wellesley College and author of a number of books and poems. She was so impressed by her first visit to the summit of Pike's Peak in Colorado that the opening lines of the poem seemed to come to her. They were printed in a magazine called *The Congregationalist* on July 4, 1895, and were subsequently set to several different tunes, but the "Materna" melody is the only one heard with the poem today.

Both the words and music for "The Stars and Stripes Forever" were the product of John Philip Sousa (1854–1932). Sousa was born in Washington, D.C., of a Portuguese father and a Bavarian mother. The first ten years of his career were spent as a violinist in a theater orchestra, but in 1880 he became leader of the U.S. Marine Corps Band. After twelve years he left that position to form his own band, which was enormously popular. He is said to have gotten the idea for the march "The Stars and Stripes Forever" while returning from a European tour. It was so well thought out in his mind that upon arriving home he wrote it down without changing a note.

Another march also became an American patriotic song. Feeling the need for a song to help unify the young country, in 1798 Joseph Hopkinson wrote the words "Hail Columbia!" and set them to a melody that had been written as an inaugural march for George Washington nine years earlier. The composer of that march is generally believed to be Philip Phile. In those days America was often referred to as "Columbia" (the feminine form of Columbus), as can be seen in the designation "District of Columbia" for the national capital area.

Cover of Sousa's Stars and Stripes Forever! *Notice the instruments for which it was available and the low prices.*

Not only did America import much of its music; it imported musicians as well. Many European virtuosos found it profitable to tour the United States. The most sensational of these was the singer Jenny Lind, who was advertised by her brilliant promoter, P. T. Barnum, as "the Swedish Nightingale."

An American piano virtuoso was Louis Moreau Gottschalk (1829–1869). He was a handsome man who cultivated some of the mannerisms of Liszt. He often left his white gloves on the piano for his female admirers to fight over. He wrote sentimental pieces with such tear-jerking titles as *The Last Hope* and *The Dying Poet.* Actually, his music is much better than its titles suggest.

Louis A. Jullien (1812–1860) chose a different approach. He kept his white gloves on as he conducted with his jewelled baton. He played some good music, including works by American composers. But his biggest success was a number entitled *Firemen's Quadrille,* during which, as flames burst from the ceiling, he brought the local fire department into the hall to dramatically quench the blaze.

For sheer spectacle he was matched only by Patrick Gilmore (1829–1892), a bandmaster who organized supercolossal extravaganzas. One was the Great National Peace Jubilee in Boston in 1869. The performers included a chorus of 10,000 and an orchestra of 1,000, with cannons and 100 firemen pounding anvils in the "Anvil Chorus" from Verdi's *Il Trovatore.* The only way for Gilmore to top that was to organize a World Peace Jubilee. For this he brought Johann Strauss from Europe to lead his *Blue Danube Waltz.* Although the orchestra was held down to 1,000 players, the chorus was increased to 20,000 singers. Strauss later described, in a letter home, his feelings of terror as he stepped before the huge aggregation.

From Jullien's orchestra emerged a young German violinist named Theodore Thomas (1835–1905). In 1862, he organized his own orchestra. He maintained high standards of performance and sought to educate the audience, and in so doing he laid the foundation for the symphony orchestras of today. He traveled widely throughout the United States and was for a while the conductor of the New York Philharmonic. Later he organized the Chicago Symphony and was its conductor for many years.

The revolutions in Europe, and especially in Germany, in the mid-1800s brought thousands of immigrants to America. Some were musicians who soon became affiliated with orchestras and opera companies throughout the country. The European immigrants constituted an interested audience for the German symphonic music that Thomas performed for them.

Stephen Collins Foster holds a special place in American music, as can be seen on page 455.

Late in the nineteenth century a few capable American composers began to write longer and more sophisticated works. Most of these composers lived around Boston, and almost all of them had studied in Germany at one time

STEPHEN FOSTER—AMERICA'S BARD

Stephen Collins Foster (1826–1864) lived for only thirty-eight years. Many of those years were not happy or easy ones for him. His family did not want him to pursue a career in music, he made little money despite the great success of his music, and finally his creative abilities seemed to leave him. However, he must have had some moments of genuine satisfaction when he thought about the lasting pleasure many of his songs brought millions of people.

Stephen Foster.

Foster was born in Lawrenceville, Pennsylvania. His grandfather had fought in the Revolutionary War and his father in the War of 1812. He received little musical training, and his family could not understand his interest in music and wished it would go away. In 1846 he went to Cincinnati to work as a bookkeeper for his brother. In his spare time he wrote songs. In 1848 he sold "Oh! Susanna" for $100. It soon became a hit with the Forty-niners on their way to the goldfields of California. In fact, it was so popular that soon twenty editions of it appeared, nineteen of them pirated.

In 1850 Foster married Jane Denny McDowell, who inspired his song "Jeanie with the Light Brown Hair." That year he moved back to Pittsburgh. The other timeless Foster songs include "Old Folks at Home," "Camptown Races," "Old Black Joe," "My Old Kentucky Home," and "Beautiful Dreamer" (published after his death).

Although his music is often associated with the South, he never lived further south than Bardstown, Kentucky, forty miles south of Louisville, and then for only short periods of time. Something about the Negro songs he heard along the Ohio River while living in Cincinnati and his stays in Kentucky must have made a great impression on him, because his music has much of the melancholy beauty of the black songs of his day. His songs idealized life in the South, especially that of the blacks. Although they detract from the songs, the idealization and attempts at black dialect cannot obscure the melodic charm of the music.

By 1860 Foster seemed to have spent his creative imagination. He tried to improve his income and career by moving to New York. The move turned out to be a bad one. He began drinking heavily and his wife left him. Although he wrote many more songs, they were uninspired imitations of his earlier successes. Almost penniless, in 1864 he died in Bellevue Hospital after an accident in a Bowery flophouse. In his pocket was a crumbled piece of paper containing the words, "Dear friends and gentle hearts." It may have been a verse for a new song; no one will ever know. We do know that it was the final written thought of the composer of some of America's favorite music.

Thomas Eakins's Home Ranch.

or another. Consequently, much of their music sounded like works of the European masters with whom they had studied. The "Boston" or "New England" group included George W. Chadwick (1854–1931), Horatio Parker (1863–1919), Arthur Foote (1853–1937), and John Knowles Paine (1839–1906), who taught Foote. Little of their music is heard today.

Edward MacDowell (1861–1908) had excellent musical training. He studied at the Paris Conservatory when he was eleven years old and was a classmate of Debussy. He also played for Liszt at Weimar in 1882. After his return to America, he was a professor of music at Columbia University for eight years. Most of his works are for piano, with *Woodland Sketches* and the ever-popular "To a Wild Rose" being representative of his style. He also wrote four piano sonatas and two piano concertos. His Suite No. 2 *(Indian Suite)* was a landmark because it was one of the first American works to use music from native sources.

THE EARLY TWENTIETH CENTURY

Soon after the turn of the century the popularity of German romanticism began to wane in America, only to be replaced by attempts to imitate impressionism. The best-known "American impressionist" was Charles Tomlinson Griffes (1884–1920). At first he wrote in the German tradition, but he later switched to the Debussy-Ravel style. "The White Peacock" from *Roman Sketches* is still a frequently performed number of his. Charles Martin Loeffler (1861–1935), who immigrated to America from Alsace at the age of twenty, also wrote music of an impressionistic nature.

As the twentieth century began, American music was in a dormant state. All around was a rich heritage of folk music in the songs of the blacks, the lumberjack, the sailor, the cowboy, the Indian, and the mountaineer, as well as the ballads and folklore brought to America by its myriad peoples. Only the American MacDowell and the Bohemian Dvořák had chosen to draw on musical resources of this country. American composers apparently had feelings of inferiority about the quality of their own culture. Not only did it seem necessary for all serious musicians to study in Europe; it was considered advisable to pattern compositions on European models.

However, one composer in America was writing modern, innovative American music prior to World War I. At the time, virtually no one had heard of him. The name Charles Ives meant nothing.

CHARLES IVES

Ives (1874–1954) was born in Danbury, Connecticut, the son of a bandmaster. His father was no ordinary town band leader. He encouraged his son to listen carefully and to write different tonal effects. "Stretch your ears," was his advice. So young Ives experimented with various acoustical effects, such as new tunings for the piano, or two bands playing different music while marching toward

Charles Ives.

and away from each other. He attended Yale as a music student and after graduation went to New York, where he literally made a fortune in the insurance business. He had a country home in Connecticut. In the evenings he would sit at his desk and compose for relaxation. As he finished a page of music he would stack it on the floor near him. When the stacks became too high, he would carry them out to the barn for storage. Because he had no need for money, he did not try to have his works published and sold. In fact, for a long time no one knew about them; they just sat there in the barn.

Shortly after the turn of the century, Ives was writing novel harmonies and rhythms that did not appear in Europe until a decade or more later. He was experimenting with such ideas as polytonality, dissonant counterpoint, atonality, polyrhythm, chords with added tones, unusual melodic intervals, and *sprechstimme,* a kind of singsong speech that Schoenberg used in *Pierrot Lunaire.*

Ives's Symphony No. 3, written between 1901 and 1904, won him the Pulitzer Prize in 1947. Another work that is often played is the Piano Sonata No. 2 *(Concord),* which contains fragments of several well-known tunes heard in Concord, Massachusetts between 1840 and 1860. The fragments Ives selected, the manner in which he employed devices such as polytonality, the character of his melodies, and his use of instruments produced music that was in no sense a copy of Stravinsky or Milhaud. It was American music. At long last, the seed planted by Billings, the tanner, was flourishing in Ives, the insurance man. But until the 1930s, no one knew it.

On July 4, 1891, at the age of sixteen, Ives improvised on the song "America" ("My Country 'Tis of Thee") in an organ recital. Later he wrote out a version of what he played. Here and there on the manuscript, the handwriting of his music teacher appears—usually remarks disapproving of some of Ives's unconventional writing. Later, Ives recalled that playing the pedals on the last variation gave him "almost as much fun as playing baseball." He also remembered being scolded for his unusual harmonies in the interludes. Some friends advised him to play them "only if all the Music Committee were asleep." In any case, his composition is a fascinating and "fun" set of variations on a familiar melody.

The work opens (Record 6, Side 2) with an introduction containing fragments of the "America" theme. Then the theme is presented in a straightforward manner, just about as one finds it in a song book. The first variation contains a contrapuntal line of continuously moving sixteenth notes. The second variation presents a new harmonization of the theme, some of which suggests barbershop quartet style with its descending chromatic phrases. They are especially noticeable in measures 4 and 5.

Next is an interlude, also based on the theme. The music is bitonal with the higher-pitched chords in F major and the lower-pitched chords in D-flat major. As if bitonality were not enough, Ives treats the melodic lines in imitation, with the lower line following one measure later.

The third variation presents a change of rhythm. This change gives the music a lilting quality, which when combined with the pedal part produces an effect something like a calliope.

Ives's sense of humor shows in the musical incongruities of the fourth variation. The usually solemn pipe organ plays the theme in the style of a polonaise, a dance popularized by Chopin. A further incongruity results from the merry character of the music in a minor key. Often the minor mode is treated somberly. Before the variation is finished Ives even adds some little chirping figures.

Another short bitonal interlude follows. The fifth variation features a contrasting line in the pedal part, one marked to be played "as fast as the pedals go."

*Notation found on an old manuscript: *"This passage was often played by the pedals while the left hand hung on to the bench."* It may, however, be played by the left hand.

The theme extends into a coda, which Ives once told someone "is in a way a kind of take-off on the Bunker Hill fight." And the music does alternate in a contesting fashion between the keyboards of the organ, sometimes sounding as though it is growling.

This very early work is typical of Ives's music in several respects. It treats a recognized American melody in a highly imaginative way.

World War I was to leave the United States a world power, if for no other reason than its size and economic wealth. Gradually, falteringly, and sometimes unwillingly America would become more world conscious and assume a greater leadership, including in the area of music. It had been a long journey from Hopkinson and Billings to Ives. However, even greater musical accomplishments lay in the future, and it is to this American music that the next chapter is devoted.

33

AMERICAN MUSIC IN THE TWENTIETH CENTURY

Charles Ives worked largely in isolation from the mainstream of American musical life. He did not know many other composers nor did he teach composition in a college. Even his influence on American music was slight until well into the 1930s. However, something about the spirit of the times must have affected not only Ives, but a number of other composers a generation younger than him. American music soon flourished, as did art. Grant Wood's *American Gothic* (plate 15) pays tribute to an aspect of the American character.

Three composers and their works have been selected to serve as examples of mainstream American music: Aaron Copland, George Gershwin, and Alan Hovhaness.

Copland's Appalachian Spring

As the biographical information on page 466 indicates, Copland composed three successful ballets. *Appalachian Spring* concerns the courtship and wedding of a couple in rural Pennsylvania in the early nineteenth century. It was written for the outstanding choreographer and teacher Martha Graham. Copland draws on several Shaker melodies to serve as themes. The overall spirit of the ballet is calm and hymnlike, as befits the character of the people being portrayed. The music is usually heard as a concert suite arranged by the composer.

Copland provides a synopsis of the score. The opening section (1.) is marked *Very Slowly.* His words continue, "Introduction of the characters, one by one, in a suffused light."* The bride enters, then the groom, a neighbor, and a revivalist and his flock. The music is built around a motive derived from the major chord. Soon a hymnlike melody emerges:

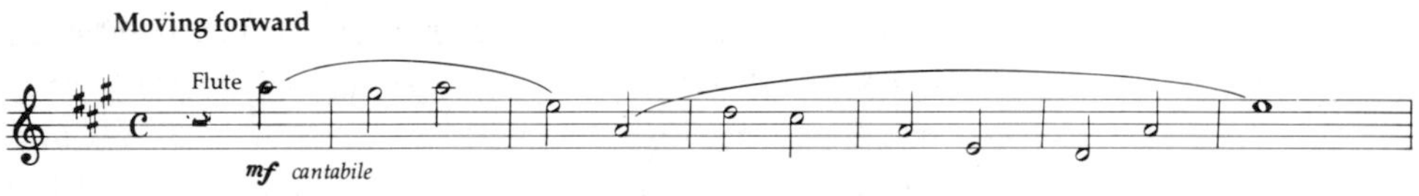

Notice that the distance between many of its tones is four or five steps. These intervals add to the open, sturdy sound of the line. Notice also that Copland writes the tempo directions in English.

"2. *Fast.* A sudden burst of unison strings in A major arpeggios starts the action. A sentiment both elated and religious gives the keynote to this scene." The theme is a lively one that could come from no other country than America:

Copland soon combines the high, rapidly moving part with the long notes in the trombones and basses. The flute plays a lovely obbligato part.

"3. Duo for bride and her intended—scene of tenderness and passion." Here Copland depicts with taste and skill the sensitivity and sincerity of feeling that pervades the scene.

"4. *Quite fast.* The Revivalist and his flock. Folksy feeling—suggestions of square dances and country fiddlers." The music here is as American as baseball and the Liberty Bell.

**Appalachian Spring,* copyright 1945 by Boosey and Hawkes, Inc. Used by permission.

"5. *Still faster.* Solo dance of the bride—presentiment of motherhood. Extremes of joy and fear and wonder." Again the music is beautifully sensitive and expressive.

"6. *Very slowly* (as at first). Transition scene to music reminiscent of the introduction." Some of the music heard in this section is derived from Section 2.

"7. *Calm and flowing.* Scenes of daily activity for the bride and her farmer husband. There are variations on a Shaker theme" (Record 6, Side 2). The Shaker song Copland has chosen is "Simple Gifts," the same song discussed in Chapter 8. It appears first in the clarinet:

Copland treats the theme to old-fashioned contrapuntal devices such as augmentation, canon, and new lines of counterpoint. The theme ends in a mighty hymn.

"8. The bride takes her place among her neighbors." The section is a quiet coda that balances the Introduction. The neighbors depart, and the newlyweds remain "quiet and strong in their new house." The music closes with a serene passage for strings, which sounds "like a prayer."

The story for the ballet *Appalachian Spring* and its music are definitely American. There is something about the way the sounds are organized that can never be confused with Russian, Spanish, or German music.

Appalachian Spring sounds simple and uncomplicated compared to Schoenberg's Variations for Orchestra or Stravinsky's *The Rite of Spring.* There is more technical sophistication in Copland's music than appears, but it does sound less complex than its European contemporaries. This is not entirely due to the demands for simplicity in the story. Most of Copland's works have this quality, and it can be observed in the music of other American composers. The lines are bolder and more clear-cut, imparting a straightforward quality to the music.

Scene from Appalachian Spring.

GEORGE GERSHWIN

Like Copland, George Gershwin (1898–1937) was born and raised in New York in less than affluent circumstances. He had little musical training but much talent, especially on piano. His early composing efforts were confined to popular songs and musical comedies. In 1924, when he wrote *Rhapsody in Blue,* he did not feel competent to write for instruments other than piano, so he asked Ferde Grofé to do the orchestration. Gershwin's writing style matured rapidly, only to be cut short by death from a brain tumor. His other well-known works, all of which show the influence of jazz and popular music, include *An*

George Gershwin.

American in Paris for orchestra, Concerto in F for Piano and Orchestra, and a folk opera *Porgy and Bess.*

Gershwin's Porgy and Bess

Gershwin was impressed by DuBose Heyward's novel *Porgy.* The story deals with the poor blacks living on Catfish Row in Charleston, South Carolina. Gershwin could see the dramatic possibilities in the story, and he decided to write an opera based on it. To make his opera more authentic, he spent the summer of 1934 in Charleston observing the ways of the people. He heard the street cries of the vendors and listened to the songs the children sang as they played. Then he returned to New York and spent another nine months writing *Porgy and Bess.*

Porgy and Bess concerns itself with the common people. To make the story as real as possible, Gershwin has the characters speak most of their lines, instead of singing in recitative style. He also incorporates the music of these people—the blues and other features of jazz—into the opera. Although he does not include actual folk songs, he does maintain a folklike quality in the music. The jazz elements are written down rather than improvised.

The story of *Porgy and Bess* is filled with tragedy. Porgy is a crippled beggar who leads a lonely life. Bess, a loose-living woman, comes to town with her lover, Crown. Neither Bess nor Crown is accepted by the people of Catfish Row. Crown kills one of the local men in a fight, and Bess takes refuge from the police in Porgy's shanty. Their relationship grows to one of genuine love.

One day a big picnic is held on a nearby island. Because he is crippled, Porgy can't attend, but he encourages Bess to go. As she is about to catch the

---

1900—A VERY GOOD YEAR

In most ways the year 1900 was like many others. Great musicians were born, others died, and music was created and performed. But 1900 was the first year of a new century, and it was also the year in which a group of musicians were born who represent the many and varied musical paths found in the twentieth century.

Louis Armstrong was born in 1900 (d. 1971). His life changed much when he was sent to a reform school for shooting off a blank pistol in Storyville, the red-light area of New Orleans where he had lived all his life to that point. At the age of thirteen he was placed in the Colored Waifs' Home, and it was there that he had the opportunity to learn how to play the cornet. His first professional playing was on Mississippi riverboats. By 1925 he had worked his way to Chicago, where he played with the band of King Oliver and made his first recordings for Columbia Records. Later he formed his own band called the "Hot Five" (later the "Hot Seven"). He influenced the style of other jazz musicians very much and was a consummate showman, who later sang as much as he played his horn.

In many ways George Antheil (d. 1959) was the opposite of Armstrong. Born the same year as Armstrong in Trenton, New Jersey, he became one of the pioneers in breaking away from conventional music and advocating "an anti-expressive, anti-romantic, coldly mechanistic aesthetic." This belief led him to create his famous (or infamous) *Ballet méchanique* in 1924. The original score specified eight pianos, a player piano, and an airplane propeller, but he later revised this score to include more pianos as well as anvils, bells, automobile horns, and buzz saws. Such compositions earned him the reputation as "the bad boy of music." He had a variety of interests outside of music, including criminology and inventions like a radio torpedo.

Aaron Copland was born in Brooklyn, the son of Russian-Jewish immigrant parents. He attended the New York City public schools, helped in his father's store, took his first piano lessons from his older sister, and often studied scores in the public library. He was the first American to travel to France to study composition with a remarkable woman named Nadia Boulanger (*Boo*-lahn-zhay). In the 1920s Copland's music showed the influence of jazz, but by 1930 his works became more abstract. The music he is best known for is nationalistic in character: *A Lincoln Portrait* (which includes a narrator reciting some of Lincoln's words) and three ballets—*Billy the Kid, Rodeo,* and *Appalachian Spring.* In these works he often cites American folk songs and the music has a distinctly American flavor. Since 1950 his music has become somewhat more intel-

---

boat back to Catfish Row, she is abducted by Crown, who has escaped from jail and is hiding on the island. When Crown learns of Bess's love for Porgy, he sets out to kill his rival. In the fight between the two men Crown is stabbed and dies. Porgy is taken off to jail on suspicion of murder.

Now is the moment Sporting Life has been waiting for. He represents the easy, evil life that Bess left behind when she moved in with Porgy. Because it is doubtful that Porgy will ever be freed from jail, Sporting Life is able to

---

Aaron Copland.

lectual, and he has even experimented with tone-row principles. In much of his music he manages to retain the interest and respect of trained musicians while at the same time pleasing the public. Not many twentieth-century composers have been able to accomplish this!

Ernst Krenek is an Austrian tone-row composer who has not found much favor with the public. After beginning with harsh atonal works, he mellowed as he adopted some jazz idioms. His *Jonny spielt auf* is a story about a black jazz violinist and is by far his most successful work. His music was not liked by Adolph Hitler and so Krenek settled in America in 1937, where he continued to compose and teach.

The Philadelphia Orchestra, one of America's greatest symphony orchestras, was founded in 1900. The first conductor was Fritz Scheel, who remained for seven years. The success of the group, however, is largely the result of two conductors, Leopold Stokowski, who led it for nearly thirty years, and Eugene Ormandy, who followed Stokowski and remained for forty years. Over the years these two men brought the Philadelphia Orchestra to heights of orchestral virtuosity.

Kurt Weill (d. 1950) was born and lived the first thirty-five years of his life in Berlin. He was motivated to write music for the theater. While in Berlin he composed such works as *The Rise and Fall of the City Mahagonny* and *Der Dreigroschenoper* ("The Three-Penny Opera"), a revival of John Gay's *The Beggar's Opera,* which was originally a successful competitor to George Handel's operas in London in the 1720s. Weill was Jewish and Hitler was in power, so in 1935 he came to the United States. He wrote a couple of Broadway musicals and a folk opera *Down in the Valley.* "September Song" and "Mack the Knife" are two of his songs.

A great jazz performer, an experimental, iconoclastic composer, a distinguished composer of American music, an Austrian composer of tone-row music, a great orchestra, and a composer of theater music—all are products of the year 1900. It was a very good year.

Porgy and Bess realize their love for each other.

persuade Bess to go back to New York with him. But Porgy is released, and when he returns home he finds Bess gone. "Where is she?" he asks. "New York," answer his neighbors. The opera closes with the pathetic scene of Porgy climbing into his goat cart to go after Bess.

Porgy and Bess opens with the lullaby "Summertime." The mood is lazy and relaxed, and the accompaniment suggests a gentle rocking motion. Short notes introduce each new idea, and the last syllable of each phrase is sustained. The effect suggests snatches of thought spoken at random. Later in the song Gershwin adds some vocal devices he heard that summer in Charleston, such as a "slide" or glissando, and a little catch on the word "cry." The rhythm on the word "jumpin'" increases the feeling of bounciness. The word "hush" is given a place of prominence so that the "sh" sound can be easily heard. Jazz harmonies are evident.

In "I've Got Plenty of Nothin'" Porgy displays a carefree spirit, telling everyone that he has everything he wants, so he doesn't have to worry about material goods.

"Bess, You Is My Woman Now" is a glorious duet between Porgy and Bess (Record 6, Side 2). It sounds more like opera than like folk music. As is typical in such duets, the man sings first to initiate the exchange of feelings, the woman answers, and then they sing together. The two lines are quite different. Porgy's part is a countermelody to what Bess is singing. This duet also contains jazz elements.

In "It Ain't Necessarily So" Sporting Life tries to con the people over to his way of life. His words are not those of an honest skeptic, but a sly salesman. The pitches of the melody seem to slink about in a manner that is just right for Sporting Life's personality. The song is in an *A B A* form. The main portion is heard twice, then there is a contrasting section, which is followed by the return of the main portion. The contrasting section features nonsense syllables rather than regular words.

Throughout *Porgy and Bess,* there is an attempt to duplicate black dialect by making some changes in grammar and pronunciation. The linguistic result is seldom accurate or realistic. But the content of the opera—its music, story line, and characterizations—is more than strong enough to make it an artistic success. It is a favorite of audiences around the world.

ALAN HOVHANESS

Alan Hovhaness Chakmakjian was born on March 8, 1911 in Somerville, Massachusetts, of Armenian-Scottish parents. From the beginning he seemed des-

Alan Hovhaness.

tined to bring together the best of two worlds, the old and the new, the Occident and the Orient. His musical training in his younger years was largely confined to Boston and the New England Conservatory of Music. He did, however, study astronomy and Far Eastern music and religions. For a while he taught theory and composition in Boston and was church organist at an Armenian church in Watertown, Massachusetts. Early in his career he dropped his long and complicated last name.

Hovhaness began receiving public attention in the late 1940s. He has received several awards and grants to study music and compose. These grants have taken him to India, Japan, and Korea. His creative work seems to have increased with these journeys. His opus numbers are well past 200.

Unlike Copland and Gershwin, Hovhaness is not interested in creating American music. He typifies the change of many American composers into more cosmopolitan or international styles. In writing about the Symphony No. 4, which he composed in 1958, he says, "I admire the giant melody of the Himalayan Mountains, seventh-century Armenian religious music, classical music of South India, orchestra music of Tang Dynasty China about 700 A.D., opera-oratorios of Handel." His Symphony No. 4 represents a synthesis of these diverse musical styles.

Hovhaness's Symphony No. 4

Symphony No. 4 is one of several works by recognized twentieth-century composers for wind ensemble/band. The presence of many fine wind groups in universities and high schools has encouraged the writing of such music.

This symphony is unusual in that it is written for what Hovhaness calls a "wind orchestra." No strings are involved, except harp. The word "band" was avoided because the instrumentation is more limited than most band music. This particular score calls for flutes, oboes, English horn, clarinets, bass clarinet, bassoon, contrabassoon, horns, trumpets, trombones, tuba, and harp, plus four percussion parts. Hovhaness specifies that no more than six instruments of any single type are to play.

Hovhaness does achieve something different from the traditional band sound. The music is filled with what he calls "points of sound"—coloristic tonal effects, mainly from the percussion section. To add even more color to the music, groups of instruments are sounded in contrast to one another in concerto grosso style. The bass clarinet, contrabassoon, marimba, and xylophone—instruments seldom heard alone—are given lengthy solos.

The first movement consists of five sections, with the first and third, and the second and fourth having a similar character. Sections one and three are hymnlike and are written for brasses. Sections two and four have an Oriental quality and feature solo bass clarinet and contrabassoon. The fifth section is like a fugue and develops contrapuntally.

The second movement opens with a marimba solo in an irregular rhythmic pattern. The middle section consists of two slow dance melodies. The first one is played by the woodwinds and the harp; the second by the vibraphone and woodwinds.

The third movement, which is presented in the Listening Guide on pages 472–73, continues the admixture of cultural influences that Hovhaness described. A chantlike theme in 7/4 meter alternates with Oriental-sounding phrases played by the English horn and oboe. Later, distinctly Baroque imitation is heard. At one place there are bells ringing freely, something that Mussorgsky had done in *Boris Godunov.* Yes, it is an American piece of music—in a sense.

LISTENING GUIDE

HOVHANESS: SYMPHONY NO. 4

Third Movement (Record 6, Side 2)

A *Section*

0:00 French horns open with *A* theme, which is somewhat like a chant.

0:26 Harp chord followed by free-sounding English horn solo; music has Oriental quality.

0:52 Horns take up *A* theme, with trumpets soon joining in.

1:20 Harp chord followed by another free-sounding solo for English horn.

1:49 Trombones continue with contrasting portion of *A* theme; some dissonant harmonies.

2:24 Oboe has free-sounding solo.

2:41 Brasses enter and soon take up portions of *A* theme.

3:11 Harp chord followed by a second oboe solo.

3:30 French horns play *A* theme as at opening of movement.

B *Section*

4:02 Two trombone parts begin accompanying *glissando* sliding figures; other trombones take up forceful *B* theme.

4:57 Very low, loud growling note played, followed by free cadenza-like passage for chimes, glockenspiel, and cymbals.

A′ *Section*

5:26 Trumpets and trombones begin and are answered by French horns on *A* theme; trombones have a contrapuntal line of eighth notes; "color" sounds are heard until end of movement from percussion instruments.

6:05	*A* theme heard in imitation, first in first trumpets, then second trumpets, then French horns, and then trombones; music is contrapuntal.
6:33	Woodwinds take up *A* theme.
6:53	French horns and then trumpets take up *A* theme.
7:11	*A* theme appears in imitation again, first in trombones, then French horns, then second trumpets, and then first trumpets; counterpoint continues, leading to full-sounding ending.
7:41	Close of movement with highly colorful final chord.

OTHER MAINSTREAM AMERICAN COMPOSERS

Walter Piston (1894–1976)	Somewhat Classical in style; writer on music theory; suite from ballet *The Incredible Flutist.*
William Grant Still (1895–1978)	First recognized black composer; various compositions including *Afro-American Symphony.*
Howard Hanson (b. 1896)	Neoromantic in style; outstanding educator and leader in American music; opera *Merry Mount* and Symphony No. 2 ("Romantic").
Virgil Thomson (b. 1896)	Music critic; operas on text of Gertrude Stein—*Four Saints in Three Acts* and *The Mother of Us All*—and two film scores.
Roger Sessions (b. 1896)	Complex abstract works that he believes express nonverbal thoughts; instrumental works.
Roy Harris (1898–1979)	Symphonies and chamber music; believed that music should be emotional but not romantic; influential teacher.
Samuel Barber (b. 1910)	Works show evidence of romanticism; vocal works and opera *Vanessa.*
Elliott Carter (b. 1908)	Complex instrumental works; shows influence of Stravinsky and Schoenberg.
William Schuman (b. 1910)	Equally successful in writing for vocal and instrumental groups; some nationalistic music including *New England Triptych* on themes by William Billings.

Norman Dello Joio (b. 1913)	Old and new elements combined in his music.
Vincent Persichetti (b. 1915)	Eclectic in his sources and techniques; piano music and seven symphonies.
Ulysses Kay (b. 1917)	Instrumental and choral music; eclectic style.
Ned Rorem (b. 1923)	Chiefly known for his songs, although has composed some instrumental music.
Gunther Schuller (b. 1925)	Leading advocate of "third stream" music in which art music and jazz are combined; also composed other abstract instrumental music.
Lukas Foss (b. 1922)	Born in Berlin but came to America at age fifteen; influenced by Hindemith, but later included improvisation in some works.

INTELLECTUALISM IN AMERICAN MUSIC

Not many American composers have been attracted to the tone-row techniques of Schoenberg as their dominant type of composition. Many of them have experimented with the idea, and some have chosen the principles of tone-row composition for a few works. Only two names are generally associated with such writing:

Wallingford Riegger (1885–1961)	Followed close upon Schoenberg's development of the tone-row idiom; more conservative than Schoenberg; several works for ballet.
Ernst Krenek (b. 1900)	See page 467.

EXPERIMENTAL AMERICAN MUSIC

Since World War II, American composers have turned more to experimental and electronic music. The nationalism evident in American music in the 1920s, 1930s, and early 1940s has given way to more international and experimental styles.

George Antheil (1900–1959)	America's earliest experimental composer. See page 466.
Edgard Varèse (1883–1965)	Born and trained in Europe, but lived in the U.S. much of his creative life. Inter-

	ested in tone colors and unusual rhythms; *Poème électronique*—composed for Brussels World Fair—is eight hours long and for 425 loudspeakers.
Henry Cowell (1897–1965)	Innovative practices for pianist, including strumming the strings and playing chords with forearm.
Otto Luening (b. 1900)	Pioneer composer of tape music; co-founder of Electronic Music Center at Columbia University.
Vladimir Ussachevsky (b. 1911)	Also pioneer composer of tape and electronic music.
Milton Babbitt (b. 1916)	Started out as tone-row composer but changed to electronic music and became director of Electronic Music Center.
Charles Wuorinen (b. 1938)	Frequent winner of composition awards; some serial works, but most works are electronic music; synthesizer with conventional instruments.
John Cage (b. 1912)	Most controversial and experimental American composer; first wrote for "prepared" piano and then turned to chance or aleatory works, including *4′33″*, in which not a single sound is made; more recently composing with computer.
George Crumb (b. 1929)	Imaginative and delicate use of tonal colors; intellectual approach to music; professor at University of Pennsylvania.
Morton Subotnik (b. 1933)	Imaginative electronic composer; teaches at California Institute of the Arts at Valencia, established by Walt Disney estate.

American music has had a rags-to-riches history. From weak imitations of European styles, American music has progressed to a place of prominence in the world. America has developed a body of music uniquely its own. With the tremendous vitality of its cultural life and the increasing attention being paid the arts, music in America should continue to change and expand.

34
JAZZ

The various types of popular music, especially jazz and rock, are among America's most recognized contributions to the world of music. Travelers to other countries—Japan, Thailand, France, Greece, and so on—hear American popular music (sometimes with the lyrics still in English). The various types of popular music have their promoters and detractors, and most of the styles have developed under a cloud of doubt about their musical quality. Regardless of their artistic merits, or lack of them, no presentation of American music can be complete without some discussion of jazz and other types of popular music.

TRADITIONAL JAZZ

The roots of jazz reach back to black Americans' African heritage. But other elements have also influenced jazz: minstrel show music, work songs, field hollers, funeral marching bands, blues, French-Creole and Spanish-American music, and more recently, West Indian music. Jazz did not develop as a type of music until about the beginning of the twentieth century. Basin Street in New Orleans is traditionally considered its birthplace, although clearly jazz did not just pop into being in one spot and at a fixed historical moment. It was brought to public attention by the funeral procession. On the way back from the cemetery the band played its tunes in a way quite different from the somber sounds that accompanied the march to the gravesite. The players shifted the emphasis from the strong to the weak beat and launched into a decorated version of the melody. When Storyville, New Orleans' red-light district, was closed down in 1917, many jazz musicians lost their jobs and sought work in other cities. Jazz moved up the Mississippi River through Memphis and St. Louis to Chicago and the rest of the United States.

Two types of Afro-American folk music existed before and with early jazz and later merged with it. One of these was *ragtime.* It featured the piano, occasionally in combination with other instruments. The music sounds like a polished, syncopated march with a decorated right-hand part. Early musicians associated with ragtime are Scott Joplin in Sedalia, Missouri, and Ben Harvey, who published his *Ragtime Instructor* in 1897. In 1974 the film *The Sting* caused a renewed interest in Joplin's rags.

The other type of music involved with early jazz was the folk *blues.* Its musical characteristics will be discussed shortly. Some of the most famous names associated with blues are Leadbelly, whose real name was Huddie Ledbetter; W. C. Handy, who was known for his "Memphis Blues" and "St. Louis Blues"; and Ferdinand "Jelly Roll" Morton, whose first published blues appeared in 1905—the "Jelly Roll Blues."

Like folk music, jazz was created by generally untutored musicians who could not have written down what they played or sang, even if they had wanted to. Jazz is different from most folk music in two respects. It has sprung from the cities rather than the fields and forests; it is an urban form of music. And for most people, it is a spectator experience. Usually only a few people perform, although listeners may contribute a little hand clapping and foot stomping.

But what is traditional jazz? It has several elements.

Melody. The most significant feature of jazz melodies is the *blue note.* These notes are derived from an altered version of the major scale. The blues scale merely lowers the third, fifth, and/or seventh steps. Many times the performer shifts between the regular note and its lower alternative as if searching for a sound, which in a sense is what is happening. The blue-note interval is an approximation of a microtone, roughly half of a half step in this case. African music is the influence behind its use in jazz. Blue notes are a source of subtle color. Their effect in jazz is further enhanced by the fact that the chord in the harmony usually contains the particular note at its expected pitch while the lowered blue note is sounded in the melody. This combination creates an interesting and characteristic dissonance.

Harmony. Traditional jazz harmony is as conservative as any church hymn. The typical chords are the same three that form the backbone of traditional tonal harmony: tonic (I), dominant (V), and subdominant (IV). More recently, sophisticated types of jazz have employed the advanced harmonic idioms of Debussy, Bartók, and Stravinsky. The appeal of jazz, however, does not lie in its harmony.

Rhythm. Here is one of the most important features of jazz. Although its meter is nearly always two beats per measure, with irregular meters occurring only rarely, the jazz musician employs an endless variety of syncopated patterns and rhythmic figures over this regular pulse. Syncopation—the redistribution of accents so that the rhythmic patterns do not occur as the listener expects—is the lifeblood of jazz.

Jazz rhythms do not fit well into the usual divisions of time into sixteenths, eighths, and quarters. Jazz musicians perform rhythm with small deviations of timing and accent that cannot be rendered in notation. Players even make slight alterations of the patterns of conventional notation when reading them. These deviations in rhythm are one reason why traditionally trained musicians often cannot achieve an authentic jazz sound.

Timbre. The basic timbre sought by jazz instrumentalists is perhaps an unconscious imitation of the black singing voice: a bit breathy with a little vibrato (rapid and slight variance of pitch on a single tone). Certain instruments, therefore, have become associated with this idiom. The saxophone was intended to be a concert instrument, but it was taken up by jazz musicians because it can produce the desired quality. Mutes—metal or fiber devices inserted in or over the bell to change the tone quality—are often used on brass instruments, and their names are as distinctive as the sounds they produce: "cup," "wah-wah," and "plunger," the latter of which is like the end of a rubber sink plunger. Many jazz trumpeters use a particular type of mouthpiece that helps them produce a more shrill sound and makes high notes easier to play. In jazz style the clarinet is played in a manner that produces a saxophonelike tone quality. The timbres of other instruments also vary according to whether they are playing orchestral music or jazz.

Some jazz timbres, like the bongo and conga drums and the Cuban cowbell, are from Afro-Cuban sources, while others, such as the Chinese woodblock, cymbals, and vibraphone, have an Oriental flavor.

Repetition of Material. Jazz has no form that is applicable to all its styles. Generally it is a series of stanzas based on the chords to a popular tune. The form of the blues is more definite. A line is sung and immediately repeated, and then a third line concludes the stanza. Sometimes the singer does not sing all the way through a section, and an instrumentalist fills in with a short solo called a *break.*

Text. The metrical scheme of the text is often one of the standard poetic meters. It is not uncommon to find iambic pentameter in verses of the blues. The texts seldom have literary significance, but some are quite moving.

Improvisation. Improvisation is a fundamental component of jazz. Traditionally jazz is not written down because it is made up on the spot. This extemporaneous creativity is what gives jazz its ever-fresh quality. Sometimes people confuse a sexy or "hot" popular song with jazz. Jazz does not exist unless someone improvises on a tune.

What happens is this: The musicians agree that they will play a certain song in a certain key. They also agree generally on the order of each player's featured section. Then the first player, while keeping in mind the harmonies and melody of the song, improvises a part that reflects the rhythmic and melodic characteristics of jazz. This procedure is followed as each player takes a turn. On the final chorus, all play together in simultaneous, semi-accidental counterpoint. It is like an improvised musical conversation. Throughout the number, no player knows exactly what the others will do, but each plays according to musical instinct so that every part fits in with the others. Nor are the individual players entirely certain what they themselves will do, because a player taking a "ride" on a number plays it somewhat differently each time.

Sometimes there seems to be so much improvisation that the melody is no longer identifiable. Why does that happen? Because the player improvises on the basic harmony as well as the melody. For example, if the song starts on the tonic chord, as it often does, and if the piece is in the key of C, then the notes of the tonic chord are C E G. The improviser may play any or all of these three notes plus tones that are nonharmonic in relation to that chord. In other words, other pitches can be woven around the notes of the chord, which may rather obscure the tune.

The particular song may get lost for another reason. Most popular songs have simple chord patterns and there is little difference between the chords of one popular song and another. When the melody is being improvised upon, the harmony is often not distinguishable from that of other songs. The rhapsodic nature of jazz improvisation also leads to a sameness of mood that makes it more difficult to distinguish the basic song.

Several jazz features are illustrated in the example that follows. It is a trumpet solo by Bubber Miley, recorded in 1927 while he was playing with Duke Ellington's band. In it can be seen blue notes (called minor third, flat fifth, and minor seventh on the coded chart), growls (indicated by the lines through the note stems), and slides (indicated by "gliss," or a wavy line). The underlying chords are identified in large letters above the melody. Syncopation occurs in measures 5, 7, 8, 10, 12, 13, 14, 15, 19, 20, 22, and 23.

BLACK AND TAN FANTASY

Gunther Schuller, *Early Jazz* (New York: Oxford University Press, 1968), p. 331. Used by permission of Belwin-Mills Music, Inc.

Blue Notes: a = minor third
b = flat fifth
c = minor seventh
d = minor ninth

e is a bent tone which goes from a flat octave through the minor seventh to the sixth degree, anticipating the return to B-flat.

TYPES OF JAZZ

The 1920s saw the real emergence of jazz, which was given impetus in 1918 by Joe "King" Oliver's famous Creole Jazz Band in Chicago. Other musicians soon became prominent: Paul Whiteman, whose band presented the first jazz concert in 1924, featuring the premiere of George Gershwin's *Rhapsody in Blue;* Bessie Smith, the famous blues singer; Fletcher Henderson and his band; Bix Beiderbecke, who started "white" jazz with his cornet and a band called the "Wolverines"; and the notable Louis Armstrong (see page 466). Through his trumpet playing and vocal renditions, Armstrong had much influence on the basic sound and style of jazz.

The prevailing style in the 1920s was *dixieland.* It is characterized by a strong upbeat, a meter of two beats to the measure, and certain tonal and stylistic qualities that are impossible to notate. It has a "busy" sound, since there is simultaneous improvisation by perhaps four to seven players. The result is a type of "accidental" counterpoint that is held together only by the song's basic harmony and the musical instincts of the players. The presence of simultaneous improvisation in both African music and jazz can hardly be a coincidence. Dixieland style is often described as "hot"; it is rather fast and usually loud.

During the depression of the 1930s the hiring of bands became prohibitively expensive. So pianists enjoyed increasing popularity, especially as they developed a jazz piano style called *boogie woogie.* It features a persistently repeated melodic figure—an ostinato—in the bass. Usually the boogie-woogie ostinato consists of eight notes per measure, which explains why this type of

King Oliver's Creole Jazz Band, 1923. Standing, left to right: Baby Dodds, Honoré Dutrey, Bill Johnson, Louis Armstrong, Johnny Dodds, Lil Hardin. Seated: Joe King Oliver. (The Record Changer)

Louis Armstrong in about 1940.

music is sometimes called "eight to the bar." Over the continuous bass the pianist plays trills, octave tremolos (the rapid alternation of pitches an octave apart), and other melodic figures.

The *swing era* in jazz lasted from 1935 to about 1950. It featured intricate arrangements and big bands of about seventeen players under the leadership of such musicians as Benny Goodman, Count Basie, and Duke Ellington. It was also the era of the featured soloist—Gene Krupa, Fats Waller, and Tommy Dorsey, to name a few. Other notable figures from the period include Artie Shaw, Harry James, Glenn Miller, Coleman Hawkins, and Fletcher Henderson. Musically, swing has four beats to the measure and rhythm with a "bounce." The swing era was one in which the audience danced. Its "concert halls" were such places as the Roseland Ballroom in New York and California's Hollywood Palladium.

There were many great bands and arrangers during the swing era. The most enduring, and the one probably still heard today more than the others, is Duke Ellington and His Orchestra. As the material on pages 483–84 points out, Ellington's group spanned nearly five decades and produced varied and interesting music. "Take the 'A' Train" (Record 4, Side 1) was not Ellington's greatest work, but it was one of his more popular ones, and it demonstrates well the style of the bands in the swing era. The melody is taken in four rather fast beats per measure. There is a contrasting phrase to the eight bars in the example. The remainder of the recorded version in the *Record Album* is the same sixteen measures repeated with new improvised solo material or played in a different key. The chord symbols in the example indicate the chords on which the soloists improvise.

Following World War II there emerged a style called *bebop,* or more commonly, *bop.* It was developed chiefly by Charlie "Bird" Parker and Dizzy Gillespie, who once defined the term by saying that in bop you go *Ba*-oo *Ba*-oo *Ba*-oo instead of *Oo*-ba *Oo*-ba *Oo*-ba. What he was describing was the nearly continuous syncopation that occurs in bop. It also features dissonant chords and freely developed melodies. Often the performers play in unison at the octave instead of presenting the traditional improvised counterpoint. In bop

TWO LONG-LIVED JAZZ GROUPS

For some reason, jazz performers have tended to change jobs a lot. A few successful bands experienced some personnel changes every few months; a performer who stayed with the same group for a couple of years was unusual. There were some exceptions to this situation, however, notably the Duke Ellington Orchestra and the Modern Jazz Quartet.

Edward Kennedy "Duke" Ellington (1899–1974) must have had an admirable way of working with his musicians, not only in achieving good human relations, but also in drawing from them their best creative and musical efforts. Although he was a successful song writer, his music seemed to lose something when played by any other group. In a sense, his music was the collective effort of the orchestra. Ellington or Billy Strayhorn, his alter ego and arranger, or one of the band members, might come up with an idea or theme. Ellington would play it on the piano. After a while the rhythm section would join in; then a saxophone or trumpet player would follow; another player like alto saxophonist Johnny Hodges or baritone saxophonist Harry Carney (with whom Ellington worked for forty-seven years!) might improvise on the musical idea; the brass section might try a suitable background. While this was going on, Ellington would sit at the piano and listen, sometimes adding chords. Suddenly he knew: That is how the piece should sound. At that point it would be put down on paper.

Ellington was born and raised in Washington, D.C., the son of a butler. At eighteen he wanted to become an artist, but finally opted for music. The notion of "musical painting" remained with him throughout his life, as many of his song titles reflect—"Mood Indigo," "Sepia Panorama," "Black and Tan Fantasy," "Diminuendo and Crescendo in Blue," and others.

Duke Ellington in 1943.

In 1923 he joined a five-piece combo called "The Washingtonians" and went to New York. They had little success. As Ellington later said, they sometimes had to split a hot dog five ways to keep from starving. Three years later Ellington tried again, and this time it worked. He soon was playing at Harlem's Cotton Club, the most expensive night spot in Harlem. At that time it catered to white audiences who wanted to listen to good jazz. The Cotton Club band stayed together well into the 1950s. Over the years it introduced many musical innovations, including echo chambers in recording to increase reverberation (now standard in popular music recordings), the flatted fifth that was to become so prominent in bop, the amplified bass, and music featuring the baritone saxophone.

By the mid-1950s Ellington's group seemed to have been declining, which might have been expected after twenty years. However, a stunning performance at the Newport Festival in 1956 seemed to revive it. Ellington overcame his grief over the death of Billy Strayhorn in 1967 and

(continued)

brought out some of his most highly regarded works, such as "Sacred Concert," "Second Sacred Concert," "Far Eastern Suite" (reflecting a State Department tour of Asia), and "New Orleans Suite" (which became the 1970 "Record of the Year"). Duke Ellington died of pneumonia in a New York hospital on May 25, 1975, just a couple of weeks before the *Down Beat* issue dedicated to him and his music was printed.

If Ellington represented the most lasting of the big-band groups, the Modern Jazz Quartet represented the most lasting of the jazz combos. The group consisted of John Lewis as leader and pianist, Percy Heath on bass, Kenny Clarke and later Connie Kay on drums, and Milt Jackson on vibraphone. It was founded in 1951 and disbanded in 1974. Like Ellington, the MJQ (as Lewis's combo was often called) was never the most successful group of its type in terms of sales in the marketplace. Rather, success was more in terms of musical influence and the esteem of musicians, both in and out of jazz. Lewis was greatly stimulated by the music of J. S. Bach. Early in the MJQ's life some art music forms were taken over almost literally. "Vendome" is a Baroque invention in style and "Versailles" a fugue. By the 1960s there were much fewer Bach influences and more jazz intensity in the MJQ's music. At times, it revealed a tendency toward light romantic music, but it never lost its unique ability to integrate different styles of music in a highly interesting and effective way.

the fifth step of the scale is lowered, which is a carry-over of the blue notes discussed earlier. The bass drum does not sound all the time—a change from earlier styles. Instead, the double bass is given the responsibility for keeping the beat. Bop bands were much smaller than the bands of the swing era.

Stan Kenton was the leader of *progressive jazz,* which is characterized by big bands and highly dissonant chords. In a sense, the progressive style is an updated, intellectual version of the swing style that prevailed about fifteen years earlier. With Miles Davis, the Modern Jazz Quartet, and Dave Brubeck, jazz turned toward a "cool" style, still intellectual and well ordered, but performed by much smaller groups. Charlie Mingus, Ornette Coleman, and John Coltrane led a movement toward *free form jazz,* in which all restraints were removed. No longer was improvisation held together by the harmony.

Over the years jazz has become more of a "listener's" type of music, in contrast to its early history. Gone is much of jazz's image as a "music of the people." It has matured in the sense that it is not always played just for fun, at least not by many jazz musicians. It is now serious business, performed by musicians who have studied Stravinsky and Bartók. One need only listen to works by jazz composers such as Miles Davis to hear how far jazz has progressed from what its "founding fathers" started.

Jazz represents the rediscovery of the art of improvising, which was largely neglected after the time of Bach and Mozart. Perhaps it was a better counterbalance to the deadly seriousness of nineteenth-century music than were the arty, chic attempts at ridicule by Satie and his followers.

35

ROCK, COUNTRY, SOUL, AND MUSICAL THEATER

The rivers that represent styles and types of music, both art and popular, flow along and at times divide into streams that sound quite different from other music, even though they may have had a common source. This fact can be seen in the great variety of music that influenced and became a part of jazz. The same thing happened to other types of popular music. Rock music is a good example of this. It seems to be a combination of the soul or rhythm-and-blues music of America's black population and the country-western style associated with Nashville, Tennessee.

ROCK

Rock music's beginning date is somewhat clearer. The theme song for a 1955 motion picture called *Blackboard Jungle* was "Rock Around the Clock," performed by a group called Bill Haley and the Comets. Haley was a bland-looking guitarist and singer of country music. The music he and his group performed was a simple twelve-bar blues played at a faster tempo. The movie was somewhat of a shocker in 1955; the setting was an urban school in which the delinquent students talked back to teachers, attempted rape, smashed the teacher's valued jazz records as they laughed at his "old-fashioned" music, and beat two teachers to death. It was rebellion plain and simple. Twenty-five years later it is hard to associate rebellion with "Rock Around the clock," considering the nostalgic and happy view people have of the 1950s.

Haley's career as a rock 'n' roll (as rock was called then) performer did not long endure, but others were soon to follow. The most famous of these was Elvis Presley (1935–1977). Presley, who had worked as a truck driver in Memphis before trying music, seemed to exude animal, sexual magnetism. Teenagers loved such songs as "You're Nothing but a Hound Dog." His outfit was leather, and he swung a guitar around his neck more as a prop than an accompanying instrument. Other groups wore glittering tuxedos in red or gold.

Physical actions were a part of the show. Some piano players jumped up and down as they played, and many singers swung microphones. Presley's swaying body earned him the nickname "Elvis the Pelvis." Later on rock and soul performances were to be choreographed with great care.

As rock developed in the 1960s it became somewhat more complex. The "twist" and discotheques came in about 1960, followed two years later by the

---

THE BEATLES: ROCK AND RIBBING

No rock group achieved the fame or sold as many records as the Beatles. The members of the group—John Lennon, Paul McCartney, George Harrison, and after 1962 Ringo Starr—were all born in Liverpool of working-class parents during World War II. In the late 1950s Liverpool was somewhat like New Orleans at the turn of the twentieth century. Sailors and longshoremen made it a tough, nightlife city with hundreds of clubs and dives that provided employment for musicians. Often these groups were called "beat groups," probably a term derived from "beatnik." The Beatles got part of their name from that word. Lennon, who was half-heartedly studying art at a local institute, met McCartney and Harrison in the late 1950s, and they decided to form the group. At the time they were just one of the 300 such groups around Liverpool hoping to make it big someday and earning about $15 a week in the meantime. They tried a variety of names in the hope that the right name would help them catch on with the public: The Cavemen, The Moondogs, The Moonshiners, The Quarrymen Skiffle Group, and they even paid tribute to the Everly Brothers with the name The Foreverly Brothers. In 1960 they played a stint on the Reeperbahn, Hamburg's red-light district, and made a recording there on an offbeat label using the name The Silver Beatles. At that time they were not very successful.

The name changes didn't help, but the acquisition in 1961 of Brian Epstein as manager made all the difference in the world. Epstein became interested in them when customers came into his father's department store asking for Beatles records. First, he designed a pseudo-choirboy outfit to replace the beatnik outfits they had worn. Next, he took them to London to try interesting some record company in the group. After a few turn-downs, EMI (Electrical Music Industries) produced "Love Me Do" in 1962. It sold respectably, but not phenomenally. The EMI executives had an idea: Bring in a new drummer, Ringo Starr. In the fall of 1962 they made their debut on British television with Starr on drums, and it was soon uphill at a dizzy pace. By April of 1963 they had their first British gold record (one million sales) and between April and December had thirteen more television appearances, plus a wildly received concert and a Royal Command Performance. The young people loved their odd hairdos, charming irreverence, brashness, and iconoclastic humor. For example, at the Command Performance before the Queen, John Lennon announced, "The people in the cheap seats can clap. The rest of you, just rattle your jewelry."

The Beatles did not enter the American rock scene until early in 1964. EMI's American affiliate, Capitol Records, did not exercise its first-refusal option rights, so the Beatles' songs were introduced on four different labels, which provided a tremendous initial market advantage. All four records boomed into the best-selling lists. By February of 1964 the Beatles were

---

"surf" music of the Beach Boys and Jay Dean. The "English invasion," as some writers refer to it, took place about 1964 with the appearance of the Beatles and the Rolling Stones. (See below.) That was also the year that the "Motown sound" was born with the Supremes and other groups. Folk rock appeared about 1965 with Bob Dylan, the Byrds, and the Mamas and the Papas. Psychedelic or "acid" rock appeared in 1966 with such groups as Jefferson Airplane

The Beatles (John Lennon, Ringo Starr, Paul McCartney, George Harrison) in about 1964.

in America in person for appearances at Carnegie Hall and a television debut on the Ed Sullivan Show. When their plane landed at Kennedy Airport, the police had to restrain some 5,000 ecstatic teenagers. At performances their music could hardly be heard over the screaming. Their main avenue of performance was, and still is for most rock groups, the recording. By 1967 the Beatles had sold twenty million singles and an equal number of long-playing records. Initially, music critics differed widely in their evaluations of the Beatles' musical talents, but warmed up considerably over the years, especially with the album *Sgt. Pepper's Lonely Hearts Club Band.*

Whatever may be said of the Beatles' music, they were very much a product of the 1960s with its sometimes irrational intellectual views, many tensions, and contradictions. Many people have tried to analyze "Beatlemania," as it has sometimes been called. Some writers tried to ascribe deep meaning and profound insight to the Beatles' music and lyrics, others saw them in sociological terms as presenting an image of "cuddly imps" who were doing away with out-of-date social inhibitions, while others saw them as a threat to morality. The Beatles did not appear to take themselves seriously. As Lennon once said of their music: "We're kidding you, we're kidding ourselves, we're kidding everybody. We don't take anything seriously except the money." Some of their music was put-down and put-on, much of it was just fun, and a little of it, despite their denials, was a real attempt at artistic expression. This was especially true in a couple of their later albums. Their introduction of Indian music and electronic psychedelic sounds led the way for innovative music by other rock groups.

The beginning of the decline for the Beatles was in 1967, when their brilliant manager Brian Epstein died accidentally. Some of their business ventures went sour, and tensions developed among the four men and their wives and girlfriends. They disbanded in 1971 and went their separate ways. Only McCartney achieved any success without the others. By 1971 the Beatles and the decade they represented had both come to an end.

(later to become Jefferson Starship). By the early 1970s there were many types of rock, including combinations of rock with religious, theatrical, blues, jazz, and other styles.

By around 1975 rock was beginning to lose its predominant position, and in a sense began to merge with the other streams of popular music. Disco dancing had become a fad and country music, which is discussed later in this chapter, had surpassed it in record sales.

How does rock differ from jazz and other popular music? One characteristic is its heavy beat, which led one critic to define rock as "music in which the bass drum carries the melody."

A second characteristic is frequent use of the modal harmonies that had fallen into disuse after the Renaissance. By 1970 more popular songs and rock pieces were in modes than were in the traditional major-minor system.

A third characteristic of rock is its departure from the standard formal schemes of the popular songs of previous decades. Most popular songs had been in an *a a b a* form, with eight measures for each portion. Rock phrases are often not symmetrical, probably to fit the blank verse of many of the texts.

A fourth significant feature of rock involves the different timbre of the music. The dance band of the preceding decades with its saxes and trumpets has been replaced by the small group with its electric guitars and electronic organ or piano. Rock is usually played through amplifiers that are turned up to a loud level. The singing, which is often done by males, is generally a little higher in pitch and lighter in quality than the singing in earlier pop music.

A fifth change in rock is the use of different chord progressions. The traditional dominant-to-tonic progression is less favored than adjacent or parallel chord movement (e.g., I-II-I-VII-I). Other nontraditional patterns are also found. The use of the modes gives the chords a different quality.

A sixth feature of rock is the dominance of small groups (many times composed of males) instead of the individual "idol" of the preceding decades. The appearance of the groups is different, too. From the dinner jacket of the 1930s and 1940s to the leather jacket of the late 1950s, the style of performers' clothes has changed to highly individual attire that ranges from dirty denim to sequins and satins of bizarre design.

A seventh characteristic is the dependence on recordings. Rock music exists primarily on records and tapes. "Live" performances are limited, and some performers never perform in person.

An eighth characteristic of rock is its folk quality. A few actual folk melodies have been revived, and new music of this type has been created. Like folk music, rock is often learned by imitation and is not written down.

A ninth characteristic of rock is its diversity. For many people rock has become synonymous with "popular music," so the word rock has lost some accuracy in definition. Some rock is in a quite conventional ballad style and is hardly rock at all; some borrows from art music; some is known as "glam/fag/drag/theatrical" rock, which features males wearing lipstick and wigs and sometimes handling boa constrictors; some is a form of social protest against injustices in society; some involves the dubbing in of electronic sounds; some is in a folk style; some is surrealistic or intentionally absurd; some is barbaric and psychedelic and is performed to flashing lights; some involves exaggerated emotions on the part of the performers; some is violent and animal-like in its primitive sounds; and some is strongly Oriental in character. There is also "bubble-gum" rock for early adolescents.

Like jazz, rock has now been around long enough for nostalgic revivals of earlier rock styles and stars.

Rock is as much a social phenomenon as it is musical. It is often identified as the music of youth. The increased number of persons between the ages of ten and twenty-five, the affluence that allows them to buy records and clothes of their choice, the youth orientation of American culture, the rapid rate of technological and social change that has increased the differences in viewpoint and orientation between young and old, the advent of mass communication, television, and especially the prevalence of recorded music—all these factors and more have contributed to a musical situation unlike anything that has ever existed before.

Another fact that makes the present popular music situation different from previous times is the importance of the recording sound engineer. Most popular music, especially rock, is nearly as much the technician's creation as it is the performer's. The development of the multiple-track tape recorder allows for the easy addition of accompanying parts and additional sounds. Also, a great deal of musical judgment is required in reducing or "mixing down" the sixteen or more tracks to the final stereo two-track version. In addition to adjusting the loudness of the various tracks, the sound engineer can add or subtract reverberation, control the sense of presence in the sound, and alter the timbre of instruments and voices. Errors can be spliced out and corrections inserted. The final record is usually quite different from the original sound—the record is likely to be far more impressive. This is one reason many rock stars avoid live performances unless similar amplification and sound enrichment is available.

COUNTRY

The country music associated with Nashville, Tennessee, has been popular for many years, and by 1975 it surpassed rock in most commercial measurements. The musical qualities of the country style reveal an ancestry in the southern mountain folk songs, which in turn grew out of English folk songs. The texts are sometimes narrative in form, and they often express sadness. The harmony, rhythm, and phrase patterns are simple and direct. The songs are often accompanied by electric guitars and fiddle, except in the bluegrass style, in which only acoustic (nonelectric) instruments are acceptable. The singing quality contains little vibrato or loudness range, and there is a tinge of melancholy in the tone. Notes are seldom sustained.

As with any popular style, the sociological factors are as significant as the musical factors. The increased interest in country music correlates to the renewed interest in "nostalgia"—the looking back with favor on the past when life seemed simpler and happier. The primary audience for country music is the white working-class population. The enthusiasm and loyalty to its stars, such as Johnny Cash, the late Hank Williams, Buck Owens, Dolly Parton, Charlie Rich, and others, is great.*

*There are several kinds of information to evaluate in determining the most popular song or type of music: record sales, gross earnings, playings on the radio, etc. Sometimes the evidence is conflicting. Also, the classifications of popular music are not precise, which adds to the difficulty of making an accurate judgment.

SOUL AND MOTOWN

Motown is probably the largest and best known of the soul or rhythm-and-blues music. The term "Motown" is a contraction of "motor town," the nickname often given Detroit. The founder of Motown Record Corporation, Berry Gordy, once described the Motown sound as "rats, roaches, struggle, talent, guts, love." It seems like an accurate description of what most of the people involved with it went through in their lives. Gordy, then an auto worker and part-time song writer, started his company in 1958 on $700 he borrowed from the credit union. Its first recording was "Way Over There" performed by Smokey Robinson and the Miracles. Initially success was limited. The real breakthrough happened in 1964 with a recording of "Where Did Our Love Go?" by the Supremes.

The Supremes, a female trio including Diana Ross, came out of a Detroit housing project and started singing together while they were in high school. Diana Ross tells about her childhood: "We were six kids, three girls and three boys. We slept in the same room, three in a bed, with a kerosene jar lighted to keep the chintzes away. . . . I got a job after school at Hudson's department store as a bus girl."

There is nothing impoverished about the way Motown Records develops its records or stars. They are carefully produced and recorded using string players from the Detroit Symphony. In a sense, the music is "slicked up" for white as well as black listeners, and it is a combination of gospel rhythms, modern harmonies, soft melodies, and bright lyrics. There is even a charm school for the girls and a choreography course for all acts.

In addition to the Supremes, some of Motown's most successful performers have been Smokey Robinson and the Miracles, whose records made it big after 1961, the Four Tops, the Temptations, and Stevie Wonder. Wonder has been blind

Soul or rhythm-and-blues is the popular music associated with America's black population. Its musical qualities reveal some aspects of African music, especially in the style of singing. It is emotional and forceful, with calls and exclaimed words. Open chords and parallel chord movement are characteristic of its harmony. The music is often loud.

Some writers include gospel music in the soul category, and the relationships are close among these styles. Prominent names in soul music include James Brown, Smokey Robinson and the Miracles, Wilson Pickett, and the groups associated with the Motown sound, which is described below.

Sometimes the same song will reach the top of popularity charts in the soul, country, and general popular music listings, but only occasionally. For example, The Beatles were never particularly popular with blacks. The ethnic associations of popular music influence its acceptance with various segments of the population. The preference is based on the style and timbre of the music rather than on the message of the words, although the background of the

Stevie Wonder.

from birth, but has become proficient on piano, organ, drums, and harmonica. He virtually grew up in the Motown organization and has continued to write and perform successfully.

Motown and the popularity of soul could not have happened without the changes in technology and social attitudes that emerged slowly in the 1950s and 1960s. When almost all the big-audience, expensive shows left radio for television, radio stations were left to survive (sometimes quite well) on the stubble of spot ads between playings of recorded music. The operation was low budget, and often stations sought a special ethnic type or age level of audience. The magnetic tape recorder made it much easier and less expensive to record, and the production costs of records were also decreasing. Therefore, it was no longer necessary to work through a few large record companies or radio stations to get one's music heard by the public.

The attitude change was in the greatly increased acceptance of black music and its performers. Whether or not it was directly related to the civil-rights feelings of the time, no one knows. What mattered was that a vast musical resource had been made available and was welcomed by much of American society.

performer makes some difference. A few songs with a message about war, poverty, or ecology achieved limited popularity in the late 1960s and early 1970s, but the trend then returned to the overwhelmingly favorite topic of popular songs: love and its pain and joy.

BROADWAY MUSICALS

The Broadway musical is an American tradition extending back well into the nineteenth century, although it has distance ancestors in the *vaudevilles* of France and *The Beggar's Opera* of Handel's London. An immediate predecessor was the operetta, which was usually based on long-ago-and-far-away subjects such as the ones in Sigmund Romberg's *The Desert Song* and Victor Herbert's *The Red Mill* (which takes place in Holland). By today's standards, the operetta seems stilted. In the past forty years musicals have become more contemporary and substantive.

West Side Story, the musical by Leonard Bernstein and Stephen Sondheim, is an example of this change. It is about the gang fights and prejudice between ethnic groups on the West Side of Manhattan. The plot is an updated version of the Romeo and Juliet story. It features Tony, a young man of Polish descent, and Maria, a Puerto Rican girl. Instead of a balcony as in Shakespeare's version, they meet on a fire escape. Before the story concludes, Tony unintentionally kills Maria's brother in a gang fight, and Tony is killed in an act of revenge by the Puerto Rican gang. He dies in Maria's arms.

The setting allows Bernstein, who was for over a decade the Musical Director of the New York Philharmonic and a recognized composer and pianist, to write in the varied styles of his cosmopolitan musical interests. Latin American music is represented by the song "America," a number in the style of a *huapango* with alternating meters, and by portions of "The Dance at the Gym," which was mentioned in Chapter 4. Jazz is especially evident in the "Jet Song" and "Cool." Popular ballad style is well represented by "Tonight" and "Maria." Operatic influences can be heard in "I Have a Love" and "One Hand, One Heart." Humor has its moment in "Gee, Officer Krupke!" The musical opens typically with an overture, which is a potpourri of the songs in the show. *West Side Story* also contains dances woven naturally into the action.

The "Quintet" is a combination of several of the types of music just mentioned, and it is presented in the Listening Guide on page 493. The music is in a tradition of operatic ensembles going back to Mozart and beyond. Each character's feelings are set in contrast to the others singing at the same time, and the five parties are somewhat separated from the others on the stage as they sing. In "Quintet" the Jets (the "native New York" gang) and the Sharks

LISTENING GUIDE

BERNSTEIN: "QUINTET" FROM *WEST SIDE STORY*

(Record 6, Side 1)

0:00 Lead-in figure from opening phrase of song; restless quality.

0:06 Jets sing melody in unpolished style (left channel).

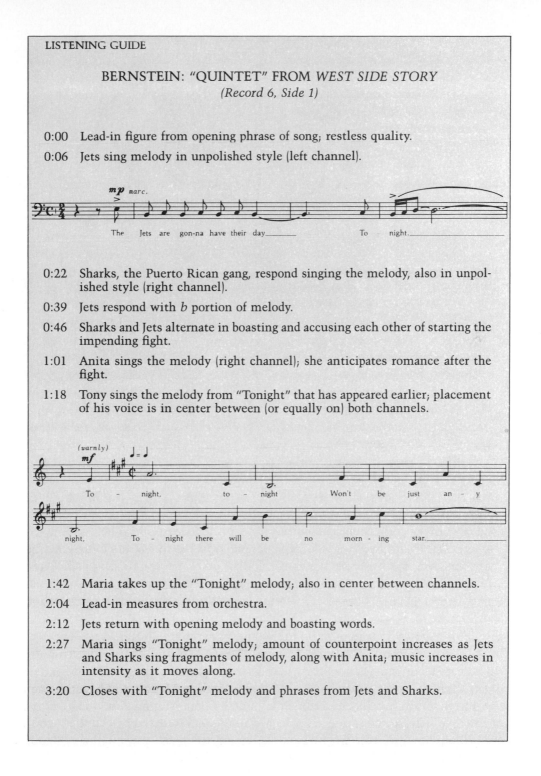

0:22 Sharks, the Puerto Rican gang, respond singing the melody, also in unpolished style (right channel).

0:39 Jets respond with *b* portion of melody.

0:46 Sharks and Jets alternate in boasting and accusing each other of starting the impending fight.

1:01 Anita sings the melody (right channel); she anticipates romance after the fight.

1:18 Tony sings the melody from "Tonight" that has appeared earlier; placement of his voice is in center between (or equally on) both channels.

1:42 Maria takes up the "Tonight" melody; also in center between channels.

2:04 Lead-in measures from orchestra.

2:12 Jets return with opening melody and boasting words.

2:27 Maria sings "Tonight" melody; amount of counterpoint increases as Jets and Sharks sing fragments of melody, along with Anita; music increases in intensity as it moves along.

3:20 Closes with "Tonight" melody and phrases from Jets and Sharks.

Maria (Natalie Wood) and Tony (Richard Beymer) meet after the dance on a fire escape in the movie version of West Side Story. *The touching of hands with the bodies behind bars seems symbolic of their ill-fated love.*

(the Puerto Rican gang) each sing boastfully about how they will beat the other gang that night and accuse each other of starting the trouble. The music they sing is restless and nervous, like the characters in the musical. Anita, singing the same restless music as the gangs, looks forward to being with her lover after the fight. Tony and Maria separately anticipate being together again that night. They repeat the warm and flowing song "Tonight" that they sang earlier in the show.

The channel placement on the recording, which is from the soundtrack of the motion picture, is "miked" much more closely and intimately than are performances of music in concert-hall settings. It gives the music a different effect than the normal-distance recordings. On the recording the Jets are on the left channel, the Sharks and Anita (sung by Rita Moreno) are on the right channel, and Tony and Maria (sung by Marni Nixon but acted by Natalie Wood) are presented equally on both channels, giving them the impression of being in the center.

Because it is live theater, the Broadway musical is tailored for its audience. A musical is normally tried out in Philadelphia, New Haven, or similar city prior to opening in New York. Portions of the musical that appear not to please the audience are deleted or rewritten. No one worries about being faithful to an artistic goal or theory because the main concern is: Is it good box office? Such a situation would appear to be harmful to creative artists and writers. Interestingly, this has not usually been the case. Composers, writers, and stage directors have been able to work around limitations of audience preferences, and have many times produced imaginative and worthy productions.

All the types of popular music have by no means been covered. In addition to jazz, rock, country-western, soul, and Broadway musicals, there are the songs of Burt Bacharach and other music for films, the big band sounds of Buddy Rich and Doc Severinsen, the staid music of Lawrence Welk, who has outlasted all other music shows on television, and many more. The world of music is larger and more interesting because of the many types of popular music.

GLOSSARY

(Terms associated with rhythm, pitch, notation, and harmony are defined in Appendix B.)

A cappella: unaccompanied choral music.

Accidental: a sharp, flat, or natural sign written in the music to show a departure from the prevailing key signature.

Acoustics: the science of sound.

Air: a song or melody.

Antiphonal: two groups performing "against" each other and from different places in the church or concert hall.

Appoggiatura: a musical ornament occurring on the beat and consisting of a nonharmonic, dissonant note that moves to an adjacent harmonic note.

Arpeggio: in "harp" style; a chord in which the notes are played one after another in an ascending or descending order instead of simultaneously.

Atonal, atonality: not in any key or tonality.

Bitonal, bitonality: two keys occurring simultaneously.

Cadence: a progression of chords (usually two or three) giving the sense of phrase ending. In poetic usage it sometimes refers to "beat" or "tempo."

Cadenza: an unaccompanied solo passage of an improvised, free nature, usually found in concertos.

Canon: strict imitation carried on between two or more lines of music for a significant amount of time.

Cantabile: in singing style.

Cembalo: harpsichord.

Chanson: song (French).

Chromatic: melodic movement by semitones.

Clavecin: harpsichord (French).

Consonance: concord; a group of sounds that the listener considers agreeable or pleasant.

Continuo: a bass line for keyboard in which the player is given only a succession of single notes and other symbols from which he fills out the remainder of the harmony. Also, the instruments that play that part.

Dissonance: discord; a group of sounds that the listener considers tense or unpleasant.

Enharmonic: two names for the same pitch; for example, E-flat sounds the same as D-sharp.

Ensemble: a group of performers; also the effect of unity achieved when they perform together.

Equal temperament: a system of tuning in which the octave is divided into twelve exactly equal segments or semitones.

Fugal: suggestive of a fugue in style, but not actually a fugue.

Glissando: ascending or descending notes occurring quickly; played on a piano by rapidly moving the hand across the keys and on a harp by plucking many strings consecutively in a single sweeping motion. Other instruments achieve the sliding sound in a variety of ways.

Grace note: an ornamental note preceding another more important pitch, and printed in smaller size. It is performed quickly.

Harmonic: a note produced by lightly touching a string at a proper place to divide it into segments. The sound is high and light in quality.

Harmony: the effect created when pitches are sounded simultaneously.

Homophony: music consisting essentially of a melody with accompanying chords.

Improvisation: music that is performed without first being written.

Intonation: the quality of sounding "in tune."

Inversion: turning a melody upside down so that an ascending interval descends, and vice versa; also, rearranging the notes in a chord so that its basic note is no longer on the bottom.

Key: the centering or relating of pitches around a particular pitch. See Appendix B.

Legato: smooth.

Leitmotiv: a motive or theme that is associated with a particular character or idea, especially in the music dramas of Wagner.

Libretto: the text of an opera.

Lied: song (German).

Manual: organ (or harpsichord) keyboard played with the hands, as opposed to pedal keyboard played by the feet.

Melody: a series of consecutive pitches that form a cohesive musical entity.

Meter: the pattern created by stressed and unstressed beats in music.

Meter signature: time signature; numbers at the beginning of a musical work that indicate the meter.

Modulation: changing key as the music progresses, usually without a break.

Monophony: a single unaccompanied melody.

Motive: a short melodic or rhythmic fragment that achieves structural importance through its frequent recurrence in a musical work.

Mute: a device for muffling or damping the sound of an instrument.

Octave: a pitch that has twice or half the frequency of vibration of another. The two pitches, if sounded simultaneously, blend into a sameness of sound.

Opus (op.): work. The opus numbers of a composer's music are generally in chronological order.

Ornament: a decorative note or a rather unimportant melodic figure.

Ostinato: a persistently repeated musical pattern.

Pedal point: a note sustained above or below changing harmonies.

Pitch: the highness or lowness of a musical sound, as largely determined by the frequency of its sound waves.

Polyphony: music in which melodies of about equal importance occur simultaneously.

Polyrhythm: several rhythms occurring simultaneously.

Polytonal, polytonality: several keys occurring simultaneously.

Range: the upper and lower pitch limits of a voice or instrument, or the pitch limits of a piece of music.

Retrograde: a theme performed backward, last note first.

Rhythm: the expression of music in terms of time; affected by the duration and strength of the various sounds.

Rubato: a performer's slight deviation from strict interpretation of rhythm.

Sequence: the immediate repetition of a phrase at higher or lower pitch level than the original.

Sforzando: a sudden accent on a sound.

Slur: a curved line grouping notes together and indicating that they are to be performed smoothly.

Staccato: notes separated from one another, usually indicated by a dot over or under each note.

Suite: a collection of stylized dances, or a collection of music from a ballet or opera.

Suspension: a nonharmonic, dissonant tone that was consonant in the preceding harmony and that eventually resolves downward to become consonant in its present harmony.

Syncopation: the displacement of accent so that accents occur where they are not normally expected and/or are lacking where they are expected.

Texture: the basic setting of the music: monophonic, homophonic, or polyphonic.

Through-composed: a melody without repetition of phrases.

Timbre: tone quality or tone color.

Tonality: key.

Transcribe: to arrange a piece for a performing medium other than the original.

Transpose: to rewrite music or perform it at a pitch level other than the original.

Tremolo: "trembling," produced in two ways: by rapid back-and-forth motion of the bow on a string instrument, or by rapid alternation between two pitches.

Trill: an ornament in which there is a rapid alternation between the written note and the note immediately above it.

Turn: an ornamental figure consisting of several notes that move above and below the main note.

Vibrato: a slight but rapid fluctuation of pitch.

APPENDIX B

THE NOTATION OF MUSIC

RHYTHM

Beat: the pulse or throb that recurs regularly in music and that is accented periodically. The beat is the unit of measurement by which we judge the duration of a musical sound.

Tempo: the rate at which the beats recur.

Meter: the way in which beats are grouped together and measured. Meter requires attention to the heaviness or lightness of the various beats:

Example:
beat beat *beat* beat *beat* beat (suggests a grouping of twos)
beat beat beat *beat* beat beat (suggests a grouping of threes)

Note Values: The passing of time in music is indicated by various kinds of notes, each one representing a particular duration. The duration of a note is always figured in relation to the beat.

Whole note	𝅝	usually lasts for 4 beats
Half note	𝅗𝅥	usually lasts for 2 beats
Quarter note	♩	usually lasts for 1 beat
Eighth note	♪	usually lasts for ½ beat
Sixteenth note	𝅘𝅥𝅯	usually lasts for ¼ beat

The mathematical relationships among these note values is illustrated by the following chart. The arrows here represent the passing of time; they do not appear in actual music.

Consecutive notes may share flags for ease in writing and reading.

Rest: a sign to indicate silence for a certain period of time. For each kind of note there is arest with the same name and time value.

Whole rest	Half rest	Quarter rest	Eighth rest	Sixteenth rest

The whole rest may also indicate an entire measure of rest, regardless of measure length. In such case it is called a "measure rest."

Dotted Notes: a dot to the right of a note indicates that the note is lengthened by half of the original note value. In other words, the value of the dot depends on the value of the note preceding it. Assuming in each case below that a quarter note receives one beat, the duration of each dotted note is:

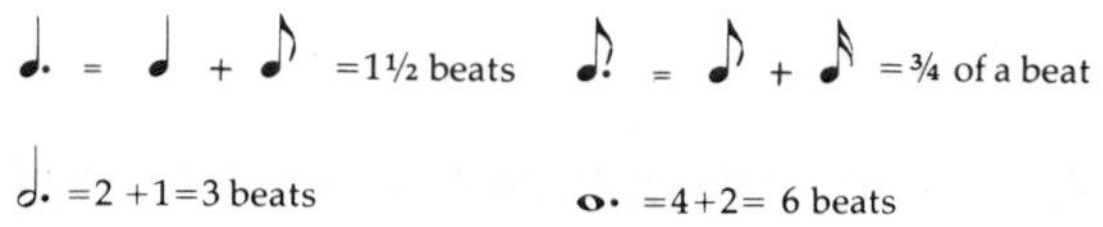

Time Signature or Meter Signature: the two numbers at the beginning of a piece of music. The meter signature indicates the meter or basic rhythmic grouping of the beats. This grouping is indicated by vertical bar lines in the music itself; the areas marked off by bar lines are called "measures." The *top number* of the time signature tells how many beats are in each measure. The *bottom number* tells what kind of note lasts for one beat. A 4 on the bottom stands for a quarter note, a 2 stands for a half note, and an 8 stands for an eighth note.

The time signature is *not* a fraction; $^{3}_{4}$ or 3/4 does *not* mean three-fourths, because it does not represent a portion of anything.

Two abbreviated time signatures are seen frequently:

C (common time) means $^{4}_{4}$
¢ (cut time, or alla breve) means $^{2}_{2}$

Meters are of two types. One has beats that are subdivided into twos; it is called *simple* time. The other, called *compound* time, subdivides the beat into threes.

The meter signature for compound time is more complex. Since the common note values are based on multiples of *two*, some type of dotted note must represent multiples of *three*. Furthermore, the meter signature must somehow indicate to the performer that the meter is compound. A signature such as 2/1½ is impracticable. So the number of beat *subdivisions* is indicated in the top number, and the note value of each of these subdivisions is indicated in the bottom number. Hence $^{6}_{8}$ usually means that there are two beats per measure, with a dotted quarter note receiving a beat:

PITCH

Note: a sign placed on the staff to indicate the pitch and duration of a particular musical sound.

Staff: the five horizontal lines and four spaces upon which the notes are written.

Leger Lines: short horizontal lines indicating the pitch of notes too high or too low to be placed on the regular staff. Leger lines extend the range of the staff.

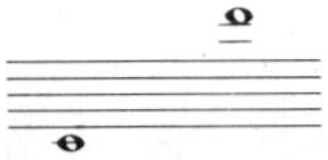

Clef: a sign placed on a staff to show the exact pitches of the notes written on the staff. The two most common clefs are:

 treble clef (or G clef, because it curls around the second line, G);

 bass clef (or F clef, because it has two dots on either side of the fourth line, F).

The treble and bass clefs indicate definite pitches, all named for letters of the alphabet from A to G:

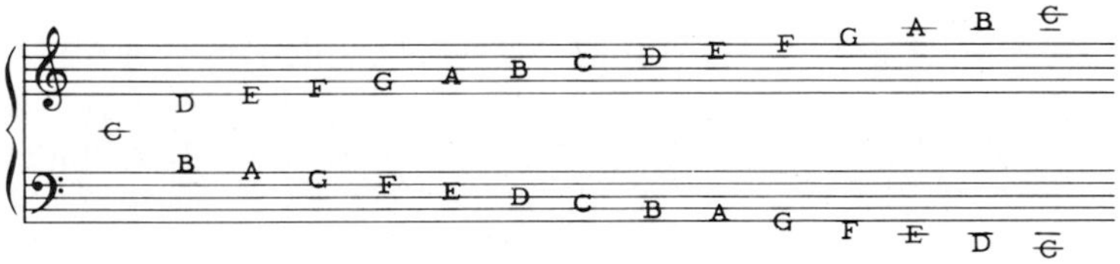

Another clef sometimes encountered in instrumental music is the alto clef (or C clef, because it indicates the position of middle C): 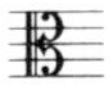

Sharp: (♯) a sign placed before a note to raise the pitch one half step.

Flat: (♭) a sign placed before a note to lower the pitch one half step.

Natural: (♮) a sign placed before a note to indicate that it is neither raised nor lowered. This sign cancels a sharp or flat previously applied to the note.

Pitches on the Piano Keyboard

The black keys of the piano are found in groups of twos and threes. All white keys are identified in relation to these groups of black keys. For example, every C on the piano is a white key immediately to the left of a two-black-keys group; every F is a white key immediately to the left of a three-black-keys group. The white keys are named consecutively from left to right, using the letters A to G:

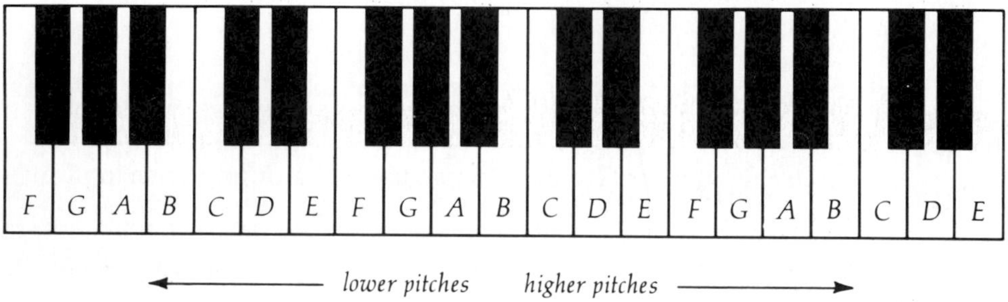

To find the sharp of any white key on the piano, find the black key touching it on the *right.* To find the flat of any white key, find the black key touching it on the *left.* If there is no black key on the side where you are looking, the nearest white key in that direction is the sharp or flat.

On the keyboard below, notice that each black key has two names, such as the key called G-sharp (because it is to the right of G) or A-flat (because it is to the left of A).

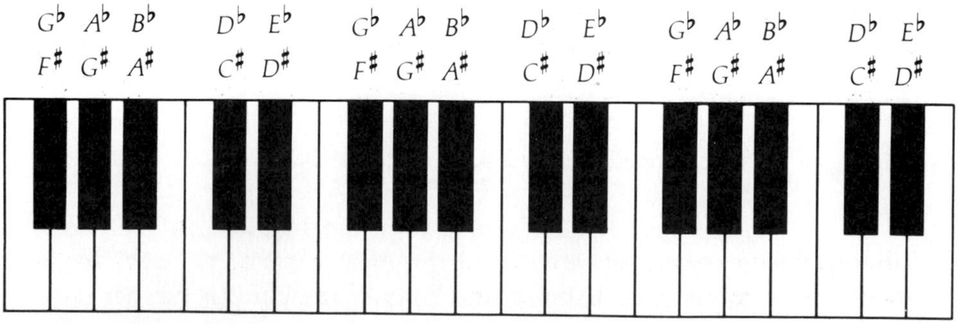

"Middle C," the note midway between the treble and bass staffs, is also the C nearest the middle of the piano keyboard. Using this as a guide, you can look at any note on the staff and find the exact pitch it represents.

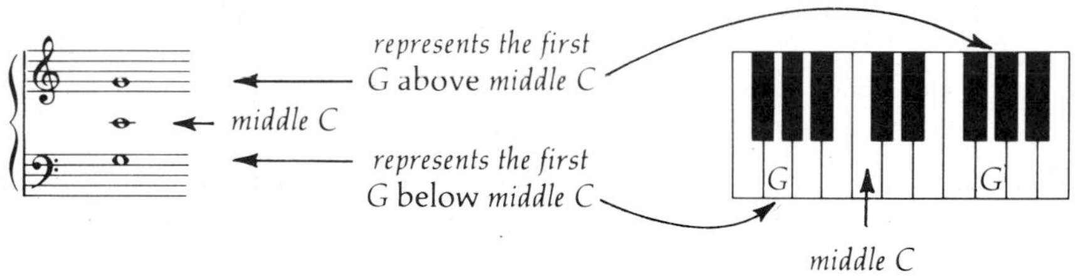

Interval: the difference in pitch between two tones. The name of an interval is determined by the number of letters it includes, counting the lower tone and the higher tone. Examples:

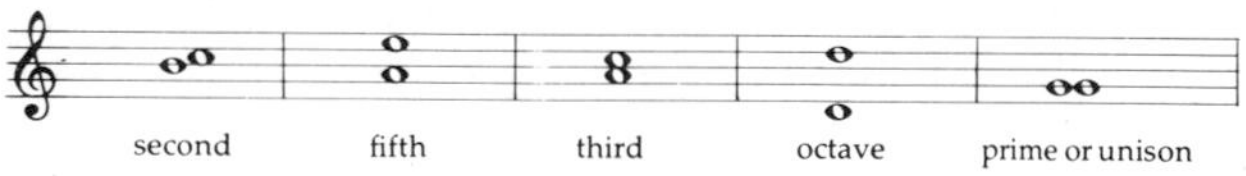

Interval names are not to be considered fractions; they are not portions of anything. The name is written in full: "a sixth" rather than "1/6."

Half Step: the smallest interval that can be played on the piano; also called a semitone or a minor second.

Whole Step: an interval of two semitones; also called a major second.

Scale: a series of pitches ascending or descending by a specific pattern of intervals; an "index" of the pitches that constitute a musical composition or a portion thereof. A scale can be built on any note, which is then called the *tonal center, tonic,* or *keynote.* A scale usually consists of eight notes, the eighth note having the same letter name as the first, or keynote. Numbers are often used to indicate the successive steps of the scale:

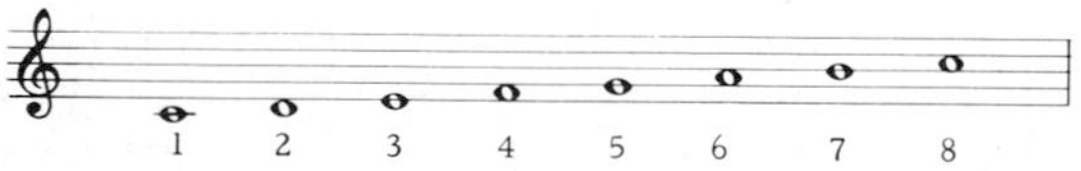

When eight-note scales are written, they must utilize each successive line and space—every letter—between the low and high keynote.

Major Scale: a scale having this pattern of whole and half steps:

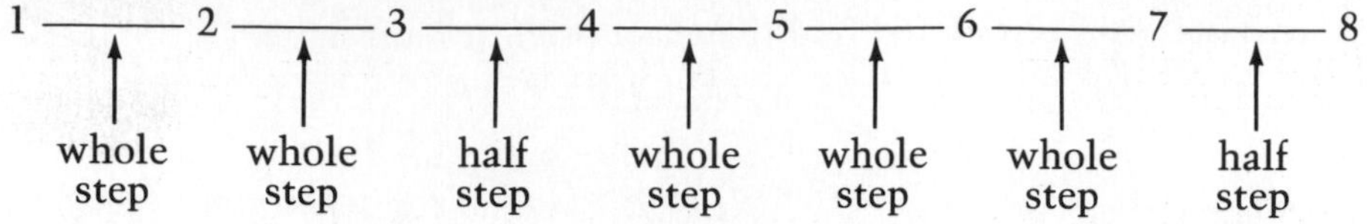

A scale can also be visualized as a flight of steps. The steps are *not* of equal height—steps 3 and 4 are close together, as are steps 7 and 8.

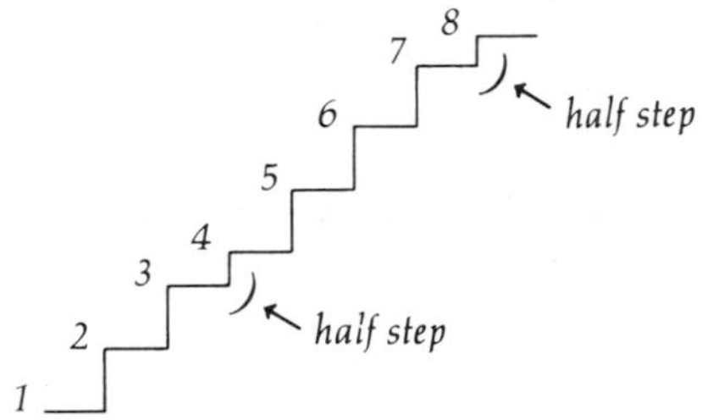

Key: the effect created when several tones are related to a common tonal center. If these notes are rearranged to form a scale, the starting note of the scale (step 1) is the name of the key.

Key Signature: a group of sharps or flats placed after the clef at the beginning of the staff. Every sharp or flat in the key signature applies to its particular note throughout the composition, unless the composer later cancels it with a natural. The key signature indicates the tonal center of the composition. If the signature is in *sharps,* the last sharp to the right is always step 7 of the major scale; therefore the eighth step, or keynote, is a half step above this last sharp. If the signature is in *flats,* the last flat to the right is always step 4 of the major scale. (If there is more than one flat, the keynote has the same name as the next-to-last flat in the signature.)

Here are the key signatures for all major keys. The order in which flats appear in a signature is exactly the reverse of the order of sharps.

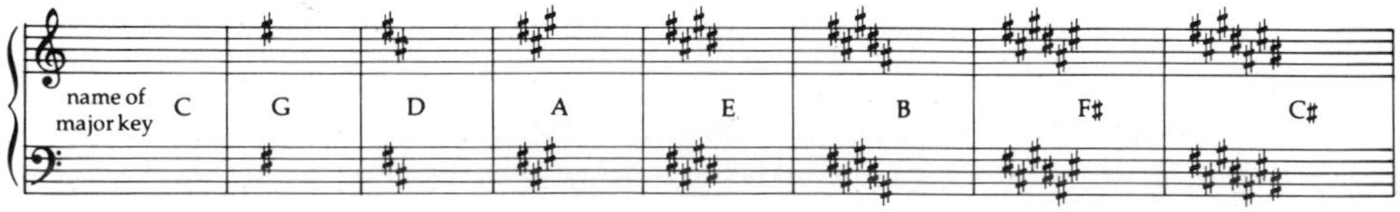

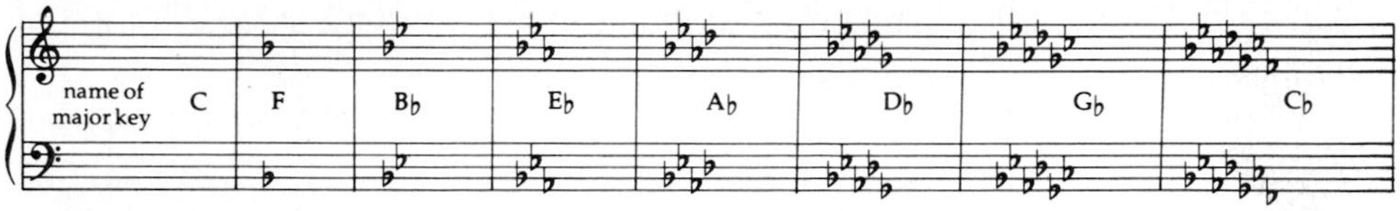

Accidental: a sharp, flat, or natural used within a composition to show a pitch not indicated by the key signature. An accidental remains in effect for one measure; after a bar line it is assumed to be canceled unless it is specifically indicated again in succeeding measures.

Modulation: changing key within a composition, usually with no break in the music.

Transposition: changing the key of an entire piece, so that it is performed at a higher or lower pitch level.

HARMONY

Chord: a combination of three or more pitches sounded simultaneously.

Triad: a chord of three pitches.

Root: the note on which a chord is built.

The harmony most familiar in Western culture is based on a specific type of chord—the triad. In any key, there are three triads that are basic because they occur so frequently. They can be better understood when they are related to the scale:

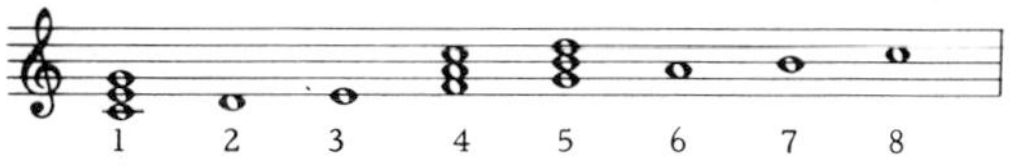

In any key: The triad built on step 1 is called I or *tonic* triad.
The triad built on step 4 is called IV or *subdominant* triad.
The triad built on step 5 is called V or *dominant* triad.

Although the I, IV, and V triads are the most common, triads can be built on any step of the scale, and are named accordingly: II, VI, etc. (In harmonic analysis, a Roman numeral indicates a *triad;* an Arabic numeral indicates only *one* tone—one particular scale step.)

Chord Function: the role of a chord in a particular key. In the music example above, the G triad (G B D) functions as V. It suggests restlessness, and the listener wants it to resolve to the home triad of C E G, which is I. However, in the key of G major, the same G B D triad has a different function; it is the home triad and gives the listener a feeling of repose and rest. The purpose of Roman numerals is to indicate chord function—to tell how a particular chord functions in a particular key.

Seventh Chord: a chord of four notes, consisting of a root plus intervals of a third, fifth, and seventh above the root:

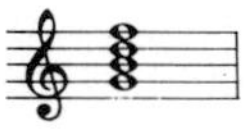

The most common seventh chord is the V^7, or dominant seventh chord. The term "seventh" refers to the interval above the root; it does not mean the seventh step of the scale.

Inverted Chord: a chord that does not have its root sounding as the lowest tone. Inversion does not affect the name or function of the chord.

A chord may be sounded in many ways. Here are the three basic methods:

MINOR KEYS

Minor Key: the effect created when the third step above the keynote is lowered. Other notes may be lowered also, but a lowered third step is a consistent feature of music in minor keys.

The basic pitch relationships in a minor piece are these:

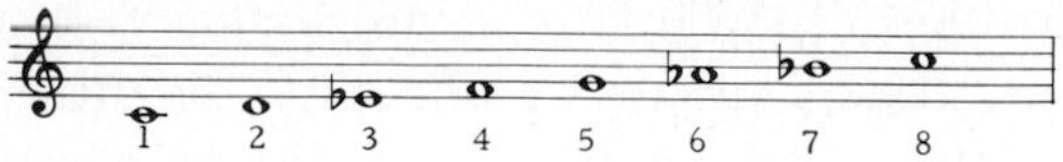

This is *natural* (or "pure") minor; steps 3, 6, and 7 are lowered a half step from their position in a comparable major key. In the diagram below, the dotted lines show at what pitch steps 3, 6, and 7 would be heard if the music were major:

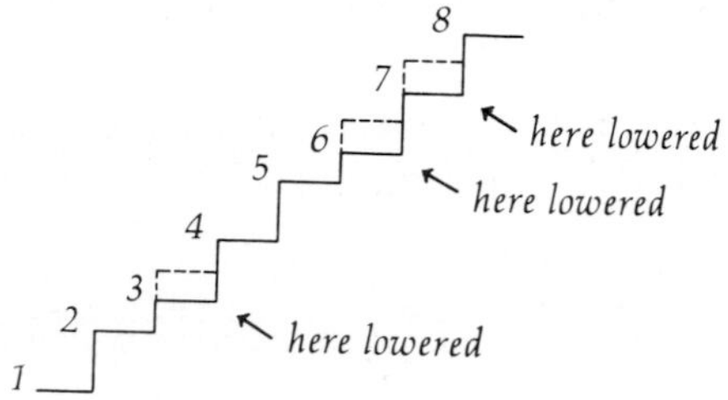

Steps 6 and 7 may be altered in a minor key. Here is one of the altered forms of minor:

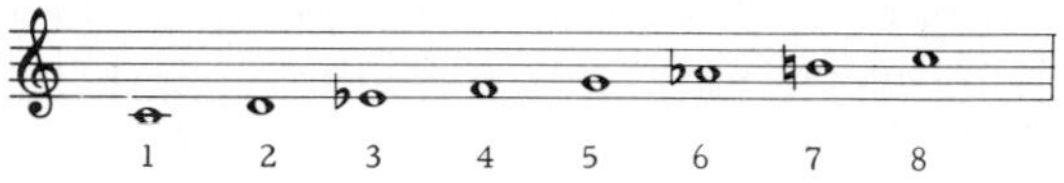

The pattern above represents *harmonic* minor: steps 3 and 6 are lowered as in natural minor, but step 7 is raised so that it is now only a half step away from the keynote. This gives a nice feeling of "leading into" the keynote, but it creates a rather large gap between steps 6 and 7. The following alteration, then, is a compromise:

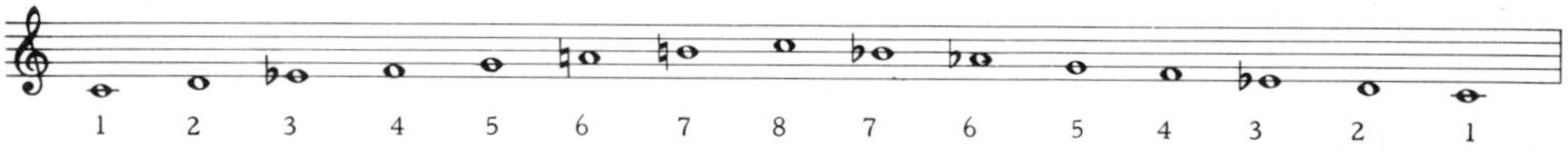

It is called *melodic* minor: steps 6 and 7 are raised when the notes ascend and lowered when the notes descend. In ascending passages, the raised step 7 serves as a "leading tone," to pull strongly into step 8. When step 6 is raised, the awkward interval found in the harmonic-minor scale is eliminated and the pattern is easier to sing or play. It is more "melodious"—hence the name. In descending passages, these two notes are lowered, so that the music sounds more distinctively minor again, as in the natural-minor form.

The key signature of a minor piece assumes that the notes will conform to the patterns of *natural* minor. Therefore any deviations from natural minor must be written in the piece as accidentals. Here are the signatures for all minor keys:

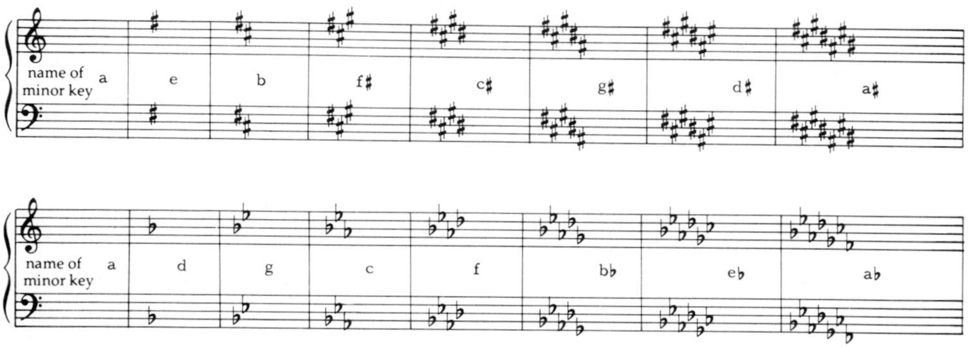

Compare the foregoing chart with the chart of major keys on pages 504–5. Notice that *each minor key has three more flats* than the major key built on the same note. These additional flats (or canceled sharps, as the case may be) indicate the lowered 3, 6, and 7 of natural minor.

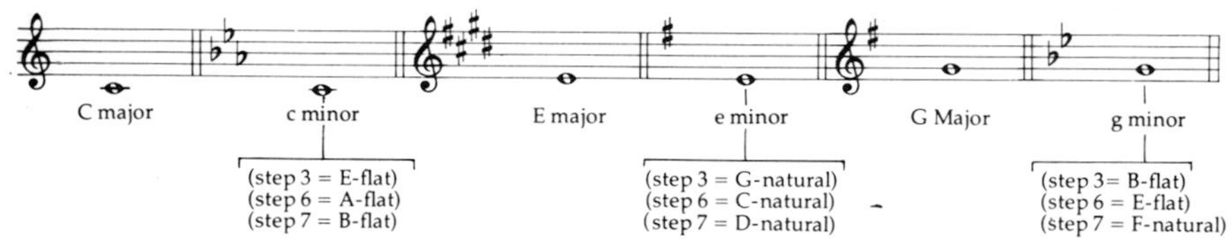

The examples above illustrate major and minor *parallel* keys: they have the same key center but require different key signatures. Think of the scales of each pair as starting on the same horizontal plane on the staff, "parallel" to each other.

As can be observed from the two signature charts, every key signature can represent either a major key or a minor key. The two keys thus related are called *relative* keys: they share the same key signature but have a different key center. The key center of a minor key is always step 6 of its relative major key. Examples of relative major and minor keys:

B-flat major and G minor each have two flats; G is step 6 in key of B-flat major.
D major and B minor each have two sharps; B is step 6 in key of D major.
F major and D minor each have one flat; D is step 6 in key of F major.

INDEX

Period	Prominent Composers	New Large Forms	New Small Forms
Gothic			
1100–1450	Machaut, Landini	Mass	Motet, secular ballades
Baroque			
1450–1600	Josquin des Prez, Palestrina, di Lasso, Byrd		Madrigal, motet, chorale melody
Renaissance			
1600–1750	Monteverdi, Corelli, Vivaldi, Purcell, Lully, Telemann, Rameau, Bach, Handel	Opera, oratorio, cantata, sonata, concerto grosso, suite	Chorale, fugue, passacaglia, toccata, prelude, overture, chorale variation, chorale prelude, recitative, aria
Rococo			
1725–1765	Couperin		
Classical			
1750–1825	Mozart, Haydn, Gluck, J. C. Bach, C. P. E. Bach	Symphony, solo concerto, sonata, string quartet	Sonata form, rondo, theme and variation, minuet and trio, scherzo
Romantic			
1825–1900	Beethoven, Schubert, von Weber, Chopin, Liszt, Mendelssohn, Berlioz, Schumann, Franck, Verdi, Brahms, Tchaikovsky, Fauré, Dvořák, Mussorgsky, Borodin, Rimsky-Korsakov, Rachmaninoff, Puccini, Wagner, Grieg, Elgar, R. Strauss, Mahler, Sibelius	Art song, symphonic poem, grand opera and music drama	Short lyric, instrumental pieces
Impressionism			
1890–1920	Debussy, Ravel		
Twentieth Century			
1900–	Stravinsky, Schoenberg, Bartók, Berg, Ives, Copland, Shostakovich, Prokofiev, Britten, Menotti, Vaughan Williams, Hindemith, Poulenc, Milhaud, Villa-Lobos, Webern, Penderecki, Cage		Jazz, electronic music, aleatory music, tone row